The Science of Philosophy

कर्मणो ह्यपि बोद्धव्यं, बोद्धव्यं च विकर्मणः।
अकर्मणश्च बोद्धव्यं, गहना कर्मणो गतिः॥
– *श्रीमद्भगवद्गीता*, 4.17

karmaṇo hyapi boddhavyaṁ, boddhavyaṁ ca vikarmaṇaḥ ।
akarmaṇaśca boddhavyaṁ, gahanā karmaṇo gatiḥ ॥
– *Śrīmad Bhagavad-Gītā*, 4.17

The truth about action must be known; the truth of prohibited action also be known; even the truth about inaction must be known. For mysterious are the ways of action.

The Science of Philosophy

Theory of Fundamental Processes in Human Behaviour and Experiences

Radhey Shyam Kaushal

D.K. Printworld (P) Ltd.
Publishers of Indian Traditions

Cataloging in Publication Data — DK
[Courtesy: D.K. Agencies (P) Ltd. <docinfo@dkagencies.com>]

Kaushal, Radhey Shyam.
Science of philosophy : theory of fundamental processes in human behaviour and experiences / Radhey Shyam Kaushal.
p. cm.
Includes bibliographical references and index.
ISBN 13: 9788124605585
ISBN 10: 8124605580

1. Science – Philosophy. 2. Human behavior – Philosophy. 3. Vedanta. 4. Karma. 5. Quantum theory. I. Title.

DDC 501 22

First published in India, 2011
ISBN 13: 978-81-246-0558-5 (HB) ISBN 10: 81-246-0558-0

Published and printed by:
D.K. Printworld (P) Ltd.
Regd. office : *'Srikunj,'* F-52, Bali Nagar
Ramesh Nagar Metro Station
New Delhi – 110 015
Phones : (011) 2545 3975; 2546 6019; *Fax* : (011) 2546 5926
E-mail: indology@dkprintworld.com
Web: www.dkprintworld.com

To my wife
Shashi

and

grand children
Sanchit, Aditya, Shruti, Pragya and Shubham

Who made it all worthwhile and joyful

If philosophy is interpreted as the quest for most general and comprehensive knowledge, it obviously becomes the mother of all scientific inquiry.

— Albert Einstein

All truths are easy to understand once they are discovered; the point is to discover them.

— Galileo Galilei

Science has proof without any certainty. Creationists have certainty without any proof.

— Ashiey Montague

Preface

In the early 1960s, Nobel Laureate Richard P. Feynman delivered lectures which were later published with the title, *The Theory of Fundamental Processes* by W.A. Benjamin, New York, 1962 in about 172 pages. The word "fundamental" was used there, perhaps for the first time, to identify, elaborate and understand the basic processes responsible for the functioning of the physical world. It is true that until that time it was the only electromagnetic interaction (that led to the subject of quantum electrodynamics) which was better understood theoretically as well as experimentally compared to the then other known interactions in Nature. Over a period of more than fifty years, a fast change of phases in physics, particularly in elementary particle physics, has taken place on both theoretical and experimental fronts. As a result, not only the problem of elementarity of the building blocks of the universe appears to be settled in terms of six quarks and six leptons (along with their antiparticle counterparts and a few field quanta) but also a reasonable understanding of several other physical interactions along with the associated or so-called "fundamental processes" has been achieved.

In fact efforts have been made to understand the functioning of the whole physical world in terms of four "fundamental" space-time mediated interactions, namely, strong, electromagnetic, weak, and gravitational. On the other hand, the physical laws derived with such an understanding of Nature have already started showing limitations in recent years when used to explain several newly discovered phenomena in physical and biosciences. As a matter of fact, the role of consciousness has started manifesting in a variety of situations. For example, the role of a conscious observer is tactfully avoided at the cost of introducing different types of probabilities in the quantum measurement theory. The occurrence of several consciousness-manifesting phenomena has been known now for quite some time in the laboratories of physiology and neurology. Even in the process of applying the laws of classical mechanics to some day-to-day practical problems involving living Beings, the role of will-power or of consciousness of the Being is tactfully avoided. In general, within the frame-work of objective sciences, no doubt the role of consciousness has been outrightly discarded but it cannot be denied indefinitely particularly when one wants to understand a phenomenon in Nature in totality and that too in view of ever-advancing technologies of modern times on the experimental front. Moreover, according to the three-world concept of Eccle and Popper, the physical world and its "physics description" offers only one aspect of the Complete Truth in Nature.

The situation described above, while leaves the question of fundamentality, whether it pertains to processes or to interactions, open, however, forces one to account for the consciousness in the physical and/or biological theories. As a matter of fact, a process cannot be a fundamental one unless the role of "ultimate" observer manifests in it. In the same vein an interaction cannot be a fundamental one unless it involves the "ultimate" observer or its derivative(s) (like consciousness) as one of the participants.

It is in the realm of consciousness of an individual that the scientific observations via the sense organs responsible for knowledge and action along with other essences of life make sense, otherwise the instrument-based data will tell only the partial truth in Nature. Now the question arises as to how to account for the consciousness in physical theories. (To some extent, this will also resolve the problem of its role in biosciences, as the measuring devices/instruments in the latter case are again physics-based). In such an attempt, difficulties may be at several stages starting with the perception or definition of consciousness itself, at least for an extrovert person, finally to the level of its quantification in the form of mathematical equations. In addition to this, the source of its origin, the plurality of its character, etc. have to be understood along with other essences of life. As a result, the "philosophy" or "psyche" of the individual participating in the process need to be understood at the deepest possible level in order to enter into the depth of fundamentality of a process or of an interaction. In fact the concept of fundamentality will not only be now limited to physical world but it will be extended to a more realistic situation in which the role of a human being also becomes transparent. To elaborate further, the essences of life in conjunction with the consciousness can provide a viable framework for understanding not only of the above-mentioned phenomena and the alike but also for an understanding of human/non-human behaviour and its experiences. It is in this spirit the present book is aimed at.

A modest attempt is made in this book, perhaps for the first time, to suggest the ways and means to incorporating the consciousness in physical theories. With regard to the concept of consciousness, Western philosophy does not have much to say. On the other hand, the Vedānta philosophy is much richer in providing the concepts regarding its origin, its plurality character, and its role in a co-ordinated functioning of various essences of life in an individual. Some of these aspects have already been investigated by the author in his earlier book, *The Philosophy of the Vedānta : A Modern Scientific Perspective,* Garibdas Oriental Series No. 179, Sri Satguru Publication, Indian Book Centre, New Delhi, 1994. (Also, see the Ph.D. Thesis "Patomic Model of Human Being in the Context of Modern Science" (unpublished), University of Delhi, 1998). In these works, a philosophical atom-type model (in brief it is called "patomic" model) for the human being is proposed. The model outlined in Chapter 2 and given in Appendix A, has strong bearing on the philosophy described in Upaniṣads and *Śrīmad Bhagavad-Gītā.* It is hoped that this little understanding of consciousness by the author when combined with his limited understanding of modern theoretical/mathematical physics, will give rise to some fruitful results for further development of the subject. As a matter of fact, this book is an attempt to find answers to many questions posed by the author in the previous book (cf. Chapters 6 and 7) in the domain of physics-philosophy interface.

Let me emphasize that after reading this book on the theory of behaviour, the reader in any case is not going to doubt the existing science or the objective reality in Nature; rather he will be convinced of the demand made hereafter for an incorporation of subjective reality. The book is divided into three parts: Part I (Chapters 2-6) describes mostly the existed tools and rules of the game of both East and West whereas Part II (Chapters 7-10) describes new developments and their workability. Part III (Chapters 11-14) highlights applications and future prospects of the theory. Chapters 11-13 are the eye-openers for a common reader who is bewildered by the modern developments of science. In fact the book will provide some sort of guiding principle to readers and researchers working in the extreme fields of social and pure sciences. Also, the book will be useful to a broad spectrum of readers, particularly physicists, biologists, psychologists, professional philosophers and philosophers of science.

Finally, with due apology to our female readers, all throughout the book the English pronouns for the human being corresponding to the masculine gender are used. This is, of course, without any prejudice on the part of the author against the feminine gender. Moreover, within the framework of patomic model they are the same essences of life beyond the biological body (B), which equally prevail in both man and woman and it is their role in the human behaviour which is highlighted in this book. In the same spirit a neutral gender is used for the consciousness/Soul, essences of life and sometimes for the living Beings in general.

Delhi, September 01, 2010 **Radhey Shyam Kaushal**

(*Kṛṣṇa Janmāṣṭamī*)

Acknowledgements

DURING the early days of my academic career an Unseen Power first created my interest in both physics and philosophy, particularly in theoretical physics and Vedānta philosophy and now, after forty years or so, the same Power has inspired me to come out with the present package; otherwise a person like me with a limited understanding about the world and its order could never have dared to explore the intricacies of Nature. Perhaps God wanted me to do so. I think I have done my job to my fullest satisfaction and capability. Yet if something is left, it is all God's desire at the inspiration part and due to my limitations at the presentation part.

During this forty-year period, I have come in contact with many saints, saintly persons, scientists of different tastes and expertise, religious leaders of different faiths within the country and abroad. I am greatly benefited from the long discussions which I had with them. I express my gratitude to them for giving a direction to my thinking process on this front from time to time during my haunt. Basically this package is the outcome of my hobby and a fruit of my part-time work during the past five years and more. This is an assimilation of knowledge of different disciplines, even though in most of them I am not an expert. Naturally, I had to learn many things from my colleagues and friends in Ramjas College and outside, mainly to seek the authenticity of some of the ideas presented in this book. As a result I had to disturb them from time to time. I am highly grateful to them. Some names I wish to mention are: Dr A.K. Shukla (Botany), Dr P.N. Dutta Gupta and Ochit Singh (Zoology), Drs Mohan Chand and P.K. Panda (Sanskrit), Drs

J.B. Gupta, A.K. Kavethkar and S.K. Bansal (Physics), Dr Man Mohan, H.G. Gupta and Ms Raj Kumari Bahl (Mathematics & Statistics). In addition to this my teacher, Prof. S.R. Bhatt and several other colleagues and friends in the University have encouraged me from time to time in this venture. In particular, I am thankful to Prof. K. Muralidhar, Dr M.C. Jain, Dr J.K. Kohli, Dr Sardar Singh, Dr R. Ramanathan, Dr Awadhesh Prasad and to my students Sunil Kumar, Manish Agrawal, Dr Ranjit Kumar and Sushil S. Chauhan, who also helped me in preparing the manuscript.

One person, without whom this project could have never been completed and who made himself available to me any time towards reading my hand written draft, is my friend, colleague, collaborator in research and co-author in a book, Dr D. Parashar of ARSD College. Words are not enough to express my gratitude to him. Thanks are also due to Dr Girish Upadhyaya for sharing many ideas on Vedic Science and to Engr. V.K. Rajoria for enlightening me with his experiences on his trainee dog, Bruno. During last six months or so I am also greatly inspired and benefited from the discourses on TV of Pujya Deepak Bhai Desai of Dada Bhagvan Foundation, Adalaj, Gujarat.

Lastly, the invaluable co-operation extended and deep sense of patience shown by my wife, Shashi and children Shraddha, Medha, Mukta and Govind and my sons-in-law Ch. Kunal, Vijay and Manoj during these years cannot be ignored. While Shraddha and Govind have helped me in preparing the manuscript, Dr Vijay and Dr Medha have taught me a bit of Ayurveda and Naturopathy.

I also thank J.S. Patwal for the excellent typing of the manuscript, oftentimes in extra hours. Thanks are also due to M/s D.K. Printworld (P) Ltd., and particularly to Mr Susheel Mittal for taking interest in bringing the book in the present shape.

R.S.K.

Abbreviations, Notations and Symbols

AA = animate-animate (interaction)
AAD = action-at-a-distance
AADT = action-at-a-distance time
AAT = action-at-a-time
AI = animate-inanimate (interaction)
b = Being (or *jīva* or life principle)
B = biological body
$\mathcal{B}$ = a composite of gross and micro bodies
BBNS = brain, body and nervous system
BPK = bio-psychokinesis
C = causal-body
CF = consciousness fraction
CM = consciousness mediated
CSTM = consciousness-space-time mediated
E = ego, self-conscience
ε = environment
EFLs = essentials for life
EOLs = essences of life
EP = epi-physical
ESP = extra-sensory perception
FOA = fruit of action
FOU = faculties of understanding
$\mathcal{G}$ = gross-body
I = intellect, faculty of decision
IA = inanimate-animate (interaction)
II = inanimate-inanimate (interaction)
ISO = "inside out"
IWB = inner-world-based (experiences)
M = mind, faculty of emotions
$\mathcal{M}$ = micro-body, mindset (function)
μ = meditation parameter (variable)
MC = mentally challenged (person)
NDEs = near-death experiences
OBEs = out-of-body experiences
OSO = "outside out"
OWE = outer-world-based (experiences)
P = physical matter/particle
PA = physical apparatus
PC = physically challenged (person)
PMs = *pañca mahābhūtas*
PMC = physically and mentally challenged (person)
PK = psychokinesis

Psi = psychic or psychical
QCD = quantum chromodynamics
QED = quantum electrodynamics
RAM = random access memory (of a computer)
ROM = read only memory
SCE = scientific circumstantial evidence
SE = senses of knowledge and action
SEA = sense organs responsible for action
SEK = sense organs responsible for Knowledge
SEP = special epi-physical (matter)
SMBG = *Śrīmad Bhagavad-Gītā*
SNP = systematic of negative pursuits
SO = soul, the inner-most existence
SOA = seed of action
SPP = systematic of positive pursuits
σ = circumstances
Σ = *Saṁjoga*
STC = space-time-consciousness
STCG = spatio-temporal Cartesian grid
STCM = space-time-consciousness mediated
STR = space-time recorder
τ = *tanmātra*
WO = worldly objects

Contents

PART I

BASICS OF EASTERN AND WESTERN VIEWS

PART II

New Analytical Methods and Workability

PART III
PREDICTIVE POWER AND FUTURE PROSPECTS

APPENDICES

1

Introducton

> Physicists are very excitable people. If they come across a new theory, they promote it as the answer to everything. Then a few years later, the same theory is replaced by yet another hypothesis.
>
> — Roger Penrose[1]

1.1 Philosophy and Science

PHILOSOPHY is the mother of all disciplines of knowledge. There is a seed of entire gamut of human experiences and observations in philosophy. Once upon a time it was all philosophy and hardly any science in its objective form. Of course, science in its subjective form was very much there in "some" of the philosophies (as every culture/religion in this world has its own philosophy in the sense that people have varying attitudes and views towards the existence and the functioning of this universe in general and this world in particular). However, tenets of some philosophies (like those of the Vedānta philosophy) do accommodate such concepts like the "ultimate truth," "reality," etc. in Nature. As a matter of fact, the plurality of knowledge of various disciplines culminates finally into the philosophy[2] and even within it the same converges[3] to a singularity limit which can be termed as "ultimate" truth — rather asymptotically.

---

1. Roger Penrose, "Physics of Tao", *Times of India* (New Delhi), 28 January, 2003.
2. Radhey Shyam Kaushal, *The Philosophy of the Vedānta: A Modern Scientific Perspective*, Garibdas Oriental Series No. 179, Delhi: Sri Satguru Publications, Indian Book Centre, 1994.
3. Radhey Shyam Kaushal, *Structural Analogies in Understanding Nature*, New Delhi: Anamaya Publishers, 2003.

The subject of philosophy (or the objects of study in it such as religions, cults, etc.) was perhaps born with the human race. There is a famous saying in the Sanskrit literature according to which it is the only finest form of the intellect in the human Being that differentiates between the human and non-human Beings; otherwise there is not much difference (except for the biological ones) between them as far as their survival in this world is concerned. Perhaps for this reason human Being created the subject of philosophy not only for understanding himself and Nature but also the associated interactions between the two in their finest possible form. As a matter of fact, the functioning of intellect (the faculty of decision) with reference to the methodology of grasping, studying the quantity and quality of contents in and an analysis of knowledge about the world-order including the human Being by the human Being himself constitutes the subject of philosophy. From certain standards, this leads to the proliferation of knowledge, but lacks in providing the "ultimate" truth that manifests in Nature from other standards.

There have been varying attitudes and views towards the study of Nature and world-order in different cultures. In Western thinking, it mainly concerns the search for objective reality. The knowledge as perceived by the organs responsible for the knowledge (such as eyes, ears, nose, tongue and skin) and human actions (such as hands, feet, power of speech and copulatory organs) or by the "man-made" (scientific) instrument has been the main theme of search. Accordingly, the so-called conventional branches of science (in physics these are optics, sound, heat, electricity and magnetism; in chemistry these are physical, organic and inorganic; in biology these are zoology and botany and in engineering these are civil, mechanical and electrical) were developed. In modern times there is a lot of intermixing and advancements in these branches of the objective science. As a result, over the years several new disciplines have emerged and a considerable knowledge about the Being (human or non-human) and the Nature has been gained. In physics particularly the modern understanding of Nature has been reduced to study of just four fundamental, space-time mediated interactions (namely strong, electromagnetic, weak and gravitational) and about two dozen building blocks (namely six quarks and six leptons and their anti-particle counter parts). We shall return to some of these concepts later.

In Eastern thinking, we shall, however, restrict ourselves to the Vedānta philosophy which, in the author's opinion, is capable of providing[4] the finest possible framework for understanding the processes responsible for the human behaviour in the day-to-day life. In addition, this also provides a full-fledged package for the description of entire gamut of human experiences and actions. A justification to this fact will be sought in Section 1.4 where the concept of various essences of life will be introduced.

Even though it varies from philosophy to philosophy of different cultures, the fact is that there exists a common methodology up to a certain stage as far as the understanding of human Being himself or of Nature[5] is concerned. A major difference between Western and Eastern philosophies, in the author's opinion, is that in the former one tries to understand the "functioning" of Being and Nature within a limited framework of postulates and assumptions whereas in the latter, one also concentrates on undertaking the working of this "functioning" in terms of certain (but precisely identified) essences of life.[6, 7] As a result, by and large the former remains extrovert philosophy.

4. Radhey Shyam Kaushal, 1994, op. cit.

5. Here the word "Nature" is used with regard to outer world only; otherwise in some philosophies (like the Vedāntic one) this word includes a part of the Being in terms of essences of life (cf. cit. 7 below).

6. Radhey Shyam Kaushal, 1994, op. cit.

7. *Śrīmad Bhagavad-Gītā* (SMBG), verse 4, chapter 7.

One commonality involved in the study of different branches of objective science without bringing in the role of the Being itself, can be described as follows: To understand Nature an objective scientist starts by having observations (measurements) on a particular phenomenon and continues with the collection of the so-called "data." These data are then classified according to a certain criterion. Then one looks for possible correlation(s) among these data and thereby makes an effort to search for a law. Once the law is found, then predictions are made and subsequently efforts are directed to verify these predictions in the laboratory. When all these stages are successfully passed through, one feels satisfied and starts modelling the phenomenon in a theoretical/mathematical framework in which the law (searched above) plays the key role. Note that this mathematical framework (the so-called "model") is constructed (recall, for example, the case of the kinetic theory of gases or of the Bohr model of atom) under some highly simplifying assumptions and interestingly the same is found to work successfully within the limitations of the measuring instrument. This is how the Nature is understood in the objective science. In the present work, unless the word "science" is qualified by an adjective it will stand for the objective science in general. However, our efforts will be there to develop a similar science (now on termed as "subjective science") for the inner-world, i.e. in the subjective domain.

1.2 Philosophy of Science: A Search for Perfect Science

After having highlighted the common methodology followed in objective sciences in the preceding section, here we try to elaborate on the heads under which the knowledge in science is gained and in fact is growing rather exponentially in this age of fast computers. From the point of view of a philosopher of science several questions that naturally arise are (i) as to what extent this knowledge is going to be helpful in understanding the Nature and the Being in totality in spite of the fact that the quality of life of a common man is improving, (ii) how scientists work to gain this knowledge, and (iii) what the final limit of this proliferation of knowledge will be as far as the search for "ultimate" truth in Nature is concerned. With regard to the last question one can again ask: can one have a science, so-called "perfect" science, possibly in terms of some minimals, which should be able to provide a basis for all these diversities of knowledge in different disciplines of science? In this section we are going to comment on these issues.

Historically, at the time of Newton, knowledge in all sciences was confined to "Natural philosophy" that included mathematics as well. Later originated the three branches of science, namely physics, chemistry and biology. Conventionally, the knowledge in chemistry was gained under the three heads, viz. organic, inorganic and physical and that in biology under the two heads, viz. zoology and botany. In recent times many interdisciplinary subjects have arisen and their number is growing at a fast rate. On the other hand in physics the conventional subjects studied for a long time are the properties of matter, heat, sound, optics, electricity and magnetism. It is only about a century ago that the "conceptual disciplines" started emerging at different points of time particularly after the advent of quantum mechanics and the theory of relativity. Under this category the subjects developed are condensed matter, molecular, atomic, nuclear, elementary particle and quark physics. The subjects of astrophysics and astronomy also fall under this category. The mathematical tools used in these conceptual disciplines of physics also grew simultaneously as and when the necessity arose. Under this class (so-called "mathematical disciplines") we have classical, quantum, statistical and stochastic mechanics, classical and quantum field theories, and string theories.

As a matter of fact this type of compartmentalization of knowledge has become the story of the past; otherwise, in recent years various branches of the so-called pure science have penetrated into each other to a non-definable extent and it has led to newer disciplines like biophysics, chemical physics, molecular biology, biochemistry, etc. and with regard to the use of tools of mathematics, several branches have emerged such as mathematical physics, mathematical biology, biostatistics, etc.

In addition to these conventional, conceptual and mathematical disciplines in physics another subject which has been growing rather independently is that of technology or engineering. Under this head three main disciplines, namely civil, mechanical and electrical engineering were studied for a long time. It is only in recent times that more than two dozen branches of engineering, mostly of interdisciplinary nature, have emerged. While physics was dominating the scene for a long time, now chemistry and biology have also started contributing to these branches of engineering in terms of concepts, methodology and tools and thereby making the life of a common man more comfortable. With regard to an individual human Being these scientific advancements have provided pleasure but not peace in the same proportion except for those who have learnt the art of living in this world.

While these programmes and developments are successfully going at the forefront, some minds (philosophers of science) are still busy in putting the available knowledge in a nut-shell by the so-called *process of abstraction*. Efforts have been there to find some sort of unity in this diversified knowledge originating from different branches of science. Search for minimals in terms of some basic principles and analogies[8] has also been there. These basic principles are expected to emerge from the combination of both physics and biology (in some sense chemistry is also an applied version of physical laws) mainly because these branches have offered and are also offering even now the challenges to scientists in terms of the questions of biggest and smallest, fastest and slowest and that of life and death, etc. with regard to the universe and the human Being himself.

---

8. Radhey Shyam Kaushal, 2003, op. cit.

The abstraction of knowledge with regard to the ultimate truth in Nature can be achieved in two possible ways — either by inward or by outward procedure. In the former case, whole knowledge will finally merge into a single source (singularity limit) rather asymptotically with respect to time by the process of abstraction at different stages. In the latter case, however, it can be assumed to be originated from the same single source and then slowly emerging and manifesting through fronts of different disciplines. It is true that for the inward procedure professional scientists are the experts and it is for them to develop such a *perfect science* which is capable of describing/explaining the working of entire universe including the role of human Being in terms of some minimum principles. On the other hand, for the outward procedure professional philosophers are the experts and they should develop such a *perfect philosophy* which is capable of accounting for the entire gamut of human experiences with regard to the working of this universe. Unfortunately, both of them are handicapped for such an endeavour in terms of their expertise and tools with which they are equipped. Perhaps the partial truths about Nature collected and experienced by both, when combined together, can give the true picture of the objective reality in Nature.

1.3 Active and Passive Sciences: How Science Progresses

It is true that the methodology of science with reference to a particular study is systematic; however, as history reveals, the growth and development of science is not quite systematic. It is only at a later stage, particularly after a sequence of discoveries in a given field that one finds the coherence in the development of ideas. Moreover, scientists keep on jumping to study newer phenomena in Nature without actually understanding the older ones in totality. Of course, in this process they sometimes improve upon the rules and tools of study in accordance with the new phenomenon and when these improved rules and tools are applied to study the old phenomenon, it sometimes provides the improved understanding of the latter. Also, the understanding of the new phenomenon at times supplies a feedback for a better understanding of the older one. This is how science progresses. One example from physics will suffice to substantiate these observations: In physics, without understanding the atom completely, nuclear physics was developed. Again without understanding the atomic nucleus in totality, the elementary particle or quark physics has been developed. (Even today we are fiddling around half a dozen models for the atomic nucleus.) Of course, in the meantime, the development in the mathematical tools (such as quantum field theory) took place which in fact has provided a satisfactory explanation of a number of newly discovered phenomena in the domain of atomic physics. In another context the tools of angular momentum algebra, developed to understand the nuclear transitions and spectroscopy about four decades ago have now found applications in atomic theory to explain the newly observed data. Similarly, the spectroscopic methods, which were once the hot topics of research in physics, now have very wide applications in chemistry and biology and surprisingly for the latter subjects these methods have become the modern tools of study, of course, after appropriate modifications.

In science there are some branches which are progressing actively with time whereas there are some in which the progress has been either slow or has not been there at all for years and decades. One never knows, this latter class of branches of science may one day become active if the rules and tools of the same get a boost or some importance of them is noticed in the context of other disciplines or of new discoveries in the same discipline. For example, the studies in lattice structure of solids remained more of less static for decades until the lattice gauge theory was developed. As a matter of fact whatever is said above for the "activeness" of branches of science the same is true with regard to the "activeness" of a scientific concept or thought. In fact one never knows when and where the newly discovered idea catches the market of research as far as its applications are concerned, if not in the same branch may be in other branches of science. In this context the concept of analogy, particularly that of structural analogy plays[9] an important role. Look at the concept of non-abelian gauge theories: The idea was given and developed by C.N. Yang and R.L. Mills in 1954. It was only after two decades or so that the importance of this concept was realized by way of developing not only a satisfactory theory of strong interactions — quantum chromodynamics but also by unifying different interactions in Nature and now by formulating a theory of everything, i.e. the string theory. In this context J.V. Narlikar's ideas are worth quoting:[10]

> Science advances through a method of trial and error, through a certain discipline in which speculations and verifications have their roles to play. Scientific theories are forever on probation and can be dislodged if new facts so warrant. But theories that have withstood the tests of experimental checks for a long enough period acquire a confidence and stability that make them harder to dislodge. The special theory of relativity, quantum theory, the study of electromagnetic force, etc. are examples of such stabilized frameworks.

In summary, in spite of so much development in science in terms of concepts and methodologies there is no hope that researches in science will come to an end in the near future. Research appears to be an ever-increasing inquiry into the great vistas in Nature. The ultimate truth is still lying in the murky depth of ideas according to the philosophers of science. It is only a bit of objective reality in Nature which scientists achieve and enjoy at every stage of their research progress and that too in pieces. Sometimes scientific thoughts, once established for ever in accordance with the existing world are also questioned in view of the advancing technologies on the experimental front. For example, the universal constancy of

---

9. Radhey Shyam Kaushal, 2003, op. cit.

10. J.V. Narlikar, "Cranks' Constant : Popular Science and Vulgar Factions", *Times of India*.

certain quantities in physics such as electronic charge and mass, gravitational constant, Planck constant, etc. accepted once forever, is now questioned in view of the new experimental results. While a common man gets amazed at the scientific discoveries, the philosopher on the other hand very well knows the limitations not only of these discoveries but also those of the discoverer.

1.4 Science of Philosophy: A Search for Perfect Philosophy

Four categories of persons, namely common man, scientist, philosopher and *yogī* can always be found[11] at all times and in all cultures of the world. Out of these four categories, common man confines mostly to his day-to-day livelihood or to the attainment of related worldly objects. His attitude towards the working of Nature in general or this world in particular, is limited only to the way they appear to him at their face value mainly because of the limited development of his essences of life. *Yogī* while remains over and above many of the happenings in and the functioning of the world, both categories of scientist and philosopher, on the other hand, show their far-sightedness with regard to the world-order and its changes. The latter are not only curious and conscious to know (with reference to the questions of "how" and "why") about the world order but often are critics as well to the changes in this respect. Thus, every

---

11. On the basis of the degree of development of one's essence of life, the people in this world can be classified into four categories, namely common man, scientist, philosopher and *yogī*. The development of essences of life in the first case is limited only to the day-to-day life, in the second (extrovert persons) the perception of the outer world is developed more than the inner, in the third case the perception of the inner world is developed more than the outer one (introvert persons) and in the case of *yogī* the perception of both inner and outer worlds is developed to its maximum possible. The existence of these categories of persons can be noticed at all times and in all cultures of the world. It is only their methodology and the degree of development of their faculties of understanding that has been changing with space and time. For further details in this connection see Chapter 1 citation 3 above.

culture has some philosophy and some science in its testament(s) and the amalgamation of the two appears as the so-called "religion." It is only the magnitude and the degree of depth of these ideas which vary from culture to culture and from time to time. In this way, a synonym of culture is also termed as "religion." In the context of Vedānta philosophy and Indian culture the word *dharma* is found more appropriate in place of religion, as it describes the way of life in totality and with so many provisions already built in it.

Human Being is the only being who could be the ultimate "realizer" or a perfect "describer" of the absolute reality in Nature via the understanding of two worlds, i.e. "inner" and "outer." As a matter of fact, the human Being acts as an "instrument" which is common to both these worlds as far as the understanding of Nature is concerned. By the *outer* world we mean the world governed by the laws of objective sciences (namely physics, chemistry, biology, etc.) and the *inner* world is the one which comes within the domain of philosophical thinking and that ultimately becomes the subject of realization. Though there is no sharp boundary between these two worlds, the methodology of studying them is however different. From the outer world while the human Being extracts objective reality, it becomes difficult for him to ignore the subjective reality of the inner world at the same time. This is true for all categories of persons irrespective of the degree of development of their essences of life. It is only the subtle part of the ego which comes on the way to suppress the realization of one over the other and thus brings the human Being in a particular category and in some cases this causes departure from the categories of *yogī* and common man. For the human Being, as a matter of fact, these realities of inner and outer worlds appear as the two sides of the same coin — the "absolute reality" or the "ultimate" truth in Nature. In some sense we can say that a philosopher deals with the knowledge of unmanifest whereas a scientist is mostly confined to the knowledge of manifest.

The working of the outer world, as mentioned earlier, appears to be describable to some extent in terms of some well-defined principles of objective science. These principles have universal acceptability in spite of some limitations on their validity and are verifiable at different space time points to a certain degree of accuracy provided the same physical conditions prevail there. On the other hand, although the laws for functioning of the inner world are also well defined[12] (from the point of view of a *yogī* — the man of perfection[13]) however they are not perceptible so easily to everybody. In fact in the latter case a certain degree of training is needed to perceive these laws of subjective science and each of us does not want to undergo such a training. A trace of these laws of subjective science can easily be looked into the philosophies of different cultures of the world. In some sense the quality of a philosophy can be judged from the extent of the depth to which these laws of subjective science are able to spell out the world-order and that too in an objective style. As a matter of fact a philosophy can be said to be a "perfect" one if it is capable of providing oneself a logical, reasonably convincing and systematic explanation of entire gamut of human experiences with reference to both inner and outer worlds at the same time and to the finest possible level. Naturally, such an explanation is possible if the philosophy originates out of some crisply defined and deep-rooted principles. Also, the creator(s) of the same must have given enough thought to them and that too in entirety.

It again depends on the ability of the creator of a testament of a particular philosophy as to what extent these laws of subjective science have been incorporated or highlighted in the concerned testament in spite of their realization by him. In this case the role of creator himself becomes crucial in terms of the development of his essences of life. If the creator happens to be

---

12. Swami Yukteswar Giri in *Autobiography of a Yogi* by Paramhans Yoganand, Bombay: Jaico Publication House, 1994.

13. Radhey Shyam Kaushal, 2003, op. cit.

a *yogī*, then the creation (testament) can be considered to be a perfect one. Thus, with regard to a perfect philosophy a few points are worth noting here:

(i) The cult or religion originated from a philosophy cannot remain in existence forever unless the *yogī*-category of persons are the creators of the testament, which is rather rare.

(ii) For an ordered lifestyle, no doubt certain tenets of religion are necessary but these tenets must be born out of a *double* realization of subjective reality in Nature, otherwise their operative part is going to be limited by the boundaries of space and time, particularly when the tenets are finite in number and do not allow much degree of freedom.

(iii) As we are fond of using models in objective science to understand the objective reality, the same is the picture here. As such the model of a religion can provide only a few glimpses of the subjective reality in Nature; otherwise the creator of a testament or the originator of a religion thereof suggests an ordered lifestyle sometimes leaving behind the absolute reality as a matter of realization. In objective science one discards a model as and when it is not ın tune with experiments. In the same way, tenets of religion (of faith) should be the subject of scrutiny from time to time, particularly for a progressive society.

(iv) Finally, note that a slight change in the postulates of a model of a religion can drastically affect the working of a common man, as all the followers of this category have not developed their essences of life to the same level. Such a change should not lead to a different religion and thereby leading to differences in the followers, in exactly the same way as in objective science the change of postulate of a model leads to just a correction and not to the different branch of science.

Every religion, in analogy with scientific methods, has[14, 15] three main ingredients (or aspects), namely (i) knowledge, (ii) methodology, and (iii) practice. If one does not go into the details of the aspects of methodology and practice, then the Indian philosophy originating from the last part of *Sāmaveda* can be considered as the "perfect" one. In this endeavour, no doubt the author may be considered as biased but the fact is that it is indeed so in view of its inherent features. It is only this Vedānta philosophy (particularly its knowledge aspect) which fulfils all the above requirements for a "perfect" philosophy. A justification for this choice is further elucidated in the next section.

1.5 Active and Passive Philosophies

As such a philosophy cannot be an active or a passive one on its own. These are the followers of the corresponding faith or religion who make it active or passive in terms of its applications in the day-to-day life. As a result, the assessment of the progress of society in terms of peace and pleasure enjoyed by the members will suggest a measure to this "activeness" of the underlying philosophy. If these standards prevail for a philosophy, then that philosophy can be said to be an *active* one; otherwise the same is reckoned as passive (may be in a certain proportion) or forgotten one in the same way as the trees on the pathway for a traveller. As a matter of fact if these standards for a philosophy prevail at all times and places, then the same is a "perfect" philosophy. Recall that the same is the case in the objective science. Theories are left behind and become passive as and when they are detuned with experiments.

On the other hand, the change in Nature is natural. The scientific advancements of modern times further supplement this rate of change. As this change affects our understanding

---

14. Radhey Shyam Kaushal, 1994, op. cit.

15. Radhey Shyam Kaushal, "Modelling in science and religion : From the point of view of Ancient Hindu Philosophy", *Science-Philosophy Interface* (Calcutta) 1 (1996) 40-53, No. 1.

of Nature from time to time, all three components of a religion, and accordingly the concerned philosophy, get affected. While the maximum change is bound to appear in the practice-aspect of a religion and comparatively less in the methodology-aspect, the knowledge-aspect in principle is expected to remain intact if the same is properly founded by the creator(s). Of course, the examples/simile/metaphor used to illustrate the tenets can be updated according to developments and environments. Most of the cultures in the world undergo this kind of change. If the knowledge-aspect in a particular religion was already poor, the same is not going to sustain against this change and the corresponding philosophy is going to be passive which might decay with time. Even among the active philosophies, those that have sound and well-founded knowledge-aspect in its religion counterpart (with regard to the finest explanation of all the fundamental processes responsible for the human behaviour and experiences) will survive relatively longer or forever.

There are only a few philosophies in the world which are ever-green within the above framework mainly because their knowledge-aspect originated perhaps after a deep thinking of the (creator) seers. This knowledge-aspect, undoubtedly, is beyond the boundaries of space and time and the same has withstood firmly against all tests of time and history. In Indian context this philosophy of Vedas prevails via "Sanātana Dharma" (cf. Sect. 12.5) meaning thereby "the (spiritual and scriptural) ordinances governing an ordered lifestyle at all times." In fact in totality it is a way of life. In this philosophy with a lot of degree of freedom, the Nature, the human and non-human Beings and their interactions have already been investigated by seers to the finest possible level. It is only a matter of putting them properly in a modern scientific perspective and this is precisely the aim of this package.

1.6 Limitations of (Objective) Science

With regard to the complete description and the understanding of the universe objective science and its laws show limitations on several fronts. As a matter of fact the laws of objective sciences offer explanation of only a limited part of the universe (which includes both inner and outer worlds) and a large part of it still remains unexplained. Further, these laws describe the functioning of the universe in pieces and not in totality. While the understanding of the universe in totality is possible only by a *yogī* (a man of perfection), scientists and philosophers jointly or independently, however, are bound to fail in this endeavour mainly because of their limitations. Even for an understanding of the world-order in pieces, objective sciences or their laws show limitations to this effect.

About 30 years ago, Victor F. Weisskopf[16] a theoretical physicist, highlighted the limits on scientific studies in general. He talked about two types of frontiers of science which respectively show the internal and external limits of science. In the former case the *creativity of Nature* itself keeps on setting the limits from time to time in view of the ever progressing scientific methodology. In the latter case, however, *human creativity* is held responsible to set the limits on scientific laws.

According to Weisskopf there are three aims of science — comprehension, explanation and prediction. Comprehension indicates the presence of a general idea of how a phenomenon comes about, what are the general causes and how it is related to other parts of the natural world. It implies a "demystification" of the part of natural world to which the phenomenon belongs. Explanation goes further, it tells us why the phenomenon or the process under consideration runs one way and not otherwise. Prediction is even more specific, it tells us what will happen to a well defined system in the future when certain conditions are fulfilled. There is also such a thing as a prediction of the past, called *retrodiction,* when conclusions are drawn in with regard to the yet unexplored previous history of a given set of objects.

16. Victor F. Weisskopf, "Frontiers and Limits of Science", *American Scientist* **65** (1977) 405.

The internal limits on science, according to Weisskopf, applies only to the possibilities of explanation and prediction. They do not restrict comprehension. The reasons for these limitations can be subsumed under the term "amplification effects." It implies that very small change causes sometimes very large effects. For example, consider the fate of a gas molecule in the atmosphere. Very small changes in the initial conditions of the molecule are quickly amplified in the effects during the course of its collisions with other molecules. In elaborating on the external limits of science Weisskopf attributes them mainly to the comprehension aspect of the phenomenon. This is with regard to the understanding of the phenomenon in the context of other human experiences which are "complementary" to scientific description. In fact there can be several mutually exclusive approaches to understand the reality in Nature and scientific approach is only one of them. Weisskopf cites only a few examples to this effect but there are many phenomena in Nature which are going to set the limits on science and scientific laws. The possibilities of combining words to form a book, colours to form a painting, views of individuals to form a cultural expression (e.g. social sciences, cult, etc.) are some cases cited by Weisskopf. Such cases indicate the discretization of a characteristic in Nature and science offers only a unique way of combining them which are again supported by ideally set experiments. We shall return to such discussions in the next chapter.

The laws of chemistry by and large constitute the subset of physics. On the other hand, a large number of working principles in biology in modern times also depend heavily on physical principles except for the explanation of a few phenomena like birth and death. In a nut-shell, the physical laws are still leading the show as far as the understanding of the Universe is concerned. Not only this, the laws of physical sciences have also found an application domain in soft disciplines in recent years.[17]

17. There are now many situations in the study of social science and humanities where the physical concepts and the corresponding →

For example, the concepts of Bose-Einstein condensation, equation of continuity in car traffic, etc. are frequently used.

With regard to the limitations of physical laws for a complete description of Nature and subsequent understanding of its functioning, the following points are worth noting:

(i) Physical laws successfully work for closed system (a system is said to be closed if it does not interact with its surroundings and this may not always by the case). For their application to open systems, corrections have been proposed but with their limited success.

(ii) The physical laws are normally framed for mathematically idealized situations. For a physicist, the gases are perfect, surfaces are smooth, conductors are perfect, etc. but in reality it is surely not so. Even the Newton's law of gravitation describes a force between two point masses (an idealized situation).

(iii) Within the framework of the three-world concept (world one — which exists, world two — which we perceive, and the world three — which physics describes by way of models), the models play an important role. In spite of the fact that a model cannot be the complete reality of Nature, models are distributed to all branches of physics (cf. Appendix B). Model can only offer some glimpses of absolute reality, or at most, they can describe the objective reality and that too asymptotically in the sense that one goes on refining the given model with a hope to obtain a better and better description of the observed facts (observations) (see, citation 3, Chapter 6).

So far most of the models used in physics are based on linearity. The non-linearity has been tactfully avoided. For

---

→ mathematical equations are applied for analysis purposes and perhaps to give a quantitative flavour to the description of the phenomenon, see sections 3.2.2; 5.2.3 and Chapter 4 of citation 3 above.

example, force law for a simple pendulum, Hooke's law in elasticity, Ohm's law in electricity, etc. are considered linear in terms of the algebraic equations. Similarly a large number of examples can be cited from the cases where only linear differential (total or partial) equations have been considered. Look at the setting of the Schrodinger equation in quantum mechanics or for that matter the Dirac equation in the relativistic case. In view of the predictive power of these mathematical settings one is amazed to see the Nature's liking for these sorts of linearities. But this cannot be the only liking of Nature. As a matter of fact, a major share of Nature's liking goes to non-linearity with regard to its objective description and the account of nonlinearity in the description of Nature cannot indefinitely be avoided in view of the advancing technologies on the experimental front. Note that Nature by and large is non-linear from the point of view of objective sciences. Non-linearity manifests in Nature more than the linearity. But human (scientist's) limitations come in the way to account for it. Moreover, there is a plurality of departures from linearity, i.e. there is no single way to account for the non-linearity in the system whether it is the case of algebraic or differential equations. Again if you identify the type of non-linearity, the methods for accounting for the same are still inadequate as far as the exact solutions of the problem are concerned.[18]

(iv) There is another dimension of limitations of physical laws, i.e. the case of "non-centrality." By and large the physical phenomena are investigated either in one (space) dimension or in the radial coordinate in the case of higher dimensions. Again this is a kind of idealization of the situation as the Nature cannot restrict itself only to these

18. See, for example, R.S. Kaushal and D. Parashar, *Advanced methods of Mathematical Physics* (New Delhi: Narosa, USA: CRC Press, London: Alpha Science, 2000); second half of the book is devoted to such problems.

situations. In many cases mathematical tools so developed (in terms of the integrability of the system) fail miserably as and when one starts accounting[19] for the non-centrality of the underlying forces governing the phenomenon. As in (iii) above, again there appears the plurality of departures from the centrality. In this case, the situation is however better because the space-dimensions are postulated to be only three in physics; therefore the plurality of departures from centrality is limited.

(v) When a phenomenon is described in terms of constituents of a system (sub-systems), the laws of statistical mechanics or that of stochastic mechanics are used. In fact these laws successfully work for the case when the number of particles (constituents) is assumed to be infinitely large or a particular type of randomness in the system is considered in the latter case (again a mathematically idealized situation) and this may not always be the case.

(vi) Physical laws work well for inanimate objects. They badly fail when applied to animate objects. As and when one brings in the role of "will power" or "consciousness" of a Being, physical laws are silent as far as the description of such a phenomenon is concerned. For example, one can easily write down the equation for the (parabolic) path of a piece of stone thrown in the field of earth's gravity. However, it is not possible so easily to write the equation for a live bird thrown in air. Force law for a pendulum also shows limitations (see, citation 3, Appendix B) when the suspended bob and/or the support is an animate (conscious) object, etc. We will come across many such examples in the next section. In fact the whole book will deal with such situations in which the living being will be part of the physical system.

19. See, for example, R.S. Kaushal, *Classical and Quantum Mechanics of Non-central Potentials: A Survey of Two-Dimensional Systems*, New Delhi: Narosa, Heidelberg: Springer-Verlag, 1998.

(vii) When a person is doing the act of running at a point in the room, this is the case of velocity/acceleration without variation in space or when a supersonic aircraft passes by a person he notices the case of velocity/acceleration without variation in time. Thus, the terms like velocity and acceleration in physics have limited meanings in terms of the definition of a closed system.

1.7 Interactions and Associated Processes in Nature

By definition the interaction means some sort of net effect produced as a result of the presence of two or more objects in Nature, particularly when they are placed in close (!) vicinity of each other. Loosely speaking, action and reaction between the objects constitute the interaction and one can say that it is a synonym of force or experience which is experienced by the objects due to the presence of each other and sometimes with reference to a third observer or instrument. In this case several terms need clarification.

The word "experience" means some sort of recording of the event occurred as a result of interaction. The recording can be made either by an instrument (which we shall consider as an inanimate object with limited capacity of recording and with a fixed level of analysing power) or by an observer (which we shall consider as an animate object with infinite capacity of recording and with various levels of analysing power depending upon the development of his essences of life). Further, this experience of interaction between the objects O_1 and O_2, in the present case, can arise as a result of two situations, namely when the experiencer is an outsider — a third (animate or inanimate) object — or when the experiencer himself is one of the two (or many) objects.

The "closeness" of vicinity or proximity within which the effect of an interaction is noticeable, to some extent, is the characteristic of the interaction itself and this is called the "range" of the respective interaction. For the interactions originating out of the space-time structure of Nature alone (physical forces), this range is again expressible in terms of space-time scales; otherwise, like the interaction, the range can also be beyond the domains of space and/or time scales. This is how one understands the closeness of the objects in order to enable them to have an interaction. The range can be infinite in the space-time domain and it can also be beyond this domain if the infinity is defined in the latter case.

The nature of compatibility of the objects or the so-called "correlation" among them also characterizes the interaction. The objects in the Universe can broadly be classified into two categories, namely the living (animate) and the non-living (inanimate) ones and accordingly this leads to three possible types of two-body interactions, viz.

(i) interaction between inanimate-inanimate objects (II-type)

(ii) interaction between inanimate-animate (or animate-inanimate) objects (IA- or AI-type)

(iii) interaction between animate-animate objects (AA-type)

Note that the difference may also arise between IA- and AI-type interactions at a subtler level, but we postpone these details for the moment. Also, animate objects in Nature are characterized by the presence of an additional element, called *consciousness*, in it and the objective sciences have yet to accept and accommodate this concept in their laws (cf. Chapter 3). The above classification of interactions is basically for two bodies; otherwise one can as well have higher-body interactions, like IIA-, IAA-, III-, AAA-type for the three bodies or IAAA-, IIAA-, IIIA-, IIII-, AAAA-type for the four bodies and so on. This will simply complicate the studies. Sometimes, as will be noticed later, the ordering (or arrangement) of objects in space-time and subsequently the ordering of letters I and A in the above abbreviations will also matter.

It may be mentioned that an animate object is not only a source of consciousness but it could as well be a conscious "participator" in the processes defined below. Of course, in the absence of consciousness (the case of a dead Being) an animate object can be considered as an inanimate object. Further, for an objective scientist the interactions not involving the letter A, namely II-, III-, IIII-type, etc. are the only ones of main interest to their theories as the same still fail to account either for consciousness or for will power of a living Being. Thus, in view of the above classification, there is a vast class of interactions which has not yet been explored by the scientists and their account is obviously necessary in order to understand Nature in totality. Before proceeding further some examples of the above interactions will be helpful. In what follows we present the cases where only two-body interactions dominate the process and the examples corresponding to three and higher body interactions are ignored for the time being. They can, however, easily be sought in the day-to-day life in a similar way. In fact these examples are the illustrative ones and as such will form a basis for our future discussions. Also, while the above classification of interactions is rather vague, one can as well have a feel for their finer distinctions through these examples.

Fig. **1.1** depicts the II-type interaction (a subject of physics) between the inanimate objects, namely electron and proton. This is a Feynman diagram for the electron-proton scattering in which the space-time mediated electromagnetic interaction occurs via the exchange of one photon between the electron and the proton. When considering the interaction between the electron and proton (cf. *fig*. 1.1) note that the presence of observer or the apparatus is ignored, then what to say of the world (or its role) in which the electron and proton are placed. In other words, the electron-proton system is considered as isolated or closed.

Fig. **1.2** presents the case of an AI-type interaction in which a boy is about to eat a slice of pizza. The interaction process in this case is somewhat simplified as the boy is already holding the pizza slice in his hand. While the boy will eat it, he has not yet made contact of pizza with his tongue. As the boy is holding the slice in his hand he is free to eat it at any time he desires, irrespective of any change in certain part of the environment. His mind is prepared to see whether the pizza is hot or cold, his intellect is ready to decide the taste of it and ego will also do its job by storing the feeling of the taste and thereby noticing a satisfaction by the process of eating. Compare this situation with a general one, when the pizza slice was lying on a table, not only the jobs of mind, intellect or ego would have increased with regard to the availability of pizza in that case but the role of other essences of life such as sense organs responsible for action would have also come into play. While the boy knows he will eat the pizza, the pizza (an inanimate object) does not know who is going to eat it or when and how it is going to be eaten or as to what would have been the fate with regard to its creation or destruction. In summary, there is no question of memory in pizza slice (so is in the case of electron or proton in the previous example) for a man of science. (However, a person from literature can personify pizza and impose or assume such a concept.) Through this example, it can be seen how an open system approaches towards the closed-ness by continuously diminishing the size of environment. Also, note the two situations: (a) when the inanimate object is in the proximity of sense organs, and (b) when it is outside the range of sense organs. Accordingly, the concepts of a contact force or those of an action-at-a-distance (AAD) or an action-at-a-time (AAT) type forces will emerge.

***Figs.* 1.3 (a), (b), (c) and (d)** represent the cases of AA-type interaction with its subtle distinctions. In *fig*. 1.3(a), two girls are bothered about their dress code — the case of interaction between their sense organs or biological bodies leading to the external appearance only. *fig*. 1.3(b) in which two persons are enjoying the scratching of each other's body — an experience at the mental level — is the case of an action-at-time (AAT) type force in addition to the contact force. *fig*. 1.3(c) displays the interactions of high order in terms of their fine-ness. Here two ladies have already arrived at (of course, without any contact so far) the peak of certain interactions (again by suppressing some others). It appears that while the oral fight (verbal duel) between them continues, they have prepared themselves enough for a physical fight — perhaps a culmination; otherwise the interactions at-a-distance or at-a-time might also continue later even if they disperse at the present stage. Such a limit of ultimate fight is further demonstrated in *fig.* 1.3(d). Here, two persons are already passing through the state of ultimate. They are not only using their body parts in the quarrel but also the external instrument(s) for the purpose.

***Fig.* 1.4** demonstrates the case of a man-machine interaction of a highly complicated nature in the sense that it appears to be a 4-body interaction, i.e. of a (man-machine)-(man-machine)-type. This picture, at present, no doubt appears to be only out of imagination but one never knows it can be the reality of tomorrow in a certain limit. In this figure a man headed with a computer (containing only limited analogue of essences of life) on the right is considered to be interacting with another man on the left who is headed with modern equipments (like sensors, etc.) which are sensitive to the signals sent by the computer. As a result there appears to be the initiation of action of the outer sense organs, like lifting up the cups of tea, etc. Note that here computer (or, for that matter, sensors, etc.) are not the ordinary (mechanical) machines but they carry a certain element of memory like that in a Being. Further, note that the memory in the computer is fixed (it is the one created in it again by a human Being) and the capacity of sensing in the equipment is also limited (limitations in designing and the limitations on the principles on which its working is based). While these machines lack in terms of certain essences of life compared to a man, they do not have much degrees of freedom to enhance or to decrease their capacity of working, i.e. they suffer from will-power and/or consciousness.

***Fig.* 1.5** depicts a case of interaction between human and non-human Beings, of course via an inanimate object, i.e. a piece of bread. We shall return to the details of these processes later.

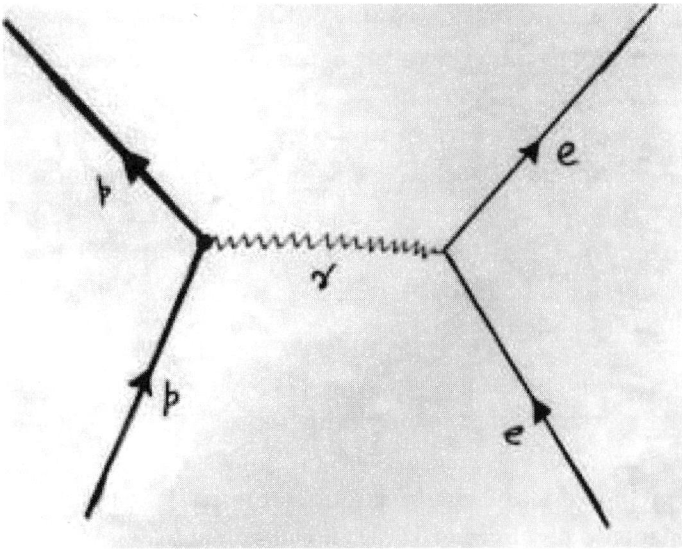

fig. 1.1: Feynman diagram for the interaction between two inanimate objects (physical forces): An example of electron-proton interaction (II-type).

fig. 1.2: An example of interaction between animate and inanimate objects; Eating of pizza piece (AI or IA-type).

fig. 1.3: Examples of interactions between two animate objects (human Beings) (AA-type).

1.3 (a): The question of dress-codes

1.3: (b) The mystery of itching

1.3 (c): Preparing a ground for the ultimate (fight).

1.3 (d): Final preparations: Exchange of blows.

fig. 1.4: Possible interactions between two computers/machines (II-type).

fig. 1.5: Example of interaction between human and non-human Beings (AA-type).

1.7.1 FUNDAMENTAL PROCESSES

From the above illustrations it is clear that except for *figs*. 1.1 and 1.4 the fundamental processes and interactions responsible for the actions of objects in this Universe, in general, are different from those discussed in modern times in the domains of objective science. In fact the processes of objective science, particularly when the human component is involved, are the outcome of somewhat more fundamental processes or interactions and about which the objective sciences are either silent or their tools are inadequate for the purposes of accounting for this fundamentality.

For physical objects the question of fundamentality of a process or an interaction was discussed as early as in 1940s by several workers. It was only in 1960s that the ideas were crystallized and Richard Feynman[20] took the lead in investigating the question of fundamentality of a process in physical terms. In fact the best-studied interaction at that time was the electromagnetic interaction and all theoretical investigations were focused around that via the elementary particles like electrons and photons. In the context of electromagnetic interaction the fundamentality of these objects, while retained even today, about a dozen more building blocks of the Universe have also been postulated to describe the other three, namely strong, weak and gravitational interactions and sometimes in a unified way with improved tools of what is now called 'string theory.' Note that in these descriptions of fundamentality of a process or an interaction only the space-time structure of Nature, which basically is an attribute of the consciousness of a Being, has been explored to its finest possible level from the timely standards. As discussed in Section 1.6, since the role of consciousness ignored in such a physical description of Nature this sets limitations on the well-tested (again from the present standards) theories of modern science. In the same spirit the concept of elementarity of physical object has been periodically

20. R.P. Feynman, *Theory of Fundamental Processes*, New York: Berjamin, 1962.

questioned in the last century. As a result newer and newer disciplines in physics, namely molecular, atomic, nuclear and quark physics have emerged with the passage of time. In biosciences the discovery of gene has also added to this trend of development. Whether those are the physical objects or the gene, they are looked upon by the scientists again in terms of space-time structure of Nature and that too in a highly restricted sense. On the other hand, in the presence of consciousness or its source, the above concept of fundamentality associated with a process or an interaction cannot be accepted by any standard for exploring the ultimate truth in Nature. Thus the role of essences of life of a Being in these theories becomes essential to seek an explanation of its behaviour in totality.

Symbolically, a "reaction" or a "process" in physical sciences depicted on a board or on a paper and going on in the mind of a scientist, is represented conventionally by,

$$A+B \underset{conditions}{\overset{physical}{\rightleftarrows}} C+D. \qquad (1.1)$$

The objects on the left are termed as "reactants" and those on the right as "products." The arrow towards right (left) is the "time arrow" representing the process in the forward (backward) direction. The phrase(s) above and below the arrow(s) represent the physical conditions (like temperature, pressure or environment, in general) favouring the occurrence of the process. Only two objects in the initial and final states are shown in (1.1) mainly for simplicity; otherwise one can equally well have more than two objects in either of the initial or final states. However, accordingly the complexity in understanding the corresponding process increases. Note that the objects A, B, C, D etc. can be composites and their constituents can also participate in the process. In that case, one can question not only the elementarity of the objects A, B, C and D but also the fundamentality of the process as the latter leads to several other sub-processes which in turn correspond to different types of interactions and energy scales. It may so happen that the reactants and products could be the same but with different arrangement of constituents in them.

The study of the process (1.1) mainly lies in its occurrence in the state of space-time mediated equilibrium and the achievement of this equilibrium is attributed to physical laws, like the conservation laws for energy (mass), momentum, angular momentum, etc. In addition to these laws several others, originating from the intrinsic properties of the participating objects are also considered to describe the reaction (1.1). It may be mentioned that only two types of interactions, namely the contact and action-at-a-distance (AAD)- type forces considered so far in physical theories conform to experiments in the science laboratory. Further, neither the laws are derived, nor the interactions or processes are investigated so far when the forces among the objects A, B, C, D (or among their constituents) are of the action-at-a-time (AAT)- or action-at-a-distance time (AADT)-type. Some of these situations arise when some or all A, B, C, D are the living Beings.

To investigate this kind of fundamentality of a process in which living Beings also participate, one has to postulate new types of interactions, (field) quanta, particles and the environment for a complete description of a process or a phenomenon. To this effect, a broad class of interactions is already outlined in the previous sections. Finer details of these interactions emerge when one defines these living Beings in terms of their essences of life. This we shall address in future chapters within the framework of Vedānta philosophy.

1.7.2 FUNDAMENTAL INTERACTIONS: QUANTA, PARTICLES AND ENVIRONMENT

As mentioned, physics at present deals with four sharply quantified fundamental, space-time mediated interactions, twenty-four elementary particles (six quarks, six leptons and their anti-counterparts), and about half-a-dozen field quanta and gauge bosons. Similarly, in biosciences (zoology and botany) the fundamental entity presently established to describe various so-called life processes is the "gene" which works through DNA and other similar objects. Gene which exhibits many life-like properties (like its reproduction in an appropriate environment, etc.) however is kept intact from the domain of consciousness-manifesting features such as free-will which are the attributes of living Beings. For the description of processes of behavioural sciences in general and those of human experiences in particular, the role of gene is no doubt important at the fundamental level, but once the life is created after the conception then it goes in the background[21] in the form of *prārabdha* or *sañcita* (long term) category of actions of a Being. For this purpose, then comes the role of essences of life of a Being. These essences of life basically are the philosophical entities the existence of which we all perceive. These essences of life, if quantified properly, can act as elementary (fundamental) entities to describe the human (or non-human) behaviour.

With regard to quantification of these essences of life there may be controversies, since philosophy has a root in culture and there is plurality of cultures in this world. But, as mentioned, we shall restrict to Vedānta philosophy and try to stick to the number and properties of these essences of life as described there. In any case, in order to develop a new theory of human behaviour in terms of these entities one has to make a beginning from somewhere. In the next chapter we shall return to the details of these essences of life.

1.8 Human Experiences and Behavioural Science: The Role of Fundamental Processes

An experience is the outcome of a decision taken on the basis of

---

21. Vedānta philosophy looks for three-types of sources of actions of a Being — *prārabdha, sañcita* and *kriyamāna*. The *prārabdha* class is attributed to those actions performed in previous birth(s); the *sañcita* class to those performed in this birth and *kriyamāna* are the ones performed in the present by the Being with the given set of essences of life. Further details can be found in Chapter 4.

stored memory in the sub-conscious part of ego. Experiences first appear at the level of mind, later materialized in this world into actions through the sense organs responsible for knowledge and action and the body as well. One can say that the revelation of experiences is some kind of a reverse process from inside to outside. As a matter of fact the knowledge gained out of this world first goes inside through the above instruments (essences of life) and then returns back again after a fine tuning and mostly in an analogous[22] manner.

In other words, after going through the examples listed in the previous section (cf. *figs*. 1.1 to 1.5) it can be noticed that all actions of a Being performed in this world are the outcome of some fundamental processes taking place inside him. In these processes, beside the roles of the world outside, biological body and sense organs, the roles of mind, intellect and ego manifest in all cases in a certain proportion. As these (philosophical) entities are fundamental not only for the existence of a Being but also in performing the actions in this outer world, the processes in which they are participating are also termed as *fundamental* in some sense, particularly the ones occurring in the microbody ($\mathcal{M}$).[23] In fact the processes occurring at the level of the gross-body ($\mathcal{G}$) can again be described, to some extent, in terms of the ones occurring at the level of microbody. However, we shall list them under the head of "fundamental processes" in this book. Note that the occurrence of all these processes makes sense in the presence of the casual body ($\mathcal{C}$).

1.9 Motivation of the Book and Arrangement of Chapters

To pinpoint the motivation of the present book, we comment

22. Radhey Shyam Kaushal, 2003, op. cit.

23. At a subtle level human Being can be considered as the union of three bodies, namely causal ($\mathcal{C}$), micro ($\mathcal{M}$) and gross ($\mathcal{G}$) according to the fineness of the essences of life constituting them. Details can be seen in Chapter 2.

on some recent works[24, 25, 26, 27, 28] published on similar concepts and ideas and pertaining respectively to the philosophies of the East and the West. With regard to the Eastern thought, Panda[29] discusses the Vedāntic concept of *māyā* in the context of modern physics more in a philosophical manner. He not only looks for the interpretation of the space time mediated concepts of modern physics, like quantum mechanics, relativity, astrophysics, particle physics, etc. in the deep-researched concepts of Vedic science, but at times also identifies these concepts in the philosophy of Advaita Vedānta, mostly on the basis of analogies.[30] Through such studies, no doubt, Panda has been able to touch many deep-rooted concepts of Vedānta philosophy, but with a view to explain modern physics which itself is based on so many assumptions and subsequently on the thus-derived models. He seems to be unaware of the intricately interwoven roles and limitations of these models in various branches of physics and biosciences (cf. Chapter 6, and Appendices B and C) as far as the search for the ultimate truth in Nature is concerned. On the other hand, whether one is a modern scientist or an age-old *ṛṣi*, human thoughts and experiences, if they originate from the same innermost existence (soul), have to reveal the same ultimate truth. The only difference remains in the methods of quantifying them. In this respect, the language of mathematics has proved

24. N.C. Panda, *Maya in Physics*, Delhi: Motilal Banarsidass, 2005.
25. Hermann Weyl, Frank Wilczek (Introduction), *Philosophy of Mathematics and Natural Science*, Princeton University Press, 2009.
26. Roger Penrose, "Physics of Tao", *Times of India* (New Delhi), 28 January, 2003.
27. Roger Penrose, *Shadows of the Mind : A Search for the Missing Science of Consciousness*, Oxford: Oxford University Press, 1994.
28. Roger Penrose, *The large, The Small and the Human Being*, Cambridge: Cambridge University Press, 1997.
29. N.C. Panda, op. cit.
30. Radhey Shyam Kaushal, 2003, op. cit.

to be a powerful tool as far as the development of objective science in the West is concerned. Similar tools, if applied to the hidden subjective science in Vedic literature, can open new vistas with regard to understanding of the role of essences of life in human behaviour and experiences. The present package is an effort in this direction.

Another recent work that clearly highlights the necessity of a subjective science (or, in particular, the role of consciousness in physical theories) and requires a discussion here is Hermann Weyl's view as summarized by the Nobel Laureate Frank Wilzcek:[31]

> The objective world simply is, it does not happen. Only to gauge of my consciousness, crawling along the lifeline of my body, does a section of this world come to life as a fleeting image in space which continuously changes with time.

After a penetrating critique of the mechanical concept of causality, that prevails and is intricately spread over in various physical theories Weyl, in the end, also feels the necessity of the concept of consciousness (particularly in understanding the dual role of ego) as the solution of the body-soul problem.

Like this, there are several other philosophers of science or physicists (who in fact generally become philosophers in the last phase of their active life) in the West, who also speculated the necessity of the concept of consciousness in physical theories, for example, in the context of the famous mind-body problem. However, the inner essences of life, mind, intellect and ego (or their roles in human actions) are not clearly identified in the Western philosophy (cf. Chapter 3). Contrarily, Vedic science has to say a lot on this front and the same now needs an analytical development.

In analogy with physical theories, an attempt is made in this book to look for a unifying mechanism of fundamental processes

---

31. Franck Wilezek, op. cit. in citation 25.

taking place inside the human Being and are responsible for all actions and behaviour in outer world. In this connection Roger Penrose's ideas are worth quoting:[32]

> The conflict between science and religion can be seen as an extension of the conflict between different religious outlooks. We need to realize that the growth of new knowledge will necessitate a revision of religious beliefs. . . . Nevertheless, the questions raised and addressed by various religions are quintessential to human existence. Although science has not made any significant headway towards answering these questions so far, I think, it needs to broaden its horizon to take on board such questions.

Further, "we have to explore within ourselves to take science forward. In principle you might be able to acquire knowledge internally, but in practice you will require help from observations in the physical world." In addition, Roger Penrose highlights[33, 34] many situations and examples whose complete understanding would require an account of the hidden concept of consciousness. In a nut-shell the net outcome of all actions of a Being performed in this world culminates into two objectives, namely peace and pleasure. While the peace is subjective in nature the pleasure is largely objective. Since pleasure too has roots in peace, the latter is more fundamental. The approach followed in this book is somewhat scientific and hence it might appeal to all categories of persons. The arrangement of chapters is as follows:

The continuous and coherent spectrum of knowledge emerging out all along from the study of Nature is discretized and accordingly compartmentalized from the point of view of its extraction, classification and simplification for all three categories of persons (except *yogī*). For a *yogī* however, true knowledge appears to be a sum total of all aspects of a

32. Roger Penrose, op. cit. in citation 26.
33. Roger Penrose, 1994, op. cit.
34. Roger Penrose, 1997, op. cit.

phenomenon and that too in entirety. In this knowledge-extraction process models play an important role. Also the models used for this purpose lie in the domains of objective and subjective sciences. The ones used in objective sciences are now already available in science textbooks, however some of them are briefly outlined in Appendices B and C. Those belonging to subjective science — and we plan to use them in this book — are outlined in the next chapter. As a matter of fact, in the language of fine arts, the models of physics (cf. Appendix B) are like the poems of a poet whose ideas are subject to verification in this world whereas the models of biosciences (cf. Appendix C) are the physical reality like the creation of a sculptor.

In Chapter 3, we plan to recapitulate the Western view and views of modern science with regard to the theory of *karma* (actions) or about the above-mentioned processes. In this connection only limited aspects will be presented because of limitations of the author.

Chapters 4 and 5 are devoted to developing the ideas which are going to be useful in the subsequent chapters. In a way they form the backbone of the book. In Chapter 4 the Vedānta theory of *karma* is presented in a logical and scientific style and in Chapter 5 a basis for the study of fundamental processes in the domain of subjective science is developed by way of highlighting the tools and rules of the game again in a logical style. The tools and rules developed in these chapters are then applied to study the varieties of processes in Chapters 6-9.

In Chapter 6, we briefly outline the interactions and processes of objective science in view of the modern physical theories, mainly for comparison in the subsequent chapters. The role of human Being in a process is introduced for the first time in Chapter 7 where we discuss the man-machine interaction. In particular, within the framework of patomic model the case of human-computer interaction is discussed. Further, mind-body and mind-body-machine interactions are investigated in this chapter. In Chapter 8, we discuss the interaction of human Being with physical world within the framework of Vedānta philosophy. In Chapter 9 the interactions among human Beings are elaborated and subsequently the emergence of the subject of social sciences is discussed.

Chapter 10 is devoted to get a feel of the behaviour of non-human Beings by way of highlighting their latent powers, of course within the framework of their limited essences of life. To this effect, the development of their essences of life and the associated fundamental processes taking place inside them are discussed. Some of the aspects of the theory developed in these chapters are then put to a test in the laboratories of human and non-human behaviours in day-to-day life in Chapters 11-14. In Chapter 11, we discuss the limitation of the above theory and the possible connection between the above fundamental processes and the biochemical processes which take place before an action is actually performed by a Being. From the application point of view these discussions are further extended in Chapter 12. Several important applications are highlighted in this chapter with reference to humanities and social sciences.

While the ideas developed in this book provide a fine, logical and scientific explanation of many processes taking place in performing the actions in the inner and outer worlds by the Being, the question of what one achieves out of it is discussed in Chapter 13. In this chapter, in the light of Vedānta philosophy, the purpose of above studies is ultimately hinted towards attaining peace in life on the basis of the principle of *neti neti*. From the point of view of a scientific mind, several important conclusions are drawn from these studies and accordingly future aspects of such a theory are discussed in Chapter 14.

Although the development of the subject is smooth, still to facilitate the reader all these chapters (except the present one) are grouped into three parts. Chapters 2-6, dealing with the basics of Eastern and Western views on the subject, constitute

Part I. In Part II (Chapters 7-10) the development of a new theory and its workability is discussed, and finally, applications and future prospects of this theory are highlighted in Part III (Chapters 11-14). In the end six appendices on certain specialized topics are also included. These appendices namely Appendix A on the details of patonic model, Appendices B and C respectively on the details of modelling game in physical and biological sciences, Appendix D on presenting a basis for the Ayurvedic treatment of diseases, Appendix E on a new style of generalization of Hamilton's principle of least action in physics, and Appendix F on a brief survey of certain exotic phenomena in the realm of human behaviour, will further facilitate and justify the above style of studies.

Part I
Basics of Eastern and Western Views

2

Modelling
Basics of Vedānta Philosophy

WITH a view to developing the tools and rules of the game to study the fundamental processes in future chapters, we present here some basic tenets of modelling carried out in Vedānta philosophy since time immemorial. In fact such modellings in both objective and subjective sciences are essential mainly because of the limitations of human essences of life (EOL) with regard to the study of Nature and the underlying processes therein and that too in entirety.[1] While the models used in objective science at different space-time scales are now available in many science texts of different standards (and some are listed in Appendices B and C), the ones needed for the development of subjective science have to be framed in an appropriate spirit for their later use.

As a matter of fact some models in humanities and social sciences have already been in use to explain and understand the proliferation of data in modern times though with their limited validity and not so deep a foundation. Moreover, a scientific and fine-tuned version of these models, if available, will be an asset as far as the development of quantitative study of fundamental processes in the domain of subjective science is concerned. Such a version of models of Nature and human Being is beautifully described in Vedānta philosophy in a variety of ways and it is just a matter of putting them in a proper scientific

---

1. See, Radhey Shyam Kaushal, *Structural Analogies in Understanding Nature*, New Delhi: Anamaya Publishers, 2003, Chapter 6.

Table 2.1 : Some Examples of Trinity, Trio and Triad in Vedānta Philosophy

S. No.	*Characteristic(s)/ Feature(s)*	*Trinity, trio or triad*		*Source/Ref.*	*Context(s)/Remark(s)*
		Sanskrit/Hindi Words	*Respective English translation*		
1.	*Guṇas* — Nature born qualities (*triguṇa*)	*Sattva* (*S*), *Rajas* (*R*), *Tamas* (*T*)	Best positive of the quality, better of the quality, negative of the quality, from the point of view of ethical/human values.	*SMBG*: 14/5-18;22-26, *SMBG*; Chap. 3, 17, 18	These three *guṇas*, in conjunction with several other features, accordingly help in identifying and classifying the personality of a human Being. In particular, these *guṇas* qualify for the following features/characteristics as sāttvic, rājasic or tāmasic; (a) *śraddhā* — faith, (b) *tapa* — penance, (c) *bhojana* — food, (d) *tyāga* — Relinquishment (e) *yajña* — sacrifice, (f) *dāna* — gift (or charity), (g) Austerity of (1) body (2) speech (senses) and (3) mind, (h) *jñāna* — the knowledge, (i) *karma* — the action (j) *karttā* — the doer

					(k) *buddhi* — the intellect (reason), (l) *dhṛti*—firmness (m) *sukha* — joy (pleasure).
2.	Basis of an action	*Prārabdha, Sañcita, Kriyamāṇa*	Destined due to previous (past) birth(s), accumulated in this birth, performed in the present.		Any action and the fruit thereof is controlled by these three factors as far as the outcome of the action is concerned.
3.	Triple gate of hell	*Kāma, Krodha, Lobha*	Passion, anger, greed	*SMBG*: 16/21	This trio suggests the beginning of the downfall of a personality.
4.	3-fold incentives to action	*Jñāta, Jñāna, Jñyeya*	The knower, the knowledge, the object of knowledge	*SMBG*: 18/18	As a result of these incentives one feels like performing an action.
5.	3-fold constituents of action	*Karttā, Karma, Karaṇa*	The doer, the action, the organ of action.	*SMBG*: 18/18	Any performed action is an outcome of the functioning of these constituents.
6.	Trio used for revelation of perception	*Manasā, Vācā, Karmaṇā*	Mind, speech (senses), action	*SMBG*: 16/1	The straightforwardness of a person is normally characterized by the degree of coordination offered by the constituents of this trio.

7.	**Other useful trios**				
(a)	Human behaviour/ social dynamics	*Deśa, Kāla, Āvasyakatā*	Space, time, necessity	—	A great deal of working conditions of a common man can be attributed to this trio, particularly with reference to personal necessities.
(b)	-do-	*Deśa, Kāla, Dhana*	Space, time, money		The functioning of a businessman or a marketing customer is the outcome of the co-ordination of the constituents of this trio.
(c)	-do- (3Ps)	*Sukha, Dukha, Śānti*	Pleasure, pain, peace		This trio controls the working of a person in his relaxing mood. This working again can be in the background of time or mind. Mind offers a universal background for attaining peace. During pleasure however time appears to be contracted, on the other hand, during pain it appears to be dilated.

(d)	*Yoga*/meditation	Deśa, Kāla, Ekāgratā	Space, time, concentration		This trio helps in sharpening the mind (see citation 1, p. 46) with respect to the availability of space and/or time towards performing an intellectual work.
(e)	Creations of consciousness	Deśa, Kāla, Jyāmiti	Space, time, Geometry		Space and/or time and consequently the geometry (as also the laws of physical science) are the creation of consciousness of a Being [see citation 1].
(f)	Trio of microbody	*Manas, Buddhi, Ahaṁkāra*	Mind, intellect, ego		Working of the constituents of this trio can be noticed by an individual while taking (hard) decision or going for *saṅkalpa*.
(g)	Three modes of respiration	*Prāṇa, Apāna, Udāna*	inhale, exhale, stable		A regulated and balanced respiration which is a link between micro and gross body (cf. Sect. 2.4); it is an asset for spiritual development.

(h)	Three states of a Being	*Jāgrata, Svapna, Suṣupti*	Awakening, dream, sound sleep		These three states of the Being differ on the basis of degree of manifestation of consciousness through the body, particularly through its three forms *G, M, C.*

Table 2.2 : Some Examples of Quadruples in Vedāntic Philosophy

S. No.	*Characteristic(s)/ Feature(s)*	*Quadruple*		*Source/Ref.*	*Context(s)/Remark(s)*
		Sanskrit/Hindi Words	*Respective English translation*		
1.	*Varṇa* — Caste	Brāhmaṇa, Kṣatriya, Vaiśya, Śūdra	Intellecturals, fighters (Ruler), Businessman, Serving class	*SMBG*: 4/13; 18/41	This was the classification of persons in a society on the basis of their duties to run the society.
2.	*Āśrama* — four stages of working of a person	*Brahmacarya, Gṛhastha Vānaprastha, Saṁnyāsa*			Assumed 100 years of lifetime of a person, these four stages for him (from childhood to death) help psychologically in accepting the challenges of life.

3.	Broad classification of actions performed by a person	*Nitya, Naimittika, Kāmya, Niṣedha*	Daily routine, social obligation, action performed according to one's own will, immoral action.		Man is free in performing *karma* (actions), particularly in *kāmya karma*. While he must perform *nitya karma*, he must not perform *niṣedha karma*. Rest are social/moral obligations.
4.	Broad classification of food which promote longevity	*Bhojya, Peya, Lehya Cosya*	To be eaten, to be drinked, like a gum, to be sucked		For a balanced working of the stomach and the digestive system, these four varieties of food are necessary.
5.	Broad classification of virtuous persons	*Ārtta, Arthārthi, Jijñāsu, Jñānī*	The sufferer, the seeker of worldly objects, the seeker of knowledge, the man of wisdom.	*SMBG*: 7/16	Of these four categories, the best is the man of wisdom who constantly remains established in the identity with Lord.

Table 2.3: Some Examples of Pentads in Vedānta Philosophy

S. No.	Characteristic(s)/ Feature(s)	Pentads		Source/Ref.	Context(s)/Remark(s)
		Sanskrit/Hindi Words	*Respective English translation*		
1.	*Pañca-mahābhūtas* (*PMs*) — five cosmic elements	*Bhūmi, Āpo, Anala, Vāyu, Khaṁ*	Earth (Ea), Water (W), Fire (F), Air (A), Ether (E_t)	*SMBG*: 7/4; 13/5	Five cosmic elements, in their generalized sense, respectively representing the five states of matter in this Universe in the context of modern physics.
2.	*Pañca-jñānendriya* — five sense of knowledge	*Nāsikā, Jivhā, Cakṣu, Kāna, Tvacā*	Nose, tongue, eye, ear skin	*SMBG*: 13/5	Their working while controlled by the presence of mind only, their presence however, guides in performing the actions by the human being in particular.
3.	*Pañca-karmendriya* — five senses of action	*Hasta, Pāda, Vāk Liṅga, Gudā*	Hands, feet, power of speech, copulatory, organ and anus	*SMBG*: 13/5	They are the real instruments which can be seen in working of a Being in general and human being in particular.
4.	*Pañca-indriya* — *Viṣaya* — five objects of senses of knowledge	*Gandha, Svāda, Raṅga, Dhvani, Sparśa*	Smell, taste, colour, sound, touch	*SMBG*: 4/8; 13/5	As a result of these objects of *jñānendriyas* (cf. entry 2 above) several branches of

					physics and bioscience have emerged.
5.	Five *tanmātras*	N/A	denoted in the text by τ_{ea}, τ_{w}, τ_{e}, τ_{f}, τ_{et}		Five quanta of interactions between the *pañca-mahābhūtas* and the five senses of knowledge in human Being.
6.	*Pañca-kośas* — five sheaths (auras)	*Annamaya, Prāṇamaya Manomaya, Vijñānamaya, Ānandamaya*	N/A		In conjunction with patomic model of human Being, they prove as assets in classifying the personalities as their attributes.
7.	Five contributory causes responsible for the accomplishment of all actions	*Adhiṣṭhānam, Karttā, Karaṇa, Ceṣṭā, Daiva*	The body (as the seat of all activity and the organ of action), the agent (*jivātmā*), and the different kinds of organs, the divergent efforts, and destiny	*SMBG*: 18/14	For the success(!) of a performed action by the human Being an account of quality of these different instruments is essential.
8.	Success of *Yoga* attributed to five regulated (appropriate) actions	*Āhāra, Vihāra, Ceṣṭā, Karma, Svapna-bodha*	Diet, recreation, efforts, actions, balanced-sleeping	*SMBG*: 6/17	For the success of a *saṅkalpa* (hard decision) all these five need to be regulated.

9.	*Pañca-yamas*	*Satya, Ahiṁsā, Brahmacarya, Āsteya, Aparigṛha*	Truth, non-violence, continence, non-stealing, want of accumulation of wealth with the sense of meum	*Rāja-Yoga* as in Patañjali's *Yoga Darśana*	Out of eight parts of *Aṣṭāṅga Yoga* of Patañjali, these are the components of the first part only, i.e., *yama*.
10.	*Pañca-niyamas*	*Śauca, Santoṣa, Svādhyāya, Satsaṅga, Sevā*	Purity, contentment, self-study, good company, helping of others with-out return	-do-	Out of eight parts of *Aṣṭāṅga Yoga* of Patañjali, these are the components of second part, i.e. *niyama*.
11.	*Pañca-mahā-yajña*	*Deva-yajña, Ṛṣi-yajña, Pitṛ-yajña, Manuṣya-yajña, Bhūta-yajña*	N/A	N/A	Keep a person busy in his daily routine for a positive pursuit and wellness.

perspective.[2] An effort will be made in this direction in the coming chapters. In particular, in Vedānta and allied philosophies a large number of trinity (union of three), trio, triad (combining power of three), quadruple, pentad etc. exist (cf. Tables 2.1 to 2.3) which, while helping in such a development of subjective concepts, also offer an easy way to remember the abstract entities in their proper perspective. It does not mean that they are the final classifications of things/features/characteristics (cf. Tables 2.1 to 2.3) but they are still sufficient to offer a certain basis to start with. With this spirit we highlight some of these models in this chapter which will enable the development of this new field of subjective science with reference to the theory of *karma* (action).

2.1 Nature and Its Description

2.1.1 VIEWPOINT OF OBJECTIVE SCIENCE

Before the systematic development of objective science, started about 350 years ago after the work of Newton and others, the same Nature and the associated natural phenomena had varieties of explanations depending on the culture of the place and time. At times the explanations appeared mystic or magical to a common man. Thanks to the systematic development of scientific studies, which has taken place over centuries, in providing a reasonably good and sometimes universally acceptable explanation of these phenomena. In recent years, while the compartmentalization of knowledge of science (cf. Section 1.3) has suggested a fairly good world-view of various phenomena at all scales, the development of interdisciplinary subjects in both science and engineering, on the other hand, has further added to this growth of knowledge.

In spite of all this, the understanding of absolute reality in Nature remains a far cry mainly because of the modelling game

---

2. Radhey Shyam Kaushal, *The Philosophy of the Vedānta : A Modern Scientific Perspective*, Garibdas Oriental Series no. 179, Delhi: Sri Sataguru Publications, Indian Book Centre, 1994.

adopted in the methodology of science. In fact a model represents[3] only a "finite" of the "infinite truth" prevailing and inherent in Nature. However, the success achieved from the use of models, possibly in a limited domain, is amazing. Thus, the Nature's liking at least for these models cannot be ignored. In spite of the fact that models provide information only in pieces, a coherent, consistent, cohesive and mutually compatible view of the Universe has now emerged. For example, quark models, nuclear models, atomic models, etc. at various micro-scales, and solar and galactic models, etc. for heavenly objects at giga scales have found their linkage in providing an understanding of the early Universe and also in the laboratory for heavy-ion collision experiments.

Further, models do exist for both "tools" and "rules of the game." By "tools" we mean constituents of a given composite system and "rules of the game" means the "functioning" of these constituents via interactions and the associated processes. Such a methodology of (objective) science is followed in both physical and biosciences. In the latter case, however, while tools are more realistic (in the sense that they are based least on the hypotheses and their direct and ready availability is there in the laboratory), the rules of the game even today are heavily based on modelling.[4] This is mainly because the role of consciousness in the description of a phenomenon in objective science is kept aside, or else scientists do not know how to account for this new ingredient. For a ready reference some typical models are briefly listed in Appendices B and C.

2.1.2 VIEWPOINT OF VEDĀNTA PHILOSOPHY

Vedānta philosophy has an altogether different framework to describe Nature and its functioning but in totality. Human Being

---

3. Radhey Shyam Kaushal, 2003, op. cit.

4. As a matter of fact a fine description and explanation of many phenomena in biosciences, to some extent, has become possible only after a great deal of use of physics instruments and the laws of physics as well. This fact has further become clear from recent researches in this field.

is also a part of this totality of realities unlike the case in objective science, particularly in physical science in which the present laws are found to work well only for a closed system and in the absence of will-power.[5, 6] For the description of Nature in this context an octal model described[7] in *Śrīmad Bhagavad-Gītā* (*SMBG*) is worth mentioning, viz.,

bhūmir āpo analo vāyuḥ khaṁ mano buddhir eva ca ।
ahaṁkāra itīyaṁ me bhinnā prakṛtir aṣṭadhā ॥ — 7.4 (2.1)

apareyam itas tv anyāṁ prakṛtiṁ viddhi me parām ।
jivabhūtāṁ mahābāho yayedaṁ dhāryate jagat ॥ — 7.5 (2.2)

In addition to five *mahābhūtas* — earth, water, fire, air and ether — the mind, the intellect, and also the ego constitute the eightfold insentient (inanimate) mode of My Nature; the other than this, by which the whole Universe is sustained, know it as My higher or sentient (animate) Nature in the form of *jīva* (the life principle), O Arjuna.

The sentient mode is the domain of soul in whose presence the entire insentient mode becomes operative (or exists).

As a matter of fact in Vedānta philosophy both these modes of Nature are essential for its working. The important point to be noted here is that in this octet model the insentient mode continues right up to ego (the self-sense). The eight ingredients constitute the tools (or instruments) of the model which start functioning in the presence of soul. The pentad of *pañca-mahābhūtas* (*PMs*) (or cosmic elements) — earth (E_a), water (W), air (A), fire (F) and ether (E_t) (cf. Table 2.3) and the triad of the

5. Radhey Shyam Kaushal, 1994, op. cit.
6. Radhey Shyam Kaushal, 2003, op. cit.
7. *Śrīmad Bhagavad-Gītā*, chapter 7, verses 4 and 5; Even in the insentient mode of Nature only a limited variety of phenomena have been understood in totality in modern science; otherwise many of them have yet to be explored from this point of view. The domain of sentient mode or its role in the insentient mode still remains unexplored.

mind (M), the intellect (I) and the ego (E) (cf. Table 2.1) indeed play an important role as far as the working of Nature and the behaviour of human Being are concerned. In the language of modern science these *PMs*, in their generalized sense, can respectively be considered as representing the five states of matter in this universe namely solid, liquid, gas, QED and QCD plasmas, and the structure of vacuum. On the other hand, modern science is silent about the account of other three ingredients of this octet model as far as the description of Nature is concerned. They however also become part of human Being as is clear from the following. We shall further elaborate on the contents of this model in Chapter 5.

With regard to the description of human being a beautiful model already exists in *SMBG*, viz.

indriyāṇi parāṇy āhur indriyebhyaḥ paraṁ manaḥ ।
manasas tu parā buddhir yo buddheḥ paratas tu saḥ ॥ — 3.42 (2.3)

The senses are said to be greater than the body; but greater than the senses is mind. Greater than the mind is the intellect; and what is greater than the intellect is He (the Self).

This verse of *SMBG* beautifully introduces the essences of life and their relative ordering as far as their role in the day-to-day actions and in human behaviour is concerned. Further, note that the ingredient soul, i.e. the source of consciousness, of this model is listed as the greatest (much beyond) of all other ingredients. In Section 2.4, we shall return back to the details of this grand model of human being, termed as patomic (philosophical atomic type) model.[8, 9]

---

8. Radhey Shyam Kaushal, "Human Being : From the Point of View of a Philosophical-type Model", *Journal of Scientific and Ind. Res.* (New Delhi) 49 (1990) 578-82; Also see, Radhey Shyam Kaushal, "Patomic Model of Human Being in the context of Modern Science", Ph.D. Thesis (unpublished), University of Delhi, 1998, and the Appendix A.

9. Radhey Shyam Kaushal, 1994, op. cit.

With a view to suggesting a formula to attain peace by a human being while remaining and working in this physical world, Lord Kṛṣṇa in *SMBG* offers a model of models of varieties of actions performed by the human Being:

> *prakṛteḥ kriyamāṇāni guṇaiḥ karmāṇi sarvaśaḥ* ।
> *ahaṁkāra vimūḍhātmā kartāham iti manyate* ॥ — 3.27 (2.4)
>
> *tatvavit tu mahābāho guṇakarma vibhāgayoḥ* ।
> *guṇā guṇeṣu vartanta iti matvā na sajjate* ॥ — 3.28 (2.5)

> All actions are being done by the modes of *prakṛti* (primordial matter). The fool, whose mind is deluded by egoism considers himself to be the doer.
>
> He, however, who knows the truth about the respective spheres of *guṇas* (modes of *prakṛti*) and actions, holding that it is the *guṇas* (in the shape of the senses, the mind, etc.) that move among the *guṇas* (objects of perception), does not get attached to them, O Arjuna.

In Chapter 5, we shall return to these tools and rules of an action. The trio of *guṇas* is already listed in Table 2.1, with some possible remarks. In a nut-shell, these two verses suggest the essence of all essences as far as the working of a human Being (described in verse (2.3)) and its behaviour in the domain of Nature (defined in verses (2.1) and (2.2)) are concerned.

2.1.3 VIEWPOINT OF OTHER PHILOSOPHIES

In various philosophies the Nature is described basically in terms of matter and energy in the Universe. While the study of energy by and large in all philosophies culminates into three forms, namely physical, mental and spiritual with regard to an individual, the matter is variously described differently in different philosophies. Even in the Indian context different descriptions of Nature do exist. For example, *bhūta* of Cārvākas, *prakṛti* of Sāṁkhya, *rūpa* of Buddhists, *māyā* of Sāṁkhya-Vedānta, *pudgal* of Jainism are the synonyms of matter in some sense. Again there are varying views about postulating the minimal number and the fundamental nature of aggregates of matter (so-called "cosmic elements") in different philosophies. For example, Chinese recognize[10] them as five, namely, wood, fire, water, earth and metal; Greeks believe[11] in four namely, earth, water, fire and air; in Jainism one comes across[12] six, namely, *jīva, pudgal, dharma, adharma, ākāśa*, and *kāla*. In fact Jainism offers[13] a much involved theory for matter in terms of *pudgals*.[14] Here, without going into controversy about the number or the nature of these (cosmic) elements, we continue with *PMs* as described in Vedānta philosophy (cf. verse (2.1)) and highlight their role in the actions performed by a human Being.

2.2 Substance in the Universe: Origin of Beings, their Experiences and Actions

With regard to the fundamental contents of the Universe Vedānta philosophy (cf. *SMBG*) starts with the concepts of *prakṛti*

10. See, for example, S. Madradihassan, "The five elements of Chinese Cosmology in the Dialecticism", *Ind. Journ. Hist. Sc.* (New Delhi) 27 (1992) 1-3; Also see, *Ind. Journ. Hist. Sc.* (New Delhi) 24 (1989) 181-85.
11. See, for example, David Harrison, *Am. J. Phys.* 46 (1978) 432; Julia H. Gaisser and T.K. Gaisser, *Am. J. Phys.* 45 (1977) 439.
12. See, for example, Srimadamritcandsurikrit, *Tattvārthasāra* ed. Pt. Pannalal Sahityacarya (Sri Ganesh Prasad Varni Granthmālā – 22, Dumarabagh, Assi, Varanasi, 1970).
13. See, for example, *Tao of Jaina Sciences* (Delhi: Arihant Publications, Dariba, 1992); Also see, J.C. Sikdar in *Study of Jainism* ed. M.P. Marathe, M.A. Kelkar and P.P. Gokhale (Pune: I.P.Q. Publication, 1984), and J.C. Sikdar, "Fabric of life: Paryatpi Pranapan in Jain Agam", *Ind. Journ. Hist. Sc.* (New Delhi) 27 (1992) 221-29.
14. In Jainism *pudgal* is the most commonly used entity. The word *pudgal* can be considered as *puda+gala*, meaning thereby "making and breaking" of matter from and into the constituents. In fact it is believed that this process of making and breaking of *pudgals* is continuously going on in this Universe. Also, it is not even possible to count the varieties of *pudgals*. Starting from earth, water, air, fire, vegetables to insects and other creatures, all are believed to be the *pudgals*. *Pudgals* can never be a (human) Being and the Being can never be an inanimate object. Of course, a relation exists between the *pudgals* and the human Being ever since the beginning of the Universe which itself is the manifestation of *pudgals*. For further details on Jain philosophy see citation 13 above.

(matter) and *puruṣa* (spirit) (of course, the existence of the former is attributed to the latter in certain schools of thinking) through,

prakṛtiṁ puruṣaṁ caiva viddhyanādi ubhāvapi ।
vikārāṁś ca guṇāṁścaiva viddhi prakṛtisambhavān ॥
— 13.19 (2.6)

Know Matter and Spirit to be both without beginning and know all modifications and qualities (*guṇas*) to be Nature-born.

The Lord in *SMBG* further emphasizes,

kāryakāraṇakartṛtve hetuḥ prakṛtir ucyate ।
puruṣaḥ sukhaduḥkhānāṁ bhoktṛtve hetur ucyate ॥ — 13.20 (2.7)

Matter is said to be the cause of production of the (physical) body and the senses; while Spirit (in its quantized version also termed as *jīvātmā*[15]) is said to be the cause of experience of pleasure and pain.

We shall further attempt to quantify this quantized version of the Cosmic Spirit (or Cosmic Consciousness) in the next section. Not only this, the Lord in the next verse clearly hints at the source of experiences and subsequently to the working of Jivātmā in this world, viz.,

puruṣaḥ prakṛtistho hi bhuṅkte prakṛtijāna guṇān ।
kāraṇaṁ guṇasaṅgo asya sad asad yoni janmasu ॥ — 13.21 (2.8)

Spirit (in the form of *jīvātmā*) when seated in Matter (physical body), enjoys all objects of the nature of the three *guṇas* (qualities) (cf. entry 1, Table 2.1) born of Matter; attachment to these qualities is the cause of his birth in good and evil wombs.

Further, the role of *jīvātmā* (the Spirit seated in Matter) *vis-à-vis* its existence and working in this world is highlighted by the Lord in the next verse in very clear terms, namely

updraṣṭā 'anumantā ca bhartā bhoktā maheśvaraḥ ।
paramātmeti cāpy ukto dehe 'sminpuruṣaḥ paraḥ ॥ — 13.22 (2.9)

Spirit, even when dwelling in this body, is really transcendent (i.e. it is beyond the domain of triple-nature of *guṇas*). He has been

---

15. Radhey Shyam Kaushal, 1994, op. cit., chapter 4, p. 40.

> declared to be the Witness, the Guide, the Sustainer, the Experiencer (of pleasure and pain), the Supreme Lord, and the Over-soul.

With such a universality of concepts in Vedānta philosophy, now we attempt to model the human Being in the forthcoming sections.

2.3 Human Being

2.3.1 HUMAN BODY

It is said that human Being is the perfect creation of God, possibly because in him there is appearance of all (!) essences of life (EOL) with an optimum co-ordination and equilibrium at least for a common man; otherwise with most non-human and some human Beings there is a problem of extra-sensory or under-sensory powers besides the fact that they may not possess all the essences of life (cf. Chapter 10).

A man of literature, particularly the poet, describes the human Being (the human body and the Nature), in a variety of ways using metaphor, simile or analogies[16] for its different parts and components. A scientist, particularly a bioscientist, has his own way of looking at the things. After removing the cover of skin of a Being, separating out flesh, bones, etc. again there are some important organs like heart, brain, lungs, liver, . . ., etc. essential for his survival. The interesting part is that there is again a beautiful and another type of co-ordination among the workings of these organs in the presence of certain fluids like oxygen and blood. However, the system with all these arrangements while originating from the womb of a mother, it is said to be dead in the absence of an extra-physical element called "consciousness." While the presently available scientific laws have beautifully described the working of these organs in a human body to its finest possible level, the element of consciousness has not yet entered into the domain of these studies.

16. Radhey Shyam Kaushal, 2003, op. cit.

With regard to the description of human Being, the Vedānta philosophy also has to offer something new via the famous saying *yathā piṇḍe tathā brahmāṇḍe* (whatever is present in the body, the same is there in the Universe or vice versa), i.e. the human Being is a microcosmos or a representation of the Universe. At another place the philosophy propounds "*vyaṣṭi* in *samaṣṭi* and *samaṣṭi* in *vyaṣṭi*," i.e. there are two equivalent but seemingly different ways of realizing the absolute reality in Nature — by way of considering the individual as a part (sample) of the Universe or by considering the Universe as an outcome of the individual. One thing is sure that for an individual the Universe exists only in the presence of the extra-physical element of consciousness in the Being. Not only this, other philosophical elements like mind, intellect, ego, etc. present and already working in the human body, are also the manifestations of consciousness (cosmic or individual(!)). Another fact which cannot be ignored is that the consciousness of different level manifests in all actions (performed by motor organs and/or biological body) of the human Being in the day-to-day life and also in its behaviour (domain of inner essences of life). It is also an observed fact that these actions sometimes are not realized by the individual in the absence of conscious seer.[17]

Thus, both the human Being (or a working human body or for that matter any Being) and its actions can be considered to have two aspects of contents in them — physical, the one accounted for by objective science and the other non-physical, about which the objective science is silent but whose role in human actions and behaviour cannot be ignored.

---

17. In Vedānta philosophy there is definite sequence of seer and scene with regard to the realization of an event which occurred in this Universe (see, citation 2, section 4.1). For example, senses of knowledge and action are the seer of worldly objects (scene). Again mind is the seer of the functioning of senses of knowledge and action with the help of intellect and ego. Finally, it is the consciousness (an attribute of soul) which actually sees (perceives) the worldly objects.

2.3.2 SPIRITUAL AND ETHICAL VALUES

While a great deal of actions of a Being are controlled by the physical content of the body of a Being, a still larger aspect is covered by its non-physical content. Further, actions themselves when analysed at their face value, can have both physical and non-physical contents in terms of their performance and motivation. In fact the appearance of these physical and non-physical contents in actions suggests an extended set of essences of life including the ones of subjective nature and these EOLs are in the background of all actions performed by the Being (cf. Chapter 4).

Goodness appears to be natural and it is built already in the human Being. This is perhaps another best and grand manifestation of consciousness. As a result each individual by nature is spiritual. It is only the ego and/or intellect — somewhat lower manifestations of the consciousness — which, after suppressing the spiritual aspect, make the individual seemingly non-spiritual. These aspects force him to use his mental and physical energies for the negative of goodness and the same reflects in his behaviour.

Spiritual values have to be placed at the highest level as far as the quality of the action of an individual is concerned. As the spirituality is the characteristic of (cosmic) consciousness, it is universal. It is not bound by space and time or by the divisions of caste, colour, creed or country.

On the other hand, a society is the collective version of individuals.[18] "Inside-out" of the patomic model of a Being[19]

---

18. Radhey Shyam Kaushal, 1994, op. cit., chapter 7, p. 84.
19. For the meanings of the phrases "inside-out" and "outside-out," the attention of the reader is drawn to Section 2.5, where the essences of life of a Being are arranged in an atom-like model of the human Being. The inner contents of the model while control the outward actions of a Being, the outer contents of the model however control the inward actions of the Being.

while contributes maximum to this collective system, "out-side out" however contributes somewhat less. For an efficient and value-based functioning of this collective system, as mentioned in Chapter 1 certain norms leading to an ordered lifestyle are necessary. These norms when framed after keeping spirituality (or spiritual values) in mind and practised for a period of time, define the ethical values for a society in general and for an individual in particular. For the intellectual component (thinkers) of a society these norms while just remain norms which for them are subjected to scrutiny from time to time, for the common man, however, these norms become scriptural ordinances and also the guiding principles in his daily working. Moreover, if these norms have some scientific and logical basis then they can serve as the guide for a society for a long time. While spirituality remains Universal, the norms or ethical values can be the function of space and time — they may be different for different caste, colour, creed or country and also at different time points in the history. Thus, while the ethical values could be relative, the spiritual values are absolute and Universal.

2.4 Human Essences of Life and the Understanding of Nature: "Who Understands What?"

After highlighting the complementarity, conjunction and inter-dependence of Beings in general and of human Beings in particular in previous sections, here we concentrate on the essences of life *vis-à-vis* their role in understanding Nature.

First note the difference between the essences of life (EOLs) and the essentials for life (EFLs). While the EFLs are objective (derived from the outer world) in nature, the EOLs on the other hand, are subjective and they play important roles in both the functioning of the Being in this world and the process of understanding the Nature side by side. With reference to the survival of a Being in this world both are essential. The EFLs are the subject of sociology whereas the EOLs are that of humanities. In the process of a systematic analysis of workings of a Being in this world, in the subsequent chapters, it will be argued that

EFLs lead to pleasure and EOLs to peace for a human Being at their end points. According to verse (2.1), the EOLs constitute Nature itself, i.e. they are "God made" and transcend with the birth of a Being. The EFLs are "man-made" and are just sufficient to nourish the "biological body" of a being. The EOLs, when identified in this biological body, help in understanding Nature.

Then what are these EOLs? One can say that it is the biological body of a Being along with sense organs in it which help in gaining knowledge about Nature. But that is not so. One cannot perceive the external world by sense organs alone in the absence of mind — the faculty of feeling and emotions, intellect — the faculty of decision, and the subtle ego — the faculty of memory. As a matter of fact this whole arrangement only offers an engine-like instrument or an electrical appliance-kind of apparatus to work. Clearly, neither the engine nor the apparatus will work in the absence of steam (energy) or electricity. It is the consciousness originating from the innermost existence in the body of a Being, that causes (in the same way as the steam or electricity respectively in the cases of steam engine or electrical appliance) the functioning of the Being in this world.

With regard to the answer to the question, "Who understands what?" we have to go by the following logic. For an observer sitting outside our Universe, our Universe might appear to him as a closed system in which the working of all constituents (both animate and inanimate) is governed by some generalized laws describing not only the life and death (for the animate objects) and the growth and decay (for the inanimate objects) of these constituents but also their functioning in a self-contained and self-consistent manner (cf. verses (2.4) and (2.5)). Note that the science (objective) identifies only a limited domain of study of Nature out of this vast sea of phenomena caused by the so-called "life" and/or "physical" energies. On the other hand, for an observer sitting in our Universe, the whole Universe can never be a closed system. It can only be an approximated-closed-system and that too in parts in different physical theories.

In this way, the understanding of Nature by a Being[20] in this Universe will always remain limited. The study of life energy or consciousness manifesting through EOLs is as important as the study of physical energy or the space-time structure of Nature working through inanimate objects. In summary, the observer of this Universe is always going to be the part of the "observed" whether the (physical) theories account for it or not. One possible hindrance to this effect could be the non-availability of adequate tools (mathematical or otherwise) for this purpose.

2.5 Patomic Model of Human Being and its Reduced Version

2.5.1 THE PATOMIC MODEL

As the human behaviour is the direct outcome of the role played by EOLs, we present here in brief a model of human being.[21]

The patomic (philosophical atom-type) model of human Being offers a framework within which a variety of laws of subjective science (cf. Section 1.4) governing the role of inner world in the human behaviour, can be made transparent to a common man. In order to have an effective analysis of human behaviour involving various processes and interactions in the following chapters, we give here a brief review of this model and postpone the details to Appendix A. Although the proposed patomic model[22] of the human being has strong bearing on the Vedānta philosophy (cf. verse (2.3)), it is equally compatible with other philosophies of the world since the reasoning followed in designing this model is logical.

In analogy with the atomic model for the structure of matter, the nucleus in the patomic model is identified (cf. *fig*. 2.1) with the worldly objects (WO) like want of desire for kith and kin,

20. Here the word "Being" can as well be considered for super-Being or a *yogī*, who has developed his EOLs to the highest possible level to command over Nature.

21. Radhey Shyam Kaushal, 1994, op. cit., chapter 3, p. 19.

22. Radhey Shyam Kaushal, 1990, 1998, op. cit., in citation 8.

money, prosperity, lust, pleasure, fame, honour, etc. The different energy levels of the electron are identified with various EOLs namely, with biological body (B) of the human being, the senses of knowledge and action (SE) (cf. Table 2.3, entries 2 and 3), mind (M), (particularly the subconscious mind), intellect (I) (the faculty of decision) and ego (E) (self-sense or micro-component of *ahaṁkāra*) (cf. *fig*. 2.1). While the continuum is identified with the soul (SO) (the innermost existence, characterized by consciousness and is responsible for the survival of the Being), the role of the electron is assumed to be played by the Being (b) (the seed of life or the life principle) itself. In spite of the fact that the exact force-law between b and WO is not known, b is assumed to perform both upward (for the limiting case of a *yogī* deeply involved in the domain of SO) and downward (for the limiting case of a person who is deeply involved in the domain of WO) transitions in the orbits B, SE, M, I, and E in the same way as the electron does in the atomic orbits. These transitions of the Being b dictate the spirit of developments of its EOLs.

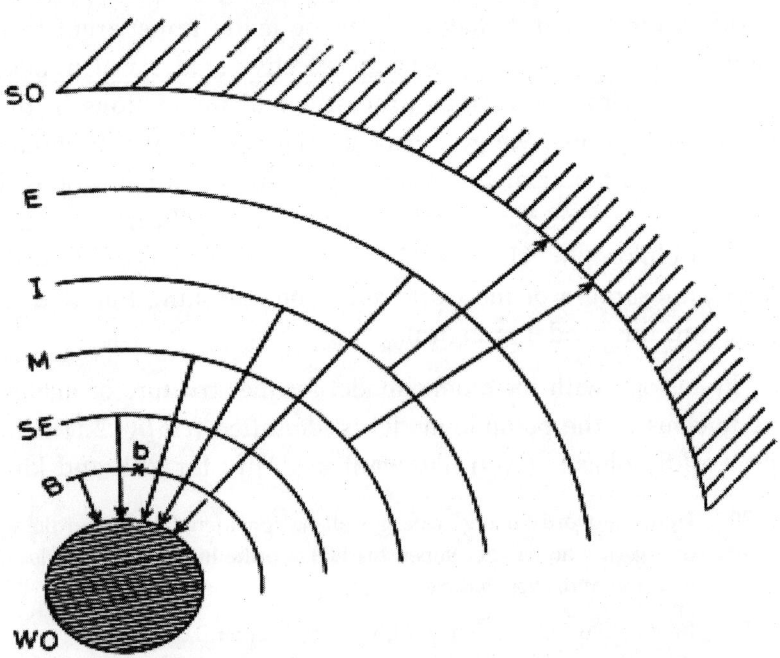

fig. 2.1: A philosophical atom-type model of human Being

The upward transitions of b lead to peace and the downward ones to pleasure for b. While the peace and pleasure are complementary for a Being, the quanta corresponding to both, in the presence of *PMs* come in three "colours" (the so called *guṇas*) of *sattva, rajas, tamas* for a common man including philosopher and scientist. However, for a *yogī* these quanta could be colour-white as he (the *yogī*) is in a fourth (*triguṇātīta*) state (beside the three *jāgrata, svapna, suṣupti* states known for all other categories of persons) also called *turīya* state. As the transitions are in the space (domain) of concentration/meditation parameter (μ), the role of these *guṇas* in the outer world basically manifests in the behaviour of b but in the philosophical domain. However, this role reflects in the behaviour of the Being, first through nonphysical interactions and then through the space-time mediated (physical) interactions. For the occurrence of the associated processes no doubt the consciousness of any degree remains in the background, but at times in certain situation, the concept of space-time at the level of outer world also goes unnoticed. This happens by suppressing those components of M, I and E which are responsive to the outer world.

With this picture of the human Being a possible explanation of several phenomena (exotic or otherwise) in behavioural sciences for which the objective science has no explanation whatsoever, has been advanced.[23] This Vedānta model clearly provides[24] 23 vertices of interactions in general through which b interacts with another b or with the outer world. Also, from the point of view of understanding Nature in "totality," this model might suggest a generalization of existing laws of objective science. We shall recapture some of these ideas later.

---

23. Radhey Shyam Kaushal, 1994, op. cit., chapter 3, 4 and 6.
24. Twenty-three vertices of interactions in Patomic model arise as follows: 5 *PMs*, 10 SEs (5 *karmendriya* and 5 *jñānendriya*) and 5 sense objects plus M, I and E, leading to 23 domains (!) of interaction. 5 *PMs* while offer a ground for survival and interaction of b, they as well constitute the biological body B.

The role of space and time in this framework needs a little clarification: As mentioned, it is the consciousness of certain order which is responsible for the creation of space, time and geometry. In fact in both the extreme cases (namely, when the Being b is dwelling in the domain of continuum, the case of a *yogī*, and when the Being b is dwelling in the domain of WO, the case of a deeply involved person in WO), these concepts have no meaning at all. It is only in the intermediate states of B, SE, M, I and E the concepts of space, time and geometry are arising and whereby help in understanding Nature mainly through analogies. The role of space and time is again important more at the level of B and SE and not that much at the levels of M, I and E and it finally reduces to zero at the level of SO. Further, such descriptions are for a bare human Being and when the same is placed in the field(s) of *PM*s, b gets dressed up and attains degeneracy or plurality of these states and from then on human Being starts interacting with Nature.

2.5.2 Reduced Version of the Patomic Model

The above description and arrangement of EOLs in a living human body is somewhat in-between the two descriptions presented in Vedānta philosophy.[25] While further fine-tuning of these EOLs is also given there, in a broad sense these EOLs are also described in terms of *sthūla, sūkṣma* and *kāraṇa śarīras* which we respectively identify here as gross ($\mathcal{G}$), micro ($\mathcal{M}$) and causal ($\mathcal{C}$) forms of the Being b. This is done mainly to simplify the descriptions of various underlying processes appearing in human behaviour and actions. This grouping in the language of set theory can be expressed as

$$\mathcal{G} \equiv \{\text{SE, B, WO}\}\ ;\ \mathcal{M} \equiv \{\text{E,I,M}\}\ ;\ \mathcal{C} \equiv \{\text{SO}\}. \tag{2.10}$$

Thus, the human Being b can be considered as the union of these three subsets (see citation 2, pages 60-62), viz.

25. See, for example, *Vivekacūḍāmaṇi* — Śrī Ādi Śaṅkarācārya viracit, verses 89, 98, 122.

$$b \equiv \mathcal{C} \cup \mathcal{M} \cup \mathcal{G}. \quad (2.11)$$

Here, the symbol "$\cup$" stands for the union of sets. For example, the right hand side of (2.11) consists of all elements of $\mathcal{C}$, $\mathcal{M}$ and $\mathcal{G}$ and can be expressed as {SO, E, I, M, SE, B, WO}. Note that although SO manifests through all the EOLs or through the three forms of b in terms of relative and absolute consciousness (cf. citation 2, chapter 4), yet it constitutes a separate subset $\mathcal{C}$. In fact it is some sort of a super or a universal set. For the working of $\mathcal{M}$ and/or $\mathcal{G}$ the presence of $\mathcal{C}$ in the background is a must. With regard to the role of space and time in the sense of objective science, the same exists only up to the level of $\mathcal{G}$ and beyond this, at the level of $\mathcal{M}$ and $\mathcal{C}$, it does not make any sense as mentioned earlier.

Within this framework the description of non-human Beings[26] can also be accommodated. For example, a Being can exist without $\mathcal{G}$ or $\mathcal{M}$ or both. These classes of Being are imperfect creations (relative to the human Being) of God. We call these classes of Beings as "beta" (β) — class. Further, one can broadly classify them as

$$\beta_1 \equiv \mathcal{C} \cup \mathcal{M} \quad , \qquad \beta_2 \equiv \mathcal{C} \cup \mathcal{G}. \quad (2.12)$$

Clearly, the existence of $\mathcal{M} \cup \mathcal{G}$ (or $\mathcal{M} \cap \mathcal{G}$) class is not possible to survive as the element SO is a prerequisite for the existence. Here, the symbol "$\cap$" represents the intersection of sets. For example, the vanishing of $\mathcal{M} \cap \mathcal{G}$ means that no element is common in the sets $\mathcal{M}$ and $\mathcal{G}$. Further sub-classes β_1 and β_2 are also possible since all the EOLs contained in $\mathcal{M}$ or in $\mathcal{G}$ may not be present in all the Beings. Note that β_1- class of creatures is not expected to have any definite physical form in this universe

26. Human Being is said to be the perfect creation of God and other Beings are generally deprived of certain EOLs. Sometimes these remaining EOLs in the non-human Beings are found to have some extra(-sensory) powers. Viruses, bacteria, etc. could be the examples in which there is no gross body or perhaps a little micro one. Vedāntic philosophy very well accommodates them in its description.

though it could be complete in all other respects, from the point of view of its survival. While the bacteria, viruses, ghosts, spirits, etc. type of entities could be the examples of β_1-class, many examples of β_2-class of Beings can be found in Nature. As β_1-class of creatures is devoid of certain interacting centres,[27] they can manifest as and when they find a convenient base of a gross body. Such manifestations through $\mathcal{G}$ can lead to abnormal behaviour of the concerned Being whose physical form is used for the routing of β_1 particularly with respect to the behaviour defined for that form. Sometimes this may appear against rules of objective science or the *pañcīkaraṇa* rule[28] of Vedic science. We shall take a fresh look at some of these discussions later.

In accordance with these three forms of b, i.e. $\mathcal{G}$, $\mathcal{M}$ and $\mathcal{C}$, there exist again three states of b, namely *jāgrat* (awakening), *svapna* (dream) and *suṣupti* (sound sleep) (see entry 7(h) in Table 2.1). In *jāgrat* state all three forms of b are actively present in a certain proportion at a given space and time. In *svapna* state $\mathcal{G}$ is more or less inactive, whereas in *suṣupti* not only $\mathcal{G}$ but also $\mathcal{M}$ is inactive and it is only $\mathcal{C}$ which remains active. There is another state of b called *turīya*, state in which the activeness and inactiveness of both $\mathcal{M}$ and $\mathcal{G}$ merge into the activeness of $\mathcal{C}$ alone by suppressing the rest. An example of *suṣupti* state is worth mentioning. A person gets up in the morning after a sound sleep and says "tonight I had good sleep." The question is when the person was sleeping then who realized the goodness or

---

27. See, note 24.

28. In order to reveal the manifestation of *PM*s, there is a built-in rule — termed as *pañcīkaraṇa* rule. According to this each *mahābhūta*, as realized by the Being b, consists of 50 per cent of its own and 12.5 per cent of each of the remaining four. For example, the earth, as we perceive it, is not the abstract earth E_a but it consists of 50 per cent of the abstract (physical) E_a and 12.5 per cent of each of water, fire, air and ether. In other words, the abstract form of each of these *mahābhūtas* is dressed up with the interaction it has with the remaining four, of course considered to be in equal proportions. For details see citation 2, Chapter 4 and the reference therein.

badness of sleeping. It is the causal body *C* of the person present and realizing the quality of sleeping.

The understanding of many phenomena in the behaviour of human Being becomes simplified within the framework of the above reduced version of the patomic model.

2.5.3 Social Aspect of the Patomic Model: Inside-out and Outside-out Cases

The patomic model described above is clearly expected to work well in understanding the processes/phenomena which involve an individual Being. However, its use for a group, a society or a collection of Beings, can be considered (in analogy with the free-electron theory of metals in physics) in the following sense. In fact with regard to the description of physical properties of metals/crystals, the contribution to electron gas comes from each individual atom (i.e. the situation of an "outside-out" (OSO) case appears in the sense that the electron(s) in the outer most orbit(s) contribute to the ensemble of electrons). On the other hand, "in-side-out" (ISO) situation arises in using the patomic model for a collection of Beings (human or otherwise). This is mainly because of the fact that, for most of the time, Beings for their survival remain involved in the worldly objects WO in terms of bodily needs. Not only this, the Being seeks co-ordination with other Beings of the same or different species and with the environment as well.

In other words, in social sciences normally the studies are carried out only in zeroth-order approximation by collecting data pertaining mainly to worldly objects like prosperity, pleasure, human relations, etc. with reference to the needs of food, housing, clothing and the like. The higher and important stages of studies of a social phenomenon have to involve basically psychology, intelligence, culture, heritage, etc. (the functionals of M, I and E) of a society in the framework of patomic model. In general, the collective (rather than the individual) role of B, SE, M, I and E appears often in the data and the same is being analysed using sociological models rather empirically. Physics can offer a guide to study the sociology in a new but exact style via patomic model by way of considering the individual interactions arising from WO, B, SE, M, I, and E of a Being rather separately. Thus, one can start with a few-body problem (two- or three-body, as one does in physics) and generate the results for a corresponding many body system. We shall revisit some of these ideas later.

2.6 Physical (P), Epiphysical (EP) and Special Epiphysical (SEP) Matter in the Universe

Earlier[29] we have attempted to understand the quantum measurement problem within the framework of the above patomic model of human Being by way of bringing the role of plurality of consciousness in the description. In fact this problem offers an example of the interaction of a Being (human) with the physical (inanimate) matter (AI or IA-type interaction, see Section 1.7). The physical matter in the presence of b cannot retain its same properties as it has in the absence of b. Therefore, we broadly classify the inanimate matter of the Universe as physical (P) and epiphysical (EP) matter. In addition to these two categories, we have postulated earlier[30] another category of special epiphysical (SEP) matter which also has a source of consciousness in it via the presence of element SO. While the physical laws work well for the P-matter, they need to be modified or else the alternatives are to be sought for the study of EP- and SEP-matters.

In other words, if x is a P-matter, then x + consciousness, is an EP-matter and x + consciousness + source of consciousness

29. Radhey Shyam Kaushal, "Plurality of Consciousness in Vedantic Philosophy and its Role in Scientific Observations" in *Scientific and Philosophical Studies in Consciousness*, ed. Sangeetha Menon et al. (National Institute of Advanced Studies (NIAS) Publication, I.I. Sc., Bangalore, India, 1999) pp. 346-61; Also see citation 2, Chapters 4 and 5 and citation 1 of Appendix B.

30. Radhey Shyam Kaushal, 1994, op. cit., p. 40.

is the SEP-matter. At a deeper level, though the last two categories might appear to be different; however for many practical purposes EP-matter can be considered as SEP-matter. This is mainly because the P-matter in the presence of consciousness gets "dressed-up" at such a fast pace that it becomes rather difficult for it to be distinguished from the field of consciousness in which it is placed and such an EP-matter sometimes becomes part of the extended (human) apparatus. Moreover, this "dressing-up" also depends not only on the nature of P-matter but also on the nature of consciousness imposed on it. We shall return to some of these discussions later in chapter 8.

2.7 Inner and Outer Worlds and the Associated Experiences

For the sake of ready use in the forthcoming chapters we also introduce here the concepts of inner and outer worlds with reference to an individual. These concepts in fact become more transparent within the framework of the patomic model for the human Being. In fact the functional domains of the essences of life M, I and E in the presence of SO while constitute the inner world, the domains of EOLs SE, B and WO in conjunction with *PM*s constitute the outer world as far as the role of consciousness in the entire functioning of b is concerned. These EOLs are in continuous action in a non-stop but co-ordinated (partly or fully) manner irrespective of the cognizance of the action by the individual. The function of B in general and that of SE in particular is twofold; namely (i) to interact with the outside world and supply the objective reality (as perceived by M and I and subsequently stored in E) to the individual, and (ii) to come out with an initially stored framework to interact with the outer world with possibly a different (better or worse as they are relative) understanding of the latter. In the latter process while B and SE assist the individual in realizing the subjective reality, however, also supply a feedback for an increasingly better understanding of the outside world. At this stage we also introduce the terms "outer-world-based" (OWB) experiences corresponding to the former case (i) and "inner-world-based"

(IWB) experiences corresponding to the case (ii) above. In this connection, at least for a common man, the role of "incoming" objective reality (knowledge) is very important since it leaves a considerable impact on the inner essences of life which, in turn, would supply a feedback for his subsequent functions.

Except for some recent attempts;[31, 32, 33] note that objective science is completely silent as far as the description and the role of inner world in explaining the physical data are concerned. On the other hand, in spite of having somewhat similar IWB experiences, different philosophies offer different explanations for the same event of subjective nature. With regard to the explanation of the OWB experiences, while different cultures had different pictures in the past, the objective science has however offered a unified (and perhaps more realistic) description of the outer world. In the forthcoming chapters we shall try to look for a similar unified and coherent description of IWB experiences within the framework of the patomic model.

Keeping the nature and complexity of the interactions involved in describing the IWB experiences and the human behaviour in mind there does not appear to be a sharp boundary line between the inner and the outer worlds at a first look. However, for analysing the underlying processes at a rather deeper level one has to be careful in identifying the domains of the two worlds, viz., inner and outer worlds.

2.8 Concluding Discussion

An introduction to various aspects of Vedānta philosophy, which is going to form the basis of our discussion in future chapters, is

---

31. Roger Penrose, *Shadows of Mind: A Search for Missing Science of Consciousness*, Oxford: Oxford University, Press, 1994.
32. Roger Penrose, *The Large, the Small and the Human being*, Cambridge: Cambridge University Press, 1997.
33. See, for example, Robert G. Jalm and B. Dunne, *Margins of Reality : The Role of Consciousness in Physical World* (Harcourt Brace Jovanovich Publishers, 1987).

furnished here under the heading of modelling. As a matter of fact, while the modelling is a must in objective science (cf. Appendices B and C) for the explanation of a physical phenomenon in the outer world, however the same cannot be ignored in the description of IWB experiences and in developing a subjective science which, in turn, can provide the explanation of more intriguing phenomena and processes involving the behaviour of a Being. In a way, the tools for description of such processes are presented in this chapter. Starting with the quantification of various human qualities and virtues in terms of trios, quadruples and pentads, the models of human Being (patomic) and of Nature are given here. These models, after combining with the models of the rules of the game, will be an asset for understanding the fundamental processes. By way of defining and introducing the concepts of different types of matter in the Universe (cf. Section 2.6) and of inner and outer worlds with reference to an individual, a basis is formed here for analysing the fundamental processes at a finer level.

An important aspect highlighted in this chapter from Vedānta philosophy is the discretization of the human characteristics or qualities in spite of the fact that the same might appear continuous with reference to the faculties of understanding of a common man. This concept of discretization (or classification) of characteristics of an individual (or of a collection of individuals) is not new; rather this has already been in use in hard disciplines for centuries. Classification or discretization in fact is an essential part (step) of scientific methods and sometimes this also helps in the modelling of the phenomenon under study irrespective of the fact that the latter belongs to the domains of soft or hard disciplines.

For example, seven colors in the white light, depicted as "VIBGYOR," is just the discretization of visible region (wavelength range, 4000-7000 Å) of the continuous electromagnetic (e-m) spectrum in terms of the wavelength. On the other hand, a broad discretization of e-m spectrum is in the form of radio waves, X-ray, visible region, γ-rays, etc. Corresponding to this latter class of discretization different models for the structure of matter are used. Another case of discretization of e-m radiation is based on the energy distribution. Different laws for energy distribution in the e-m radiation (Rayleigh-Jeans and Wien's Laws) work in different wavelength regions. In an analogous way, the discretization of human qualities in the different domains of EOLs can be visualized. In summary, the discretization of a characteristic is an attempt in the direction of its quantification[34] and mathematics plays an important role in this process. Further, limits do exist on this kind of quantification both in mathematical terms (e.g. ε-δ language for understanding the concepts of limit and continuity in mathematics) and in terms of the development of faculties of understanding[35] of a Being.

---

34. Radhey Shyam Kaushal, *Discretization of Characteristics: A Concept Prevailing in Mathematical and Behavioural Sciences*, presented in National Conference on History of Mathematics and Recent Developments, held at Rohtak, Dec. 20-23, 2006, (to be published).
35. Faculty of understanding (FOU) is an elevated version of the faculty of memory (E). In fact the net experiences gained by a conscious Being through a combined role of E, I, M, SE and B about WO and SO elevates the E to a higher level.

3

Fundamental Processes and the Theory of Karma (Action)

Western View and the Views of Modern Science

BEFORE embarking upon the theory of *karma* as described in Indian (Vedānta) philosophy in the next chapter, we briefly outline here the Western way of thinking about it, particularly the view(s) of modern scientist/philosophers. One thing is clear, as mentioned in chapter 1, that there is not enough philosophical (or analytical) content in the Western theory of *karma*. As such no analytical explanation of the process of performing an action by a human Being in finer terms exists in Western philosophy. To the best of the author's knowledge there is no deep basis to describe the processes highlighted in chapter 1 (cf. *figs*. 1.1 to 1.5).

In his 1950 speech to the International Congress of Surgeons in Cleveland, Ohio, Albert Einstein summarizes[1] his views as follows:

> The spatiotemporal laws are *complete*. This means, there is not a single law of Nature that, in principle, could not be reduced to a law within the domain of space-time concepts. This principle implies, for instance, the conviction that psychic entities and relations can be reduced, in the last analysis, to processes of a physical and chemical nature within the nervous system. According to this principle, there are no non-physical elements in the causal system of the processes of nature. In this sense there is no room for

1. Quoted from the speech of Albert Einstein, "Physics, Philosophy and Scieintific Progress" appeared in *Physics Today*, June 2005, pp. 46-48, the World Year of Physics 2005 issue.

> "free will" within the framework of scientific thought, nor for an escape into "vitalism."

This view of Einstein clearly reflects the basis of thinking of the Western philosophers as far as the handling of the processes involving the human actions is concerned. The reduction of outer-world processes in their last analysis to the space-time structure of Nature is definitely understandable in terms of objective science (bottom-up!); but what about the reduction of inner-world processes to the space-time structure of Nature (top-down!)? This is something missing in Western philosophy. One definitely needs a parallel subjective science for this purpose and it is there in Vedānta philosophy. As will be elaborated below these ideas of Einstein in 1950s, in fact, have also been the tenets of Western philosophy since its development in historical perspective.

No doubt, in recent years, there is an enormous indication[2, 3, 4, 5, 6] of occurrence of the element of consciousness in the description of certain physical processes involving the human Being in the domain of objective science (such as quantum measurement problem, mind-brain problem, etc. for further details see the Ph.D. Thesis of D.J. Chalmers[7]); but again in these descriptions this element of consciousness appears only uniquely whereas the Vedānta philosophy repeatedly emphasizes (cf. chapter 4) the plurality of this concept in a distinctive style.

---

2. Roger Peorose, *Shadows of Mind: A search for Missing Science of Consciousness* (Oxford: Oxford University Press, 1994).

3. G.F.R. Ellis, "Physics and the Real World", *Physics Today*, July 2005, pp. 49-54, the World Year of Physics 2005 issue.

4. T. Pink, *Free Will: A Very short Introduction* (New York: Oxford University Press, 2004).

5. D.J. Chalmers, *The Conscious Mind: In Search of a Fundamental Theory* (New York: Oxford University Press, 1996).

6. Roger Penrose, *The Large, The Small and the Human Mind* (Cambridge: Cambridge University Press, 1997).

7. D.J. Chalmers, op. cit.

From this point of view we shall just make a brief survey in this chapter of certain areas where there is a hint to the possibility of accounting for the consciousness in the description of certain processes of the outer world through which the same manifest in objective science. It is only recently (cf. Section 3.6) that scientists have started realizing the importance of these higher levels of understanding in the hierarchy mainly in the context of studying the complex systems.

In what follows we shall first outline the basics of Western philosophy and then continue the discussion on the work of Emmanuel Kant with regard to human actions in Section 3.2. In fact in modern times Kant's ideas on space, time, Nature and objective reality have become the authority in the development of philosophical thinking in the West. Sections 3.3 to 3.5 are devoted to make a quest for the roots of human actions in modern scientific theories developed in different contexts. While the limitations of Darwin's concept of natural selection are argued in Section 3.3 by emphasizing the role of Intelligent Design, the concept of rebirth is strengthened from the genetical studies in Section 3.4. After highlighting the studies pertaining to mind-brain problem in Section 3.5, a survey of recent studies in complex systems is presented in Section 3.6. Finally, concluding remarks are made in Section 3.7.

3.1 Philosophical Perspective

Western philosophy is generally considered to have begun in ancient Greece as speculation about the underlying nature of the physical world. Technically, philosophy is defined as the "love of wisdom." In its earliest form it was indistinguishable from natural science. The writings of the earliest philosophers no longer exist, except for a few fragments cited by Aristotle and other writers of later times.

One of the seven wise men of Greece is Thales (580 BC) who was interested in astronomical, physical and meteorological phenomena. In fact several philosophical schools started later after the Ionian School of Thales; for example, Pythagorean school started by Pythagorus, Heraclitean school started by Heraclitus, among others. They were just differing in terms of certain postulates about the existence of physical world.

Western philosophy basically emerged and grew under the four heads, namely metaphysics, epistemology, ethics and aesthetics. In metaphysics knowledge developed around the search for ultimate reality; in epistemology one looks for the origin, validity and limits of that knowledge; ethics deals with the question of morality and judgement in a society, and finally a beautiful description of Nature (mostly described in the domain of objective science) forms the part of aesthetics.

No doubt Einstein's summary view mentioned above does not leave any room open for the subjective component in the description of ultimate reality in Nature, but a great deal of development of its objective component has been in existence in the West for thousands of years. Perhaps this has been there to avoid the account of multifaceted and arbitrary character which a subjective component of reality may have with reference to an individual and the same can be a problem not only from the point of view of quantification but also in bringing the common man under the same "umbrella." On the other hand, if a philosophy starts with an objective basis alone then it is not complete in spite of the fact that such a philosophy is subject to a better scrutiny since the ideas thereof can easily be put to a test and subsequent verification from time to time. Our common experience tells that such a testing and verification of ideas can as well be there if not for all that but for a certain subjective component present in the ultimate reality. As a result one cannot deny the role of subjective science in understanding the working of Nature in totality.

While the tools of subjective science are better developed in the Eastern (particularly in the Indian) philosophy, their quantification has not been carried out to the same extent as is the case with objective science in the West. In spite of all this a very fine philosophy of space, time, Nature and objective reality has been developed in the West over a period of time which, in fact, has been supplying a fairly strong basis for the practitioners of the objective science. Often Emmanuel Kant of recent times is quoted on this front and we briefly review his work in the next section in this context.

3.2 Objective Reality: Space-time Structure in Nature and Morality in Society

In the development of Western philosophy, the considerations of the subjective component in understanding the working of Nature while remained at low pitch, the description of objective reality has been persisted beyond bounds. In fact for the latter, the main credit goes to the great German philosopher Emmanuel Kant who, about 250 years ago, advocated a fine description of objective component of ultimate reality in Nature in terms of its space-time constituents and in society in terms of moral values. Here we outline briefly Kant's ideas and other recent views on this aspect.

3.2.1 PHILOSOPHY OF EMMANUEL KANT

Kant's philosophy focuses[8, 9] around the development of a viable methodology that can be used to put the available (objective) knowledge about the working of the Universe in a nutshell. This abstraction process finally ended with the exploration of space-time structure of Nature and the same later became the basis for the development of theories of modern science. Kant in fact made an attempt to estimate the achievements of new sciences which at that time were offering conflicting claims and ideals with reference to a common man. No doubt such thinking began with Descartes and Galileo, but Kant was the first to become conscious of these things. This kind of stock taking of knowledge

8. Emmanuel Kant, *Metaphysical Foundation of Natural Sciences* (London: Bell Publishers, 1883).

9. A.D. Lindsay, *The Philosophy of Immanuel Kant* (T.C. & E.C. Jack, 67 Long Acre, W.C. and Dodge Publishing Co. Edinburgh and New York) Rare collection.

was basically a criticism and Kant himself called his great books as critiques — the "Critique of Pure Reason"; the "Critique of Practical Reason," the "Critique of Judgement." He called his philosophy as the "Critical Philosophy," or "Critical Idealism." As far as the actions of an individual and their execution in the day-to-day life are concerned, the same appear in the philosophy of Kant through the principle of morality which he has advocated in great detail in his later "Critiques." Kant regarded human actions as "phenomenal," when looked at from an anthropological point of view. As a result these actions are subject to the law of cause and effect.

According to him, we are born and grow with different natures, which in turn lead to different "likes and dislikes," "inclination and disinclination," temptations, temperaments, abilities to perform an act, etc. These differences, though dealing with matters of fact over which we have no control, are attributed to different external environments to which an individual is subjected and responds differently in accordance with the principle of causality. Human actions, thus, are considered as the result of interaction of character and environment, and are not to be praised or blamed but understood.

On the other hand, in view of moral judgements, we seem to be in a different world and the obligations of this world have nothing to do with an individual's likes and dislikes, particularly when one analyses his past actions within the framework of rules of this new world according to which a society (collection of human Beings) is supposed to work. At this stage of "ought to be and not ought to be done," one assumes and follows another type of law of cause and effect. For the claim of duty now, one should not act as a creature of "inclination and disinclination" or of "likes and dislikes," etc. in this domain of different causality. The motive to do what duty demands comes from elsewhere. Kant here makes a sharp separation between phenomenal and moral worlds. In fact a man in this latter case is a moral agent — he is an observer and understander of other men.

In the domain of morality, according to Kant, many commands and principles are hypothetical. They are derived solely from the nature of man as a moral agent and assume that men desire certain ends — happiness, health or success and the actions they advise — are suggested as means to such ends. Commands and principles appeal to man simply because he is a rational Being. In another context, Kant indicates[10] more clearly the relation of duty to a society of moral agents responsible to one another, viz. "Act so that you treat humanity, in your person and in the person of every one else, always as an end as well as a means, never merely as a means." Following such imperatives, according to Kant, one can rise above the promptings of circumstance since he has to act as a self-legislative. Kant further emphasizes that the "principles of right action" can be deduced directly from the imperative he has formulated and need therefore take no account of historical circumstance.

In his "Critique of Judgement" Kant discusses the role of faculty of judgement in human actions and experiences. The principle of causation is again found to play an important role in the working of the faculty of judgement of an individual. The judgement of beauty in Nature is discussed by Kant in great detail and considered as the supreme act of the faculty of judgement.

According to Lindsay's interpretations of Kant's ideas,[11] "all knowledge needs imagination, the power of seeing resemblances and differences in objects which by concepts give unity and rules to the imagination. In science the imagination is subordinate to the understanding, for the aim of science is definiteness and precision. In arts (in the context of beauty) the imagination is free and yet art is not the mere seeing of resemblances and differences; it also has its unity. It aims at the best proportion of variety and unity. This is independent of varying nature of individual person and therefore the judgement of beauty can claim to be universally valid." "We enjoy art not

10. A.D. Lindsay, op. cit., chapter VI.

11. Ibid., chapter VII.

because it serves any of our individual desires and purposes, it is enjoyed by something in us that is universal." "The faculty of judgement, as we saw, is concerned with the attempt to give unity to the detail of the natural world." Thus, art carries some subjectivity in its understanding which leaves certain scope of imprecision and uncertainty whereas science develops on the pillars of definiteness and precision.

With regard to the search of reality in Nature, it is not for a definite purpose, rather it is considered as subordinate to the well-being of man. Lindsay transcribes,[12] the *principle of purposiveness* that arises properly from the contemplation of living things, from the perception of the difference between an *organism* and a *machine*. An organism is purposive in the sense in which a work of art is. Unlike the principle of machine, the working of an organism (or a work of art) can only be understood by studying the individual relations of all its parts. We can never know the Universe as an organism, for we can never know all of its parts. We can understand and put together more and more of these parts, but we never come to an end.

3.2.2 CAUSALITY AT DIFFERENT PLANES AND MISSING LINKS IN KANT PHILOSOPHY

Kant brought in the role of the faculty of judgement (an entity of subjective domain) to find a basis for the working of the moral world, but the incorporation of other constituents of the faculty of understanding[13] of an individual is largely missing in his philosophy. No doubt he realized the difference in the working principles of an organism (or an act of art) and a machine; he still could not go deeper in the former case perhaps due to the ignorance about the existence of other essences of life and their working.

12. A.D. Lindsay, op. cit., chapter VII.

13. Faculty of understanding is an elevated version of E (the faculty of memory). The net experiences gained by a conscious Being are the result of a combined role played by E, I, M, SE and B in the process of perception.

Kant's sharp separation of moral and phenomenal worlds, which manifests in his discussion of motives, also creates certain difficulties, in that he brings in different causality principles in the two cases. The causes and effects of the two worlds (despite their sequential link) are of different scales and magnitudes and sometimes form disjoint sets. Kant conceived the individual as a phenomenal who is to be determined solely by pleasure and pain. He has not bothered himself to understand either the underlying complexity of his "phenomenal individual" or the role of other essences of life in its functioning. No doubt the moral world often conquers the phenomenal world in the sense that the motive of respect for moral law is there by suppressing an individual's inclination and likes and dislikes but only to a certain extent. Moreover, in some way an individual has to reflect collectively in a society. Like this, there are many inconsistencies and gaps that appear in the philosophy of Kant from the point of view of providing a unified theory of human actions and that too at different scales (i.e. as an individual and as its collection). As we shall see in the forthcoming chapters Vedānta philosophy offers a full-fledged package for such descriptions.

3.3 Intelligent Design and Darwin Theory: Do They go Together?

In Western theories of recent times controversies have started emerging with regard to the evolution of man. Both the cases of Intelligent Design and natural selection of Darwin are under scrutiny. Now some schools of thought are convinced that Universe was possibly created not out of random mutation and natural selection as suggested by Charles Darwin long ago but by an Intelligent Design of an unseen power. Bharat Jhunjhunuwala[14] finds a beautiful solution to this problem in *Māṇḍūkya Upaniṣad* (Mantras 2-5) where *ṛṣis* emphasize the manifestation of *Brahman* (unseen power) at the levels of *Īśvara, Hiraṇyagarbha* and *Virāṭ*. Clearly, "Intelligent Design" can be argued

14. Bharat Jhunjhunwala, "Intelligent Design and Darwin go together", The Speaking Tree, *Times of India*, 21 December, 2005.

to operate at the level of *Brahman* while natural selection works later, i.e. at the level of the material world (the *Virāṭ*). Several convincing and appealing arguments to this concept are brought together by Jhunjhunuwala in this regard. Some of the analogies advanced by him are as follows:

(i) If one wants to reach the top of the highest mountain, he can proceed in a specific direction with the highest point in view, or, he can as well start walking in a random direction with a finite probability of reaching the top. In both cases the chance of reaching the top is equal if one keeps aside the question of space and time. In fact the difference in the two cases arises when the role of space and time is brought in and that is important in the material world and perhaps not that much important at higher levels. The former case corresponds to Intelligent Design and the latter to natural selection and their choice depends again on the development of the faculties of understanding of the individual and accordingly his actions or *karma* will emerge.

(ii) The theory of Jay Richards,[15] as Jhunjhunuwala puts it, is more convincing and logical in the context of theory of *karma*. According to Jay Richards, "If we are nothing more than sum of chance, impersonal law and environment, then we are not free and responsible individuals, endowed by our Creator with certain inalienable rights. Because we are not free, we are not responsible; so paradoxically, we can do whatever we want."

The fact that a number of licensing powers are working behind every action performed for an ordered lifestyle puts the Darwin concept of natural selection alone in a cold storage as far as the creation and the working of Universe is concerned.

---

15. Jay Richards, "Intelligent Design Theory: Why it Matters?", an Article by Jay Richards, Sr. Fellow, Discovery Institute's Centre for the Renewal of Science and Culture in Seattle, USA, on Thursday, 25 February 1999, available at Google and Speatout.com pages.

Just as a class teacher divides the students into two groups to hold a friendly test match and encourages them for a competition, the Creator, in the same way, divides us into many separate Beings at the conscious level and leaves us for the survival of the fittest with a varying degree of free will and licensing powers. While the quantity of actions or *karma* originates in either of the two situations mentioned above, the quality of these actions goes by the intelligent design in terms of free will, licensing powers and experiences gained therefrom. Thus, the theories of the Intelligent Design and the natural selection have to be complementary to each other as far as the actions of a Being in this world are concerned. In some sense this concept of complementarity is further strengthened in the next section in the light of advancing modern theories in genetics.

The interesting part is that in the Western world the experts of law and order (and that too of the man-made material world) are going to decide the imparting of these realities of facts to school kids. In addition the views of Judge, which are against the introduction of the component of Intelligent Design in the curriculum, are supported[16, 17] by Vatican office. In a way this shows a lack of foresightedness on the part of Western thinkers in view of the globalization of spirituality in modern times.

3.4 Genetics, Theory of Rebirth and Human Actions

In recent years, efforts have also been made to look for the origin of *karma* in modern genetics by way of decoding the human genome. This also gives an opportunity to re-examine our belief in fate, predestination, free will and the law of *karma*. It is found that some genes determine our mood, some predispose us to diseases, some determine our faithfulness to our companions and there are some which determine our spirituality or religiosity. If genes predetermine our behaviour

---

16. Ian Fisher and Correlia Dean, "Darwin Vs. 'Design': Evolution Still Rules", The Speaking Tree, *Times of India*, 20 January 2006, p. 25.

17. See, citation 15.

in terms of kārmic destiny encoded in them, then the question arises whether we have a choice, or what will be the role of free will? In fact through our efforts dormant genes could get activated. For example, spirituality gene (VMAT 2 or God Gene) gets activated when a person feels an inner need for God and devotes himself wholeheartedly to spiritual pursuits.

According to Lord Kṛṣṇa in *Śrīmad Bhagavad-Gītā* (chapter 6, verses 40-45), the deeds of a person are never annulled even when they are discontinued. In fact in his next birth the negligent seeker of excellence recollects his unfinished project of previous birth and hereafter continues with it starting from the point where he left the same in the previous birth. Not only this, he is born again in such households that are congenial to his inclination. In his present birth, his free will and dedicated efforts could be guided by what is encoded in his genes. It will not be wrong to say that the encoding on gene (an "intelligent design") could be the outcome of deeds of previous birth(s) and the same is now subject to change by a scientist or by the role of free will(!). While religious person calls this as *latencies*, it could be the attribute of *prārabdha* (see entry 2 in Table 2.1 and Section 4.7) in Vedānta philosophy.

Extensive neuropsychological research on patients with near death experience has shown that they experience an expanding consciousness while their brains register no activity at all. A majority think hundred times faster with greater clarity than is humanly possible. They go back to their childhood days and experience an intense connection with everything and everyone around them instantly as before. It is now empirically proved that people can think and feel when they are clinically unconscious due to acute pancerebral ischemia. M.N. Kundu[18] summarizes these observations as follows:

---

18. M.N. Kundu, "Death Does not Mean the End of consciousness", The Speaking Tree, *Times of India*, 4 April 2006.

> All our experiences are systematically stored in phase-space from where the same is retrieved by our DNA in the mind-body complex. When we lose the body we lose only the mortal substance, the real architect or the user of the system, our individual consciousness limited in space continues in a different state of consciousness.

As a matter of fact the theory of action only attempts to make sense of the mysterious by way of systematizing the randomness of happenings and to give a sense of purpose to life. In this regard, the deeds, a person performs by choice as a free agent, determine the body in which his soul would inhabit and the family in which he would be born in his next life to finish the unfinished task(s) of previous birth(s). In general he would be given according to what he deserves — the worst possible (hell) or the best possible (heaven) or something in between the two on this earth itself. There are also persons endowed with an ability to transform adversity into advantage, to compromise with all fluctuations of fortune with stoic calm. We shall return to these discussions later.

Thus, it is yet to become clear whether gene decodes the outcome of actions of the previous birth(s) of an individual or of his parents (or forefathers) or of both. Despite mysterious ways of actions of a human Being, it appears that modern scientific studies have also started taking turn in the direction of age-old Vedānta philosophy. Only future studies can throw more light on these issues.

3.5 Mind-Brain Complex: Quantum Neurodynamics

The mind-body interaction and related problems have been the subject of study in the Western philosophy for a long time but without having a complete understanding of the highly complex object like the human Being. While the laws of physics are found to show their limitations[19] in general, their viability is further questioned when applied to understand the working of

19. See, for example, Victor F. Weisskopf, "Frontiers and Limits of Science", in *American Scientist* **65** (1977) 405.

biological systems.[20, 21] In spite of all this a considerable interest has been generated in recent years to investigate the role of mind in explaining a physical phenomenon[22, 23, 24] or conversely in searching for the effect of physical phenomenon on human mind. The age-old mind-body problem now seems to be focused around the mind-brain problem and has given birth to a new branch of study called "quantum neurodynamics," particularly after the development of language of quantum mechanics and of improved computer techniques in terms of network studies.[25, 26, 27] Very recently, efforts have also been made[28] to apply the laws of physics to various aspects of human behaviour and to mathematize the functioning of limbs, of course via the process of modelling. Computer modelling of the blood flow through veins and arteries has been carried out. Nuclear magnetic resonance imaging (MRI) has become an important device in this regard. While it has become possible to detect magnetic fields of magnitude 10^{-13} tesla using superconducting sensors,

20. Hermann Haken, *Synergetics*, 2nd edn. (Springer-Verlag, 1978), vol. 1.
21. G. Nicolis and I. Prigogine, *Self Organization in Non-equilibrium Systems* (Wiley, 1977).
22. T. Pink, op. cit.
23. D.J. Chalmers, op. cit.
24. Roger Penrose, 1997, op. cit.
25. J. Searle, "Minds, Brains and Programs", *Behaviour and Brain Sc.* **3** (1980) 412; P. Churchland, *Neurophilosophy* (Bradford Books, 1986).
26. J.G. Taylor, Can Neural Networks Ever be Made to Think, NNW1/91, 4-12, and the references cited therein.
27. N. Fragopanagos and J.G. Taylor, "Emotion Recognition in Human-Computer Interaction", *Neural Networks* **18** (2005) 389-405 (Special Issue), also see other Articles in this issue.
28. See, for example, R. Balasubramaniam and M.T. Turvey, "Co-ordination Modes in the Multisegmental Dynamics of Hula Hoping", Bio, Cybern. **90** (2004) 176-90 and the references therein; H.-I. Pai, C.-Y. Tseng and H.C. Lee, "Identifying Biomagnetic sources in the brain by the maximum entropy approach", arXiv : q-bio.NC/0508040, August 2005.

brain imaging can tell us whether a thought — a subject of mind, is good or bad.

From the point of view of accounting consciousness in physical theories the present studies in quantum neurodynamics emerge in two (perhaps) connected ways. These ways discussed by Roger Penrose and Stephen Hawking are the outcome of an attempt to understand gravity forces in Nature at the level of quantum mechanics.[29] In one case Penrose advocates for a uniform full-fledged theory in physics which accommodates consciousness and the other one having support of Stephen Hawking is in terms of "patchwork" picture of physics (a picture in which physical phenomena are understood in isolation and very often in ideal conditions). In the "patchwork" case, however, different brain or intelligence (artificial or otherwise) related phenomena pertaining to the action of a Being find explanation in different (and often disconnected) concepts and models in a patchwork style. Further, Hawking believes in a transparent reduction of the law of biology to those of chemistry and those of chemistry to those of physics. There is no scope of consciousness in these reductions. On the other hand, Penrose talks of an objective reduction of the (quantum) wave function to explain the physical reality (the one which is realizable in the space-time world and also leaves behind an unexplained, latent part of it) aspect of the phenomenon and he is silent (and perhaps has no theory) about how the subjective aspect of the reality can be accommodated in spite of the fact that he clearly feels a necessity of its introduction in the theory in terms of an "extra" parameter. Further, this objective reduction of Penrose is needed in order to explain self-awareness in view of Godel theorem and the same implies that a conscious mind is not computable. According to Penrose consciousness is something special to living Beings and the same cannot be simulated on a computer.

With regard to the ways of introducing consciousness in physical theories, Penrose suggests four possible viewpoints, of

29. Roger Penrose, 1997, op. cit. Chapters 6 and 7.

course without defining the terms like consciousness or awareness. His four alternatives A, B, C, and D (now prefixed by P, to retain the name of Penrose) are the following:[30]

PA : All thinking is computation; in particular, feelings of conscious awareness are evoked merely by carrying out of appropriate computations.

PB : Awareness is a feature of the brain's physical action; and, whereas any physical action can be simulated computationally, computation simulation cannot by itself evoke awareness.

PC : Appropriate physical action of the brain evokes awareness, but this physical action cannot even be properly simulated computationally.

PD : Awareness cannot be explained by physical, computation, or any other scientific terms.

In the viewpoint PD, the consciousness or awareness is kept aside from the physical theory, though it is attributed to the brain action in the viewpoint PC. Even the physical action — an outcome of brain action is not completely understandable. The viewpoint PB is not independent; it is rather a mixture of PC and PD. There is definitely a role of cause and effect at a very fine level, particularly in the phrase at the beginning of PB. The viewpoint PA is misleading in the sense as to how the all-thinking can be computational, particularly when the "thinker" is not defined. In fact it becomes computable only after an objective reduction is carried out.

In recent times efforts have also been made to investigate the role of consciousness, manifesting in the processes attributed to the mind-brain complex by way of postulating an attention-emotion interaction. With a view to understanding the human-computer interaction better, the modelling and corresponding mathematization has also been carried out by Fragopanagos and

30. Roger Penrose, 1997, op. cit., p. 101.

Taylor[31, 32] for emotion recognition. We shall take stock of some of these details in Chapter 7.

3.6 Recent Theories: Levels of Hierarchy in Complex Systems

The subject of physics represents a model of what a successful science should be. As mentioned in Chapter 1, it provides the basis for other physical and biological sciences because everything in this (physical) world, including our biological body, is believed to be made up of the same fundamental particles, whose interactions are again governed by the same fundamental forces. Physicists follow the reductionist's approach, i.e. their goal has been to reduce complexity to simplicity. They reduce matter to molecules, then to atoms, then to nuclei and electron and so on (cf. Appendix B) and this is done on the basis of the concept of isolated system. According to G.F.R. Ellis,[33]

> The problem is that no real physical or biological system is truly isolated, physically or historically. Consequently, reductionism tends to ignore the kinds of interactions that can trigger the emergence of order, patterns, or properties that do not pre-exist in the underlying physical substratum. Biological complexity and consciousness — as products of evolutionary adaptation — are just two examples. Physics might provide the *necessary* conditions for such phenomena to exist, but not the *sufficient* conditions for specifying the behaviours that emerge at those higher levels of complexity. Indeed the laws of behaviour in complex systems emerge from, but are to a large degree independent of, the underlying low-level physics. . . .

Thus, despite physics being a successful science in providing the necessary conditions to exist it does not, however, provide sufficient conditions for the *causes* to exist. As a matter of fact the causes at those higher levels in the hierarchy of complexity

---

31. N. Fragopanagos and J.G. Taylor, op. cit.
32. See the Introduction of the Special Issue on "Emotion and Brain : Understanding Emotions and Modeling Their Recognition", *Neural Networks* **18** (2005) 313-16.
33. G.F.R. Ellis, op. cit.

have real effects at lower levels but just the converse is not true. Clearly, objective science has limitations[34] to describe the real world. Further, it is believed that true complexity, with the emergence of higher levels of order and meaning (including life) occurs in modular, hierarchical structures[35] and one can talk of different levels of meaning embodied in the same complex structure. These higher levels display new properties which are not evident at the lower levels. Unique properties of the organized matter, however, arise from how the constituent parts are arranged and interact. Also, these specific properties cannot be fully explained[36, 37] by breaking that order down into its component parts.[38] In fact one cannot describe the higher levels in terms of the language of lower levels. As a result there is a clear hint for the emergence of a new science to describe the framework of these higher levels.

3.6.1 LEVELS OF HIERARCHY VS. "FROM BOTTOM-UP TO TOP-DOWN" ACTIONS

In the levels of hierarchy mentioned above, higher level variables are not only the aggregates of lower-level variables but are determined by them. On the other hand, the higher level variables reveal important properties of the hierarchy that are otherwise hidden. In fact an appropriate choice of higher level variables offers the key to a phenomenological understanding of the higher levels themselves. What happens at each higher level the description is, of course, based in the chain of causes and effects

---

34. Victor F. Weisskopf, op. cit.

35. See, for example, *The Re-Emergence of Emergence*, eds. P. Clayton and P.C.W. Davies, New York: Oxford University Press (in Press); Also see http://www.math.uct.ac.za/~ellis/ermerge.doc.

36. See the introduction of the Special issue of Neural Networks, **18** (2005), p. 313-16, op. cit. in citation 32.

37. R.B. Laughlin, *A Different Universe : Re-inventing Physics from the Bottom Down* (New York: Basic Books, 2005).

38. R.B. Laughlin, op. cit.

from the levels below it and thereby *suggesting a "bottom-up"* action. On the other hand, higher level variables can control what happens at the lower level — a case of *"top-down"* action. Such a top-down action affects the nature of causality significantly because of the possibility of inter-level feedback loops.

From the study of complex systems (including the living Beings) it is found that the causal models of the real world remain incomplete unless they account for various effects arising from nonphysical parameters like intentions, purposes, and goals. It is noticed that multiple top-down actions allow various causal chains in higher levels of a complex system to co-ordinate the action at lower levels but in a coherent way. Also the causal hierarchy bifurcates because of the effectiveness of human minds at controlling the lower levels of structure. Some of these ideas of recently discussed theories of complex systems (of which the human being is also an example) will be clear from the examples discussed below from the domains of both animate and inanimate objects.

3.6.2 "FROM BOTTOM-UP TO TOP-DOWN" PICTURE IN PRACTICE: EXAMPLES

In general, the reduction of laws of physics to those of chemistry, and those of chemistry to those of biochemistry or to those of biology and to those of limb actions and so forth could be the example of bottom-up action. On the other hand, higher level variables can control what happens at the lower levels. For example, when one moves his arm he moves because he has decided to move it. The intention thus instructs many millions of electrons and protons to come into action in a particular way. Further detailed structure of this system of hierarchy can be attributed to the physiology of the nervous system which makes the movement possible and then to psychology of the person and so on. Such a top-down action affects the nature of causality at different levels. Further examples of top-down effects from physical sciences are as follows:

(i) The case of top-down action can be visualized in the quantum measurement process through the collapse of the wave function to an eigenstate of a chosen measurement basis. One chooses the details of the measurement such as preparing the initial states, aligning axes of polarization and so on and those choices determine what set of microstates can result from a measurement.

(ii) Top-down effects occur because an *ordered structure underlies the causal relations*. For example, (a) electrons flow in specific wires that connect specific components or specific neurons connect to other specific neurons. However, the externally applied potentials may represent top-down effects that the environment imposes on a system; (b) the gravitational field of massive planet affects the motion of particles measured in a laboratory on the surface of the planet; (c) potential functions in the Schrodinger equation or in the action (function) of a system, generally, are the outcome of aggregate effects from particles and their interactions (potential *vs.* field theoretic or Feynman diagram approach). These approaches provide the nature of the system, at least in principle, as simple as a particle in a box or as complex as computers and brains.

(iii) A classic case of top-down action from environment to microstructure is that of the difference in the DNA codings. For example, polar bears have genes for white fur whereas those living in a forest have genes for brown or black fur. Thus, the environment leads to the difference in the microstructures, i.e. the difference in the DNA codings of their genes.

(iv) The cases of top-down and bottom-up action can be further understood from the single example of searching for the answer to the question as to why an aircraft is flying. In the bottom-up case, it flies because air molecules move at different speeds over the top and the bottom wing surfaces to create a pressure difference that lifts the aeroplane against gravity — Bernoulli's principle. In the same-level terms, the aeroplane flies because the pilot is flying it, after a rigorous training and testing process to develop the requisite skills. However, in the top-down picture, an aeroplane flies because it was designed to fly! A team of engineers at the same point worked within a historical context of the development of metallurgy, combustion, lubrication, aeronautics, machine tools, computer aided design and so on. All this occurred in the economic context of a society with a transportation need. On the other hand, a brick cannot fly as it is not designed to fly — intentions.

While many such examples can also be sought from the soft disciplines and day-to-day life the main point is that causal models of the real world remain incomplete unless they account for various effects of intention, purposes, and goals. In fact multiple top-down actions allow various causal chains in higher levels of a complex system to co-ordinate action at lower levels in a coherent way. It is the causal hierarchy which is responsible for the bifurcation of choices and intentions involved therein.

3.7 Concluding Discussion

The survey made in this chapter corroborates the ideas outlined in Chapter 1, and however suggests that the existing laws of objective science are inadequate with regard to providing explanation of many phenomena in Nature. In fact they explain only a few phenomena and many remain unexplained. The limitations of the laws, in particular, can be noticed when applied to understand the behaviour not only of an individual but also of the collection of individual objects. While this is true with most animate objects, several processes involving inanimate objects also do not abide by them, particularly when the role of surroundings or of circumstances need to be accounted for.

While Western philosophy has very little to say with regard to the understanding of human behaviour and experiences, modern science, on the other hand, has started penetrating into this domain. In particular, in the development of new physical theories, the studies in genetics via the details of cell structure and in mind-brain complex via neural networks computer analogues, the introduction of levels of hierarchy in case of complex systems via the concept of "from top-down to bottom-up" action, etc. offer clear evidence of realizing the need of an extra dimension of consciousness. In spite of all this, an account of plurality of consciousness in these theories remains a far cry. This, in fact, is required because the consciousness in human actions manifest in ways more than one through EOLs and at different levels of understanding.

Physical theories such as the gas laws or Ohm's law provide only a phenomenological understanding of the behaviour of atoms or charges. In particular, these are the examples of laws that emerge out of the joint (collective) behaviour of particles rather than the individual ones. The higher many-body levels are more complex and less predictable than the lower levels. In fact the above-mentioned phenomenological laws are reliable to describe the behaviour at the level of physics and chemistry but not at the level of psychology or sociology.

To account for human purpose, according to G.F.R. Ellis, one would have to include some kind of consciousness — intention function Ψ, dependent on lower level variables that would, at least in principle, cover higher level mind effects and subsequently will help in mathematizing the problem. As a whole this exercise is going to be equally tedious since mind also gets affected by the presence of biological or physical phenomenon. Ellis further emphasizes, "no current physics experiment or theory explains the Nature — or even the existence — of emotions, money, fine art, foot ball games or people." Long ago, Emmanuel Kant also arrived at similar conclusions while talking of causality at different planes. He also suggested the different working principles for an organism and a machine. Thus, it appears that in philosophical terms the progress made in understanding Nature over a period of 250 years comes to a naught.

There are two important actions, which take the human Being to higher levels — concentration and meditation. In concentration, the consciousness is focused on to a particular object in an objective (outward) style by way of controlling other actions of EOLs of a Being. On the other hand, in meditation consciousness must be pushed to the source or to the roots in a subjective (an inward) style for a possibility of transformation again by controlling the actions of the Being. In fact "ultimate" cannot be known only through the brain processes, mainly because when one is functioning through the brain he is in conflict with the roots.

Hegel also tried[39] to look for a science of philosophy but strictly in a scientific form. These developments however remained incomplete without actaully knowing as how to scientifically deal with a reality that is personal.

In summary it may be emphasized that (i) intelligent design and Darwin theory have to go together; (ii) the fact that gene contains a lot of pre-history of the Being, the theory or rebirth/ intelligent design cannot be discarded out rightly, and (iii) in "from bottom-up to top-down" theories one can foresee emerging new fields of research.

---

39. G.W.F. Hegel Resource site; http://www.gwfhegel.org/intro-cont.html.

4

Fundamental Processes and the Theory of Karma
Vedānta Philosophy in Modern Perspective

In technical terms, in physics, the "action" is defined as the time integral of an energy measure — called Lagrangian functional over a certain period of time and the dynamics of the system is derived by extremizing this functional integral with respect to an external (arbitrary) parameter which is required to vanish at the end points of the trajectories. Thus, out of infinitely many possibilities Nature is found to follow the one along which the action turns out to be minimum — *the principle of least action*.

In the day-to-day life, however, the *karma* or action with reference to a (human) Being can be understood as the outcome of engagement(s) of some or all essences of life (EOLs) of that Being in their respective domains in the presence of consciousness. In particular, in the language of the patomic model (cf. Appendix A), the outcome of engagements of EOLs E, I, M, SE and B in their respective domains could be either towards WO or towards SO depending on the developments of the faculties of understanding (FOU)[1] of that individual. In other words, if the Being b performs upward transitions, i.e. towards SO (cf. *fig*. 2.1), spirituality develops in life. On the other hand, if b performs downward transitions, i.e. towards WO (which are more likely) then worldliness in the behaviour of the

1. Faculty of understanding (FOU) is an elevated version of the faculty of memory (E). In fact the net experiences gained by a conscious Being through a combined role of E, I, M, SE and B about WO and SO lifts the E to a highter level.

individual reflects. In fact when the functions of these EOLs of the Being become repetitive at the space-time level with respect to the external environment and/or circumstances as the result of a sequence of cause and effect, then they constitute the *behaviour* of that individual either in totality or in parts if only a few EOLs of that Being play the role in performing the action. Again in these actions of EOLs, *the principle of minimum efforts* is followed at various stages and in the guidance of the faculty of decision I. Now the question arises as to what are the directed efforts or with respect to what these efforts be minimized. Is there any link between the arbitrary parameter used in physics and the one required here? To maintain these efforts, different EOLs have to perform actions. We shall try to look for possible answers to some of these questions in this chapter within the framework of Vedānta philosophy.

Before proceeding further it may be recalled that in Vedānta philosophy the human Being is said to be the perfect creation of God and the difference between human Being and other species arises mainly due to the levels of development of some or all EOLs (in view of the Darwin's theory), particularly that of the faculty of decision I. This EOL, I, plays a very important role not only in the actions performed by a Being but also in arriving at a definite outcome at the end of these actions.

4.1 Origin of Karma vis-à-vis Survival of Body

While the physical (man-made) instrument waits for a command from a living Being to act, the actions of the (God-made) living instrument, i.e. the body of a Being are the outcome of its free will and the consciousness which is injected by the Creator at the time of its creation. Once the consciousness is there in the instrument of body of a Being, then some or all EOLs start working automatically in their respective domains. Since these actions finally appear through SE and B at the space time level it is natural that these actions by and large be directed towards WO which, in turn, will help in maintaining B and SE. Thus, to maintain B and SE, it is necessary to fulfil their basic needs and for doing so not only a non-human Being but also a common man pass their whole lifetime. In this respect it will not be wrong to say that all species (including the human Being) follow the principle of survival of the fittest and most of the actions of a Being originate for the survival of B and SE.

However, other categories of persons do think of something above these domains of actions of the Being. Vedānta philosophy clearly presents a systematic and fixes the priorities of these actions performed by the EOLs of a Being, in general. Those actions of EOLs which end up in favouring the upward transitions of b are put at a higher level in terms of values. Also, of them the better ones are directed to attain the knowledge (worldly or otherwise) and the same are put at a relatively higher level in Vedānta philosophy, in fact, at the highest level, if the EOLs are directed to attain the ultimate knowledge (cf. verse (4.2) below).

4.1.1 SUPREMACY OF KNOWLEDGE

In *SMBG*, the attainment of knowledge is said[2] to be the supreme goal of life, not because it is the best purifier of the self but because it is the purest of the pure goals of life, viz.

na hi jñānena sadraśaṁ pavitrama iha vidyate ।
tat svayaṁ yoga saṁsiddhaḥ kālenātmani vindati ॥ — 4.38 (4.1)

In this world, there is no purifier like knowledge; he who has attained purity of heart through practice of *karmayoga*, automatically realizes it in the Self in the course of time.

4.1.2 WHAT IS TRUE (ULTIMATE) KNOWLEDGE?

Again this knowledge may concern to attain worldly objects (cf. Appendix A) or to understand the Self and the Universe. In Sanskrit literature the question of true knowledge is answered beautifully through the following verse:[3]

2. *Śrīmad Bhagavad-Gītā* (*SMBG*), chapter 4, verse 38, Gorakhpur: Gita Press.

3. Quoted in the work of Kālidāsa.

ātma jñānaṁ vidurjñānaṁ jñānānyāni yāni tu ।
tāni jñānāvabhāṣāni sārasyānava bodhanāt ॥ (4.2)

The knowledge of self is the only true knowledge; the rest of knowledge is mirage that does not lead us to the absolute truth.

4.1.3 WHO IS QUALIFIED TO ATTAIN THIS (TRUE) KNOWLEDGE?

In *SMBG*, Lord Kr̥ṣṇa suggests in very clear terms the methodology and the purpose of attaining the knowledge. In a universally acceptable style, he dictates the qualities of a deserving seeker of the ultimate knowledge through the following verse:[4]

śraddhāvān labhate jñānaṁ tatparaḥ saṁyatendriyaḥ ।
jñānaṁ labdhvā parāmśāntiṁ achireṇādhi gacchati ॥ — 4.39 (4.3)

He, who has fully controlled his senses, is exclusively devoted to spiritual practice and is full of faith, attains knowledge; having gained knowledge he immediately attains supreme peace (in the form of realization of God). One who is devoid of faith, not alert and full of doubts cannot be on the spiritual path and hence no peace and subsequently no pleasure is attained. In another verse,[5] the Lord further indicates the use of knowledge in clearing one's own doubts. As a result, it helps in purifying the heart and intellect, leading to a personality who is either not attached or least attached to the actions he performs or to the fruits thereof, viz.

yoga sannyasta karmāṇaṁ jñāna sañcchinna saṁśayaṁ ।
ātmavantaṁ na karmāṇi nibadhnanti dhanañjaya ॥ — 4.41 (4.4)

Here, again the Lord addresses his friend and disciple, Arjuna, as "Arjuna, he who has dedicated all his actions to God (or to the highest goal) according to the spirit of *karma-yoga*, whose doubts have been dispelled by wisdom, and who is self-

---

4. *SMBG*: chapter 4, verse 39.

5. *SMBG*: chapter 4, verse 41.

possessed, actions do not bind him." This verse clearly suggests a basis for attaining peace in modern times provided one digests its meaning. Not only this, the Lord at several other places clearly highlights, sometimes using analogies, the art and logic of dispelling out actions (and thus becoming a perfect doer, so-called *karmayogī*) by way of reducing the proliferation of actions merely to ashes in the form of fruits thereof again by using the fire of wisdom. We shall return to some of these discussions later.

At another place, Lord Kṛṣṇa spells out in clear terms the incentive to perform an action and the main constituents of an action through the verse:[6]

> *jñānaṁ jñeyaṁ parijñātā trividhā karmacodanā* ।
> *karaṇaṁ karma karteti trividhaḥ karma saṅgrahaḥ* ॥ — 18.18 (4.5)

In other words, "the knowledge, the object of knowledge and the knower — these are threefold incentives to action; and the doer, the action and the organ(s) of action — these are the threefold constituents of action" (cf. entries 4 and 5 in Table 2.1).

For the accomplishment of all actions, the Lord further highlights the five contributory causes (cf. entry 7 in Table 2.3) through the following verse,[7]

> *adhiṣṭhānaṁ tathā kartā karaṇaṁ ca pṛthagvidhaṁ* ।
> *vividhāśca pṛthakceṣṭā daivaṁ caivātra pañcamam* ॥ — 18.14 (4.6)

> The body (as the seat of all activity and the organs of action), the agent (*jīvātmā*) and the different kinds of organs, as also the divergent activities of various kinds and the fifth, destiny — these are the causes (operating) here.

The actions of EOLs can broadly be classified as (i) directed and (ii) arbitrary. Fruit or gain of an action is always positively definite; however, it may be good or bad according to the standards or the value system defined for a society. In the

---

6. *SMBG*: chapter 18, verse 18.

7. *SMBG*: chapter 18, verse 14; now onward the citations of the verses of *SMBG* is given at the respective places.

process of performing a "directed" action, the role of a large number of EOLs is regulated, whereas in the case of "arbitrary" action only a few EOLs and that too temporarily need be regulated. The arbitrary actions are not as arbitrary as they appear; rather they originate out of a limited domain of cause and effect and give temporary satisfaction to the individual after their performance. Sometimes there is no coherence between cause and effect in this case. On the other hand, the directed action of EOLs gives long-term positive gains with a greater degree of satisfaction. The knowledge and the outcome attained out of the directed actions are said to be the best and are the finest possible ones in the world. Out of them, those that lead to spirituality or spiritual knowledge are still better compared to the ones resulting in the worldliness and the worldly knowledge.

In either case, in order to attain knowledge, the EOLs need to be trained in the same universal style. For example, this is possible by B with a controlled set of SE and a pointed and concentrated M using a fine analysing power of I. Such knowledge when stored in E, gives a satisfaction (peace) at the level of SO — an aim dictated by *SMBG* through the verses (4.1) and (4.5).

Whether it is the case of directed or arbitrary action, in either situation, *kāma* (or deep-rooted desire) plays an important role in giving rise to the performance of an action either of some or all the EOLs of Being. Broadly speaking desires can be of three categories, desiring of *knowledge*, desiring of *talent* and desiring of *sense-objects*. Efforts can again be positive or negative for these categories depending upon the nature of the systematics (cf. Section 4.4) followed. However, the first two are expected to result in the upward transitions of the Being in the patomic model whereas the third will result in the downward transitions of the Being.

While for the details of these discussions we shall return later, in summary it may be mentioned that the *karma* or the actions performed by a common man, scientist, philosopher or a *yogī* originate from different sources in the set of EOLs but in a self-consistent manner. Further, the directed actions are the outcome of directed efforts extremized with respect to the parameters associated with different EOLs.[8]

4.2 Types of Karma

4.2.1 LINEAR AND NON-LINEAR ACTIONS

When an action is performed by EOLs then a chain of cause and effect immediately comes into play separately at the levels of mind (M), senses of knowledge and action (SE) and of body (B) with a decreasing degree of fineness. In fact the role of cause and effect is clearly noticeable at the B-level, and then it is a little less at the SE-level and further less at the M-level. Even if a person decides not to perform an action, he may do so at the B-(physical) level, but the action must have definitely been performed by him initially at the M-level according to the causality at that level. However, when an action becomes a routine, then it can also be performed at the B-and/or SE-level without a notice by the individual at the M-level. One can call an action a *linear* one if it is the outcome of a true and honest co-ordination of M, SE and B, particularly in accordance with the norms defined from outside (i.e. by a society); otherwise for the fulfilment of the *kāma* (deep-rooted desire) one sometimes adopts amoral or unethical (again from the point of view of external social standards) means that give rise to an action at the level of B which may be termed as *non-linear* since it could be the outcome of false, unethical co-ordination of EOLs. While the *yogī* category of persons is free from such a non-linearity, common man sometimes has it in a certain proportion, but philosopher and scientist categories of persons always live with it as a part of their profession. These latter categories, very often use non-linearity of an action as a part of their analysing power to

8. We shall later consider that the efforts are the functions of certain parameters representing the contribution of different EOLs towards the performance of an action. Directed effort is the result of minimizing the efforts with respect to these parameters and the directed action in some sense is another name for such an effort.

establish the truth in Nature in an objective style,[9] but within the framework of defined ethical values.

For example, whatever one thinks (good or bad in view of the ethical values), and expresses the same by senses of knowledge and accordingly brings the same in action by B with all the honesty, then such performances are termed as *linear*; otherwise any disproportionate role of these EOLs yields a non-linear action in day to day life. In Indian lore this is the case of an ideal co-ordination of *manasā, vācā, karmaṇā* — the trio of components of an action (cf. entry 6, Table 2.1).

4.2.2 BINDING EFFECT OF AN ACTION

It is true that all actions of a Being, in principle, end up in providing the fruits which make the society or world better not only in terms of ethical values (which are functions of space and time) but also in terms of working of Nature through *pañca-mahābhūtas* (five cosmic elements) (*PMs*) (cf. entry 1, Table 2.3). Note that any disturbance (local or global) in the equilibrium maintained by these *PMs* can cause the elimination of human race, then what to say of other species on this planet? Therefore, now the question is as to what is a right action so that such equilibrium is maintained all over and forever? With regard to the nature of an action even wise men are confused, i.e. at the very beginning of the chain of cause and effect, they are not able to decide as to what is right or wrong, since these are relative words and their meanings are fixed from the prevalent values. However, they (wise men) take decision within the limitations of their faculty of decision I, which is guided by the experiences stored in E. Moreover, whatever may be the nature of an action, it is bound to bear fruit and the same leave a binding effect on all categories of persons except on the ones who have understood the "art of living." In *SMBG* such a person is called *karmayogī* —

9. Subjective style of expression of truth in Nature is ultimately the matter of realization only, however a part of it is often expressed through simile, metaphor or analogies.

a subclass of *yogī* category of persons. One who becomes free from the binding effect of an action, is qualified for the salvation in this world itself.

To become a *karmayogī*, Lord Kṛṣṇa in *SMBG* further suggests some tips in very clear terms and in a universal style. While such tips are distributed all over in *SMBG* in different contexts and in a variety of ways, they are intensified at certain places. For example, for an individual, the Lord presents a logical sequence of concepts through the following verses which are, if followed and practised, can convert that individual into a *yogī* — the man of perfection or a liberated soul (free from the binding effect of an action):

karmaṇo hyapi boddhavyaṁ, boddhavyaṁ ca vikarmaṇaḥ ।
akarmaṇaśca boddhavyaṁ gahanā karmaṇo gatiaḥ ॥ — 4.17 (4.7)

The truth about action must be known; and the truth of prohibited action must also be known; even so, the truth about inaction must be known. For mysterious are the ways of action.

The Lord further adds that,

karmaṇy akarma yaḥ paśyed akarmaṇi ca karma yaḥ ।
sa buddhimān manuṣ eṣu sa yuktaḥ kṛtsna karma kṛt ॥ — 4.18 (4.8)

In other words, "he who sees inaction in action, and action in inaction, is wise among men; he is a *yogī* who has accomplished all actions."

The verses (4.7) and (4.8) present a deeper analysis of the nature of action and a classification of the same at a subtle level. Further suggested are the ways and by following them an individual can become a liberated soul, i.e. free from the binding effect of an action, through

yasya sarve samārambhāḥ kāma saṅkalpa varjitāḥ ।
jñānāgni dagdhakarmāṇaṁ tam āhuḥ paṇḍitaṁ budhāḥ । — 4.19 (4.9)

He whose undertakings are free from desire and thought of the world, and whose actions are burnt up by the fire of wisdom, him even the wise call a sage.

In an alternative style, the Lord further emphasizes,

> *tyaktvā karma phalāsamgaṁ nityatr̥pto nirāśrayaḥ* ।
> *karmaṇy abhipravr̥tto api naiva kiñcit karoti saḥ* ॥ — 4.20 (4.10)
>
> He who, having totally given up attachment to actions and their fruits, has got over the dependence on the world, and is ever satisfied, does nothing at all, though he may ever be engaged in action.

The ways of action are truly mysterious in the sense that an action is sometimes made an inaction by discarding the fruits of the same, whereas, an inaction in another situation, becomes an action if one looks at the *saṅkalpa*-level alone and not at the level of its actual performance by SE and/or B. A third category of action, introduced by the Lord in (4.7) is that of a prohibited action (*niṣedha karma*) (cf. entry 3 in Table 2.2). An action may be a right action for one category of persons or an individual and the same may be prohibited for another category of persons or individual. On the other hand, a prohibited action for one becomes the duty for another. Therefore, one who knows such finer details of the subtleties of an action is said to be a man of wisdom (cf. verse (4.8)).

The verses (4.9) and (4.10) throw some light on the "Art of Living" in this world. In fact for an individual to become a liberated soul (*yogī* or a man of perfection) the ways suggested in these verses may appear to be difficult, but not the impossible ones, definitely they are within the reach of human efforts. If one practises them, then in a gradual process one is bound to achieve such a state of perfection. In some sense, the case of a liberated soul no doubt may appear as an ideal limit but the fact is that the same does exist (or it is at least necessary to exist to set the standards in a society in the same way as one does in physics by way of postulating the perfect gases, super conductors, perfectly smooth surfaces, or perfectly black bodies, etc.). In verse (4.9), the Lord has even used a simile to elaborate the underlying point that leads one to such a state of perfection. The Lord, however, suggests to discard both *karma* and *saṅkalpa*

(*saṅkalpa* in fact is a sub-class of *kāma*[10]) to make doubly sure of the success of efforts. Recall that *kāma* is the source of all actions in the form of a deep-rooted desire. In verse (4.10), the Lord does not ask to leave a *karma* as such; rather advises to discard the attachment to the outcome of that *karma*. If the actions are performed with this spirit then the same are bound to become inaction. At another place, the Lord further advocates this theory of *karma* in an alternative style, viz.

karmaṇy evādhikāraste mā phaleṣu kadācana ।
mā karmaphala heturbhūr mā te saṅgo astva karmaṇi ॥ — 2.47 (4.11)

Your right is only to work, but never to the fruit thereof. Let not the fruit of action be your object, nor let your attachment be to inaction.

Thus, the attachment (keen passion) either to action or to the fruit thereof, is the main cause of worry leading to the binding effect of an action. However, by sacrificing fruit to the Lord one becomes a *karmayogī* and in this way the action becomes an inaction.

As a matter of fact even a common man can be a *yogī* at a particular time and a particular place, but if the above practice of discarding *saṅkalpa*s or the outcome of actions becomes the habit of a person in a rather intensive manner, then that person tends to become a true *yogī* and this is well within the reach of human efforts.

4.3 The Case of a Liberated Soul vis-à-vis the Art of Living

4.3.1 THE MAN OF PERFECTION: A LIBERATED SOUL

As mentioned above, an action always has a binding effect on an individual unless the latter knows the "art of living" in this world. By eliminating or minimizing this binding effect an individual can become a liberated soul and that too in a limiting case. As a matter of fact, the actions of a Being are necessary to

10. While *kāma* and *saṅkalpa* appear to be synonym, the former can be considered as belonging to the domain of I and the latter to the domain of M.

maintain the body and they as such are born with the Being itself. The effect of these actions stay long as one is alive as per declaration by the Lord, viz.

niyataṁ kuru karma tvaṁ karma jyāyo hyakarmaṇaḥ ।
śarīrayātrāpī ca te na prasiddha yed akarmaṇaḥ ॥ — 3.8 (4.12)

Therefore do you (Lord addressing Arjuna) perform your alloted duty; for action is superior to inaction. Desisting from action you cannot even maintain your body.

Here the word "inaction" is used in another context. It means that the *saṅkalpa* at the M-level is not to perform any outward action; in fact, it is going to be the part of any of the four categories of actions (cf. entry 3, Table 2.2). Further, with regard to an outward form of an action, the Lord advances a definition of a true renouncer of the fruits of an action, viz.

na hi dehabhratā śakyaṁ tyaktuṁ karmānyaśeṣataḥ,
yastu karmaphalatyāgī satyāgī tyabhidhī yate. — 18.11 (4.13)

Since it is not possible for the embodied Beings to renounce all actions completely, hence it is said that he who renounces the fruit of action has truly renounced.

Thus, the actions are bound to be there (and so are their binding effects) at least to maintain the body. However, such a gross form of actions falls under somewhat lower category and mostly confined to the domains of B and/or SE.

Out of the four categories of the outward class of actions, namely *nitya, naimittika, kāmya* and *niṣedha* (cf. entry 3 in Table 2.2), only the *kāmya* category of actions has somė linkage with the generalized definition of an inaction of the previous section. For an individual to become a liberated soul, the attachment to the fruits, even of this class of actions, needs to be discarded. At other places the Lord suggests some more formulae to the individual to become a liberated soul, particularly by way of eliminating the binding effects of an action. For example, the Lord suggests a universal formula for this purpose as in verse

(4.4). This verse advocates a universal truth of the highest level. It may be difficult for a common man to attain such a state but it is not an impossible one. In the same spirit, the Lord at another place defines the best (*sāttvika*) doer of an action, viz.

mukta saṅgo anahamvādi dhṛty utsāha samanvitaḥ ।
siddhy asiddhyor nirvikāraḥ kartā sāttvika ucyate ॥ — 18.26 (4.14)

Freed from attachment, unegoistic, endowed with firmness and vigour and unaffected by success or failure, such a doer is said to be *sāttvika*.

Here, the best doer of an action is defined as an unattached (free from the binding effect of an action) person who is capable of remaining neutral with respect to the success and failure.

4.3.2 WORKING OF EOLs AS A SELF-CONSISTENT MECHANISM: THEN WHERE IS THE WORRY?

In the process of attaining the state of perfection, one has to learn and follow certain "art of living" in this world. To teach this art, the Lord has adopted different styles in *SMBG* and in different contexts. In one case, already highlighted in the previous section, the Lord attacks both ends of the process of performing an action, i.e. at the beginning — *saṅkalpa* level, and at the end — fruit of action level. The Lord advises to discard both and asks to keep on doing a desireless and fruit-less action but with full use of EOLs. In this regard the Lord wants to be doubly sure of the success of efforts. On the other hand, this appears contradictory as all actions have basis in the deep-rooted desire (*kāma*) and are bound to give some outcome. So what he actually suggests is that, let there be desire and let there be fruit of action, but do not bring in the attachment or keen passion to either of them. In fact this is the working principle of a person defined as *karmayogī* by the Lord. In practice, this method is going to reduce the level of worry and could prove to be a source of peace in the day-to-day life. The easiest way of discarding the desires and the fruits of action, as suggested in *SMBG*, is to sacrifice them to the Lord instead of bothering himself about them.

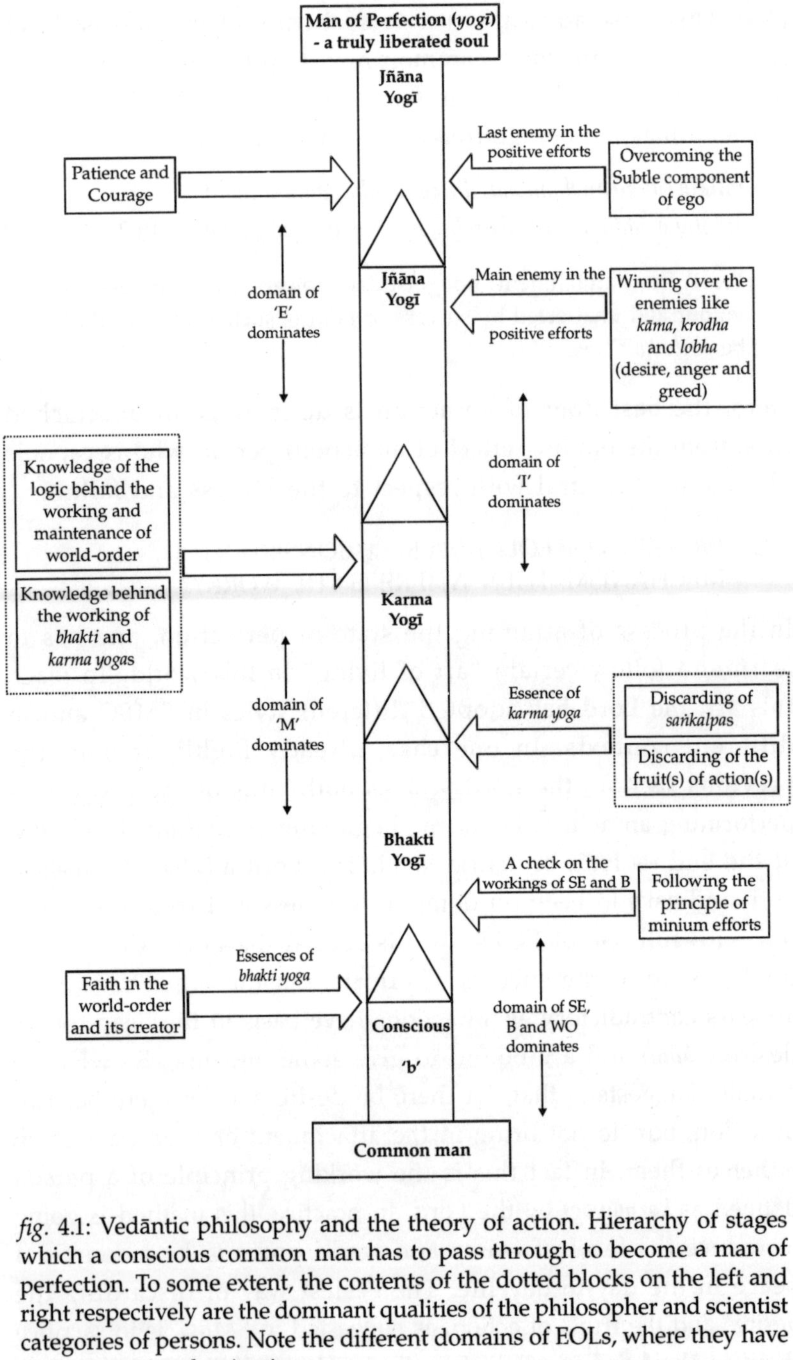

fig. 4.1: Vedāntic philosophy and the theory of action. Hierarchy of stages which a conscious common man has to pass through to become a man of perfection. To some extent, the contents of the dotted blocks on the left and right respectively are the dominant qualities of the philosopher and scientist categories of persons. Note the different domains of EOLs, where they have their respective domination.

In another case, verses (4.4) and (4.14) also imply a similar art of living but in an extended style. In (4.4), the Lord emphasizes that becoming a *karmayogī* is not just sufficient since the doer follows the principle of a sacrificed action and at this stage of hierarchy, based mainly on the faith of the individual (cf. *fig.* 4.1) there is every chance to deviate from it as and when Being comes down to the levels of SE, B or WO (cf. *fig.* 2.1). Therefore, the Lord further advises to have the knowledge (*jñāna*) of the logic behind the theory of action and its role in the maintenance of world-order. When this knowledge component is combined with the prerequisites of a *karmayogī*, then that person is termed as *jñāna-yogī* — the next stage of hierarchy to become a "man of perfection." A simple simile will suffice to clarify this concept: one can learn a language without resorting to grammar merely out of faith. The chances of forgetting the language in this case are much more than in the case when one learns the language with grammar also. Though it becomes a difficult task to learn grammar for a common man but it is an asset as far as the command over the language is concerned. Similar is the case with a *karmayogī*. He has to have a command on *jñāna* to become a *jñāna-yogī* — the stage from where the deviation is rather difficult.

While for a common man "blind" faith alone can lead to success in efforts to a certain degree (as there is a great power in faith also), for philosopher and scientist categories of persons however the *karma-yoga* combined with faith definitely gives success in efforts of a higher degree. As it is clear from *fig.* 4.1, this success in efforts will be of the highest degree for a person who follows *karma-yoga* in conjunction with knowledge. All this is possible only up to a certain limit; after that deviations from the path are still possible due to the working of some other negatives, like the subtle component of ego (cf. *fig.* 4.1) and before that other enemies of positive efforts, like *kāma, krodha, lobha, moha, mada, mātsarya* also find their way. Out of these six enemies the first three are the main ones and it requires a lot of practice to overcome them. Therefore, the Lord in verse (4.14) advises not only to have patience and courage at this stage of hierarchy but also to subside the effect of subtle ego. Such a doer is the true (*sāttvika*) doer and gradually moves towards the stage of a "man of perfection" or of a "liberated soul" in the real sense. Note that the philosopher and scientist categories of persons do appear in between the two limiting cases of the common man and the man of perfection as depicted in *fig.* 4.1.

The art of living means a way of life which is free from tension and worries in spite of one's involvement in all actions and day-to-day activities. This art basically relates to the question of mental training which needs to be exercised in view of an appropriate logic with regard to the performance of all actions by EOLs. Above-mentioned are the certain ways suggested by the Lord in *SMBG*. There is yet another method in *SMBG* based on the formula *guṇā guṇeṣu vartanti* and whose essence is already given in verses (2.4) and (2.5). According to verse (2.4) all actions by EOLs are performed as a result of various modes of *prakṛti* (Nature) in a self-consistent manner. This fact is not realized by an ignorant person mainly due to the subtle component of ego which is always present in him. As a result that person lives a life full of worries and tension.

To describe the logic behind this art of living and the meaning of the above formula, the Lord in *SMBG* defines *guṇa-vibhāga* and *karma-vibhāga*. While the former pertains to the collection of certain objects of perception (which later will be termed as "interacting centres"), the latter however belongs to the working of these objects of perceptions in an internally consistent manner. The one who realizes this fact at the minutest possible level and follows accordingly in life becomes the candidate to be entitled as the "man of perfection." In fact this is an alternative to eliminating the binding effect of an action on the individual. While we postpone the details of working of these objects of perception to future chapters, a brief recounting of them here will be helpful to understand the underlying self-consistent mechanism. In all there are 23 interacting centres (see Appendix

A) consisting of *five* senses of knowledge, *five* sense organs responsible for body-actions, *five* objects of senses of knowledge, the trio of mind, intellect, ego and *five mahābhūtas* (cosmic elements) which constitute the *guṇa-vibhāga* in Vedānta philosophy and their mutual interactions/co-ordination with reference to the performance of an action constitute the *karma-vibhāga*. As a matter of fact, any action performed by a conscious human (non-human) Being does not go beyond the domain of this *karma-vibhāga*.

In a nutshell, in this self-consistent method *kāma* originates at the I-level in the language of patomic model, *saṅkalpas* are taken at M-level and accordingly directed action is performed not only at the M-level but also at the lower hierarchy, i.e. at the SE-, B- and WO-levels naturally by following the principle of minimum efforts (cf. Section 4.4) in the space time domain. The outcome of the actions so performed is analysed by I which subsequently supplies a feedback to intensify the *saṅkalpas* and thereby improving the quality of actions (in terms of positive efforts) in the next cycle, particularly at the lower levels of hierarchy. All this happens in a natural and self-consistent manner but only for a conscious Being. For the one who is not conscious and aware of this mechanism, self-ego E enters at all stages and contributes to negative efforts by way of leaving some binding effect behind at every stage — this causes tension and worries for that individual. To elaborate this mechanism many examples can be cited from the day-to-day life and we shall return to them later.

4.4 The Principle of Minimum Efforts

For a conscious Being, the principle of minimum efforts is a key to success in both short-term as well as long-term goals in life. The principle of minimum efforts coherently works in both mental and physical domains and in a co-ordinated manner. Note that this minimization of efforts takes place with respect to certain variables. These variables are the intensity (or degree) of concentration (which will be accounted later through a meditation parameter μ) in the case of mental domain (the trio of mind, intellect and ego) and the space time variables in the case of physical domains of SE, B and WO. As a matter of fact it is the mental domain which on the one hand controls the workings of the physical domains and gets a feedback to improve upon the quality of actions to be performed by the EOLs in the next cycle on the other.

In *SMBG*, the Lord has suggested a variety of ways to an individual to intensify his concentration which in turn will help him in minimizing the efforts at both mental and physical levels.[11] The concentration indeed is the backbone in the working of a *karmayogī* (cf. *fig.* 4.1) as per *SMBG*. In response to a question posed by Arjuna pertaining to the symptoms and definition of a person with "stable mind,"[12] the Lord has described the methodology for attaining the concentration in a logical manner. The turbulent nature of senses of knowledge *vis-à-vis* their involvement in their respective sense objects is the main cause of diversions of one's attention — an object of mind. The Lord suggests a systematic method to control not only the senses of knowledge and action but also the mind. Recall that the working of organs responsible for physical actions is immediately guided by the senses of knowledge and ultimately by M and I.

While one can physically withdraw the senses of knowledge from their respective sense objects, their withdrawal at the mental level is a difficult task. For a person to become a man of stable mind, the Lord advises to control SEs at the mental level by way of discarding both the attachment to and detachment from their sense objects as a part of positive pursuits. As a matter of fact with whichever sense of knowledge the mind flows, the same is found to control the intellect I as well, mainly due to the turbulent nature of mind and thereby the *kāma* — an object of I and a natural source of all actions gets affected. Therefore, the Lord empathetically suggests that the one who has controlled

11. *SMBG*: chapter 2, verses 55-71.

12. *SMBG*: chapter 2, verse 54.

the senses by way of withdrawing them from their respective sense objects, is qualified to become a man of wisdom (or the man with a "stable mind" or "man of perfection"). This mechanism is analogous to the process of rowing a boat upstream; otherwise the senses (and so is the mind) have the natural tendency for the downstream flow with regard to their involvement in the respective sense objects; namely, tongue runs after taste, nose after smell, skin after touch, ears run after sound, eyes after glitter (beauty) and so becomes the tendency of the sense organs responsible for physical action. It is only a controlled mind which in the guidance of I can change the flow from downstream to upstream. Therefore, the Lord advises to control mind and to think of higher objects decided at the level of I, i.e. at the *kāma* or at the level of M itself as a *saṅkalpa*.

In brief, the principle of minimum efforts deals with the directed efforts which consequently lead to directed actions of EOLs and the same is possible by controlling M and subsequently the SEs and B. Note that this controlling of M, SEs and B does not mean inaction on their part; rather they are made to work in a regulated manner so that the efforts are minimized by resorting appropriately to space time variables in the physical domain(s) and to meditation parameter μ in the mental domain.

SYSTEMATICS OF NEGATIVE PURSUIT (SNP)

If the mind is not controlled by an individual (and so are SEs) from its (their) downward (i.e. towards WO) flow, then it results in the negative pursuits and arbitrary actions and ultimately going to disturb peace of his mind. A systematics to this effect is described beautifully by the Lord in the following verses:

dhyāyato viṣayān puṁsaḥ saṅgasteṣūpajāyate ।
saṅgātsañjāyate kāmaḥ kāmāt krodho abhijāyate ॥ — 2.62 (4.15)

The man dwelling on sense objects develops attachment for them; from attachment springs up desire; and from (unfulfilled) desire ensues anger.

Further,

> *krodhādbhavati sammohaḥ sammohātsmr̥ti vibhramaḥ* ।
> *smr̥tibhraṁśād buddhināśo buddhināśātpraṇaśyati* ॥ — 2.63 (4.16)

> From anger arises infatuation; from infatuation, confusion of memory; from confusion of memory, loss of reason; and from loss of reason one goes to complete ruination.

Fundamental processes to this effect keep on taking place inside an individual and often without him noticing it, their effects do reflect in his behaviour. This is how the downward flow of energy (negative efforts or negative pursuits) of an individual takes place and consequently results in an arbitrary action. Further, for such a person, the Lord continues to emphasize the following consequences:

> *nāsti buddhir ayuktasya na cāyuktasya bhāvanā* ।
> *na cābhāvayataḥ śāntir aśānt sya kutaḥ sukhaṁ* ॥ — 2.66 (4.17)

> He who has not controlled his mind and senses can have no determinate reason; nor can such an undisciplined man have belief (in Creator/God). The unbelieving man can have no peace and how can there be happiness for one lacking peace of mind?

SYSTEMATICS OF POSITIVE PURSUITS (SPP)

Contrary to the above, one who has controlled his mind and SEs enjoys the fruits of positive (directed) efforts; this is what the Lord emphasizes in the following verses:

> *rāga dveṣa vimuktaistu viṣayānindrayaiścaran* ।
> *ātmavaśyairvidheyātmā praśādamadhigacchati* ॥ — 2.64 (4.18)

> *prasāde sarvaduḥkhānāṁ hānirasyopajāyate* ।
> *prasannacetaso hyāśu buddhiḥ paryavatiṣṭhate* ॥ — 2.65 (4.19)

> But the self-controlled practiser, while enjoying the various sense objects through his senses, which are (again) disciplined and free from likes and dislikes, attains placidity of mind.

Further,

> with the attainment of such placidity of mind, all his sorrows come to an end; and the intellect of such a person of tranquil mind, soon withdrawing itself from all sides, becomes firmly established in God (higher goal).

Whether one realizes or not, the above sequence of processes under different systematics continues and the effect of the same reflects in the behaviour of that individual at different space-time points and in different circumstances.

4.5 Co-ordination among the Working of Different EOLs:The Role of Consciousness

Once the *kāma* is originated at the level of I and *saṅkalpa*s are taken at the level of M, the fundamental processes associated with other EOLs (of course I and M themselves in this mechanism are also involved as they receive feedback from the lower hierarchy) start taking place even if their occurrence for many of us goes unnoticed. Only a conscious Being is able to realize these facts. Note that there is a wonderful co-ordination not only in the workings of different EOLs but also among the associated processes taking place at different levels. All this happens in the background of consciousness whose source is much beyond E (cf. Appendix A) and the same manifests differently at different levels of hierarchy. In spite of the fact that the *plurality of consciousness* appears in the outward actions of a Being, it however originates from the same source within, which is designated as "soul" (SO).

It is true that only a conscious human Being in general and his conscious EOLs in particular are able to notice the occurrence of these processes taking place inside an individual; otherwise such processes do take place not only in any individual irrespective of his caste, colour, creed or country but also in non-human Beings. Such a universality of processes is talked about in Vedānta philosophy and attempts are made to quantify them through the systematics of positive and negative pursuits mentioned in Section 4.4. It is also true that consciousness is distributed in the whole physical body of a living Being; it is also distributed among all living Beings — a characteristic of the living (animate) world which inspires and allows the co-ordination of interaction among them. However, there are localized sources in the individuals which could be a part of a cosmic source of consciousness and as a result of certain mechanism these localized sources of Beings are created out of the grand cosmic source. It is quite possible that this cosmic source of consciousness is distributed all over in the Universe in the form of the most fundamental and the finest possible field and the localized sources of consciousness (Beings) are created out of it in the same way as the fields in physics are there, and the second quantization process creates the localized matter particles.[13] Vedānta philosophy has been repeatedly emphasizing this fact in various forms. For example, in *SMBG* the Lord clearly points out that,

mamaivāṁśo jīvaloke jīvabhūtaḥ sanātanaḥ ।
manaḥ ṣaṣṭhān īndriyāṇi prakṛtiṣṭhāni karṣati ॥ — 15.7 (4.20)

The soul (SO) in the body is an eternal portion of Myself; it draws with it the mind and the five senses that rest in matter.

At another place in *SMBG* the Lord again emphasizes that Nature works on its own but only in the presence of Him and this is particularly true with its working in the sentient mode, viz.:

na kartṛtvaṁ na karmāṇi lokasya sṛjati prabhuḥ ।
na karmaphala saṁyogaṁ svabhāvastu pravartate ॥ — 5.14 (4.21)

---

13. If one extends this analogy further, then the concept of matter and energy of physics is very much similar to that of *jaḍa* and *cetana* (or inanimate matter and consciousness) of Vedānta philosophy and about which a lot is said in Indian philosophy, i.e. in *Brahmasūtra* and Upaniṣads. However, we restrict ourself here from such comparative studies. But one thing is clear that like the energy creates the dynamism in the matter particle, the consciousness in the same way can be considered as bringing the life in the body (inanimate matter) except for some methodological details.

> The Lord determines neither the doership nor the doings of Beings, nor even their contact with the fruit of actions. It is Nature that functions (deriving its motive power from God).

In fact one should couple the meaning of this verse with that of verse (2.5) which[14] clearly suggests the working of EOLs only in the presence of God (cosmic consciousness) in general and the soul in particular, but in a self-consistent manner.

Some examples would suffice to elaborate the role of consciousness in the above self-consistent mechanism suggested for the workings of EOLs and also highlighted in Section 4.3.2. In fact while a man of perfection is expected to be free from all desires, for other categories of persons the nature of *kāma* can broadly be classified under three heads, namely (a) desiring of sense objects, (b) desiring of talent, and (c) desiring of (true) knowledge. Note that, as one goes from the head (a) to (c), the quality of desire increases from the points of view of social values and positive pursuits. In what follows, we discuss an example for each of these cases to demonstrate the workings of EOLs towards a successful pursuit in spite of the fact that the underlying mechanism is more or less the same for all the cases.

(a) In view of verse (4.13) it is impossible for a Being in general and the human Being in particular to discard the actions leading to the survival of the body itself. They need to be performed in an optimum style to maintain the body fit. Not only this, a viable and dynamic body is the basis of all sorts of development of the FOUs or EOLs. For keeping the body fit, while non-human Beings appear to be wiser (in the sense that their actions are mostly confined according to their (minimum) body requirements since they have limited *kāma* or *saṅkalpas*), the human Being, on the other hand, makes full use of his extra sense — "intellect" to fulfil maximum requirements, for his survival. As a result he keeps on running after the sense objects or in

14. *SMBG*: chapter 3, verse 28.

arranging the accessories to this effect. Of course, in this endeavour he discovers many new ideas and technologies which in turn lead to pleasure out of these developments but only when he is conscious of these happenings.

Suppose that a person decides (at the level of I) to have a taste of a particular dish and accordingly takes *saṅkalpa*s (at the level of M) to arrange the things for this purpose sometimes by taking extra pains or using his particular resources. For arranging the necessary ingredients he makes repeated use of SE, B, and WO and also of other EOLs until he succeeds in attaining the desired sense object, i.e. the taste of his liking or the enjoyment of the same by M but with a reference to I in this regard. In enjoying the dish, the person must have used his past experience or has stored a liking for this new taste in E. If the taste or the fruit of action is not up to the mark, he takes lessons for future preparation(s)/ arrangements. Similar examples can be narrated with reference to other single or multiple sense objects. If these actions (or the fruits of actions) are there to keep the body fit and are in accord with the norms of society in ethical terms, then they are the cases of positive pursuit; otherwise they are very likely to be the cases of negative pursuits from the point of view of world-order or ethical values, leading to the downfall of the individual or the society as a whole.

(b) For a person who is desiring of talent (say a position in a particular society in absolute or relative terms), the role of gross body (i.e. of SE, B and WO) remains only optimum whereas that of micro-body (i.e. of M, I and E) becomes maximum. In this case *saṅkalpa*s belong to the higher hierarchy and correspond to somewhat long-term goals compared to the ones belonging to the case (a) above (where the goals by and large are the short-term ones). In quest of talent, the individual is hardly bothered by the *saṅkalpa*s of lower hierarchy (i.e. the ones belonging to the domains of SE, B and WO). The fulfilment of the latter becomes necessary but not sufficient unlike the case in the head (a) above. No doubt the same sequence of steps has to be followed to fulfil these necessary *saṅkalpa*s but always with an eye on the *saṅkalpa*s of higher hierarchy. On the other hand, the roles of EOLs M, I and E now become more crucial at times, respectively in terms of concentration, short- or long-term decisions and use of past experiences.

(c) A person who desires knowledge goes ahead with *saṅkalpa*s of the highest order at the level of SO, particularly when he is in quest of true knowledge (cf. verse (4.2)). Knowledge of any form in this world is said to be pure (cf. verse (4.1)) but the purest one is that which belongs to the Self itself. This is done by keeping the (fulfilment of) *saṅkalpa*s of lower hierarchy, i.e. those belonging to domains of micro- and/or gross-body at low pitch as they now become necessary but not sufficient. They, however, need to be fulfilled by following the same steps as in (a) or in (b) above but with a spirit of constructive pursuits. Again one can have a desire of knowledge of the man-made world (in terms of scientific methods) or of the God-made world (in terms of the methods suggested for spirituality); however, the basic steps to be followed to this effect turn out to be the same as far as the methodology is concerned.

4.6 Trinity of Guṇas and the Nature of Human Actions in Vedānta Philosophy

While human Beings have freedom of exercising their intellect to improve upon the quality of their actions according to certain standards, the non-humans, on the other hand, are devoid of such a freedom. From the point of view of quantifying the quality of the positive definite out put of the performed action, the three degrees of qualitative adjective, namely superlative, comparative and positive are translated in Vedāntic philosophy into three *guṇa*s namely *sattva* (S), *rajas* (R) and *tamas* (T), respectively (cf. entry 1, Table 2.1). It may be just a coincidence or Vedāntic thought might be nursing some deeper meaning(s) of the analogy which we note here between the nature of human actions in terms of the above trio of *guṇa*s and the three interesting examples of the previous section used to demonstrate the role of consciousness in human actions.

As a matter of fact the desiring of knowledge, talent and sense objects by a human Being can be considered respectively as the effect of *sattva, rajas* and *tamas* modes of human efforts in general and the three different levels of hierarchy of EOLs. The role of *guṇa*s, in fact, definitely appears in the workings of all three causal, micro and gross bodies constituting the human Being. While *kāma* at the highest level remains intact, the three *guṇa*s start playing their role right from the level of *saṅkalpa*s, i.e. a *saṅkalpa* can appear in any of the three "colours" such as *sat-saṅkalpa, rajas-saṅkalpa*s or the *tamas-saṅkalpa*s or their mixtures. Once the *saṅkalpa* is enveloped by a particular *guṇa*, the same continues to affect the workings of the lower hierarchy of EOLs. As a result, the role of this particular *guṇa* finally starts reflecting in the behaviour of the individual in his day-to-day life.

Only a conscious human in his observer mode can realize such developments in his actions and improve upon them in repeated trials; otherwise for a common man all this happens in an unnoticed manner and sometimes the outcome of actions so affected by these *guṇa*s, is attributed by him to some exotic gods and goddesses in different cultures. In summary, the role of *guṇa*s in human actions is highly intricate. We shall return to such discussions in later chapters.

4.7 Concluding Discussion

With a view to having a rather rich and powerful alternative to the Western thinking with regard to the theory of actions performed by a human Being, a nutshell summary of the Vedāntic thought is presented in this chapter. While the intricacies and variants of Vedānta philosophy in this regard are kept aside, the over simplified picture of patomic model (cf. Appendix A) appears capable of providing the framework within which the explanation of various human actions can be found in a coherent and consistent manner. It is noticed that not only the scattered Western thoughts but some of the views of modern science discussed in the previous chapter can also be accommodated consistently and in a natural manner in this rather logical framework.

The Vedānta philosophy suggests a final focusing of all divergent efforts of EOLs leading to actions of an individual on the attainment of supreme knowledge (cf. Section 4.1). This is possible by using the principle of minimum efforts and the systematics of positive pursuits. Although the attainment of such a state is not an easy task (cf. *fig*. 4.1), however the efforts made by the human Being in this direction provide peace at every stage of its evolution (cf. *fig*. 4.1), by way of diminishing the binding effect of an action on him. As a matter of fact, the following of different systematics of constructive pursuits by the human Being at different levels of hierarchy in the patomic model further adds to such directed efforts and later to directed actions of the person. All this is possible when the *sat-saṅkalpa*s are there in the background of the action.

For having a *sat-saṅkalpa* in the background of any action Vedānta philosophy further highlights the ways and means in terms of another basis of any action, that is through the trio of *prārabdha, sañcita,* and *kriyamāṇa* (cf. entry 2, Table 2.1). As a matter of fact the success of the outcome of any action (particularly the one performed towards a long-term goal) is attributed to the efforts made by an individual at three distinct levels, namely in the previous birth(s) (*prārabdha* or destiny), in the present birth itself (*sañcita*) and in the present tense itself (*kriyamāṇa*). While the *prārabdha* is also supposed to contribute to the nature of *saṅkalpa*s in some sense, most of the contribution to it comes from *sañcita* and *kriyamāṇa* ingredients of actions. If one is honest in the performance of his actions, particularly in the *sañcita* and *kriyamāṇa* domains, then note that the *prārabdha* also has to play its role in the success of an action. Such a philosophy helps in minimizing the binding effect(s) of an action and yields peace to an individual. Not only this, the Lord at one place in *SMBG* has clearly dictated His role (perhaps through *prārabdha*) in providing the environment and the household in which an individual is born, according to his deeds performed in the previous birth(s). This can be noticed from the following verse:

prakṛtiṁ svām avaṣṭabhya visṛjāmi punaḥ punaḥ ।
bhūtagrāmam imaṁ kṛtsnam avaśaṁ prakṛtervaśāt ॥ — 9.8 (4.22)

Laying hold of My nature, I bring forth, again and again (according to their respective *karma*) this whole multitude of Beings subject to the influence of their own nature.

In the subsequent verse 9.9 in *SMBG* the Lord emphasizes that He remains unattached and indifferent while doing all this as all this is the game of Nature.

A few remarks about the systematics of positive and negative pursuits/efforts are in order:

(i) The role of these concepts is like a third party[15] observations as we have in physics. For example, the theoretically calculated trajectory of a particle can be seen in the laboratory by an outsider observer. In the same way, it is an outsider who, on the basis of his space- and time-tested experiences, will extract the nature of these systematics. The latter is easily verifiable in the laboratory of human experiences with a provision of a few exceptions as in physics.[16]

---

15. Third party in the sense that dynamics allows the movement of the particle from one space-time point to another space-time point (which in some sense can be considered as isolated from the first one) and an outsider watches this movement (trajectory). This all happens in the force field of gravity. In the same way, an individual passes from one mental state (a composite of the constituents of the systematics) to another one however in the field of consciousness of the outsider. Thus, it is the outsider who notices these changes and decides the nature of the systematics, i.e. whether it is positive or negative.

16. In physics, exception to the parabolic trajectory are there in several cases as it is the manifestation of the force field in which the particle

(ii) These systematics may work at the level of all the three causal, micro and gross bodies; only the role of underlying parameter(s) makes them differ, i.e. positive or negative. For example, in the causal domain, it is the suppression of the subtle component of ego; in the micro domain it is the control of mind; or in the gross domain it is the control of SE and B, which matters in deciding the nature of these systematics. It is going to be positive if these situations are favourable; otherwise the same will be negative for the opposites, i.e. for the cases when subtle component of ego is present or the mind, or SE and B are not controlled by the performer of the action.

As a matter of fact the environment and/or circumstances in which an individual is placed also play an important role in the quantification of his behaviour in terms of systematics. Sometimes the circumstances force one to adopt certain negative constituents of systematics even if they are not part of his nature. This is needed by the (conscious) individual mainly to maintain the world order in terms of moral values. In this case one invites these negative constituents, use them, and as and when the purpose is solved, ask them to leave as if they were the invited guests. Only a conscious performer is capable of doing this and it is also a part of the "art of living"; otherwise a common man is lost in the game of these negatives of a particular systematic. In fact such a presence of negatives, if it is there temporarily, does not leave any impact (or the binding effect) on the (conscious) performer. This methodology is good if followed, for example, by parents on their wards, and teachers on their students by way of inviting the negatives like anger, passion, etc.

As a final remark, we mention about the source of these negatives of a systematic. They are all born out of the subtle component of ego, namely "I-ideology" which propounds that

is moving. The same may be the case in the present context as the degree of consciousness of the conscious-outsider (third party) may be different.

no one other than self is supreme and all powerful. This leads to a feeling of pride and fuels greed, selfishness, and later anger for a common man. However, a conscious performer of the action is capable of overcoming these negatives by suppressing this "I-ness" right in the beginning (and thereby creating the positives of a systematic out of negatives) and uses this non-physical (spiritual) energy to achieve higher objects in life and finally attain peace.

5

Concepts and Facts Dominating the Human Behaviour

WHILE objective sciences at the level of their abstraction are already looking for (i) the universality of certain concepts and constants; (ii) the super-grand unified theories heading towards the theory of everything; and (iii) a common basis for workings of living organisms and the plant kingdom in terms of genetical codes, etc. Subjective science — a theme of this book is also searching for the most fundamental tools and framework in terms of which an explanation of entire gamut of human experiences and behaviour can be found. To this effect, as hints are already given in previous chapters, Vedānta philosophy offers a lot in terms of tools and methodology. In the present chapter an attempt is made to show the availability of these tools in a more objective manner at different levels of patomic model (cf. Appendix A). For this purpose, we first establish the universality of the force of attraction in Nature in the form of love and affection and then categorize the behavioural facts and look for their multiplicity and interpretation(s) in terms of these tools. An analogy of these tools and their working with those in objective science will pave a way for further development of the subject in future chapters.

5.1 Universality of Love and the Forces of Attraction in Nature

Although modern theories of origin of Universe suggest its expansion via inflationary models, the fact is that this accelerated expansion is going to be controlled by certain mechanism so that the existence of the Universe can be understood in terms of an overall attractive force. The force of attraction in Nature appears to be universal and so are the love and affection among the living Beings through their behaviour. If at all there is repulsion or hatred, it is man-made, localized and temporary. According to a Hindi poet, *prem nā hotā is dharatī par to sārā jag bañjar hotā* meaning thereby "without love and affection, this whole world would have been a desert" which clearly supports the above viewpoint.

It is the force of attraction which, through the Mach principle, defines the inertial property of matter in the universe and subsequently forms the basis of the laws of motion for the inanimate matter in physics and perhaps for the animate matter as well. Not only this, this attractive nature of the force through inverse square law continues to work well for the galactic systems, stars and for planetary motion. On the other hand, at the macro and micro levels this force, in its varied forms, binds atoms (Morse potential) to give rise to molecules; electrons and nucleus to give atoms (Coulomb Law), nucleons to form nuclei, quarks to form nucleons and so on.

In the domain of physics this attractive force is, although quantifiable to a great extent, however not so in the domain of behavioural science, particularly with regard to the co-existence of living Beings in spite of the fact that the love and affection among them are all-pervading in one form or the other. As a matter of fact there exists a hierarchy of bonds for an individual in this world. First of all the love and affection bind the individual to his self and body through the functions of mind, then to his family, his society, his state, his nation and so on through one or the other type of binding forces (e.g. terms of duties and responsibilities or via moral and ethical values). While the attachment or binding appears to be natural, the detachment or the hatred clearly is the man-made quality. This attraction of an individual or of a collection of individuals (i.e. society) could be on par with both, i.e. to an inanimate or to an animate object in this world.

In the language of modern physics, i.e. in the light of many-body theories, these binding forces could be (i) one-to-one, (ii) one-to-many, (iii) many-to-one, and (iv) many-to-many. In the context of human Beings, examples can be cited with regard to one-to-zero or many-to-zero case when an individual is interacting with the self (such as a person sitting in *samādhi*) or a group of persons are sitting in *samādhi*. Upaniṣads and other Vedic literature have suggested the rules of the game in very clear terms for all the above four possibilities. In *Bṛahadāraṇyaka Upaniṣad*[1] Yājñavalkya tells his wife, Maitreyī, the reasons for the love and affection between a husband and wife, a son and father and the likes. As a matter of fact a particular form of love and affection between persons also appears as a part of their duties and responsibilities towards each other mainly for a successful co-existence. On the other hand, at another place Upaniṣads clearly highlight the nature of binding forces in the one-to-one case of course with reference to a teacher and taught but in a generalized manner through the verse:[2]

auṁ sahanāvavatu sahnau bhunaktu sahavīryam karavāvahai
tejasvināvadhītamastu mā vidviṣāvahai
Auṁ śāntiḥ ! śāntiḥ !! śāntiḥ !!! (5.1)

Let him protect us both. May He bless us with Bliss of knowledge. Let us exert together. May what we study be well studied. May we not hate (quarrel with each other). *Oṁ* Peace! Peace !! Peace !!!

In verse (5.1), the coexistence is desired in the field of cosmic consciousness, i.e. as a prayer to God.

The force of attraction among inanimate objects and the love and affection among living Beings are universal and are the prerequisites for their coexistence and harmony. For the human Beings, however, there may be a case of pseudo-love or pseudo-

---

1. *Bṛhadāraṇyaka Upaniṣad*, Gorakhpur: Gita Press, chapter 2, particularly, see verses 2.4.5 and 2.5.14.

2. Prayer for peace as performed and narrated in opening and closing verses of *Śvetāśvatara Upaniṣad*, *Kaṭhopaniṣad* and *Taittirīyopaniṣad*.

harmony. In this case the love and affection may be based on material gains and not through interior awakening and profound search of the within. This kind of love and affection could be an illusion. In fact there are attributes like selfishness, greed, compassion, etc. which affect the natural binding between husband and wife, parents and children, between friends, colleagues and the likes. However, an intro-inspection and certain adjustments can change the things drastically. Love manifests its reality in deeds and not just in words.

According to Sri Sri Ravi Shankar (The Speaking Tree, *Times of India*, 30 May 2008), love is a state of Being rather than an act and knowledge is an aid to develop your innermost state, which is love. We are all made up of love. When the mind is in the present moment, we are in a state of love. So live in the present moment.

In summary, the element of love or the force of attraction is the characteristic of soul and it rests in there. However it manifests differently for living and non-living Beings. For non-living Beings while it is quantifiable and better understood in modern science, the same is not the case for living Beings mainly due to the occurrence of a large number of uncontrollable parameters. In fact for them the love appears at hierarchy of levels and again at relative and absolute scales. It is the absolute love which is the property of soul and it takes different forms and scales at various levels of the patomic model. In other words, in the language of patomic model, the love in the Being originates from soul SO, flows through the mind M within the boundaries as defined by the intellect I and ego E and finally manifests through the senses of knowledge and action, SE, and the body, B, in the domain of the worldly objects, WO (cf. Appendix A). Conversely, in the presence of SO, SE and B of a Being, b, find attachment to the objects of WO via M and decide its fineness and subtlety using I and E and realizes finally in SO itself as the "beauty of Nature." In fact it is the worldly knowledge and its applications in the day-to-day life that bind the individual even to the so-called "spiritual liberates." Finally, it is worthwhile to recall the distortions of love. They originate from negative emotions like lust, pride, attachment, anger, ego, greed and jealousy. These distortions manifest in animals also, but they have no way to go beyond them as they are bound by Nature. Gifted with the power of discrimination, human Being, on the other hand, can overcome these distortions and attain a state of pure love.

5.2 Behavioural Facts: Question of Their Origin and Interpretation

It is true that the behavioural facts might have originated with the human race and at all the levels of the patomic model namely $\mathcal{C}$, $\mathcal{M}$ and $\mathcal{G}$, where $\mathcal{C}$ = {SO}, $\mathcal{M}$ = {M, I, E}, $\mathcal{G}$ = {WO, B, SE} (cf. Appendix A). Broadly speaking these facts arise due to the projection of experience of an individual at the level of Self (when the Self himself is an analyser) or at the level of Self of other person(s) (when the other person(s) is an analyser) in the domain of space and time. Again at the level of space and time, these experiences could be temporal and local or permanent and global. In fact the worth of these experiences (in terms of ethical values, their multiplicity, and the plurality of their interpretations) in different cultures are somehow better recognized only in recent times, particularly after the rapid development in the means of communications. Behavioural facts exist at all levels but are minimal at the level of $\mathcal{C}$ and are more or less universal with reference to different cultures in the world. At the level of $\mathcal{M}$, they are many in number and philosophers and psychologists are trying to make them Universal even if they are not. The number of behavioural facts at the level of $\mathcal{G}$ are enormous and infinitely many and objective sciences (like physics and biology) in conjunction with technologies developed from time to time, are constantly trying to understand them again in terms of certain minimal. These behavioural facts at times become the guiding and working principles to an individual in his day-to-day activities. Here we list some representative examples of behavioural facts from different categories for the purposes of their subsequent analysis in the forthcoming chapters.

5.2.1 FACTS AT THE LEVEL OF CAUSAL BODY C ={SO}

In general, all universal facts regarding the actions and behaviour of a living Being are the attributes of soul and pertain to C. As they are independent of space and time variables, they consistently manifest at all times and in all cultures of the world in one form or the other sometimes in the folklore or the wisdom of old ladies. In literary terms, if not exactly, they analogously appear through proverbs, idioms, sayings or writings, etc. often by using metaphors or similes.

As mentioned earlier (cf. Chapter 4), all positive constructs and the characteristics thereof in the individual are the properties of soul, e.g. truth, goodness, love, beauty, silence, peace, joy, etc. Negative constructs/pursuits appear just like bubbles on the surface of water of positivity. Everybody feels that love and kindness are the best and not war and hatred, since the former belong to the domain of C. All behavioural facts about an individual which uplift the FOUs to the level of spirituality — a domain of C, belong to this class. All so-called eternal truths regarding an individual or Nature have roots in the domain of C, e.g. *God has provided enough for everyone's need but not for everyone's greed*. Since human race (or for that matter any other species) is surviving for millions of years (could be a case of survival of the fittest) the above statement is eternal; otherwise a common man always argues in either way. Thus, the words eternity and universality are relative and they have to be interpreted in the light of development of FOUs of an individual.

Another important fact which has been considered in the domain of C is that of the cases of "near-death or out-of-body experiences" by a dying person. These experiences are also universal and noticed by persons of different cultures (cf. Section 6.3 and Appendix E). A near-death person, after regaining consciousness (or after coming out of comma) describes his feeling as if a shadowy figure was standing behind him, then turning around to find that none is there. Similarly, in some cases a person feels himself leaving his body and floating in space looking down on his corporeal self. Such experiences are often attributed by those who experience them to some paranormal forces or powers. In fact these phenomena while once considered as having links with the theories of memories after death or of rebirth, or in the existence of death-god or the likes, have now found some explanations in the modern theories of brain-functioning.[3] We shall however carry out some of these discussions in later chapters.

5.2.2 FACTS AT THE LEVEL OF MICRO-BODY $\mathcal{M}$ = {M, I, E}

Facts at the level of $\mathcal{M}$ are mainly attributed to the functions of mind, intellect and ego, and they are concerned with the feelings, emotions, decisions, intellectual exercises, memories, self-expressions, etc. In the literary language one can say that the first category of them belongs to the domain of heart, the second one to the domain of brain and the third one belongs to an overlap of domains of both heart and brain as the facts in this last category are selectively stored in the subconscious mind. Normally, idioms, proverbs, sayings, folklore, or wisdom of old ladies (*Buṛhīya Purāṇa*), poems, etc. are the medium of expression of these facts and one applies or uses them as and when he desires in solving the problems of his day-to-day life. Sometimes these philosophical truths of life become the guiding principle in one's career or in the tenets of a cult or religion. Since the micro-body $\mathcal{M}$ links the inner (the domain of $\mathcal{C}$) and the outer (the domain of $\mathcal{G}$) worlds, the facts can be of two broad categories, namely with subjective meanings and with objective meanings (cf. *fig.* 5.1). While a whole bunch of objective sciences is devoted to find explanation(s) of or to establish objective facts (cf.

3. Sandra Blakeslee, "Out-of-body experience? Blame the Brain", *Times of India*, 4 October 2006, p. 33; Also see, "Plagued by Near-death Visions? Read on . . .", Reporting in *Times of India*, 20 April 2006.

Facts at the level of micro-body

Facts with objective content (they pertain to the study of Nature and the associated laws for its working; also a consistent search for their universality has been prevalent through all these years) (cf. Section 5.2.3)

Facts with subjective content (they pertain to the behaviour of an individual or of a group of individuals and are derived with respect to (a) an individual and his Self, (b) his relatives and family, (c) his friend and society, (d) his citizenship and and the laws of land, (e) his interaction with Nature *vis-à-vis* his geographical surroundings, and (f) his existence in this world and the Universe.

fig. 5.1: A categorization of facts at the level of $\mathcal{M}$ with objective and subjective contents or meanings. Note that the boundaries of sub-categories of facts with subjective meaning(s) are not very sharp, rather they are intertwined or fuzzy.

Chapter 1), many of the subjective facts are still taken as granted and sometimes without seeking any logic. But the facts are facts, they have to be accepted. A lot has been said about the objective reality, facts and their meanings in chapters 1 and 3, and about the existence of an individual in this world and Universe (cf. last sub-category of subjective facts) in various religions. In what follow we list a few representative examples of various categories of subjective facts.

(a): *Facts with reference to an individual and his Self*:

(i) According to the Hindi poet, Tulsīdāsa, in *Rāmāyaṇa*,

jākī rahī bhāvanā jaisī, prabhu mūrati dekhī tin taisī । (5.2)

In terms of faith, trust and confidence whatever feelings one has in a deity, in an individual or in an idol, he worships (or pleases) him accordingly.

(ii) Another Sanskrit verse emphasizes —

mantre, tīrthe, dvije, deve, deivajñe, bheṣaje gurauḥ ।
yādṛsi bhāvanā bhavati, siddhiḥ bhavati tādṛsi ॥ (5.3)

In hymn, place of pilgrimage (or worship), priest, god or deity, goddess, medicine, and in teacher whatever types of feelings one has created about them, he gets success accordingly after their use in life.

(iii) *As you sow so you mow* or *Might is right* are the well-known idioms which carry a lot of subjective meanings and that too in a logical manner.

(iv) *All charming people have something to conceal, usually their total dependence on the appreciation of others* (a fact pertains to the domain of mind).

(v) *Efforts may fail, but do not fail to make efforts* — a fact of the domain of intellect and useful for the success of an individual or of a group of individuals.

(vi) *To handle yourself, use your head; to handle others use your heart* (Donald Laird) — a fact which beautifully defines the self-discipline and the role of an individual while behaving with others.

(vii) *Knowledge is gained by prostrating at the feet of wise* (*SMBG*: 4.34) — clearly the experience of the "wise" is added to the knowledge available already in the scriptures.

(viii) *All sins are crossed over by a raft of knowledge* (*SMBG*: 4.36) — sin often is an act of ignorance and this ignorance goes on minimizing as one proceeds on the ladder of knowledge.

Like (vii) and (viii) there are millions of facts about life and its existence all throughout in *SMBG*. Modern physics again provides a large number of facts about Nature which lie in the domains of I and E and they have hardly to do anything with the domain of M. In fact a great deal of them is established at the level of $\mathcal{G}$ via SE and B in the context of WO.

(b), (c) and (d): *Facts with reference to one's relatives and family, one's friend and society and one's citizenship and the laws of land*: In terms of duties and rights of individual towards his relatives (say towards mother, father, brother, sister, etc.) and the family as a whole a variety of universal facts are described in different cultures and religions. In Indian context the great epics of *Rāmāyaṇa* and *Mahābhārata* do offer such ideals and role-models to an individual and also to a family to follow. Not only this, other scriptures like *Hitopadeśa*, Smṛtis, Nīti's and the creations of several modern poets do exist for this purpose. The wisdom of old ladies with regard to these facts also passes from one generation to the next. Often the facts are transferred without return but to maintain the prevailing value system in a family, society or a country. Some of these facts of course, have logical basis. In order to maintain the survival of a family in an ideal manner these norms need to be observed and the facts have to be followed by an individual. Similar is the case to maintain an ideal friendship with a person or the relations with a society for a long time or to become an ideal citizen or the law abider. These norms whether for an individual, or a society while have many things in common at the higher (philosophical) level of understanding, their applications in practice, however, might differ from place to place, time to time and from culture to culture.

(e): *Facts with reference to one's interaction with Nature*: For his survival the human Being has to live with Nature rather harmoniously. Wisdom of old people throws light on many facts (of course, some of them do not have much of the logic but in practice are found to work successfully). They often pertain to weather and agriculture. In fact so many sayings and proverbs pertaining to forecasts of rain, flood, and climate in general, earth-quake, nature of tides in ocean, effect of the direction of wind flow, etc. are known even to uneducated farmers and fishermen.

(f): *Fact with reference to one's existence in this world and the Universe in general*: There are numerous facts about this aspect which are transmitted from one generation to another by the old people and sometimes they form part of the prevailing philosophy of a given culture. For example, a faith in astrology, a faith in the boon or curse from the worship of a deity or a goddess, a faith in the effect as a result of the visibility of a particular star or the group of stars in the sky at a particular space-time point, etc. are some such facts common in various cultures.

While the use and the follow-up of these facts depend on the development of FOUs of an individual or a group of individuals, their parallelisms through metaphors or similes in the form of sayings and proverbs also exist mainly to impress upon the deeper meanings of these facts.

5.2.3 FACTS AT THE LEVEL OF GROSS BODY $\mathcal{G}$ = {WO, B, SE}

Facts at the level of gross body are the creations out of the experiences obtained mostly by senses of knowledge and biological body in the background of worldly objects which also include the realm of *pañca mahābhūtas*. This domain of $\mathcal{G}$ in fact helps in extracting the subjective component of reality in Nature out of the objective reality and the material world which in turn is supplied to the domain of $\mathcal{M}$. To this effect, $\mathcal{M}$ is again used to establish the facts and to analyse the data collected using standard scientific methods. Various branches of objective science are full of such facts about Nature and its working. Some glimpses of these facts in physics and biology can be traced in the models and modelling games as described in Appendices B and C, respectively.

5.2.4 NARRATING FACTS THROUGH STORY TELLING

Storytelling is a wonderful art of transferring knowledge and teach the persons of all age groups but they also help them construct identities for themselves and communities to learn, to grow, to find options and meanings, to heal, and to understand and honour the world — its environment, creatures and its different kinds of people. Story pitches a person into a space of multiple realities in addition to the one in which he already lives. According to Marguerite Theophil,[4]

> unlike in this "reality" where everything must fit and make sense, story offers us other realities, allowing for the unexpected, the magical, for awakenings and insights, clarity and direction, and sometimes for the persistently inexplicable to stay just that way!.

Further,

> story communicates through images. Among storytellers, it is a known fact that stories are received image by image, not word by word. Our most enduring learning happens through thoughts, feelings and connections generated by images.

Indian scriptures, not only the Purāṇas in the religious context but also *Pañcatantra* and *Hitopadeśa* in the context of moral and ethical values, are full of such stories. In fact sermons and gospels communicated to a person become more effective if told or exemplified through stories. Since stories are received image by image, characters in the story could be imagined in any form like humans, animals, birds or even the plant kingdom. When one starts telling "once upon a time or long, long ago when animals used to speak to men or men to animals, and both to God," etc. then such beginnings toss us into another, more receptive space than the defined one we live and work in. Often it is the moral of the story which is important and not even the storyteller, his words, the characters in the story or even the images for an elderly person; but for youngsters it matters a lot as to what extent the FOUs of the storyteller are developed. The listener, in fact, gets benefited in the same proportion. The moral or the essence of a story often becomes a fact which finally might belong to any of the above mentioned categories (cf. Sections 5.2.1 to 5.2.3), or conversely a story can be created in order to communicate a moral to a listener in an effective manner.

---

4. Marguerite Theophil, "Bonding and Understanding Through Storytelling" "The Speaking Tree" column, *Times of India*, 5 July 2007; also see, ibid., 6 August 2007.

In some sense storytelling offers some sort of inter-generational bonding. Personal storytelling provides us with options and solutions. Sometimes listening to steps others have taken can show us alternative ways of behaving, or gives options to choose from, and often gives us courage too. Personal storytelling helps us know each other better; it can help create a precious gift and it is healing and releasing from tension.

In brief, there exist a delightful world of myths and fables which are there in all cultures not only as a time-pass item but many of them are full of moral values and guidance with respect to that culture. Myths and fables, fairy tales and legends — and the way they are told to us or interpreted — have played an invisible role in shaping our lives.

5.2.5 A FACT AND ITS SPHERE OF INFLUENCE

Whether the affected or benefited person is an individual or a group of individuals, in either case a fact carries a "sphere of influence." Meaning thereby, out of infinity many actions performed by an individual during the day only a selective few of them get affected by the guidance of a given fact and this defines its sphere of influence. Similarly, corresponding to another fact there is another sphere of influence among the actions of a person. At the level of inner EOLs, while these spheres of influence have somewhat hard boundaries, the same become softer as they come out to the level of outer EOLs, and spheres start overlapping or penetrating into each other and thus affecting the behaviour of the individual rather collectively. In fact there is a kind of assimilation or amalgamation of different categories of facts and the diffusion of different spheres of influence takes place at different stages. Whatever is said here for an individual the same logic with little modifications can be extended to describe the behaviour of a group of individuals as far as the effect of a fact on a society or community is concerned.

5.3 Plurality of Interpretations: Limitations at Different Levels

Certain types of facts particularly the ones that guide at the levels of $\mathcal{M}$ and $\mathcal{G}$ (cf. Sections 5.2.2 and 5.2.3) have more than one interpretation and some of them sometimes get multiplied by the use of various metaphors and similes in different contexts, languages and cultures. As a matter of fact such a plurality of facts leads to proliferation of knowledge, which otherwise was at its minimal at the level of abstraction[5] in the domains of both $\mathcal{M}$ and $\mathcal{G}$. This kind of plurality while maximum for the facts in the domain of $\mathcal{G}$, and somewhat less in the domain of $\mathcal{M}$, it is minimal in the domain of $\mathcal{C}$. Further, the subjectivity of the contents of a fact increases as one proceeds from the domain of $\mathcal{G}$ to $\mathcal{C}$.

With regard to the multiplicity of facts in the domain of $\mathcal{G}$ it has no limit in soft disciplines whereas in hard disciplines like objective sciences and mathematics the established facts are finite at the level of their abstractions and foundations. For example, one can find infinitely many applications of a few established conservation laws of physics in the day-to-day life. Similarly, one can find infinitely many applications of the concepts in mathematical disciplines in the conceptual, conventional and the engineering disciplines of physics. The facts in soft disciplines, no doubt manifest in different forms on the basis of analogy at the level of applications but can again be considered as originated from a finite number of postulates at the level of the philosophy of that discipline. For example, different social or political models are the outcome of a few postulates, or various religions in the world differ in terms of nature of their finite number of postulates. Similar is the case with the facts in the domain of $\mathcal{M}$. For an individual his entire behaviour in a variety of space, time and circumstance- dependent situations originates from his mental set-up consisting of a few basic principles which

5. Radhey Shyam Kaushal, *Structural Analogies in Understanding Nature*, New Delhi: Anamaya Publishers, 2003, chapter 5.

are created out of appropriate combination of his mind, intellect and ego.

With regard to interpretation(s) of these facts, particularly when they are multiplied, it depends on the development of FOUs of the "analyser" (the person using the fact(s)). It is not necessary that the analyser of a fact has equally developed FOUs as the "user" (the person who has used or realized the fact for the first time in its essence at the level of subjective content or in summary has "got an idea") of the fact. The interesting part is that the subjective content or the essence of the fact (related finally to a space-time event) does not change by the change of context, language or culture, provided the user and analyser of the fact have a matching frequency of their FOUs. In the same spirit one can say that while objective meaning(s) of a fact may have limit in view of limitation of the measuring instruments (physical or human being), the subjective meanings can be limitless and varying with the development of FOUs of the analyser. This is true for all categories of facts because certain degree of arbitrariness does exist in the tools of subjective science.

5.4 Possibility of an Absolute Interpretation of Facts in Vedānta Philosophy

It may be mentioned that various concepts and facts that are categorized in Section 5.2 can have an absolute and consistent interpretation within the framework of the patomic model in spite of their multiplicity and plurality. In fact Vedānta philosophy is capable of providing a logically consistent meaning to a fact in terms of the working of EOLs which, in turn, will help in explaining the behaviour of a person. For this purpose, rules and tools of the game can be sought at a more fundamental level by way of analysing the structure of a fact.

As depicted in *fig*. 5.2, the structural details of a fact consist of three components — words, ordering or composition of words, and the context to which the fact is cited. While the meaning of the word itself could be of two types namely objective

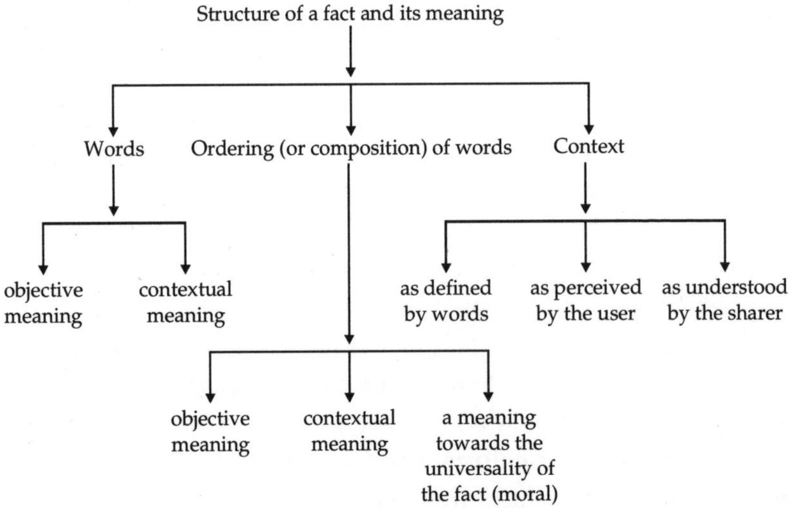

fig. 5.2: Structural details of a fact and its context-dependent meaning(s).

and contextual, that of the ordering of the words is of three types, i.e. objective, contextual and a hidden meaning, called the moral of the fact and the same leads to its universality. However, the context with which the fact deals can again appear in three different ways, i.e. as it is defined by the words, as it is perceived by the user and as it is understood by the sharer or listener. The fact is said to be transmitted in a true sense, if both the user and the sharer identify or visualize the same context and this depends on the levels of development of their FOUs and the matching of the respective levels in the patomic model.

With regard to the use of a fact note the involvement of three parties, viz.

Supplier — one who has designed (or created) the fact,

User — one who is using/applying/transmitting the fact, and

Sharer/listener — one who is receiving or sharing the fact (may be an individual or a group of individuals).

The person who designs the fact definitely has highly developed FOUs whereas the subsequent user (or the listener for that matter) may not be of the same level. Further, note that once the fact is available and settled in one's faculty of memory, E, then this faculty itself can act as a supplier. Not only this, the mind of the individual at times can act as both user and sharer of the fact. In fact during meditation or in the process of taking decisions the mind divides itself into two parts — one of them acts as an observer and the other as a decision-maker in the light of the given fact. These decision maker and observer parts can respectively be identified as the user and sharer of the given fact. This is the case with an individual, but in a gathering of two or more than two, the user and sharer could be different personalities. Note that each fact consists of a sequence of words which in a collective manner leaves an impact on the mind of a listener in terms of moral and ethical values. The magnitude of this impact depends on the context and the level of development of FOUs of the listener with reference to that context. The magnitude of this impact in turn also helps in producing a sphere of influence at the level of inner EOLs (cf. Section 5.2.5) and the same later manifests through outer EOLs and in the actions performed by an individual.

Swami Muktanand ("The Speaking Tree", *Times of India*, 3 May 2008), emphasizes as to how the psyche of a person gets affected even by the letters and words. According to him,

> Letters and words create our thoughts, and thoughts create our feelings — our joys and sorrows, depression and elation, desire, pride, expectation and jealousy. You can experience for yourself the power of language. If you sit quietly, you will notice how letters and words continually arise within.

5.5 Possibility of a Predictive Metaphysical Theory of Human Behaviour

Once the structure of concepts, facts, anecdotes, stories, examples, sayings, etc. and the mechanism of their grasping by an individual becomes clear then it is not difficult to look for a metaphysical theory of human behaviour and this is possible within the framework of the patomic model of human Being. In this regard an analysis of the mechanism, which works behind leaving an impact of a fact on the FOUs of an individual, will be of great help.

As discussed in Appendix D, the deficiency or excess of a *mahābhūta* in the body is the main cause of a disease — physical or mental. In either case, an individual seeks a guidance from the world in order to have a peaceful and regulated life by way of maintaining a super equilibrium with *PM*s. While Nature, since the time of his birth, already provides enough guidance to this effect in terms of his survival, another important source of this guidance is through parents, teachers and texts in terms of facts. Plenty of these facts and their varieties are available in this world. Depending upon the nature of his requirement an individual (to cure of his physical or mental disease) picks up suitable facts out of the available pool. At times these facts are imposed on an individual by his parents or teachers to obey, particularly when his FOUs are not fully developed. Once the suitable facts are digested/accepted by an individual, he defines norms for himself and also a domain of their applications via the sphere of influence of a fact (cf. Section 5.2.5). While many facts cure his physical diseases (requirements) pertaining to SE, B and WO constituents of the patomic model, a few of them treat his mental disease by way of accepting[6] them at the level of micro-body consisting of M, I and E. These facts stored in E, offer guidance to the workings of M and I, not only in the day-to-day life but also in the year-to-year life. In fact year-to-year behaviour is generated out of his day-to-day behaviour with an effect of environment. It is also true that one can live the whole life by resorting only to a few facts. In the future chapters we elaborate on the tools and rules which participate in the above said mechanism of grasping a fact.

5.6 Concluding Discussion

Since the behaviour of an individual is an outcome of the

6. Note that the acceptance of a fact itself is a complicated process. It is linked with the liking or disliking of a person which again has roots in the theory of *karma* via *prārabdha, sañcita* and *kriyamāṇa* (cf. chapter 4).

guidance which he has sought from this world and his environment in terms of certain concepts, facts and truths, the study of structure, meanings, implications and an analysis of these facts has been the aim of this chapter. With a view to finding a source for liking or disliking of these facts by an individual, the universality of love and affection is demonstrated in terms of forces of attraction in Nature. A broad classification of facts is presented to this effect with some representative examples. It is argued that in the practical life of an individual each fact has its own sphere of influence and the superposition of such spheres of flexible boundaries leaves an impact in the behaviour of that person. In spite of the fact that these facts have plurality of interpretations and structures in different languages and cultures (often in the form of stories, myths and fables, fairy tales, etc.), the possibility of an absolute interpretation and of the grasping mechanism of these facts by an individual is highlighted within the framework of the patomic model. This suggests a way to develop a metaphysical theory of human actions and this is precisely what we plan to pursue in the chapters ahead.

To elaborate further on the impact of these facts on the behaviour of an individual an analogy from physics may be helpful. In physics, varieties of atoms of the periodic table of elements are describable in terms of the same force law (Coulomb's law) and the constituents electron, proton and neutron. However, an account of finer details leads to distinct features of these varieties of atoms. In the same way, all individuals, in spite of having the same set of EOLs and their arrangement in the form of patomic model, reveal their behaviour differently because of the finer details involved in the grasping mechanisms and capacity of these facts with reference to an individual. Not only this, as the collection of atoms behaves differently from the individual atom in terms of the properties of the produced composite structures, i.e. molecules (many-body effects), the same is the case with a collection of individuals. The analogy can further be extended to the case of newly discovered nanostructures and macromolecules and the bigger and bigger human societies. We shall return to some of these details in Chapter 9.

According to Aristotle,[7] "All human actions have one or more of the seven causes: chance, nature, compulsion, habit, reason, passion and desire." Indeed there exist facts in different cultures pertaining to each of these causes for an action performed by an individual and the same provide guidance to this effect. As mentioned earlier (cf. Chapter 4, verse (4.6)) in *SMBG* these seven causes are further abstracted into five. Further, William Penn[8] gives the national-level importance to proverbs, when he says, "The wisdom of nations lies in their Proverbs, which are brief and pithy."

Facts are the facts; their effect on the actions of an individual depends on the fact whether that individual wants to use them for negative or positive pursuit (cf. Chapter 4). Amitava Basu[9] advises to marshall one's thought for tranquillity and writes,

> A series of sad thoughts significantly dampens energy, creates pensiveness and, at times, leads to depression. Thoughts of being mistreated, cheated, oppressed seed the feeling of hatred and vengeance against the offender. All this could lead to anguish — even violence.

On the other hand, "thoughts on love, care and camaraderie bring calmness and sobriety. Thought has bearing on desires and consequently actions to satisfy wants generated." While this sequence of events follows naturally towards the down-fall or the upliftment of an individual in general, Basu further summarily advises, "rein your thoughts to prevent disturbance of mind and undesirable behaviour; and the consequent effect that mind has on health." In fact it is the intellect of an individual that decides the choice of a fact or concept out of the pool

7. A quotation cited in *Times of India*, 24 December 2006.

8. A quotation cited in *Times of India*, 8 February 2009.

9. Amitava Basu, "The Speaking Tree", *Times of India*, 4 January 2007.

available for the purpose. To a great extent, this choice of facts depends on the circumstances in which one is left in his present; otherwise, however small it may be, there is definitely a guidance from the "past," i.e. from *prārabdha*. Once the facts are chosen then they play their role rather equally with respect to both negative and positive constructs, of course, with drastically different outputs.

The sequence of negative virtues, if followed by an individual, leads to some sort of imperfection in him and imperfection is a disease — it could be physical or mental (cf. Appendix D). On the other hand, the following of positive virtues leads to perfection, because the positive virtues are the characteristics of the inner-most existence, i.e. of the soul. But somehow the imperfection is a reality and the perfection remains only an ideality as far as the common man is concerned; that is why many of us are imperfect persons. If one knows the "art of living" then imperfection can be converted into strength and made useful in the day-to-day life. Even if one is successful, negativity can crop up in his attitude at any time for unknown reasons. But note that (i) he alone is responsible for his attitude, (ii) as is his attitude, so are his perceptions, (iii) as is his perception, so is his interaction with the world, (iv) as is the interaction, so is the experience of life, and (v) as is the experience, so is the quality of his life and actions. Not only this, whatever is the quality of his life, the same he transfers to coming generation(s) and that leads to the downfall or the upliftment of a family or society. This is how the attitude of an individual, derived from a fact, affects the community as a whole. This kind of analysis started from a fact again ends up in the facts like *as you sow, so you mow* or *as you think, so you become*. The same universal fact or experience has different effects on different individuals. This is because the grasping capacity of the same fact by different individuals is different as they have varying degrees of development of their FOUs. As a result, the art of expressing or practising the same experience or fact becomes different for different persons.

Einstein's special theory of relativity has suggested a way to see the effect of a physical fact (law) in different, so-called "inertial frames" of reference. Sometimes a law also gets distorted or modified in different frames but within the range of the measuring (inanimate) instrument. In these studies the effect of several uncontrollable parameters which are the characteristics of a living observer in the rest or in the moving frame is ignored and the theory gets a beautiful support from experiments. In the present case of human Beings, however, both observer (who may also act just as a spectator) and performer (experiencer) of an action are fully equipped with several uncontrollable parameters and this leads to distortions of a fact sometimes to several orders. In the process of transferring the experience to newer generations such distortions of a fact multiply to such an extent that the original spirit of the fact is lost. In view of the fact that the patomic model can now provide certain absolute frames of reference, it will be possible to quantify the action of a performer in the same way as one does in objective science.

6

Revisiting the Limitations of Theories of Physical and Biological Sciences

At the outset, we once again highlight the motivation of the book and also of this chapter by citing the quotations,[1]

> How on earth are you ever going to explain in terms of chemistry and physics so important a biological phenomenon as first love?
>
> — Albert Einstein

On the other hand,

> Love at the first sight is easy to understand; it is when two people have been looking at each other for a lifetime that becomes a miracle.
>
> — Amy Bloom

Clearly, both Albert Einstein and Amy Bloom are pretty sure of the limitations of the tools and working of objective sciences as far as the explanation and understanding of human actions and behaviour are concerned. In other words, not only the tools but also the laws of objective science appear inadequate when applied to understand a phenomenon in biology or in the domain of subjective science.

To this effect, while a lot has been said in chapter 1 (cf. Sections 1.6 and 1.7) and Appendices B and C, in this chapter, in view of some recent researches of inter-disciplinary nature, we once again analyse these limits at a somewhat finer level so that the role, limitations and domain of working of the tools of objective science to explain such phenomena become more transparent. In fact this will enable us to apply rather judiciously

1. As quoted in *Times of India*, 10 December, 2006, p. 19.

the tools, concepts and principles of physical sciences in the analysis of such phenomenon in an analogous manner. For this purpose, here we first highlight the available tools of physical science and then of behavioural sciences for their ready use in future chapters. Next we discuss the extent to which the tools of former category can be applied to understand certain phenomena which appear to have their basis in the biological domain but also have a link with the domain of subjective science. The study of such phenomena in recent times has become crucial in deciding the role of certain hidden parameters/variables (which are the attribute of the subjective science) in the theory. These hidden parameters are believed to be the manifestation of the consciousness of the living Being who in fact becomes an active participator in the phenomenon under study.

6.1 Physical Science and its Domain of Working

In continuation of chapter 1 (cf. Section 1.6) we once again emphasize here on the domains of working of subjective and objective sciences. In objective science, a scientist acts as a single unit but with a composite structure in the process of collecting data on a phenomenon, analysing them and at a later stage developing models and theories to understand the phenomenon though within a restricted framework. This restricted framework, broadly speaking, arises from the following fact. Since the human Being as a whole works as an intelligent apparatus in a systematic manner and studies Nature under some highly simplifying assumptions, this apparatus in fact becomes the ultimate observer (subject). In physical science, the ultimate aim of study is confined only to the inanimate aspect of Nature. Also, in the analysis of data collected on a living Being there is no scope for accounting the roles of mind, intellect or ego, which are present in the object under study. On the other hand, in subjective science both the end-points are redefined, i.e. the object of study could be an animate one and/or the observer (subject) is no more the single unit of human Being; it has a composite structure in terms of the patomic model (cf. Appendix A) whose role needs to be considered and thereby the soul becomes the ultimate experiencer. Thus, the spectrum of study of a phenomenon in subjective science is much wider and deeper as well compared to that in objective science. To be more specific, we recapitulate the constraints on the framework of objective science which inadvertently enter into its designing at various stages.

In fact the constraints on the framework used in studying a phenomenon in physical science can arise at different steps of quantification of a characteristic, namely (i) at the level of basic postulates used in framing a model or theory, (ii) at the level of using the logic, and (iii) at the level of language used for analyses and predictions, i.e. mathematics. Various limitations discussed in Section 1.6 can easily be categorized under these heads.

No doubt the theories and models of objective science appear to be ground-level realities from the point of view of understanding a phenomenon in Nature but the fact is that they all start with certain postulates and axioms about both the observer and the observed and also about the method used in taking observations. While the individual's intention, foresightedness, and his power of augmentation reflect in steps (i) and (ii), his versatility with the language of mathematics goes with step (iii). Even if the first two steps come out of a deeper philosophy of the individual, the tools of the third one may be beyond his control. Sometimes, inadequacy of the existing tools also comes on the way to describe the phenomenon in totality. Then one attempts to search for newer tools on both the fronts — theory and experiments, with a view to having a certain degree of agreement between the predicted and experimental results at their end-points. This is how the objective science has been progressing.

Whether it is with regard to the observed or the observer himself in either case the logic followed in objective science does not permit the study of Nature beyond its space-time structure. This applies equally to both tools and rules of the game (cf.

Appendices B and C) in any branch of objective science. If at all any departure from space-time structure of Nature is required to be considered in understanding a phenomenon (for example, in quantum measurement problem or in the problems pertaining to human Being(s) in psychological or sociological studies again as a single unit or as a many-body system) then the same is accounted through the probability or the statistical concepts of mathematics, mainly because of the lack of knowledge of exact nature of laws of Nature. Thus, the use of probability or statistical theories in the description of a phenomenon is also an indication of human ignorance of "precise dynamics" of Nature.

In physics, for example, the tools (the constituents of matter) and the rules of the game (i.e. the interactions among these constituents) keep on changing with respect to both space and time scales (e.g. starting from elementary particles like quarks, then nucleons, through nuclei, atoms, molecules and so on) but to the extent that space-time structure (in view of Kant philosophy) is restored at all stages. There is hardly any scope to account for the role of essences of life of the observer or of the observed in the theory if the same manifests in the phenomenon under study. Similarly, in modern times in biological sciences the studies are confined to the investigation of the arrangement of organs in the body, their structure and the working but within the framework of physical and chemical laws. In fact biologists also hesitate in accepting in clear terms the role, if any, of the essences of life of philosophical domain like consciousness, mind, etc. In spite of all this there are certain phenomena whose understanding in totality would require a crucial role of the overlapping domain of objective and subjective science. For this purpose, naturally one has to go beyond the built-in limits of objective science. In the next section we provide glimpses of such phenomena and emphasize on the limits on their description within the framework of objective science.

Even in the domain of space-time structure of Nature many departures from the well established laws of physics have been noticed in recent times.[2] For example, (i) non-linear character of theories required to describe certain phenomena under some relaxed assumptions, demands the existence of many more conservation laws; (ii) the physics of non-equilibrium or complex systems demands new frameworks to investigate them; (iii) there are quite a few experimental evidences which support the departure from the constancy of the so-called universal constants (some of them are found to vary with time or are allowed to take different values from the prescribed ones). There is growing evidence that light moved much faster during the early stages of our Universe.[3] Depending upon the situation, electron assumes different masses from the prescribed one.[4] According to Stephen Hawking,[5] "it is becoming increasingly likely that the rules we had thought were fundamental through time and space are actually just by-laws for our bit of it." Further, "it could be that the laws that govern our Universe are unchangeable but it is a remarkable coincidence that these laws are also exactly what is needed to produce life."

---

2. See, for example, David Ruelle, *Physics Today*, May 2004, p. 48; G.F.R. Ellis, *Physics Today*, July 2005, p. 49; Roger Penrose, *Times of India*, http://timesofIndia.Indiantimes.com/articleshow/306035.cms

3. See, for example, Avnish Kumar Sisodiya, R.S. Kaushal, D. Parashar and V.S. Bhasin, *Journ. Phys.* **G:** Nucl & Part **34** (2007) 929, and the references therein.

4. See, for example, S.N. Lea, "Limits to Time Variation of Fundamental Constants from Comparison of Atomic Frequency Standards", *Reports on Progress in Phys.* **70** (2007) 1473-1523; B. Bagchi, "Position Dependent Mass Models and Their Nonlinear Characterization", *Journ. Phys.* **A**: Math & Gen **40** (2007) F1041; For further work on effective mass Hamiltonian in solids, see B. Gonul et al., *Mod. Phys. Lett.* **A17** (2002) 2453, and the references therein.

5. Stephen Hawking, as quoted in "Nature Rewrites Laws of Universe" and reported by Jonathan Leake in *Times of India*, 10 September 2001.

6.2 Biological sciences and their Domain of Working: Biochemical and Biophysical Processes

As mentioned, the understanding of the functioning of inner organs of a body relies heavily on the laws developed and used in physical and chemical sciences. Since these laws do have certain limitations (cf. previous section) even in the domain of physical science, then how far it is justified to use them to biological systems which otherwise in themselves are more complex and allow the departure rather more frequently from the basic postulates of the underlying physical theory in which both the observed and the observer are considered as inanimate entities. If at all the application of these laws is going to provide some meaningful results for biological systems, then they are acceptable only in a limited order of accuracy. On the other hand, there are quite a few phenomena in the biological domain which remain unexplained thus far without a proper account of consciousness in their analysis. In what follows we pinpoint some such phenomena and areas where not only the use of physical laws but also the physiological/neurological descriptions break down in providing the complete understanding of the phenomenon and perhaps (!) the role of consciousness via inner essences of life becomes desirable.

6.2.1 BIOCHEMISTRY

This branch of chemistry deals with the chemical reactions taking place inside the body in which enzymes act as catalyzer. In these reactions, reactants and products are identified with the conventional organic or inorganic compounds under certain approximation, i.e. the constituents of soft matter (having life) are considered to behave in the same way as the constituents of the hard matter (inanimate entities). In fact to understand the chemistry of living cells the tools of conventional chemistry are employed for various processes. Such an analysis no doubt helps in preparing the medicine and drugs for treatment of various diseases but again in certain limits. The reason being, neither the soft matter of all living Beings (on which the experimentation of the prepared medicine is carried out) is the same nor do the consumers of the same drug have identical external and internal biological environment in which the medicine is supposed to work. A statistical analysis of clinical results (derived from the studies on different species) becomes the guiding factor for the use, prescription and the implementation of the products. This is how the studies in biochemistry are carried out to prepare medicines. In spite of this, in some diseases of serious nature only prayer to God is amazingly found to cure the disease in the end (cf. Appendix D). The occurrence of such miracles can be noticed everyday in society.

6.2.2 BIOMECHANICS

There can be three broad categories of mechanical systems: One which totally deals with body actions and movements of living Beings; second which involves the living Being or its body parts as one of the components of the system, and third in which the system is independent of any role of living Being except for watching the space-time evolution of the system, i.e. as a spectator. If one ignores the effect of consciousness, then the laws of mechanics neatly work only for the third category; otherwise for the first and the second categories the applications are bound to show some limitations. Several examples can be cited to this effect. The cases of Chevreul (hand-held) pendulum,[6] conscious pendulum,[7] conscious double-pendulum in the games

---

6. E. Chevreul, Lettre' A. M. Ampere', "Surne Classe Particuliere de Mouvemens Muscularies", *Revue des Deus Mondes* **2** (1833) 249-57, 2nd edn. Also see, H.H. Spitz and Y. Marcuard, "Chevereul's Report on the Mysterious Oscillations of the Hand-held Pendulum". A French Chemist's report 1833 open letter to Ampere (Translated from French), *Skeptical Inquirer* **25** (2001) 35-39, No. 4. This is the magazine for Science and Reason published by the International Organization "Committee for Scientific Investigations of Claim of the Paranormal" (CSICOP).

7. Radhey Shyam Kaushal, "The Conscious Pendulum: A Physicist's Approach", *Indian Philosophical Quarterly* (Poona) **29** (2002) 65-78, no.1.

of golf[8] and hockey are well known. Several other phenomena mentioned by Chevreul are (i) bird in flight, (ii) billiard players, and (iii) movement on a slippery surface. The self-organizing forces play an important role in categories first and second.[9] The exercises in school texts, like computing the effective height covered by a climbing monkey or a bear on a pole, who also undergo slipping downward at the same time, also offer examples of this category. No doubt consciousness plays a role in these cases but its account is avoided at the cost of some simplifying assumptions.

6.2.3 BIOELECTRICITY

About two centuries ago Italian physicist, L. Galvani, demonstrated the effect of electric current on a living Being like frog. On the other hand, later about a century ago Indian botanist, Sir J.C. Bose, demonstrated the existence of a "life-like" character in plants using electroscope. These observations, in recent years, have led to a great deal of researches in this interdisciplinary subject of electrophysiology. An electrophysiologist generally studies two aspects — one which pertains to the production of electricity by living tissues while going about their normal activities and the second deals with the study of effect of electric current when it passes through living tissues and arouses responses in them. In fact both the approaches have given valuable insights into life processes.[10] With regard to the former aspect the following simple laboratory experiment using ballistic galvanometer (B.G.) is worth mentioning:

A ballistic galvanometer is a device which is capable of detecting charges as small as of micro-coulomb magnitude.

---

8. A. Raymond Penner, "The Physics of Golf", *Reports on Progress in Physics* **66** (2003) 131.

9. Radhey Shyam Kaushal, *Structural Analogies in Understanding Nature*, New Delhi: Anamaya Publishers, 2003, p. 158, Appendix B.

10. See, for example, Robert Galambos, *Nerves and Muscles*, Bombay: Vakil, Fefferand Simons Pvt. Ltd., 1972, Chapters 4 and 5.

When one presses the connecting leads of B.G. by hands or touches them with tongue, it starts showing deflection on a scale placed at a distance from B.G. and illuminated by a focused light of a lamp. The deflection of spot on the scale from the rest position depends on how forcefully the ends of the wires are pressed by hands or touched with tongue; accordingly more and more tissues come into action. This shows the existence of electric charge in the body.

From the above observations certain questions immediately come to one's mind: In the Galvani-type experiments while the body behaves like a conductor, then does this conductor have the same features as a metallic conductor of electricity or is it different? Similarly, in *B.G.* experiment has the detected bio-charge by the instrument the same feature as the charge produced by the battery current or is it different? The answer to these questions is an emphatic No. The bio-charge or bio-conductivity as shown by a living body cannot be the same as physical charge or physical conductivity. The former are more complex characteristics of a living body and the physical instruments detect only one aspect of that complexity, i.e. the physical component of these features, which ends up at the level of existence of electromagnetic forces inside the body. But there is something more in them. In fact a major content of these features, which definitely is of non-electromagnetic nature and perhaps is the attribute of say a deeper neurodynamics, brain functioning, or mind functioning, etc. remains undetected by the physical instrument.

Wherever they look, biophysicists experimenting on plants and animals find biological batteries. Sometimes they study large collection of such cells — as in the brain, or in heart muscles. The interesting point is that whatever the biological preparation may be, a measurable electrical phenomenon turns up as it goes about its process of living.

6.2.4 BIOMAGNETISM

Like the electric character present in certain responses of a living body, the presence of an element of magnetic character in some of them has also been known. In fact modern researches to this effect have been carried out and a cure of several diseases (cf. Appendix D) using magnetic therapy has been found. This is mainly because of the presence of element of iron or its compounds not only in blood but also in other organs as well. (As a matter of fact out of the entire periodic table of elements, it is only the iron that is available in abundance in Nature, the reason being that the nucleus of iron atom is the most stable one in terms of its binding energy.)

Like the bio-charge and bio-conductivity, the biomagnetism is also a complex characteristic of a living being, of which the detected physical magnetism is only one component and the rest is attributed to non-physical aspects of the phenomenon under study. In recent years, attempts have been there to identify biomagnetic sources in brain.[11] Magnetoencephalographic measurements record magnetic fields generated from small currents in the neural systems while information is being processed in the brain (see, for example, Hamalainen et al.[12]).

6.2.5 BIO-FLUID, BIO-ACOUSTICS, BIO-OPTICS AND BIO-HEAT

Whether it is the respiratory system, blood flow or the blood with oxygen content flow, in none of the cases physical laws are precisely applicable in explaining these phenomena (cf. Appendix C). The functioning of ears and eyes also cannot be understood completely in terms of physics-based laws alone. If these organs were designed ideally only as physical instrument (as a replica) then it is a different thing; otherwise the understanding of their working in terms of the functioning of nerves and muscles which at their end-point are linked with

---

11. Hung-I. Pai, Chih-Yuan Tseng and H.C. Lee, "Identifying Biomagnetic Sources in the Brain by Maximum Entropy Approach", arXiv.q-bio.NC/0508040 v1, 29 August 2005; M. Hamalainen, R. Hari, R.J. Lmoniemi, J. Kanuutila, and O.V. Lounasmaa, *Rev. Mod. Phys.* **65** (1993) 413-97.

12. M. Hamalainen et al., cited in 11 above.

the brain or heart, etc. is definitely beyond the domain of physical laws. Similar is the case with bio-heat. Whatever cold or hot food we eat, cold or hot water we drink, cold or hot air we inhale, cold or hot environment we live in, this all gives rise to an aggregate temperature of human body as 37° C or 98.4° F. Such are the fast complex processes taking place inside the body which immediately restore this magic temperature. It is true that not all inner parts of the body have this temperature at the same time, but the kind of bio-thermodynamics which is working inside the body is not necessarily governed by the standard laws of physical-thermodynamics. In summary, there remains a major component in the data taken in bio-fluid dynamics, bio-acoustics, bio-optics, and bio-thermodynamics which cannot be explained just in terms of existing physical laws.

6.3 Some Biological Phenomena of Interdisciplinary Nature

In this section we highlight certain bio-phenomena of inter-disciplinary nature whose origin and explanation appear to lie outside the domain of modern theories of biology.

6.3.1 OUT-OF-BODY AND NEAR-DEATH EXPERIENCES: AN ENIGMA

Out-of-body experiences (OBEs) and/or near-death experiences (NDEs) of humans (since they are capable of narrating these experiences) have a long history, perhaps as old as human race. While these experiences do not occur so frequently, the description of these experiences by all persons who had them is found to be common. During the OBEs even an ordinary, healthy person feels like floating in space or has a sensation of drifting outside of his own body when he is in a particular mental state. On the other hand, during NDEs a person who has been in the throes of severe and sudden injury or illness (or in comma) reports the sensation of floating over his body, travelling through tunnels and seeing some extraordinary lights after the exit from them, etc. (for details, see Appendix F). No doubt, such experiences do occur with some individuals but the understanding of the phenomenon responsible for such experiences is still inadequate. It is not known whether these phenomena are of biological origin or their roots lie outside the domain of objective science. With regard to these experiences different cultures of the world have been having different explanations. At times, the occurrence of these experiences to an individual is attributed to the role of death-god or of some superpowers in relation to his life. In recent times neuroscientists in co-ordination with psychologists are trying to find out some plausible explanation (if at all it is there) of these experiences within the framework of objective science, but with a limited success thus far.

According to a British psychotherapist,[13] Nandini Gulati, who herself had OBEs and dealing in past-life regression,

> OBEs are usually induced when a person is undergoing an intense emotion or stress, like pain, grief or love, even in those who are otherwise not spiritually inclined. I do not think science has definite explanation of OBEs. Moreover, if spirituality offers better insight into the cycle of life and death and offers comforts and strength, a scientific explanation is not required. I think it is a great insight into the meaning of being alive and human.

In summary, "it strengthens my belief that we are more than just our corporeal selves, and consciousness can exist beyond the physical body."

On the other hand, in recent times efforts have been made to find a physical basis of philosophical concepts like thoughts, emotions, feelings, etc. in terms of brain functions and neural networking.[14] Evolutionary biologists and cognitive neuroscientists are discovering more and more genes, brain structures and other

---

13. A Reporting by Shatarupa Chakraborty, "Out-of-body Experiences Remain an Enigma", *Times of India*, 15 July 2007.

14. A Reporting by Sandra Blakeslee, "Experts Recreate Out-of-body Experience", in *Times of India*, 25 August 2007, "Times Trends" p. 21 (Also see the reporting in the *Journal Science*, Friday, August issue, 2007).

physical correlates to feelings like empathy, disgust and joy. In fact from feelings emerges the moral sense — not just in humans but in other animals as well, and a physical basis to these concepts, if available, will be an asset to develop a theory of morality.

With regard to the understanding of OBEs, recent researches have shown[15] that they are the outcome of certain types of illusions. Studies carried out by the neuroscientist, Mathew M. Botvinick at Princeton University, reveal that, "the sense of having a body, of being in a bodily self" is actually constructed from multiple sensory streams. Usually these sensory streams, which include vision, touch, balance and the sense of where one's body is positioned in space, work together seamlessly. But when the pieces of information coming from various sensory sources do not match up, the sense of being embodied as a whole comes apart; this leads to an illusion. The brain, which abhors ambiguity, then forces a decision that can involve the sense of being in a different body. Such studies are the first step in figuring out exactly as to how the brain creates this sensation. In fact similar reasons are advanced by the neuroscientists for the data on NDEs collected on different persons at different times. Several experiments, which help in arriving at such conclusions, can be traced in day-to-day life to this effect. A couple of common experiments demonstrating the vision and touch illusion are the following:

(i) When a person gazes at an illusory image of himself through the goggles and prods in just the right way with a stick, he feels as if he has left his body.

(ii) **Rubber-hand illusion**: When a person A hides one hand in his lap and looks at a rubber hand set on a table in front of him. If another person B strikes the real hand and rubber hand simultaneously with a stick, then A feels the vivid sense that rubber hand is his own; but when the rubber hand is whacked with a hammer he winces and sometimes cries out.

15. Sandra Blakeslee, op. cit.

(iii) **Feeling of two balls of one**: If a person A keeps a small, preferably a spherical object of the size of a grain of pea (say a ball of ball-bearing system) in his palm and shows the same to another person B. Now A asks B to close his eyes and to come forward to touch the grain with a cusp kind of contact created by the two crossed-fingers (say by the middle one and the index finger) of B. The person B will have feeling of two grains (or of two balls), while in reality it is only one. Some cases of optical illusions are worth citing here:

(iv) **Mirage**: feeling of water in a desert during summer time due to phenomenon of total internal reflection.

(v) Sometimes two-dimensional drawings/paintings appear to be three-dimensional, as if they have thickness in them.

(vi) A properly drawn zebra-crossing on a plain smooth road at the red-light signal sometimes gives a feeling of a bump, leading to slowing down of traffic.

Similarly, the examples can be traced which are based on sound illusion — like the case of echo in a valley. Next we present somewhat generalized definitions of illusion or hallucination.

6.3.2 ILLUSION/DELUSION AND HALLUCINATION

A non-co-ordination in the working of various EOLs of an individual at a particular space-time point in general leads to illusion or hallucination depending upon whether the non-coordinating EOLs belong to (i) $\mathcal{G}$ = {SE, B, WO} alone, or to (ii) $\mathcal{M}$ = {M, I, E} alone or to (iii) the union set of $\mathcal{G}$ and $\mathcal{M}$, i.e. $\mathcal{G} \cup \mathcal{M}$. As such there is no sharp boundary between the feelings of illusion and hallucination as far as the perception by an individual is concerned. A long-term illusion can become hallucination when the understanding about an object/a phenomenon via M and I, after a critical analysis, is stored in E permanently or for a long time. In fact illusion is defined for the case (i) where the roles of mind M and intellect I are only implicit and minimal and the simultaneous mismatch between the observation and perception processes by at least two EOLs takes place. It is often due to the workings of 10 SEs, and B and in the field of WO. Illusion is normally momentary and in it "appearing (virtual) reality" converts into actual reality in no time as and when one is able to restore the co-ordination among the concerned EOLs. Several examples/demonstrations to this effect can be cited; some such situations are already listed in Section 6.3.1.

On the other hand, hallucination is an outcome of a detailed analysis of the understanding about a perceived object/ phenomenon by I and the same is kept in the faculty of memory E for a considerable period of time. It is just a kind of fanaticism. It is broken as and when a case of counter experience occurs in life. By and large one's ignorance or the lack of understanding about a physical object or the occurrence of a phenomenon completely in terms of observations on it, or the lack of quality of analysis of these observations that leads to some confusing conclusions, is responsible for hallucination. For that matter, a study in totality of a particular phenomenon carried for a very long time may also turn out to be a failure at a certain point of time and the same can be declared as hallucination. Here the level of development of FOUs of an individual and also of a community as a whole plays a crucial role. Sometimes a single exception to a general prescription or in the working of a theory is sufficient to break the hallucination. Many examples to this effect can be found not only in the theoretical development of objective science (particularly in the modelling game) but also in the tenets of different religions.

Vedānta philosophy offers a unique case of hallucination in which the entire physical world and its working is considered as hallucination from the point of view of an "enlightened person" in terms of spirituality. As we plan to concentrate mostly on the physical reality involved in the working of a human Being, we refrain ourselves from going into these details here.

To overcome an illusion or a hallucination, a complete knowledge of the concerned phenomenon (in terms of its objective and subjective contents) is necessary and that tantamounts to raise the level of developments of one's FOUs. In fact in order to experience life in full one has to activate various senses or EOLs in general to their maximum capacity; otherwise the fragmented use of senses will lead to errors, illusions and hallucination.

It is noticed that some people (and some animals as well) do have extraordinary sensation power corresponding to a particular sense organ, since they have either developed the concerned sense organ to the highest degree or else God has gifted them with such a specific feature. On the other hand, it has been found that in spite of some common features each member of a particular species exhibits certain unique characteristics.

6.3.3 EVERY PERSON HAS A UNIQUE ODOUR

Biological or life processes taking place inside the body of a given species, though they appear to be similar at the gross level, are however different for each individual at the micro level. If these processes would have been understandable completely within the framework of objective science in an ideal manner (just like the "machine products") then a given species must have identical inner processes and the products as each individual. But that is not actually the case. It has been found that each individual differs from another in a given species not only in the philosophical domain but also in the domain of objective science, particularly in their bio-structural details. Some scientific evidences to this effect have now become available in a variety of contexts.

For example, researches in recent years have shown that each individual has a unique odour. Dustin Penn from the Konrad Lorenz Institute of Enthology (Vienna, Austria) has provided an experimental support to this fact. The researchers took samples of armpit, urine and spit from 197 adults. Each subject was sampled five times over a ten-week collecting period. They extracted thousands of volatile chemicals from the samples — the type of compound most likely to have an odour, and identified them by chromatography and mass spectroscopy. As per a report in *Journal of Royal Society Interface* (2007), researchers found many more different volatile chemicals in sweat than in urine or saliva. It could be because humans have a reason to be able to distinguish themselves by general body odour, more than by marking territory as many animals do. Although individual's cocktail of odours are found to change all the time, researchers had been able to identify nearly 400 compounds that persisted in sweat samples taken at different times.

In another context, Hiroaki Matsunami and his co-workers of Duke University in North Carolina (work published in *Nature*, September 2007) have attributed the perception of body odour by an individual to his single gene and it is shown that any human odourant receptor is associated with the way we experience odours. In other words, when it comes to a man's body odour, the fragrance (or stench) is in the nose of the beholder. In fact the same individual can smell as vanilla to some, like urine to some others and for about a third of adults no smell at all.

There are just a few studies carried out pertaining to the functions of the sense organ nose; otherwise a great vista of studies at micro-level are due pertaining to functions of other senses of knowledge namely tongue (regarding uniqueness of taste), eyes (regarding uniqueness of sight), ears (regarding uniqueness of listening), and skin (regarding uniqueness of touch), etc. In general, there still remains a question as to what extent the genetics or neuroscience will be able to provide explanation to such bio-phenomena, or else one has to account for the roles of "mind sets" of both fragmenting person and the person who perceives, in the explanation of such uniqueness features associated with an individual. According to neurologists, the perception of outer world lays the substrate for thoughts, responses and actions. Hence perception and thought initiation must have some source code which is unique for every individual.[16]

6.4. Can the Dark Energy of Modern Cosmology Comprise of Spiritual Energy?

At present, it is only the received electromagnetic radiation of different wavelength ranges (say of radio waves, microwave, optical wave, etc.) from various galactic systems that gives the feeling and details of their existence in the universe. In fact in view of the present understanding of physical theories, there cannot be a better choice than this since out of the four fundamental interactions (cf. Section 1.7.2) only two, namely gravitational and electromagnetic forces, are of long (infinite) range and the other two (namely weak and strong) are of short range. Again, gravity force is beautifully assimilated with and merged into the redefined geometry of space-time in terms of its curvature. Thus, the only physical force left is the electromagnetic one which supplies background for all recent discoveries with regard to exploring the universe and its origin. Since physicists, in their description of Nature, still hesitate in accepting the role of any other force, which is beyond the domain of space-time, the study of the universe carried out so far using the above limited tools remains rather incomplete. Not only this, the existing physical laws, which have great experimental support in recent times and have worked successfully for terrestrial systems, may not work so well for galactic systems. Perhaps, the recent discoveries of existence of "dark matter" and "dark energy" in the universe are the indications to this effect.

Recently, there have been many reports in scientific literature (see, for example, *The Early Universe: Facts and Fiction*, Springer Verlag, Berlin, 1992, Chap. 10; For a recent review on the subject also see, E.J. Copeland, M. Sami, and S. Tsujikawa, "Dynamics of Dark Energy", *Int. Journ. Mod. Phys.* D15 (2006) 1753) which show that most of the universe (96 per cent to be exact) is made of

16. M. Hamalainen et al., cited in 11 above.

dark matter and dark energy. According to Nobel laureate, James Watson Cronin (who won the 1980 Nobel Prize for physics by proving that certain subatomic reactions escape the laws of fundamental symmetry), "We think we understand the universe, but we only understand four per cent of everything." Some recent models reveal that 73 per cent of cosmic energy seems to consist of "dark energy" and 23 per cent of "dark matter" — the pervasive but unidentified stuff that holds the universe together and accelerates its expansion. The remaining 4 per cent consists of so-called "normal matter" such as atoms and molecules. Dark matter cannot be detected directly as it does not emit or reflect light or radiation — or not sensitive enough to be picked up by available tools, except that gravitational force deflects light from distant galaxies.

We still do not know as to what the dark matter is made of. Astro-particle physicists feel that its basic ingredient is probably as yet undiscovered elementary particle — a relic of Big-Bang, namely neutralino (a super symmetric partner of neutrino). In addition to dark matter, the other phenomena which need to be understood beyond the so-called "standard model" of particle physics and can possibly provide an explanation for such a new feature of the universe are: origin of cosmic rays, the existence of gravitational waves (described as "ripples" in space-time) and the mass of neutrinos. It is believed that neutrinos (least understood objects in particle physics and can prove to be good as cosmological probes) can play an important role in testing the evolution of dark energy in the universe.

Now the question arises as to what extent the above-mentioned possible three reasons will suffice in explaining the existence of dark matter and dark energy in the universe to the tune of 96 per cent. The answer is that these explanations will remain inadequate, because (i) the received cosmic rays on earth are already of very weak intensity (of course, their origin, if understood, might provide a better clue in this respect), (ii) gravitational waves are the ripples in the background of space-time — a kind of perturbative correction, and (iii) the mass of neutrino is already negligibly small as it is found to travel with velocity comparable to that of light. Clearly, in such a situation astrophysicists either have to find some better reasons for the existence of dark matter and dark energy in the universe, or else have to resort to account for phenomena whose explanations lie outside the domain of space-time structure of Nature. For example, in the universe, in addition to the inanimate matter, there does exist animate matter too and the same might contribute to the stock of dark matter and dark energy. In fact it is the huge amount of "bio-energy" comprising spiritual energy of living Beings and the same goes undetected by a physical instrument but might contribute to the stock of dark matter and dark energy via action-at-a-time and action-at-a-space-time interactions (cf. Section 1.7).

6.5 Limits on Neuroscience and Brain Studies

As we have only electromagnetic signals received from distant galactic systems in space to tell us about the anatomy and physiology of the universe, electrical events received from brain in response to external or internal stimuli are the only signals at present to tell us about the anatomy and physiology of the brain. That means whether it is the explanation of dark energy or dark matter in the universe or of the attributes of essences of life like emotions, thought, memory, etc. in the brain, the problem is all the same. In fact in either case, the tools and devices used for the purpose at present are bound to show the limitations since both their sensitivity and design basically correspond to the electromagnetic interaction — a physical force — that lies within the domain of space-time structure of Nature; whereas any exploration of emotion, thought and memory, respectively the objects of M, I and E, in the brain would require a different type of device based on interactions beyond space and time. Modern researches in neuroscience have shown that various nerve centres in the brain are responsible for such features of a living Being. We continue our survey here on this aspect of brain studies.

6.5.1 BIOLOGICAL BATTERIES, BRAIN WAVES AND THE BRAIN FUNCTIONING

Human brain contains approximately ten billion nerve cells, each of which can generate a sizeable electrical discharge. In addition to these nerve cells the brain also contains about 100 billion glia cells, each of them is a small biological battery. As a matter of fact a successful packing of such an enormous number of electrical generators into an object — the size of head — is surely a grand design and outstanding feat of Nature. This is especially because the cells co-operate and collaborate so beautifully with one another that make the assembly work successfully. Interestingly, with so many tightly packed electrical generators simultaneously in action, some net electrical output could be measured with recording devices such as those used on single cells. The electrical output of human brain recorded in this way is termed as *brain wave.* The study of such brain waves tapped off the skull of man provides a powerful tool to study further the interactions of brain neurons and glia cells. The nature of brain wave patterns (Doctors call them electroencephalograms or in brief EEGs) while representing the brain functioning in a statistical manner, however, keep on changing with different situations or with different modes of action of the person under study. For example, the patterns are found to be different when a person is asleep and awake, relaxed and excited, solving problems and with his mind "a blank." In fact in these statistical studies, the patterns are standardized for the so-called normal situations over a number of persons and then used for abnormal situations (like the case of an excited or a "mind blank" person, etc.) by way of comparison. Such studies help in tracing diseases (physical or mental, see Appendix D) and in recommending accordingly the medicine by the doctor.

A great deal of modern researches are focused around the fine-tuning of these brain wave patterns and identifying the different nerve centres in the brain responsible for a particular act of behaviour of a human Being. Note that these biological batteries remain in the background of all these studies. It is quite possible that the electrical energy exhibited by these nerve or glia cells is only one aspect of the energy content of the brain and a great deal of the latter remains undetected by the instruments sensitive to electrical or magnetic energy, in the same way as is the case with the dark energy in the universe. To summarize, the devices are still inadequate for the purpose.

6.5.2 COMPUTER, NEURAL NETWORKS AND THE BRAIN

The computer is one of the best gifts to society given by modern science. Particularly, its memory component, microchip in the form of "hard disc," is a wonderful discovery of the time. In spite of the fact that the design and working of a computer in many ways resembles the neural networks and the working of a human brain in the body, the former can never be a complete substitute for the latter. In fact the computer can act the way in which it has been told to act in terms of accumulating the knowledge and taking decisions out of the pool of alternatives supplied already to it. Creativity part in the computer machine is there but to the extent that it has been fed or taught earlier to it and not beyond that. On the other hand, the working of a human brain displays many new creative aspects every moment which can never be expected from a computer. It may be noted that neuroscientists, in spite of their best efforts, could not yet find explanation of the concepts like emotion, thought, memory, etc. which are obvious features of a living Being (and are the functions of inner EOLs namely mind, intellect and ego). However, efforts have been there to locate the nerve centres in the brain which are responsible for such human attributes. After all, the computer is a man-made tool whereas the brain is a God-gifted device. Since computers closely mimic neural networks, one can analyse their functioning to shed some light on the functioning of the human brain. In what follows, we try to understand these human attributes in terms of some analogous ideas from computer workings. In particular, the analogies noted recently by neurosurgeon,

Deepak Ranade[17] in search of a basis for all the three human attributes (namely thought, emotion and memory) in the computer working are discussed below.

6.5.3 RAM-ROM STORY AND THE FREE WILL

Consider the memory aspects of a computer: It has *Read Only Memory* (ROM) and *Random Access Memory* (RAM). ROM is a pre-set programme which cannot be modified and it has the blueprint of basic operations as well as anagrams for processing data. ROM operates and controls vital processes. On the other hand, RAM is a storage device for data and can be erased or modified during its use. While the former comes in the domain of hardware engineer while designing the machine, the latter is meant for the user of the computer. In the same way, every human Being comes with an inbuilt ROM programme and also provided with a RAM, which records all events as they take place in the day-to-day life. RAM serves as input for subsequent encryption into ROM and the latter is then formatted onto the "hard disc" of the individual in successive births. In fact ROM can be considered as the database of all past *karma*s (taken care of at the time of designing) so-called *prārabdha*, whereas RAM corresponds to *sañcita* and *kriyamāṇa* components of an action (cf., entry 2, Table 2.1). The working of a computer is further analysed to understand the role of inner EOLs in human actions, namely of M, I and E.

While thinking appears to be a constant involuntary drone in our working state, often it is the root of many psychosomatic ailments. The process of thinking, on the other hand, is essentially quasi-voluntary and in spiritual life one aims at the state of thoughtlessness. According to neurosurgeons, there is no specific centre in the brain that has been identified as the originator of thoughts. It is also not true that thoughts arise empirically and randomly, rather there is some cause-effect basis for their arising. In fact the perception of outer world lays the

---

17. Deepak Ranade, "Of Memory Templates and Free Will", The Speaking Tree Column, *Times of India*, 12 Sptember 2007.

substrate for thoughts, responses and subsequent actions of a human Being. Thus, perception and thought initiation must have some source code which is *unique* for every individual. Note that such uniqueness is also there with regard to one's emotions and memory as they have different ROMs. Within the framework of patomic model (cf. Appendix A) each of the states M, I and E form a doublet in the sense that all three offer their two aspects as far as the behaviour of b is concerned — short-term and long-term. Short-term (conscious) aspect relates to immediate (moment-to-moment or even day-to-day) actions and reactions whereas long-term (sub-conscious) one relates to their well digested actions and reactions. Analogy of brain functioning with that of a computer emphasizes only the doublet of state E by way of identifying its short-term aspect by RAM and the long-term one by ROM. The latter gives birth to *vāsanā*s.

Each individual has a unique inbuilt ROM programme which contributes not only to thought imitation and perception but also to programme the responses of the individual. As a result, different individuals behave differently to the same external stimuli. The varying reactions are therefore also a function of the operative system.

In fact *vāsanā*s precede thought and thought precedes action and action thereafter generates further *vāsanā*s and this cause and effect cycle produces *karma* for the next generation of ROM. Thus, in principle a human Being should act like an operative system having an inbuilt programme, an encryption of all previous *karma*s and *vāsanā*s. However, he also has free will (a unique feature with the human Being which is not there in the computer) to ignore the inbuilt programme and script a new programme which subsequently gets transferred to the ROM. As a matter of fact free will represents the ability to rebel against the inbuilt programme. A "hardware engineer" has the ability to tap the ROM, but by no means can "he" predict what is going to be written in the RAM.

Ranade[18] further beautifully traces the role of mind in this whole process as follows, "mind is the effecter of ROM. It generates all thoughts as a function of the unique source code of ROM. Unbridled execution of ROM results in impulsive actions. But volitional control can help us overcome the diktat of ROM. With intense determination and control, it can be forbidden to enforce the encrypted script. If efforts are not taken to counter this performed template, life travels along the uncontrolled path determined by the sum total of the past. To script a new ROM is the aim of all *sādhanā*, discipline and meditation. Life vacillates between surrendering to the programme and endeavour to exercise the free will" (see Section 7.4.1).

Generally, the knowledge about brain functioning is extracted by way of modelling its various aspects of study (cf. Section 3.5 and Appendix C). As mentioned, modelling process itself suffers from having some assumptions and approximations, but in a logical manner. Thus arise the limits on these models of neuroscience in providing the true picture of the brain functioning.

6.6 A Living Being is a Continuous Process and not the Product

According to recent guesstimates by biologists there are between 8 and 10 million species present in the world. On the other hand, in Indian philosophy it is generally held that a soul passes through 8.4 million births before it aspires to become a human. What a coincidence? Imagine the foresightedness of Indian *ṛṣis* while they were defining the stage of *mokṣa* (liberation) for a species in general and the human Being in particular and postulating this magical number which has yet to be confirmed by modern researches. Undoubtedly, Indian philosophy supports the theory of rebirth and for that matter each of us must have passed through 8.4 million cycles of births and deaths obviously of different durations corresponding to the lifespan of each species. In each birth, no

18. Deepak Ranade, op. cit.

doubt, there is a possibility of evolution but the maximum is in the form of human. Now the question is, the evolution of what? In fact a living Being is born, and in general passes through various stages like those of a baby, child, adult, youth (with a full growth to contribute in bringing the new generation of the same species), old-age and finally the stage of death, then another birth, and so on. In this sequence there is growth, decay and evolution of various essences of life of a Being while it is in the field of WO. As a result, there is a redevelopment of various FOUs which in turn guide the Being to perform newer and perhaps better (!) actions in each cycle and the same becomes the base for its rebirth in a new or in the same species. Further, growth, decay and evolution are relative with reference to the three forms of gross, micro and causal bodies of a Being. While the gross body and its constituents SE and B undergo the growth and decay in terms of different chemical, biochemical and physiological changes with various reactants and products from time to time, the constituents of the micro-body M, I and E always grow and evolve. However, the causal body remains intact and invariant with respect to such changes in the lower strata, but carries with it some selective experiences to the next cycle of birth and death. As such there is no final product in the process[19] at the highest level except for a continuous evolution of a being for which again feedback comes from the actions performed in a particular lifespan.

Thus, in the context of human Being, each individual is a process and not the product. The process varies from person to person. The enlightened one recognizes and so remains compassionate. That is why we find enlightened souls taking the risk of talking or preaching. In fact teaching to an individual means disturbing the process (hopefully for positive pursuit) of evolution of consciousness which is going on inside him. This evolution of consciousness continues without any end-product, according to Vedānta philosophy, until the soul assimilates with cosmic consciousness, i.e. until the state of *mokṣa* is achieved.

19. Santosh Kumar Kana, "You are a Continuous Process, not Product", The Speaking Tree Column, *Times of India*, 25 August 2007.

6.7 Concluding Discussion

While some glimpses of limitations on the laws of objective science are already given earlier at various places (cf. Section 1.6, Chapter 3, Appendices B and C), here in this chapter we have once again highlighted certain intricate phenomena in the domain of physical and biological sciences whose complete understanding still remains outside the realm of objective science. In view of the fact that the tools of objective science for this purpose are still inadequate, one is naturally inclined to look for other alternatives or to sharpen the existing tools. This might include an account of parameters responsible for the roles of M, I and E of a Being in the study of a given phenomenon.

In the process of analysing once again at a deeper level the domains of working of physical and biological sciences in Sections 6.1 and 6.2, we pinpointed limitations on the study of various branches in these sciences. Whether it is the study of the universe or of the brain, in either case the measuring devices are based only on the knowledge of electromagnetic interactions (cf. Sections 6.4 and 6.5). This clearly indicates the need for other dimensions of study by way of investigating the newer tools sensitive to action-at-a-time or the likes. To this effect several phenomena of interdisciplinary nature are discussed, particularly the limitations of objective science are reviewed in the studies pertaining to OBEs, NDEs, illusion, hallucination and several others. In these cases while sufficient data now exist, the theories available are only speculative and often without a deeper reasoning.

In spite of the fact that all humans have the same set of EOLs, each human Being offers unique and distinct characteristics at a subtle level. This is what the recent researches (cf. Sections 6.3.3 and 6.5.3) are indicating with regard to sense-perceptions, thinking and emotions. Further, the analogy of brain functioning with the computer working (cf. Sections 6.5.2 and 6.5.3) in terms of memory aspects RAM and ROM, strongly supports this fact and suggest a way out to understand rather better the functioning of the most complex human organ like brain. In the philosophical domain, this clearly points to a study of degeneracy of levels of patomic model (cf. Appendix A) to the extent that the behaviour of each individual can be understood distinctly.

The fact that a living Being is a continuous process and not the product is discussed in the context of Vedānta philosophy (cf. Section 6.5). Since there is enough free will attached with each individual, accordingly there are enough opportunities to improve upon the quality of evolution in a given birth so that a good deal of feedback is supplied to "ROM" (cf. Section 6.5.3) of the next birth. Such attempts by an individual might lead him to the state of *mokṣa* (total liberation) at least as a limiting case, if not in practice. In *SMBG*, the Lord clearly brings out this fact through the following verse:[20]

> *prayatnād yatamānas tu yogī saṁśuddha kilbiṣaḥ* ।
> *aneka janma samsiddhas tato yāti parāṁ gatim* ॥ — 6.45 (6.1)

> The *yogī*, however, who diligently takes up the practice, attaining perfection in this very life through the help of latencies of many births, and being thoroughly purged of sin, forthwith reaches the supreme state.

In summary, to experience life in full, in general one has to activate all his EOLs to their maximum extent (which perhaps is possible only by a *yogī*). A common man, however, only activates his SE and B to experience and enjoy the so-called good life. In recent times evolutionary biologists and cognitive neuroscientists are constantly trying[21] to peer ever deeper into the brain with a view to finding physical bases for the concepts like feeling, emotions, moral thoughts, etc. It is found that each individual has his distinct experience of the same sense object mainly because each of us goes with distinct ROM and RAM and has different levels of development of our EOLs in terms of their functions.

---

20. *Śrīmad Bhagavad-Gītā*, (*SMBG*), chapter 6, verse 45, Gorakhpur: Gita Press.

21. N. Fragopanagos and J.G. Taylor, "Emotion Recognition in Human-computer Interaction", *Neural Networks* **18** (2005) 389-405.

Part II
New Analytical Methods and Workability

7

Man-machine Interaction and its Impact on Human Behaviour

In modern times, machines and their use in the life of a common man, whatever may be his profession, or whether he is inside house, or in office or on a job outside anywhere, play an important role. The development of better and better machines and electronic devices and their use by a common man are partly responsible for his changed behaviour in modern society. Use of machines has increased the work-efficiency of a person and made life easy-going but luxurious in several respects. Out of this luxurious life one draws pleasure but often without peace. With this best gift of science, i.e. machine, some people are so much impressed that they do not hesitate in denying the existence of a Super Power or its role in maintaining the world order. But ask the designer of the man-made machines and he will point out the limitations of his designed machine when he compares the same with many God-made machines available around, e.g. the body of a Being (human or otherwise) or its parts like heart, brain, etc. While we postpone the discussion of fundamental processes involving the interaction between animate and inanimate objects (micro-features) leading to man-machine interaction to the next chapter, here we concentrate on the gross features of this interaction responsible for the occurrence of many behavioural aspects of man. For this purpose, we first introduce somewhat elaborative meanings of the terms like "human being," machine and "man-machine interaction" and then discuss the impact of these interactions on the actions and behaviour of a man.

7.1 Man, Woman and Human Being

As per dictionary meaning, a man with feminine characteristic is called "woman" whereas a man with distinct qualities is called "human." Although there might arise a slight difference in the behaviour (at the philosophical level) of a man and woman when they interact with machine, we ignore the same and for all practical purposes we shall consider here the human-machine interaction. In fact distinct qualities can exist in both man and woman to make them human. It is just a matter of developing them in oneself and employing them in day-to-day life. With regard to human Being b a lot has been said earlier (cf. Sections 2.2. and 2.4, and Appendix A) and we emphasize again that it is a complete creation of God consisting of gross, micro and causal bodies, i.e. b $\equiv \mathcal{G} \cup \mathcal{M} \cup \mathcal{C}$ with $\mathcal{G} \equiv$ {SE, B, WO}, $\mathcal{M} \equiv$ {M, I, E}, $\mathcal{C} \equiv$ {SO}. Certainly, such a philosophical definition of a man will throw more light on its interaction with a machine and subsequently on its behaviour in terms of the work-efficiency so achieved. In what follows, we just append some more facts about the biological structure of a human Being — a God-made machine.

- The human brain is 80 per cent water. The brain also uses more than 25 per cent of the oxygen consumed by the human body.
- About 15 million blood cells are produced and destroyed in the human body every second.
- Of all living Beings, only humans sleep on their back. On an average, it takes seven minutes for a human to fall asleep.
- People blink about 17000 times a day. Size of our eyes does not change in our lifetime but nose and ears keep growing.
- Every minute, 40,000 dead skin cells fall from our body. 70 per cent of the dust in our home consists of shed human skin.

- There are more living organisms on the skin of one human Being than there are human Beings on the earth.
- If our mouth was completely dry, we would not be able to distinguish the taste of anything.
- Healthy nails grow about 2 cm every year. Finger nails grow four times as fast as toenails.
- An average person has 100,000 strands of hair on his head. Each hair grows about 5 inches every year.
- Astronauts become 2 inches taller on return from space as the cartilage disks in their spine expand in zero-gravity.
- The body has 1,20,000 km of blood vessels. The heart pumps blood through this labyrinth and back again once every minute.

In fact there are many such peculiarities with human body which God has gifted at the time of its "design." For example, another fact is that sweat helps us in coping with warming. Sweat is our interior coolant — part of a unique human biological machine. The human machine drips and occasionally stalls; at times it acts like an air conditioner — although leaky but efficient. According to researchers in the field, millions of glands in the skin produce sweat, acting as the body's cooling system. The brain controls the process, monitoring body temperature and sending signals through the nervous system to the glands.

7.2 Machine and its Use

A machine or a device is the assembly of a single or several component parts whose working is based on certain physical principles. A device designed normally for a specific purpose, works generally on the basis of a single principle with the same kind of input and output energies. On the other hand, a machine, meant for multipurpose may involve more than one working principles with a possibility of different energies in the input and output domains. This all happens when the component parts of the machine are considered as basic units and isolated systems.

The simplest machine taught in schools is the lever of three kinds. To understand the working of this machine at the school level, one introduces the concepts of load, fulcrum and power. While wheel barrow, handle of a hand-pump and several other such cases are cited as examples of these three varieties of levers, a simple stick or rod can also act as a machine. By definition a machine simplifies and expedites the work to be performed by a person. Even a simple stick can simplify and expedite the work of lifting or shifting a heavy mass, if used intelligently; or a properly designed handle of a hand-pump can lift a huge quantity of water from inside the ground, etc.

Haken, Karlquist and Svedin sometime back discussed[1] the role of machine metaphor in Western culture and its frequent use in interpreting complex systems in Nature and society. The changing conception of machine over time in terms of limitations and pitfalls of machine metaphor are beautifully highlighted.

Historically, the development of machines has passed through a long journey starting from these mechanical levers to the most ultra-modern supercomputers. Although machines may have been used by the early man, yet it appears that a systematic development, motivated towards the welfare of human race, took place mainly after the scientific advancements in the West, i.e. during the last 200 years or so. These developments were accelerated from time to time only after the discovery of several important milestones in science, like that of electricity, electronic devices, solid state devices and transistors, integrated circuits, micro-chip and now nano systems, among others. During this long journey, varieties of energy sources in Nature are exploited by scientists and accordingly they have been used as a guide to improve the models of machines and

---

1. H. Haken, A. Karlquist and U. Svedin (eds.), *The Machine as Metaphor and Tool*, Springer series on Frontiers in Science and Philosophy, 1993.

consequently in making the life of a common man more comfortable and fast. Usefulness of machines can be noted on both the fronts, i.e. in the laboratory research work, in directly assisting in developing newer machines, and in the domain of industry in providing useful appliances for the day-to-day life.

When a machine works, human Being as a single unit has to play a role somewhere in its working and use because the machine is basically meant for his benefit. While in manually driven machines there is a direct role of human Being in their operations, in other large number of machines it is the electricity that supplies the energy and finally get the same converted into other desired forms of energies. It will not be an exaggeration if one says that now electricity is fulfilling the desires of a man which were once fulfilled by a limited manpower and that too not up to his satisfaction. Next, we elaborate on the nature of man-machine interaction and its role in human behaviour.

7.3 Man-Machine Interaction in Physical and Metaphysical domains

At a subtle level the nature of man-machine interaction reduces to that of AI- or IA-type interactions (cf. Section 1.7), the discussion of which we postpone to the next chapter. However, by considering the man as a composite structure in view of patomic model some gross features of this interaction in the physical and metaphysical domains can be explored, which in turn will naturally affect the behaviour of a man in day-to-day life. For this purpose, we consider the machine as an inanimate system working in the domain of WO.

7.3.1 INTERACTION OF B AND SE IN THE PRESENCE OF M

Although an aware biological body, B (note that awareness or alertness is the synonym of consciousness — a property of SO) or the senses of knowledge and action, SE can interact with a machine for a particular purpose, but the role of mind, M, is important. This is because M suggests the purpose of operation and the same categorizes the operating domain of the machine;

otherwise in the absence of M machine may be operated without purpose and perhaps indefinitely. Since the machine is designed by the engineer after taking due care of various pros and cons with regard to its utility without hardly any role of the intellect, similarly, the role of memory, E, is only to the extent that machine is made to operate properly; otherwise a great deal of necessary memory part is already fed in the machine as a recipe for its use at the time of designing. Thus, B and SE interact with the machine either by a direct contact force or by an indirect operation through a remote control apparatus or an agent. While remote control apparatus itself is an inanimate object (or a type of another machine) and its use introduces another new interaction between this apparatus and the machine, the agent on the other hand could be another living Being. The use of these intermediaries leads to a more complex situation and therefore we ignore their role at present.

7.3.2 INTERACTION OF $\mathcal{M}$ IN THE PRESENCE OF B AND SE

When a machine is available for its use, the man interacts with it and the interaction starts at the level of his micro-body, $\mathcal{M}$, (consisting of elements M, I and E) by creating different types of mindsets. In fact in the two cases, when the man has to perform a given action manually or by using a machine, his psychologies differ in terms of gain (output *versus* input energies) and production (product *versus* time). Even if the man is not actually in contact with machine, the forces of the type action-at-a-distance (AAD) and action-at-a-time (AAT) come into existence. The former is attributed to the roles of M and I and the latter to that of E (the constituents of $\mathcal{M}$). In this case the constituents of $\mathcal{M}$ go through all sorts of pros and cons and decide finally about the gain and production by using the machine in actual practice. Thus, the quality and quantity of gain and production by the machine affects a lot the behaviour of the man as an individual and also as a member of his community. If this is the case of a housewife using the kitchen appliances, then such an impact on her behaviour as an individual or as a member of the family can be easily noticed, particularly when she is preparing herself to entertain guests.

In the above case $\mathcal{M}$ directly takes over the machine when B and SE of the man are either passive or spectator; otherwise B and SE in terms of their limitations and fitness can also come on the way to affect the gain and production and subsequently the behaviour of the man.

7.3.3 THE CASE OF MIND-BODY AND BODY-MACHINE INTERACTIONS

Here one should understand the "mind" as $\mathcal{M}$ and the "body" as B and SE. While for the subtle character of mind-body interaction we shall return in the next chapter, here we just discuss the role of these intermediaries in the man-machine interaction. Now the use of a machine becomes a two-stage process and the latter becomes dominant when the same machine needs to be operated by more than one organ of the body. This is normally the case with manually operated machines, like the sewing machine, the apparatus used by the blacksmith to melt the iron, etc. In this case the physical fitness of B and SE (in addition to the mental fitness of the user) is necessary for the desired gain and production. This will accordingly affect the behaviour of the person in both short-term and long-term domains.

There is another interesting situation in which the different organs of the man are operating on different machines as in *fig*. 7.1, or the case of a modern singer playing with different musical instruments with different organs at the same time. During the practice the singer must have had dominating mind-body interactions whereas during the show it is just the body-machine interaction which dominates the scene. The same is the case with the lady in *fig*. 7.1 who is doing hard work in producing the files which are ready for despatch.

fig. 7.1: A case of mind-body and body-machine interactions where different organs are operating on different machines.

7.3.4 MACHINE-MACHINE INTERACTIONS

In modern times two or more machines (robots) can also be allowed to interact, of course, with the possibility that they are operated by the same or different persons at the juncture point. If they are operated by different persons then again the situation as such becomes highly complicated and we ignore here such a case. Such interactions however will finally reduce at the fundamental level to mind-body or body-machine type interactions under certain approximations. Machines can again be of two kinds — one with memory content like the computer (electronically driven instrument) and the other without memory content like manually or electrically driven machines. These days, although the function of several computers can be synchronized conveniently, the case of two interacting computers is personified in *fig*. 1.4. In fact this may be a case of communication between two robots — artificial intelligent machines.

Note that a computer, unlike a human Being, exhibits only the supplied memory content and a limited power of decision-making which in fact is already fed to it. The case of computer showing emotions remains a far cry. As a matter of fact there is no creative aspect of any level in a computer machine. From this point of view, irrespective of the progress in the computer designing, it is never going to replace the function of a (biological) human Being in totality.

7.4 Can the Human Being be a Machine?

In this section we analyse the working of body of a human Being as a machine — physical (working only on the basis of physical laws) or organic (working as a replica of artificially intelligent systems). In the former case, we once again highlight the role of non-physical components in the working and discuss the adaptability of human body to the external appliances placed inside the body from time to time to cure a disease or to improve the working efficiency of an organ, in the second case.

7.4.1 HUMAN BEING AS A PHYSICAL MACHINE WITH ADDITIONAL NON-PHYSICAL COMPONENTS

Note that the body of a human Being (or of any other Being for that matter) in many respects acts as a physical machine. Of course, its working is not completely governed by the physical or biological principles alone. There exist now several concepts and phenomena whose great deal of understanding still remains obscure but requires some new non-physical and non-biological concepts and frameworks for their explanation. While researches are in progress on several fronts in this context, here we just comment on a couple of such cases.

A simple analysis reveals the failure of mass-energy relation or of the law of conservation of energy. Let a person, on an average, consume M kg of mass and excrete m kg per day. Under normal conditions note that M > m. Thus, an excess mass δ = (M-m) kg is being added to the body everyday. If the person lives for, say 60 years, and then the extra mass acquired by the person turns out to be 259600δ kg. Even for δ = 0.1 kg, this figure of acquired mass, i.e. 25960 kg is beyond comprehension in view of the fact that the mass of a 60-year old person is only about 70-80 kg. Now if one accounts for the muscular forces and all the physiological movements derived from the chemical energy produced by the intake mass, even then this huge figure of acquired mass is not understandable. No doubt, a good deal of acquired mass would convert into different types of bio-energies (cf. Section 6.2), yet there exists enough[2] for something called non-physical energy and that could be the energy associated with the elements of micro-body, i.e. M, I and E or as a whole the spiritual energy.

Within the framework of patomic model one can, in principle, visualize the human Being acting as a physical machine consisting of B and SE alone. This is possible by suppressing the roles of soul and $\mathcal{M}$ in the behaviour. This normally happens to a "physically challenged" or "mentally retarded" person or to a person near death, when even though B and SE are present but they stop working because of their non-co-ordination with the elements of $\mathcal{M}$. In such a situation "external agents" (like drugs and medicines) help in activating B and SE but only for a limited duration. Sometimes even the elements of $\mathcal{M}$ also get activated in the background of SO but again for a limited period or during the period for which the external agents are working. Even in this case, the Being does not truly behave like a physical machine, since symbolically:

2. Rabindranath Chattopadhyay, "On the mas-energy relation within human body", *Bulletin Ind. Association of Phys. Teachers*, January 1997, pp. 7-8.

a physical machine consisting of B and SE alone = (human Being)′
= human Being-soul-$\mathcal{M}$
= human organs + workforce among organs,
workforce among human organs = physical force + non-physical force.

This non-physical force is the attribute of micro-body, $\mathcal{M}$, or of soul. In fact the elements of $\mathcal{M}$, combined together in the field of SO, produce a new element called, "will power." In a normal or conscious person, while both "free will" and "will power" are always present in a certain proportion, the former comes to an end in the above situations. A few remarks about these new elements in the context of human Being are in order here:

Free will and will power: "Will power" is some sort of determination (a manifestation of spiritual energy) derived from the innermost existence (i.e. soul) of a Being. It is normally used in overcoming the downward transitions of b in the patomic model. On the other hand, "free will" is the extra dimension attached with a Being which he exercises for his survival between the fields of WO and SO in the language of patomic model. Free will comes with the birth of a Being and the same assists him in creating an "order" out of "chaos" in this world at various stages despite so many constraints and odds during his growth and evolution. In fact life travels along the uncontrolled path determined by the sum total of the past, sometimes as the diktat of ROM (cf, Section 6.5.3). With intense determination and control, it can be forbidden to enforce the encrypted script of ROM. In this process comes the role of free will for its best use so that a new (perhaps better) ROM can be scripted for the next birth; otherwise one surrenders to the programme of the existing ROM.

7.4.2 HUMAN BEING AS AN ORGANIC MACHINE VIS-Ĕ-VIS NEURO-ELECTRONIC SYSTEMS

As a boon of modern science, it has now become possible to replace a body part or an inner organ in the body by its replica mainly to cure a disease or to enhance one's work efficiency. The most important organ of the body is the brain which by and large controls all actions and behaviour of a Being. Even the slightest fault in the working of this controller affects the nature of actions drastically. In the case of a paralysed person, the brain-functioning either stops in parts or becomes faulty. Modern researchers have made it possible to repair such a fault in the brain by way of implanting certain sensors. Not only this, a paralysed person with sensors implanted in his brain has been able to use his thought to move cursor of a computer, to control a television set or a robot. Thus, he can click various software files on the screen and view or operate whatever he wants.

Researchers at the Max Planck Institute, Munich, Germany have been able to develop a working interface between the living tissues of individual neurons and the inorganic compounds of silicon by placing some 16000 transistors and hundreds of capacitors on a tiny 1 mm chip using special proteins (an organic compound) found in the brain to glue the neurons onto it. These proteins not only acted like an adhesive but also provided a link between the ionic channels of neurons and the semiconductor material in a way that electrical signals could be passed to the silicon chip. In fact for the first time the signals were made to establish a two-way electronic dialogue, i.e. from neuron to chip and from chip to neuron.

While such studies with "brain-chip" could be helpful at present in testing the effect of new drugs, they could offer a step further in the direction of developing artificially intelligent systems. Such neuro-electronic systems can possibly help scientists to develop a map of the human brain which in turn might throw light on the way thoughts and emotions rise into consciousness, thereby enabling a complete understanding of how memories are formed. For such fascinating studies, naturally new type of physical-biological-computational models will be required. According to Peter Fromhertz from Max Planck

Institute[3] the discoveries of bio-electronic neuro-computers and microelectronic neuro-prostheses are unavoidable. Although such discoveries may still be years away, the fact is that the studies of man-machine interface at a subtle level has indeed begun.

7.4.3 INTELLIGENT MACHINES AND COMPUTER SIMULATION

It is worthwhile to report several other recent discoveries on artificial intelligence:

(a) Computer pillow to stop snoring:[4] A computerized pillow that shifts the head's sleeping position until the noise stops is discovered by a German computer scientist. It is argued that the smoking — active or passive — enhances the chances of snoring during sleep (reported in *American Journal of Respiratory and Critical Care Medicine*).

(b) Robots with emotions could be the next sapiens:[5] The question whether an intelligent machine can have emotions is under investigation by a European team of researchers consisting of psychologists and neuroscientists. Even if the machine may not feel emotions it can detect whether the emotions felt by a person were genuine or just pretentions; or as to what will happen when a neuroscientist replaces a damaged part of the brain that controls emotions with an artificial implant, etc. In another case, Tufts University researchers are developing technology that could allow computer to read the mind of users. The computers are programmed to respond to user's thoughts of frustration — too much work, boredom, or too little work.

(c) Virtual science laboratories and virtual observatories: With the advent of online scanning, schools are increasingly

---

3. "Organic Machines," Reporting by Mukul Sharma, in *Times of India*, 12 July 2001.
4. "Scientist Invents 'Computer Pillow' to Stop Snoring", reporting in *Times of India*, October 2007, p. 19.
5. "Feeling Good", reporting in *Times of India*, 3 March 2007; Also see, "Coming Soon, PCs that can Read Your Mind", reporting in *Times of India*, 4 October 2007, p. 21.

grappling (particularly in American education system) to strike the right balance between the traditional systems of learning and harnessing the power of the virtual world. Such virtual laboratories will allow students to perform simulated chemical experiments and dissect virtual animals. Similarly, in another case virtual observatories, as an outcome of science of computer simulation, are coming up to supply some virtual (perhaps reliable) data on the galactic systems in the universe. Such developments are still the topics of debate in teaching methods.

(d) Human can still beat a computer:[6] In a poker match against computer machine (i.e. in video games) it is found that humans are better bluffers. Unlike the chess competition, which is marked by extreme concentration and long moments of silence, the video games are based on a fast decision. It is believed that computers may soon dominate the felt-top table, as they have on the chessboard.

(e) A new theory questions whether humans are for real:[7] According to the philosopher Nick Bostrom, Director of the Future of Humanity Institute at the University of Oxford, future civilizations will have enough computing power and programming skills to be able to create what he calls "ancestor simulations." These would be detailed simulations of the simulators' predecessors — detailed enough for the computer-generated minds to be conscious and having the same kinds of experiences we have. It would in fact be an ultra-realistic virtual reality environment, but one where the brains inhabiting the world would themselves be part of the simulation. In such domains of simulated worlds (one after the other) even the existence of real human Being becomes questionable. As in Matrix movies, the intelligent machines in that case will be using the humans (who are living out illusions created in their brains

6. "In Poker Match Against Machine, Humans are Better Bluffers", reporting in *Times of India*, 27 July 2007.

7. "Worlds without End: A New Theory Questions Whether Humans are for Real", reporting in *Times of India*, 20 August 2007.

and they may not have bodies made of flesh) for sinister purposes. The brain would exist only as a network of computer circuitry. This situation can be compared with the Hindu concept of *līlā* — a cosmic game played by the Supreme Power on human Beings. In fact *līlā* describes all reality, including the cosmos, as the outcome of creative play by the Divine Absolute.

These intelligent machines (robots) pre-loaded with programmed responses, are to interact with humans emotionally. Instead of responding from a massive and passive memory bank of reactions, these robots will get into a dynamic feedback loop, receiving sensory inputs from humans they interact with and then, adapting their behaviour accordingly. With computer controlled humanoid facial characteristics to match, they might ultimately appear no different from *homo-sapiens*. As mentioned before, these concepts do not appear more than a science fiction at present.

7.5 Meditation: A Case of Diffusing the Mind-Body Interaction

In this section we discuss a case of self-interaction of human Being. In fact a human Being consisting of B and SE, as argued in Section 7.4.1, can be considered as a physical machine in a restricted sense. In the process of meditation one concentrates himself on watching the dynamics of mind and tries to control or channellize these dynamic (but non-physical) forces. In some sense there is a kind of interaction between the micro-body $\mathcal{M}$ and the gross-body $\mathcal{G}$ of a Being that persists. Note that the SE has the natural tendency to interact with external sense objects in the field of WO, but only in the presence of mind. During meditation, this tendency of theirs needs to be checked and the same happens only after consistent efforts of mind particularly, by engaging the latter in the objects higher than those of sensual nature. This may not be a difficult task to achieve such a state of concentration by a common man for a short while. Difficulty, however, arises in attaining such a state forever and everywhere while living in this world. This requires a lot of practice by an individual. The task may be difficult but not impossible, particularly by those who know the "art of living" (cf. Section 4.3) in this world.

In meditation while mind keeps on making such efforts under the guidance of intellect (or in the presence of *saṅkalpa*) SEs, on the other hand, look for a chance to involve in sense objects, since the human Being has to eat, to see, to smell, to hear, and to touch in the domain of WO for his survival in this world. This continues for the nourishment of his gross body and as long as he is alive. However, he can keep on diffusing this kind of mind-body interaction via meditation everyday provided he has determination (*saṅkalpa*) of doing so and understands the limits not only of SEs but also of enjoying the sense objects. A time comes when the mind is silenced and there are no thoughts or desires, whatsoever. At this stage one realizes as to who and what he really is — the vast, eternal consciousness.

7.6 Concluding Discussion

As an example of surface-level study of IA- or AI-type (cf. Section 1.7) interactions of day-to-day life, the case of man-machine interaction is presented in this chapter. While we continue our discussion at a more fundamental level in the next chapter, from the survey made here it can be noticed that man-machine interaction do affect the working and the lifestyle of a common man of modern society.

After introducing a detailed meaning of the words "man" and "machine," the concept of non-physical interactions between the man and machine is proposed. For a situation when a person is interacting with a more sophisticated machine of recent times, i.e. a computer or a robot, the existing physical forces alone are found to be inadequate to understand the resulting interaction. For this purpose, an account of AAD- and/or AAT-type forces in addition to the contact force becomes necessary.

Within the framework of patomic model a "microscopic" analysis of the nature of man-machine interaction is carried out with reference to micro and gross bodies of a man. In some cases the two-stage interaction, i.e. of mind-body and body-machine, is found to play a role. In view of a considerable progress on artificial intelligence or on robot technology, the importance of the cases like man-machine-machine or man-man-machine interactions is suggested. The important question whether a human Being can act as a physical machine is addressed. In this context the role of additional non-physical components (like the elements of the micro-body $\mathcal{M}$), present in a human Being, is discussed. These non-physical elements in a man in fact make him a "distinct machine" from a physical one. In view of several successful transplantations of human organs by the artificial ones or successfully affecting the memory aspect of brain by inserting/glueing a microchip in it, the case of a new type of human machine is discussed. In particular, the limitation of the predictive power of neuroelectronic systems *vis-à-vis* brain functioning are highlighted. On the other hand, the machines with artificial intelligence, i.e. robots equipped with a variety of sensors and working on the basis of computer simulation, are expected as a good replacement of a human or a non-human Being in several situations. No doubt these artificial machines can act as a living Being but they can never be a corresponding human or non-human because there will always remain a lack of non-physical components in these machines, no matter to whatever extent science advances.

It may be mentioned that like the man-machine interaction man-medicine (which in general may be a chemical or a drug) interaction also affects the human behaviour. As a matter of fact, the behaviour of a common man, as mentioned on earlier occasions, is very sensitive to the access to sense objects. For that matter why only the medicines but any sense object to which the person has weakness or addicted to, could be a good cause for a change in his behaviour. Even non-humans are not free from this disease. For example, several animals, birds and insects are found to be sensitive not only to chemicals, eatables, musical sounds, etc. but also to machines. The presence of a gun or stick affects their behaviour as one can note in a circus. There are many cases where insects are found sensitive to eatables whereas several animals like elephant, deer, snake, etc. are sensitive to music or to other sense objects even sometimes more than a man. In summary, man-machine interactions as well as man-medicine interaction do affect the behaviour of both a man and also a non-human.

8

Interaction Between Human Being and Physical World

As discussed in Chapter 1, out of AA, AI, IA and II type two-body systems it is only the II type along with AAD-type forces that is successfully investigated in physical theories. For other systems and associated interactions physical theories however have not been pursued to the same extent and depth. In this chapter we shall focus on the case of AI (or IA) type systems and investigate the associated interactions originating as a result of their detailed structures in the realm of consciousness.

It is the consciousness present inside a Being in general and in the human Being (b) in particular that creates not only the (outer) physical world but also the concepts of space, time, geometry and other related physical properties. In this chapter, the outer physical world consists of inanimate (I) objects and the animate (A) object is the human Being of patomic model (cf. Appendix A) and they constitute an IA-type system in general. As a single unit, no doubt, the human Being perceives the physical world but the fact is that both (human Being and physical world) have composite structures and their interaction via the process of perception is not so simple as it appears. Vedic sciences have clearly suggested the description of both — for the human Being it is the patomic model and for the physical world in terms of *pañca mahābhūtas* (*PM*s). With regard to their interaction, it is the outcome of many intricately interwoven processes taking place between the EOLs of b and the *PM*s of physical world. While the biological body B alone has been considered as composite of *PM*s in Vedānta philosophy, the effect of *PMs* has also been hinted on other EOL in astrological sciences (cf. Appendix D). Thus, the detailed structures of both play a dominant role in the realization of physical world by a living Being in general and by the human Being in particular.

It may be reminded here that the objective science — gifted mainly by the West — has developed and established certain pictures of the outer world in terms of laws of physics and also of human Being in terms of laws of biology. No doubt this "setting" seems to work beyond one's expectations today but the fact is that these descriptions, as argued earlier (cf. chapter 6), remain incomplete and the laws show limitations in the context of larger number of phenomena in Nature than the ones understood so far. Therefore, new frameworks for physical world, human Being and their interaction(s) become desirable and the same may serve either as an alternative or a supplement to the existing "setting" and that too in terms of the philosophy of the East.

The arrangement of the chapter is as follows: After revisiting the physics aspect of the interaction between human Being and physical world in Section 8.1, the phenomenon of consciousness and its role in human actions is discussed in Sections 8.2 and 8.3 in a variety of ways. In particular, with regard to its manifestation in various actions, performed by EOLs and body parts, a 3/2-rule is proposed in Section 8.3.3. A fine-tuning of the classical *pañcīkaraṇa* rule is carried out in Section 8.4 by suggesting its repeated use in generating highly dressed EOLs with consciousness. This helps in bringing them in a dynamic mode towards the performance of an action. The proposed *trikaraṇa* rule for inner EOLs and *dvikaraṇa* rule for outer EOLs as the off-shoots of the *pañcīkaraṇa* rule further define several new inner EOLs which in turn participate in the interactions inside a human Being. In Sections 8.5 to 8.8 altogether new methods of analysing the human actions in rigorous mathematical terms are presented. The derived space-time-consciousness (STC) evolution equations in Section 8.7 are expected to provide explanation of various human actions and experiences. Similar are the hopes from the derived mathematical conditions for an optimum mindset in Section 8.8 towards the performance of an action. Section 8.9 is devoted to develop a model to understand the role of mindset in human actions by way of setting a non-linear differential equation for its evolution. Once again we classify the interactions between EP-matter particles on the basis of details of consciousness involved in Section 8.10. By way of discussing the universality of sex and sexual processes as the roles of *prakṛti, puruṣa* and their interactions in Section 8.11, we bring out another important aspect of the interaction between human Being and physical world. Finally, concluding remarks are made in Section 8.12.

8.1 Revisiting the Physics-Aspect of the Interaction

It is only the II type case along with AAD-type interactions which is investigated in physics (cf. Sections 1.6 and 1.7). Again these are certain specific characteristics of the object in physics like the mass, Coulomb charge, weak charge or the colour charge which characterize the nature of interaction between the inanimate objects, viz. gravitational, electromagnetic, weak or strong, respectively. If the objects also carry consciousness or are the source of consciousness (like a living Being), then the physical laws remain silent in spite of the fact that consciousness is there in the background of the creation of mass, Coulomb charge, weak charge or the colour charge. On the other hand, certain physical theories (like the Kaluja-Klein case in grand unified theories) also argue that these specific characteristics of an object are the outcome of compactification of the original infinite dimensions present in space-time continuum to the finite ones and the hierarchy of these characteristics appears at different levels of compactifications depending upon the relative strength and range of the underlying interaction.

If one understands the infinity in a broad sense, then the word "infinite dimensions" is the other name of continuum of some fundamental field. Now the questions that arise are: what creates and who realizes this fundamental field? The answer is simple. It is the individual's conscious mind (i.e. M in conjunction with I and E) that supplies the idea of fundamental field and the same is accepted by a selective community of persons whose "mindset" is already tuned to the same degree of evolution of consciousness. It is the source of consciousness present in an individual who is capable of realizing the fundamental field of physics. In fact this fundamental field and the field of cosmic consciousness are synonymous. It is quite possible that the process of second quantization (the conversion of continuum into a discrete or granular form) takes place in the same cosmic consciousness field at the two fronts (depending upon one's approach) — one directly in the space-time domain by physicists leading to the origin of inanimate objects and the other by spiritualists first in the domain of consciousness itself leading to life (a quantum of consciousness) in an individual Being (of course, with varying degree and magnitude of consciousness) then in the next stage, this consciousness creates space and time. Perhaps human Being turns out to be a "perfect" product of this later process as it is equipped with a complete set of EOLs capable of creating a "perfect" physical world. However, due to the limitations of physical instrument or of these EOLs with regard to their developments, an individual is not able to visualize the "perfectness" of this world.

Needless to say, a living Being is also an inanimate object of physics in the absence of consciousness. Since the living Being and the inanimate object are created out of the same fundamental field, they can be considered as bubbles in the same medium as a result of a semblance of nucleation mechanism. As they have a common factor in the root, they cannot remain in isolation, particularly a "conscious" bubble is better equipped compared to the unconscious one since the former also has a component of the latter present in it. It is the physicist's conscious mind that has created the inanimate bubble; otherwise unconscious physicist himself is an inanimate object. Not only this, some physicists knowingly or unknowingly or rather judiciously suppress such a feeling of universality of consciousness while framing their laws in terms of probability or indeterminism.

With these pictures of human Being and physical world in mind we now proceed to discuss their interactions in the following sections. However, before that to happen, an elaboration of the intricately interwoven network of consciousness and space-time is needed.

8.2 Further Remarks on Consciousness

In the context of interaction between human Being and physical world, it is better to have a broad picture of consciousness which in fact is quality-specific of a Being in general and the human Being in particular. Beside that the element of consciousness in a human Being is discussed in Vedānta philosophy to the finest degree, it has also been the subject of formal study in modern times.[1] While the temporality and eternity aspects of consciousness have been the subject of study through human time-consciousness and human space-consciousness phenomena, their studies at the absolute scale somehow have not gone beyond the Vedāntic thought. Recent Article by Anthony Savari Raj[2] based on the thesis of R. Panikkar[3] is a good eye-opener on such a particular aspect of human time-consciousness. Here, however, our survey will focus on the studies of consciousness at an absolute scale.

8.2.1 CONSCIOUSNESS: AN ABSOLUTE REALITY

Consciousness is more of a phenomenon than a concept. As the switching on of a bulb in a dark apartment makes the household items visible and realizable, in the way the invoking of consciousness in the EOLs of a Being brings in the entirety of physical world. No doubt the household items were already there

---

1. L. Anthony Savari Raj, "Towards Trans-historical existence: Cross-cultural Relations on Human Time-consciousness", *Indian Philosophical Quarterly*, 34 (2007) no. 1, pp. 61-74.
2. L. Anthony Savari Raj, op. cit.
3. R. Panikkar, "Towards a Typology of Time and Temporality in the Ancient Indian Tradition", *Philosophy East and West*, 24 (1994) no. 2, pp. 161-64.

in the apartment in the absence of light but a part of electromagnetic radiation emanating from the bulb (VIBGYOR) makes the items visible and its infra-red and ultra-violet parts also contribute to their physical realization if not to visualization. Similarly, the space-time and the interplay thereof could be only one of the multifaceted aspects of consciousness which makes the world realizable, otherwise other aspects are equally responsible for working of EOLs in the domain of non-physical world inclusive of the inner EOLs. As mentioned in previous chapters, in the presence of consciousness EOLs of a Being however start playing a dual role, i.e. as an observer and also as a realizer through the process of scrutiny of actions. Secondly, the consciousness manifests differently through different EOLs in terms of the varying value of μ (the meditation parameter) in the same way as the varying values of the incoming photon-frequency resolves the matter at different levels of its structure.

Ramesh S. Balsekar establishes[4] consciousness as the absolute reality which pervades the real (physical) and unreal (non-physical) through several examples and logical arguments. According to him, "the appearance of universe exists in infinite consciousness, just as the notion of distance or emptiness exists in space. . . . Consciousness alone exists. It creates the illusion of the world appearance and the ego-sense, and perceives the illusion of diversity in what is truly pure Oneness." He further elaborates, "The universe exists in consciousness like future waves in a calm sea — only apparently different in potentiality." Similarly, "while the shadow of an object by itself has no existence and is therefore unreal, the shadow is not different from the object when seen together."

In fact Beings in general and human Beings in particular are like bubbles in the sea of consciousness which are constantly formed and subsequently decay in the sea itself. Balsekar further comments on the working and dreaming states of consciousness,

4. Ramesh S. Balsekar, "Consciousness Pervades the Real and Unreal", The Speaking Tree Column, *Times of India*, 20 Ferbruary 2008.

"The phenomenal objectification of this pure subjectivity appears and functions in our outer world of consciousness in the *waking state* precisely like sentient and insentient objects seem to exist and function in the inner world of consciousness in the *dream state*. Nothing really happens."

Thus, the theory of Balsekar hints at the infinity of consciousness which turns out to be an absolute reality out of which the sentient and insentient modes of Nature not only originate but their interplay in the inner world becomes the biggest truth of one's life. It is worth comparing some of these ideas with the ones advanced earlier in terms of cosmic consciousness and the existence of an all-pervading fundamental field.

8.2.2 POSSIBILITY OF A NEW AGE OF CONSCIOUSNESS AND THE YOGĪ OF VEDIC SCIENCE

According to biologists[5] an evolutionary mutation of consciousness is just round the corner. In the history of evolution, whenever a critical mass of members of a species adapts to a new way of being, mutation happens and the species evolves. It is believed that a new level of human consciousness is on the verge of emerging. The existing human race is fast approaching the critical mass. In fact there must have been a period, just before we became full-fledged *homo-erectus*, when some of us were still using our forelegs for walking while others were using these as hands with increasing dexterity and perhaps already walking on two's. And when suddenly a critical mass was reached, every-one started following the new model. Accordingly mutated off-springs were born with erect walk and dexterity already programmed into their DNA. Even today one finds a host of individuals around us who are struggling with challenges of unconsciousness in terms of multiple identities of ego we live from. As soon as enough of us become consciousness-conscious, that critical mass will be achieved.

5. Neelam Mehta, "Age of Consciousness Just Round the Corner", The Speaking Tree Column, *Times of India*, 13 March 2007.

While this picture of new age of consciousness has emerged and is supported by consciousness pioneers in the light of advancing technologies and developments in the science of psychology, it is based on certain observations and researches in this field. For example, it has been found that "human brain works only at a tenth of its capacity" or "the quantum of conscious memory is far far greater than the conscious material in the human mind." Tripping or the use of stimulants enhances our mind capacity only marginally and results are dramatic: creative insights, spiritual highs and, even ecstasy. Imagine a new reality where instead of marginal access, the whole domain of consciousness is accessible. No doubt, such may be the speculations of biologists and consciousness pioneers of present times, but the fact is that Vedic sciences have already been advocating the existence of such a human race — called *yogīs* who also have evolved their consciousness to the highest degree as a result of their practice and sacrifice but not necessarily genetically.

8.3 Consciousness and Space-Time

8.3.1 AN INTRICATELY INTERWOVEN CONNECTION: THREE ASPECTS OF CONSCIOUSNESS ON THE SUBSTRATUM OF SELF

No doubt the space and time are the creation of consciousness (as argued earlier) but the point is that the process which creates them is very intricate. Often this creation goes unnoticed to an individual and becomes difficult to realize as to at which stage of human actions and expressions in the outer world the space time oı its notion comes into existence. It is only in the reverse process when one withdraws the senses of knowledge and action from their objects of the outer world and undergoes a thought process in the "mood" of meditation. The limitations of the concept of space-time are noticed as the mental processes now start superseding the space-time-mediated processes. Vedānta philosophy emphasizes three basic stages of consciousness that exist at the substratum of Self, and through which an individual undergoes during his

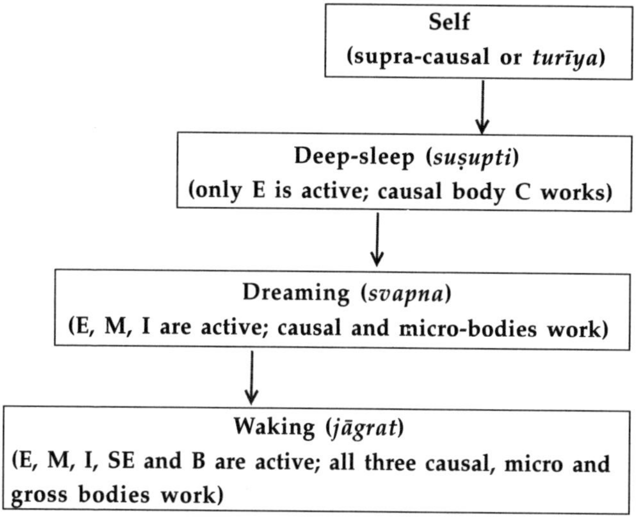

fig. 8.1: Chart displaying the grading of three stages of consciousness namely waking, dreaming and deep-sleep on the substratum of Self.

daily routine. *Fig*. 8.1 displays a kind of grading of these stages of consciousness.

Spirituality basically focuses on understanding the true nature of our inner self or pure consciousness (a second quantized version of its infiniteness discussed in Section 8.2) and is concerned with delving into the source from which the ego E (or "I-thought") emanates.[6] This stage of consciousness is outside the domain of *cause* and *effect*. This is the supra-causal or *turīya* state achieved by a *yogī* as a result of his deep meditation. In fact at this stage the cause and effect (or the seen and seer) merge into one and become inseparable. The next stage is deep-sleep or *suṣupti* in which only the ego E remains active and the rest of EOLs are passive. Note that the ego E or the feeling of Self or the "I-thought" is a representative of the causal body. In fact E identifies itself with the causal body and is not aware of physical ($\mathcal{G}$) or micro ($\mathcal{M}$) bodies. In the dreaming (*svapna*) state the ego loses identity with the physical body of the waking state and identifies itself with micro, subtle or astral body. It perceives

6. Deepak Chopra, "Time is an Illusion", a reporting in the Times Wellness Column, *Times of India*, 31 December 2007.

the dream world at a subtle level. The EOLs, E, M and I are active. The "I-thought" continues to be in operation in the form of perceiver.

In the *waking* state, the ego E or the "I-thought" identifies itself with the gross body *G*, and perceives as well as experiences the physical universe through the senses of knowledge and action (SEs) and the biological body B. All the EOLs are active in this case in the field of WO. It may be mentioned that in both dreaming and waking states, the duality of consciousness is observed in the form of perceiver and the perceived. It is only in the *turīya* state (which represents the highest form of knowledge) that the perceiver and the perceived become one and the ego E is traced back to its source, i.e. Self (soul). In this process ego loses its identity. This in fact is the state of self-realization which one attains only after a long practice.

As one passes through the stages from *suṣupti* to *jāgrat*, the notion of space-time starts emerging in a manner which is really so fine that it goes unnoticed to a common man. While there is no feeling for space-time in the *suṣupti state*, it manifests in *svapna state* but in the imaginary plane (cf. Section 8.4), of course, with a component in real life. At the level of *jāgrat state* it is all space-time of physicists which hardly has any imaginary part of philosophers.

While space may be a reality in terms of existence of distance or emptiness in it, time is only an illusion. It is just a notion. For this reason, Einstein perhaps considered time variable along the imaginary axis of space-time continuum. Deepak Chopra beautifully comments[7] on the connection between space-time and consciousness in terms of non-locality. According to him "though we might find expressions in localized terms and phenomena, the mind is non-local which means it is not confined to one location. Time, too, is non-local. The fact that we localize time is a perceptual artifact based on the quality of attention." Note that in the present context, the quality of

---

7. Deepak Chopra, op. cit.

attention means the degree of concentration or the value of meditation parameter μ. At another place he emphasizes,

> . . . time is illusion, it is an internal dialogue we use to explain our experience or perception of change and relationship. Consciousness is infinite, unbounded and eternal, which means it has no beginning, no end and no edges or boundaries in time. . . . Time is the way consciousness measures the space or gap between one experience and another. Consciousness creates the experience of time and space.

This is how one understands the intricately interwoven connection between space-time and consciousness and the creation of the former in the domain of the latter. As a matter of fact the space-time continuum creates the experience of cause and effect and the same in turn creates the experience of physical world of *jāgrat* state.

8.3.2 STATIC AND DYNAMIC MODES OF CONSCIOUSNESS

(a) Changes in Space-time: Inertia, Inertial Force and Inertial Frames: In an attempt to quantify the natural phenomena occurring in the space-time domain, Newton advanced his three laws of motion about 350 years ago. According to Newton's first law, if a body is at rest or in motion it will remain in the same state unless an external force is applied on it. When such an external force is applied, according to the second law, it causes change in the velocity and this change with respect to time defines the applied force itself after accounting for the inertial property of the body, i.e. mass. If the applied force does not produce a change in the velocity, then force is said to be inertial force and the co-ordinate system in which the motion is described is called inertial frame. If not only the rate of change but also the rate of the rate of change of velocity of the body does not vanish, then this reference co-ordinate system defines the non-inertial frame. Root of these notions lies in the concept of *absolute space* perceived by Newton. Then the question arises as to who is the realizer or perceiver of this absolute space. Further, why only the first derivative of position (i.e. velocity) or the first derivative of velocity (i.e. acceleration) becomes important in these descriptions of nature. Perhaps nature likes it this way; otherwise there is no reason as to why one should ignore the role of higher derivatives of position or velocities in these descriptions. It is quite possible that some of these features of space-time are already compacted into the concept of inertia or the inertial property of the body, i.e. mass. Mach noticed such problems with the Newtonian dynamics and came out with a generalized concept of inertia and inertial property.

According to Mach principle,[8] the property of inertia is not an intrinsic property of the particle but it depends on the existence of a background. The contribution to this background comes from other distant masses present in the Universe. This was the kind of generalization of the concept of absolute space of Newton in terms of non-locality. Cosmos is nothing but an absolute space in which the universe itself exists. For physicists the absolute space is a reality and the notion of time in it is imaginary. On the other hand, for philosophers or spiritualists, this absolute space is in the background of another all-pervading field called cosmic consciousness field which in turn supplies the "perceiver" of this absolute space.

(b) Changes in the Sea of Consciousness: While the changes in the space-time sector of the fundamental field of cosmic consciousness are explored by physicists, the changes in the fundamental field itself are explored by spiritualists. This latter class of changes does occur in two major stages. First at the creation stage of a Being in which the Being appears as a kind of second-quantization of the fundamental field of cosmic consciousness. Thus, the seed of consciousness is carried through this process and the same continuously manifests in the living Beings. When a living Being performs actions through its EOLs in this world, it also produces changes in the field of cosmic consciousness at the second stage. Note that in its original version the seed of consciousness in a Being was a pure quantum.

---

8. See, for example, J.V. Narlikar, *General Relativity and Cosmology* (The Macmillan Company of India, Ltd. 1978), Lecture 1.

However, its purity gets polluted as a result of repeated impact of actions of EOLs during its various cycles of births and deaths. In fact in a particular cycle this seed, in conjunction with the action of inner EOLs, gathers with it the effect of actions performed (*saṁskāras*) and carries the same to the next cycle and then to the next, and so on. It is quite possible for a human Being to restore the purity of such a polluted quantum or the seed of consciousness by repeated efforts in only one or in several cycles. Once it is done, then it becomes ready for the merger in the sea of consciousness or for the liberation. Only a conscious human Being is capable of recognizing these changes in the sea of consciousness; otherwise for many of us these changes go unnoticed.

(c) Consciousness at Rest and Consciousness in Action: Consciousness in human actions (or for that matter in the actions of any living Being) manifests through two modes — static and dynamic. (Note that this dynamism[9] is not with respect to time alone but also with respect to the meditation parameter, μ). When the actions of a Being become routine type, the static mode of consciousness at a certain level of EOLs is sufficient to perform them. However, a desire for any change in the routine actions brings in the role of dynamic mode of consciousness. Again this dynamism could arise at any level of EOLs namely inner or outer EOLs. The following two examples will elaborate this point further:

Example 1: A person who is walking straight along the footpath (static mode of consciousness) wishes to take a turn on the next crossing of a road. This wishing (role of E) will bring the dynamism in his intellect. Not only this, dynamism

9. In the Newtonian world it is the time parameter and the implicit or explicit dependence of the physical observables on this parameter that brings in the dynamism in the system. However, in the spiritual domain we talk of meditation parameter μ and the implicit or explicit dependence of actions on this parameter brings in a kind of dynamism in the actions. No doubt space and time can also play a role in the actions of outer EOLs, namely SE and B but for inner EOLs, namely E, I and M, it is only μ that plays the dominant role and defines the "quality" of actions.

will further act through his senses and body so that he can actually and safely take the turn at the crossing. Moreover, if the person is getting late to his office or the assignment he is given, then this dynamism will be of different nature — varieties of provisions will come to this intellect with a dressing by his mind particularly with regard to the modes of transport if available. In the absence of provisions for transport, he can think of speeding up his walk by keeping the time-factor in mind. Thus, in human actions dynamic mode of consciousness dominates and it is more frequent than the static one. The efficiency of this dynamism is obviously linked with the trio of space-time-consciousness (cf. Entry 7d, Table 2.1).

Example 2: For the walking person in example 1, if another person happens to meet him on the way (or a non-human Being for that matter), then the Pandora box of his consciousness opens up in a different style. Not only this, if the second person is a neighbour, relation (among relations again happens to be his spouse), friend (boy or girl), co-passenger, office colleague, or a stranger, then the dynamics of consciousness becomes accordingly different in different situations. We shall return to some of these discussions in the next chapter.

(d) A Practical Realization of Consciousness: If one is tuned to the right frequency only then he can realize the source or the cosmic source of consciousness. Think of yourself as a radio set. The God station is speaking to you at frequencies that you are not tuned into, otherwise a simple remembrance of God can bring you in tune with Him. Recent experiments in higher consciousness show that people begin to have holy experiences and vision while vibrating (!) at above 200,000 cycles per second, whereas non-meditator vibrates at about 350 cycles per second. To realize the God force (or to raise the vibration frequency), daily prayer, silent meditation, choosing love over hatred and fear, etc. are necessary.

(e) The Trio of Space-time-consciousness: Like several triads known in the Vedānta philosophy with regard to the action of a human Being (cf. Table 2.1), the trio of space-time-concentration (or of space-time-consciousness) (cf. Entry 7d, Table 2.1) is essentially a pivotal one. In fact for the case when the consciousness is in action, its role in the space-time mediated events becomes important. This happens in spite of the fact that space-time has hardly any role in the workings of inner EOLs and a maximum role in the workings of outer EOLs. It is only in the overlapping region where the consciousness (through the "intensity" of meditation or concentration) shows dramatic effects on the output of actions performed by EOLs in a coherent manner. To this effect, several examples can be cited from day-to-day life: (i) "time sharpens the mind" — when a person is approaching a crucial or auspicious date and time at which an action needs to be performed (e.g. the date of examination for a student, a date of lecture for a Professor, or a date of ceremonial function, etc.), then it is found that EOLs like E, I, M in general are aligned and become more efficient respectively in terms of memory, decisions and grasp, etc. (in a way it is the example of consciousness in action). (ii) "Space and time appear to be elongated when two loving hearts are approaching to meet." These loving hearts could be of husband and wife, mother and son, two close friends, etc. (iii) Many such examples can be traced in human behaviour, particularly from the analysis of "chemistry of love" or from the "code of body-actions" used to communicate with deaf and dumb.

In summary, not only the birth-death cycles of a Being but also the actions performed by a conscious person in the space-time domain of day-to-day life produce ripples (or leave some impact) in the sea of consciousness. It is a different thing that these ripples are of different "intensity" and "durations" in certain terms. Contrary to this, space and time are the creations of consciousness. There are indications in modern scientific researches that thoughts create matter or influence the dance of atom.[10]

---

10. Kambiz Naficy, "Are You Tuned into the Right Frequency?", The Speaking Tree Column, *Times of India*, 31 December 2007; Also see, "Metaphysics of the Physical World", The Speaking Tree Column, *Times of India*, 23 January 2007.

8.3.3 POSSIBILITY OF A (3/2)-RULE IN MANIFESTATION OF CONSCIOUSNESS

The quantum of cosmic consciousness present in a living Being manifests differently through various EOLs and the actions performed by them in the field of WO. For a conscious person (who is aware of the working of various EOLs and their interactions with WO), this manifestation is noticeable even by the tip of his hair on the body as far as the contact force is concerned; otherwise the roles of AAD, AAT, or AADT-type forces in various actions of day-to-day life are also known. For example, consciousness (in the form of sensation or through the associated bio sensors) is found to work for a blind person in having a feeling for the presence of his near and dear (kith and kin); or similarly, for a deaf person, in having a feeling for hearing his near and dear.

Peculiar are the ways of combination and co-ordination of the fragmented components of consciousness in a body particularly when it is in action through different EOLs. What a beautiful network of co-ordination among these fragmented components of consciousness is provided by God that leads to the success of an action! Physical or biological theories are apparently incapable of explaining these workings and co-ordinations and also their impact on the nature and quality of an action. To understand this, an analogy with the concept of "collapse of wave-function" in the quantum measurement problem is perhaps worth quoting here.

In the probabilistic interpretation of quantum mechanics, the wave-function (also called probability amplitude) and its space-time evolution describe the motion of a microscopic physical particle. In order that the particle be localized both in space and time the wave function is made to vanish at large distances. On the other hand, a quantum state (wave-function) of the particle expressible as a superposition of a class of rather well defined states (called eigenstates) instantaneously collapses or reduces to a particular well defined state out of many possibilities. This happens by way of suspending its evolution during the process of measurement. This feature of quantum measurement (popularly known as the "collapse" of the wave function), though suffers from some drawbacks can, however, be extended to understand the collapse of consciousness in the present case. In fact the consciousness, while manifesting (or emanating) through different outlets of EOLs including the tips of hair on the body in varying proportions, however, collapses (or reduces) to its maximum fraction (i.e. unity) along a particular outlet of EOLs or along a tip of a strand on the body. This happens for a conscious person who is in direct interaction with the elements of WO through that particular outlet of EOLs. Whole consciousness in fact gets focused through that outlet and provides the perception of the object concerned.

As such it is difficult to quantify the fraction of consciousness attached to a particular EOL especially when it is in action, however, a simple "3/2-rule" of its fragmentation is suggested here for the case when the consciousness works in its static mode. According to this "3/2-rule" the considered one unit of consciousness with the root, SO, divides in the 3:2 ratio between the important and less important EOLs at every stage of its fragmentation. Although it is difficult to decide the importance of one organ over the other, author's common sense has prevailed in taking such a decision. After all, one has to start from somewhere in order to have a feel for the quantification of such an abstract phenomenon like consciousness.

To start with, first division of consciousness in the ratio 3:2 takes place between the micro body $\mathcal{M}$(={E, I, M}) and the gross body $\mathcal{G}$(={SE, B}) with fractions (3/5) and (2/5), respectively. At the next stage 3/5 of 3/5 (i.e. 9/25) fraction goes with the mind M and 2/5 of 3/5 (i.e. 6/25) goes jointly with ego E and intellect I. On the other hand, 3/5 of 2/5, i.e. 6/25, goes with the senses of knowledge and action (SE) and 2/5 of 2/5, i.e. 4/25 goes with the biological body.

As shown in the "inverted tree" of consciousness in *fig.* 8.2, this kind of division of consciousness continues in the ratio 3:2 at every stage of its fragmentation. Finally, it turns out that a very small fraction goes with the tip of fingers or of a strand. Note that in *fig*. 8.2, the expansion of some of the branches of inverted tree is not shown, but the corresponding extension, among further finer details of an organ or an EOL can be carried out and the corresponding fraction of consciousness can be attached according to the same 3/2-rule. For example, the branch at skin carrying the consciousness fraction (CF) as (72/3125) can be extended to pores and flat parts of the skin, then the fractions of consciousness attached with them turns out to be as 3/5 of 72/3125, i.e. (216/15625) with pores and 2/5 of (72/3125), i.e. (144/15625) with the flat part respectively. Now if one gives more weightage to the pores in the head (which have links directly with the brain) than those in the rest of the body, and assumes that there is a strand attached with every pore throughout the body, then 3/5 of (216/15625), i.e. 648/78125 fraction of consciousness goes with the hair in the head and the rest 2/5 of (216/15625), i.e. (432/78125) goes with strands in the rest of the body. Now if the average number of strands in the head of a person is about 10^5, then the fraction of consciousness attached with the tip of a strand is $648 \times 10^{-5}/78125$ units ~ 8.3×10^{-8} units. This fraction will be progressively smaller with the strands on the other parts of body. The interesting point is that this small fraction collapses to one unit as and when the consciousness of mind is aligned with a particular strand in the event of its stretching, etc.

8.3.4 ACTIVE AND PASSIVE ESSENCES OF LIFE

One can say that there are three modes of consciousness which play the roles in the actions performed by various EOLs. In addition to the static and dynamic modes discussed in Section 8.3.2, there is also a zero mode of consciousness. The case of a dead body is the example of zero mode of consciousness. Note that the dynamism in the EOLs is the result of *saṅkalpa*s which originate at a higher level and the implementation of the same

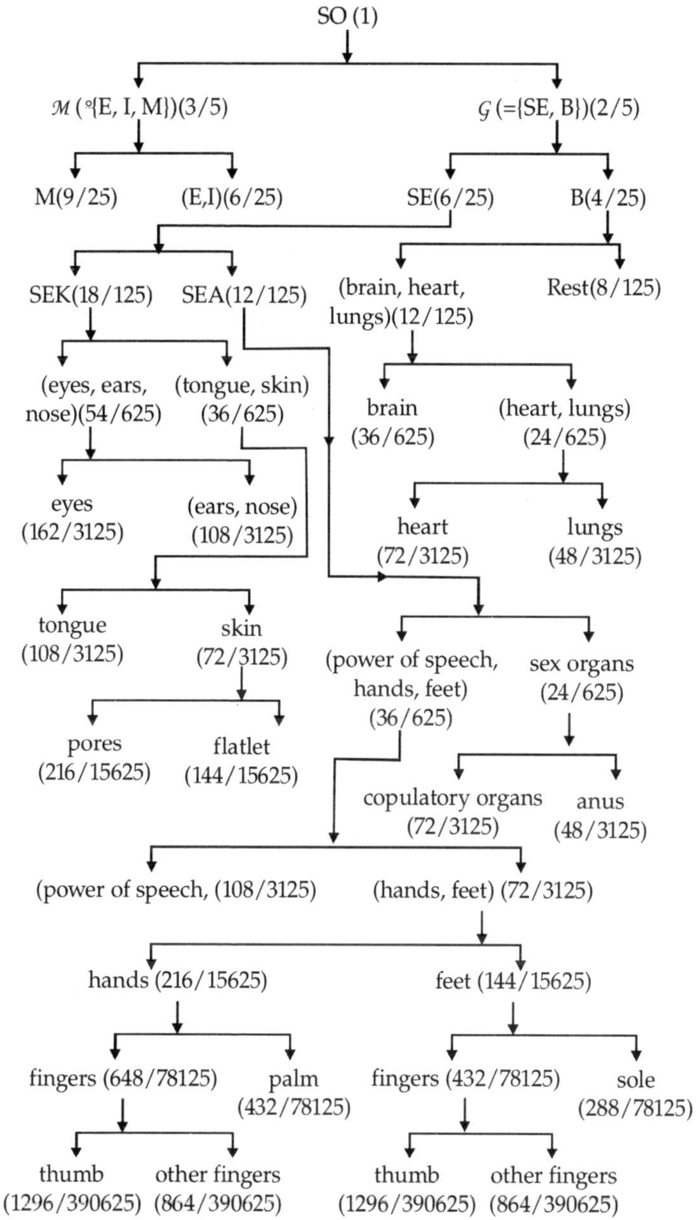

fig. 8.2: An "inverted tree" of consciousness: A "three-by-two" rule is expected to divide the consciousness between important and less important organs at every stage in the static mode of consciousness. Fraction allocated to an EOL is shown in the bracket after considering it unity with the root, SO.

characterizes the dynamic mode of consciousness in terms of its accelerated role in actions. In the static mode, no doubt, the actions are also the result of *saṅkalpa*s but the accelerated role of consciousness in this case comes to an end just by leaving behind a constant role. Although this constancy is there all throughout the body but at the level of an individual EOL there may still exist an accelerated role of consciousness however only at a low pitch. Note that a person in comma is also in the static mode of consciousness. Zero mode defines a dead body in the sense that a fully developed and grown up body is lying before us but there are no actions of any EOL in the absence of consciousness.

It may be mentioned that in the static mode the accelerated and constant versions of consciousness accordingly define the active and passive nature of EOLs. This happens through the alignment of micro-body $\mathcal{M}$ in general and that of mind in particular with an outer EOL and the same makes the latter active. In the absence of co-ordination with $\mathcal{M}$ even the functioning of the outer EOLs becomes passive. Similarly, the *saṅkalpa*s manifesting through E make the inner EOLs, namely M, I and E itself active. For example, an open eye cannot perceive the outer world unless it is activated by the co-ordination with the mind, it cannot analyse the perceived object unless co-ordinated by I, or cannot add anything to the store of information unless co-ordinated by E. In fact a part of each of M, I and E constitutes the so-called subconscious mind which, in fact, later becomes the source of *saṅkalpa*s.

8.4 Interaction of a Human being with Physical world

In this section we discuss the interaction of a human Being described by patomic model (cf. Appendix A) with the physical world described by *pañca-mahābhūta*s (*PM*s) of Vedānta philosophy (cf. Appendix D). These interactions are described basically in terms of five *tanmātra*s (five quanta of interaction) corresponding to and associated with each *mahābhūta*. Here, however, we shall introduce a few more *tanmātra*s while discussing the self-interaction or the interactions among inner EOLs.

8.4.1 HUMAN BEING, PAÑCA-MAHĀBHŪTAS AND THEIR INTERACTION

As mentioned earlier (cf. Section 2.5), human Being is an SEP-matter which is composed of several essences of life including the source of consciousness (cf. Appendix A) as shown in *fig.* 8.3(i). On the other hand, in Vedānta philosophy the description of physical world does not go beyond the domain of five cosmic elements (called *pañca-mahābhūtas* (*PMs*)). Not only this, human body including the essences of life is also considered as composed of *PMs*. As discussed in Appendix D these *PMs* are nothing but a kind of generalization of five physical states of matter. As one proceeds in the order earth (E_a), water (W), air (A), fire (F) and ether (E_t), the subtle property of a *mahābhūta* increases [cf. *fig.* 8.3 (ii)]. Similarly, with regards to EOLs as one proceeds in the order B, SE, M, I and E, the subtle character of an EOL increases. Human Being (b) as a whole in fact interacts with *five PMs*, namely E_t, F, A, W and E_a through *five tanmātras* (quanta of interactions) τ_{et}, τ_f, τ_a, τ_w and τ_{ea} respectively as shown in *fig.* 8.3(iii). These *tanmātras* of course have different characteristics depending upon the interacting *mahābhūta*. Further, the physical *mahābhūtas* (E_t, F, A, W and E_a) are different from the perceived ones (namely $\tilde{E}_t$, $\tilde{F}$, $\tilde{A}$, $\tilde{W}$ and $\tilde{E}_a$) and they are connected through *pañcīkaraṇa* rule (cf. eq. (D1)). One gains the experience of the outer world through *five* senses of knowledge (SEK) in terms of five sense objects (cf. Appendix D) and the same becomes realizable to b first via these *tanmātras* and later by inner EOLs, namely M, I and E. This is the process of interaction of b with *PMs*.

8.4.2 DRESSING-UP OF EOLS WITH CONSCIOUSNESS: A NEW PAÑCIKARAṆA RULE

To create the perceived *mahābhūtas* from the physical one a *pañcīkaraṇa* rule is known in Vedānta philosophy and the same is discussed in Appendix D. A similar *pañcīkaraṇa* rule is proposed here to create active EOLs (or the ones dressed up with consciousness) from the passive (or nascent) ones (cf. Section

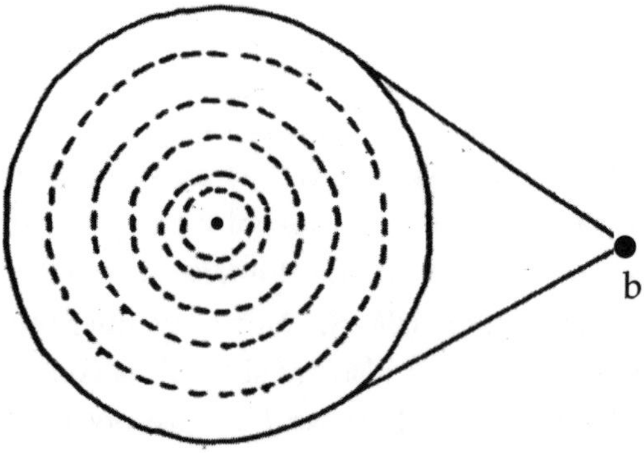

(i) Human being (b): Special EP (SEP)-matter.

(ii) *Pañca-mahābhūtas*: P-matter
↑ subtle property increases
↓ gross property increases.

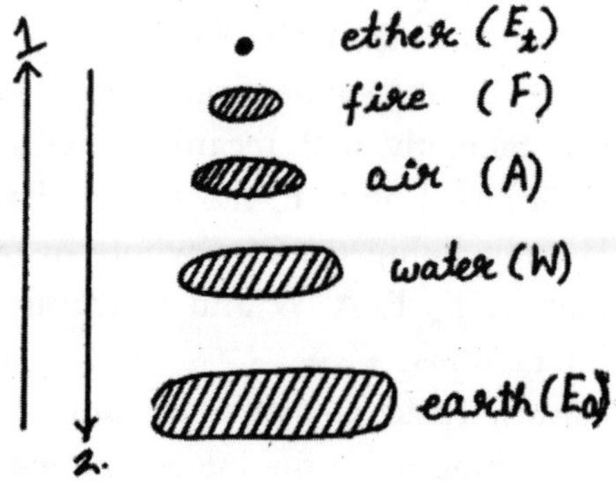

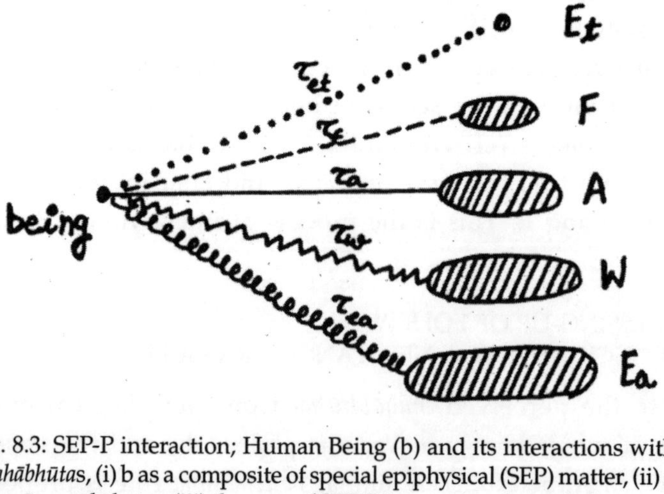

(iii)

fig. 8.3: SEP-P interaction; Human Being (b) and its interactions with *pañca-mahābhūtas*, (i) b as a composite of special epiphysical (SEP) matter, (ii) subtlety of *pañca-mahābūtas*, (iii) the case of SEP-P interaction through five *tanmātras* of Vedic science.

8.3.4). Note that passive EOLs also have some consciousness but in its static mode. However, we shall first employ the *pañcīkaraṇa* rule on the nascent EOLs to create the active EOLs and then employ *trikaraṇa* and *dvikaraṇa* rules respectively on these active inner and outer EOLs separately to create super-active EOLs. This, in fact, is a step in the direction of creating more intense or focused EOLs. As a matter of fact, the interaction of b with WO comes into existence when all the EOLs in general become conscious. It is only at the next stage that inner or outer or both EOLs readjust themselves according to the environment in the field of WO and become more active than earlier.

Let $\widetilde{B}^{(1)}$, $\widetilde{SE}^{(1)}$, $\widetilde{M}^{(1)}$, $\widetilde{I}^{(1)}$ *and* $\widetilde{E}^{(1)}$ be the once dressed EOLs. Then according to the new *pañcīkaraṇa* rule for EOLs we express them in terms of passive (nascent) EOLs as

$$\left.\begin{aligned}
\widetilde{B}^{(1)} &= \frac{1}{2}B + \frac{1}{8}SE + \frac{1}{8}M + \frac{1}{8}I + \frac{1}{8}E, \\
\widetilde{SE}^{(1)} &= \frac{1}{2}SE + \frac{1}{8}M + \frac{1}{8}I + \frac{1}{8}E + \frac{1}{8}B, \\
\widetilde{M}^{(1)} &= \frac{1}{2}M + \frac{1}{8}I + \frac{1}{8}E + \frac{1}{8}B + \frac{1}{8}SE, \\
\widetilde{I}^{(1)} &= \frac{1}{2}I + \frac{1}{8}E + \frac{1}{8}B + \frac{1}{8}SE + \frac{1}{8}M, \\
\widetilde{E}^{(1)} &= \frac{1}{2}E + \frac{1}{8}B + \frac{1}{8}SE + \frac{1}{8}M + \frac{1}{8}I.
\end{aligned}\right\} \quad (8.1)$$

In other words conscious B, i.e. $\widetilde{B}^{(1)}$ consists of 50 per cent of nascent B and the 12.5 per cent of each of nascent SE, M, I and E. Similar are the definitions of $\widetilde{SE}^{(1)}, \widetilde{M}^{(1)}, \widetilde{I}^{(1)}$ *and* $\widetilde{E}^{(1)}$. As for the case of *PMs* (cf. eq. (D2)), note here that

$$\widetilde{B}^{(1)} + \widetilde{SE}^{(1)} + \widetilde{M}^{(1)} + \widetilde{I}^{(1)} + \widetilde{E}^{(1)} = B + SE + M + I + E. \quad (8.2)$$

Eq. (8.2) throws light on the role of consciousness in co-ordinating the working of various EOLs. It is such that the Being b, while remains unaffected from the games of consciousness, however enjoys the success of actions performed by the active EOLs particularly after the fulfilment of *saṅkalpa*s.

This is not the end of the story. Since the inner EOLs M, I and E and the outer EOLs B and SE belong to different scales (as they are the constituents of micro and gross bodies respectively) another stage of a *trīkaraṇa* rule for inner EOLs and a *dvikaraṇa* rule for outer EOLs becomes desirable for the fulfilment of certain class of *saṅkalpa*s. Thus, the doubly dressed inner EOLs, $\widetilde{M}^{(2)}, \widetilde{I}^{(2)}$ *and* $\widetilde{E}^{(2)}$ can be derived from the singly dressed ones according to a *trikaraṇa* rule *as*

$$\left.\begin{aligned} \widetilde{M}^{(2)} &= \frac{1}{2}\widetilde{M}^{(1)} + \frac{1}{4}\widetilde{I}^{(1)} + \frac{1}{4}\widetilde{E}^{(1)}, \\ \widetilde{I}^{(2)} &= \frac{1}{2}\widetilde{I}^{(1)} + \frac{1}{4}\widetilde{E}^{(1)} + \frac{1}{4}\widetilde{M}^{(1)}, \\ \widetilde{E}^{(2)} &= \frac{1}{2}\widetilde{E}^{(1)} + \frac{1}{4}\widetilde{M}^{(1)} + \frac{1}{4}\widetilde{I}^{(1)}, \end{aligned}\right\} \tag{8.3}$$

i.e. $\widetilde{M}^{(2)}$ consists of 50 per cent of $\widetilde{M}^{(1)}$ and 25 per cent each of $\widetilde{I}^{(1)}$ *and* $\widetilde{E}^{(1)}$ and so on. Similarly, a *dvikaraṇa* rule provides $\widetilde{B}^{(2)}$ *and* $\widetilde{SE}^{(2)}$ as

$$\left.\begin{aligned} \widetilde{B}^{(2)} &= \frac{1}{2}\widetilde{B}^{(1)} + \frac{1}{2}\widetilde{SE}^{(1)} \\ \widetilde{SE}^{(2)} &= \frac{1}{2}\widetilde{SE}^{(1)} + \frac{1}{2}\widetilde{B}^{(1)} \end{aligned}\right\} \tag{8.4}$$

i.e. each of $\widetilde{B}^{(2)}$ *and* $\widetilde{SE}^{(2)}$ now consists of 50 per cent of each of $\widetilde{B}^{(1)}$ *and* $\widetilde{SE}^{(1)}$.

In fact it is the type of *saṅkalpa* that decides the role, which consciousness has to play in its fulfilment through EOLs. Often passive EOLs do the job, but at times not only the active but super-active EOLs are also brought into action by b so that its *saṅkalpa*s are fulfilled. In some sense this leads to an intense focusing (or a step towards collapse) of consciousness (cf. Section 8.3.3) along a specific EOL. This is what one notices in the day-to-day life. Eqs. (8.3) and (8.4) also lead to

$$\widetilde{M}^{(2)}+\widetilde{I}^{(2)}+\widetilde{E}^{(2)}=\widetilde{M}^{(1)}+\widetilde{I}^{(1)}+\widetilde{E}^{(1)} \text{ and } \widetilde{B}^{(2)}+\widetilde{SE}^{(2)}=\widetilde{B}^{(1)}+\widetilde{SE}^{(1)}, \quad (8.5a,b)$$

which imply that in further activating the inner and outer EOLs, the consciousness readjusts itself in each domain separately in such a way that it goes unnoticed to b but by fulfilling the *saṅkalpas* of b.

Next, use of eq. (8.1) in eqs. (8.3) and (8.4) yields

$$\widetilde{M}^{(2)}=\frac{10}{32}M+\frac{7}{32}I+\frac{7}{32}E+\frac{4}{32}B+\frac{4}{32}SE, \quad (8.6a)$$

$$\widetilde{I}^{(2)}=\frac{10}{32}I+\frac{7}{32}E+\frac{7}{32}M+\frac{4}{32}B+\frac{4}{32}SE, \quad (8.6b)$$

$$\widetilde{E}^{(2)}=\frac{10}{32}E+\frac{7}{32}M+\frac{7}{32}I+\frac{4}{32}B+\frac{4}{32}SE, \quad (8.6c)$$

$$\widetilde{B}^{(2)}=\frac{10}{32}B+\frac{10}{32}SE+\frac{4}{32}M+\frac{4}{32}I+\frac{4}{32}SE, \quad (8.6d)$$

$$\widetilde{SE}^{(2)}=\frac{10}{32}SE+\frac{10}{32}B+\frac{4}{32}M+\frac{4}{32}I+\frac{4}{32}SE, \quad (8.6e)$$

Similarly, the repeated use of *trikaraṇa* and *dvikaraṇa* rules on (8.6) leads to third and fourth order dressings of EOLs with consciousness and the results are as follows:

$$\widetilde{M}^{(3)}=\frac{17}{64}M+\frac{31}{128}I+\frac{31}{128}E+\frac{4}{32}B+\frac{4}{32}SE, \quad (8.7a)$$

$$\widetilde{I}^{(3)}=\frac{17}{64}I+\frac{31}{128}E+\frac{31}{128}M+\frac{4}{32}B+\frac{4}{32}SE, \quad (8.7b)$$

$$\widetilde{E}^{(3)}=\frac{17}{64}E+\frac{31}{128}M+\frac{31}{128}I+\frac{4}{32}B+\frac{4}{32}SE, \quad (8.7c)$$

and $$\widetilde{M}^{(4)} = \frac{65}{256}M + \frac{127}{512}I + \frac{127}{512}E + \frac{4}{32}B + \frac{4}{32}SE \,, \qquad (8.8a)$$

$$\widetilde{I}^{(4)} = \frac{65}{256}I + \frac{127}{512}E + \frac{127}{512}M + \frac{4}{32}B + \frac{4}{32}SE \,, \qquad (8.8b)$$

$$\widetilde{E}^{(4)} = \frac{65}{256}E + \frac{127}{512}M + \frac{127}{512}I + \frac{4}{32}B + \frac{4}{32}SE \,, \qquad (8.8c)$$

Where the expressions for $\widetilde{B}^{(3)}$ *and* $\widetilde{\widetilde{SE}}^{(3)}$, $\widetilde{B}^{(4)}$ *and* $\widetilde{\widetilde{SE}}^{(4)}$ are not listed. In fact they remain the same as for $\widetilde{B}^{(2)}$ *and* $\widetilde{\widetilde{SE}}^{(2)}$ in (8.6d) and (8.6e). In general, n^{th} order dressings of inner EOLs are derivable from the $(n-1)^{th}$ order dressed EOLs using the formulae

$$\widetilde{M}^{(n)} = \frac{1}{2}\widetilde{M}^{(n-1)} + \frac{1}{4}\widetilde{I}^{(n-1)} + \frac{1}{4}\widetilde{E}^{(n-1)} \,,$$

$$\widetilde{I}^{(n)} = \frac{1}{2}\widetilde{I}^{(n-1)} + \frac{1}{4}\widetilde{E}^{(n-1)} + \frac{1}{4}\widetilde{M}^{(n-1)} \,,$$

$$\widetilde{E}^{(n)} = \frac{1}{2}\widetilde{E}^{(n-1)} + \frac{1}{4}\widetilde{M}^{(n-1)} + \frac{1}{4}\widetilde{I}^{(n-1)} \,,$$

where for $n = 0$, $\widetilde{M}^{(0)} = M$, $\widetilde{I}^{(0)} = I$ *and* $\widetilde{E}^{(0)} = E$. The results for $\widetilde{\widetilde{SE}}^{(n)}$ *and* $\widetilde{B}^{(n)}$ remain the same as for $\widetilde{\widetilde{SE}}^{(2)}$ *and* $\widetilde{B}^{(2)}$ in eqs. (8.6d) and (8.6e). Further note that

$\widetilde{M}^{(n)} + \widetilde{I}^{(n)} + \widetilde{E}^{(n)} = \widetilde{M}^{(n-1)} + \widetilde{I}^{(n-1)} + \widetilde{E}^{(n-1)}$, (for n = 2, 3, . . .), is also valid in general.

With regard to human behaviour and experiences, several interesting conclusions can be drawn from eqs. (8.6)-(8.8).

(i) At any order of dressing of an EOL, the maximum contribution to it comes from the nascent form of the corresponding EOL by construction.

(ii) As a result of *pañcīkaraṇa, trikaraṇa* and *dvikaraṇa* rules, one can now arrive at active and hyperactive versions of gross and micro bodies depending on the orders of dressing of their constituents. For example, the first two orders of dressing for the gross body $\mathcal{G}$ are

$$\mathcal{G}^{(1)} = \left\{\widetilde{B}^{(1)}, \widetilde{S}\widetilde{E}^{(1)}, \widetilde{W}\widetilde{O}^{(1)}\right\}, \quad \mathcal{G}^{(2)} = \left\{\widetilde{B}^{(2)}, \widetilde{S}\widetilde{E}^{(2)}, \widetilde{W}\widetilde{O}^{(1)}\right\};$$

whereas various orders of dressing for the micro body $\mathcal{M}$ are

$$\widetilde{\mathcal{M}}^{(1)} \equiv \left\{\widetilde{M}^{(1)}, \widetilde{I}^{(1)}, \widetilde{E}^{(1)}\right\};\ \widetilde{\mathcal{M}}^{(2)} \equiv \left\{\widetilde{M}^{(2)}, \widetilde{I}^{(2)}, \widetilde{E}^{(2)}\right\}; \ldots\ldots;\ \widetilde{M}^{(n)} \equiv \left\{\widetilde{M}^{(n)}, \widetilde{I}^{(n)}, \widetilde{E}^{(n)}\right\}$$

Here $\widetilde{W}\widetilde{O}$ now consists of EP-matter, i.e. the P-matter combined with consciousness. Note that while only up to second order dressing goes with the gross body by construction, for the micro body however it continues up to any, say n[th] order or up to infinite orders in general leading to $\widetilde{\mathcal{M}}^{(\infty)}$.

(iii) In Table 8.1 we list the relative contributions of the nascent EOLs, M, I, E, B and SE to the so-called dressed micro bodies up to n=4. As one proceeds from $\widetilde{\mathcal{M}}^{(1)}$ to $\widetilde{\mathcal{M}}^{(4)}$ it is easy to see from this Table that (a) the relative contribution of all the three M, I and E decreases in the same proportion from (256/512) to (130/512), (b) dressed B and SE contain the same relative contribution of M, I and E as (64/512) in all orders of dressing, (c) while in $\widetilde{\mathcal{M}}^{(1)}$, the relative contributions of M, I and E are (256, 64, 64), they become (130, 127, 127) in $\widetilde{\mathcal{M}}^{(4)}$ for the dressed M, I and E. This means that in the higher orders of dressing of M (or for that matter of I or E) the contribution of nascent I or E becomes comparable to that of M. It is quite possible that in the limit $n \rightarrow \infty$ (i.e. in $\widetilde{\mathcal{M}}^{(\infty)}$), the dressed $\widetilde{\mathcal{M}}^{(\infty)}$ will contain equal contributions from nascent M, I and E. The construct $\widetilde{\mathcal{M}}^{(\infty)}$ becomes interesting.

Vedānta philosophy presents only the case of subconscious mind and that perhaps could be $\widetilde{\mathcal{M}}^{(1)}$. However, in the present scheme we are able to generate a variety of subconscious minds depending upon the

Table 8.1: Relative contributions of the nascent M, I and E in the construction of dressed micro-bodies $\mathcal{M}^{(1)}$, $\mathcal{M}^{(2)}$, $\mathcal{M}^{(3)}$ and $\mathcal{M}^{(4)}$. The bracketed three numbers are the coeffiecients of M, I and E respectively in the expressions for the dressed M, I and E up to fourth order and with the common denominator 512.

Dressing of the EOL	$\mathcal{M}^{(1)} \equiv \{\tilde{M}^{(1)}, \tilde{I}^{(1)}, \tilde{E}^{(1)}\}$	$\mathcal{M}^{(2)} \equiv \{\tilde{M}^{(2)}, \tilde{I}^{(2)}, \tilde{E}^{(2)}\}$	$\mathcal{M}^{(3)} \equiv \{\tilde{M}^{(3)}, \tilde{I}^{(3)}, \tilde{E}^{(3)}\}$	$\mathcal{M}^{(4)} \equiv \{\tilde{M}^{(4)}, \tilde{I}^{(4)}, \tilde{E}^{(4)}\}$
M	(256, 64, 64)	(160, 112, 112)	(136, 124, 124)	(130, 127, 127)
I	(64, 256, 64)	(112, 160, 112)	(124, 136, 124)	(127, 130, 127)
E	(64, 64, 256)	(112, 112, 160)	(124, 124, 136)	(127, 127, 130)
B	(64, 64, 64)	(64, 64, 64)	(64, 64, 64)	(64, 64, 64)
SE	(64, 64, 64)	(64, 64, 64)	(64, 64, 64)	(64, 64, 64)

order of dressing them with consciousness. In the limiting case, $\tilde{\mathcal{M}}^{(\infty)}$ could be the most intense composite of M, I and E in which all the three constituents in their nascent form contribute equally. It could be very close to the source of consciousness, i.e. SO and perhaps also is the source of *saṅkalpas*.

(iv) Different actions of EOLs in the day-to-day life demand the different roles of the dressed micro and gross bodies with consciousness. While there could be a limit to become physically active (in terms of $\tilde{\mathcal{G}}^{(1)}$ and $\tilde{\mathcal{G}}^{(2)}$), there is no limit on becoming mentally active (in terms of $\tilde{\mathcal{M}}^{(1)}, \tilde{\mathcal{M}}^{(2)}, \dots, \tilde{\mathcal{M}}^{(\infty)}$). Several examples can be cited to this effect from the behaviour and actions of a human Being.

8.4.3 INTERACTIONS INSIDE THE HUMAN BEING

As mentioned earlier, the outward actions of a human Being are the result of a large number of processes taking place inside the human Being at the level of conscious (or dressed) micro and gross bodies. These processes in fact are the outcome of combination and re-combinations of inner EOLs dressed with consciousness of varying degree according to *pañcīkaraṇa, trikaraṇa* and *dvikaraṇa* rules discussed above. In this section we shall be more precise in quantifying the consciousness and the underlying interactions which in turn lead to these processes. To this effect, we shall introduce several new sets of quanta of interactions (or *tanmātras*). As a matter of fact these processes or interactions become more realizable or transparent to a conscious person, $\widetilde{b} = \widetilde{\mathcal{M}}^{(1)} \cup \mathcal{G}^{(1)}$, who starts enjoying the meditations of higher and higher levels. Schematically, these interactions are depicted in *fig.* 8.4 as a function of the meditation parameter μ.

To start with, at low μ the micro and gross bodies with corresponding dressed EOLs at the lowest order unite together

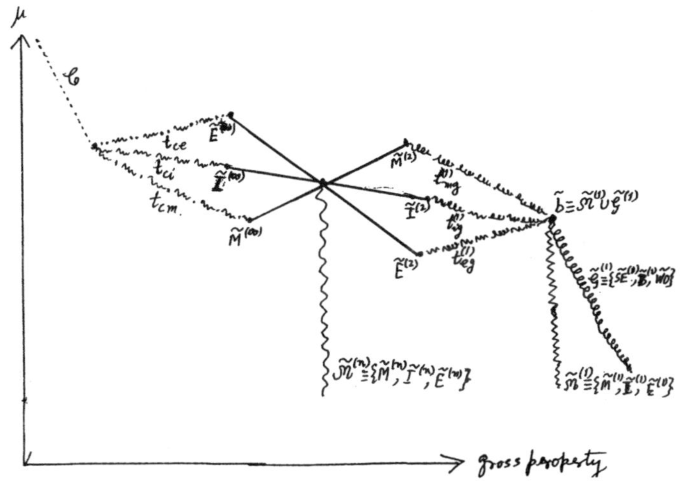

fig. 8.4: Interaction inside the human Being.

to form a conscious Being $\widetilde{b}$. As μ increases, the dressed constituents of $\widetilde{\mathcal{G}}^{(1)}$, namely $\widetilde{\text{SE}}^{(1)}$, $\widetilde{\text{B}}^{(1)}$, $\widetilde{\text{WO}}$ remain unaffected whereas those of $\widetilde{\mathcal{M}}^{(1)}$ namely $\widetilde{M}^{(1)}$, $\widetilde{I}^{(1)}$, $\widetilde{E}^{(1)}$ undergo the next order dressing with consciousness according to the *trikaraṇa* rule and thus giving rise to a doubly dressed micro body $\widetilde{\mathcal{M}}^{(2)}=\{\widetilde{M}^{(2)}, \widetilde{I}^{(2)}, \widetilde{E}^{(2)}\}$. This occurs through the three quanta of interaction or *tanmātras*, namely $t^{(1)}_{mg}$, $t^{(1)}_{ig}$ *and* $t^{(1)}_{eg}$ labelled with mg, ig, eg corresponding to the mind-gross body, intellect-gross body and the ego-gross body interactions. Here the bracketed superscript 1 indicates the *tanmātra* corresponding to the interaction with singly-dressed constituents of $\widetilde{\mathcal{M}}^{(1)}$. Symbolically, one writes

$$\widetilde{M}^{(2)} \sim \widetilde{M}^{(1)} + t_{mg}^{(1)};\ \widetilde{I}^{(2)} \sim \widetilde{I}^{(1)} + t_{ig}^{(1)};\ \widetilde{E}^{(2)} \sim \widetilde{E}^{(1)} + t_{eg}^{(1)}$$

Similarly, the third-order dressing of inner EOLs can be expressed as

$$\widetilde{M}^{(3)} \sim \widetilde{M}^{(2)} + t_{mg}^{(2)};\ \widetilde{I}^{(3)} \sim \widetilde{I}^{(2)} + t_{ig}^{(2)};\ \widetilde{E}^{(3)} \sim \widetilde{E}^{(2)} + t_{eg}^{(2)}$$

and so on. In general, the nth order dressed inner EOLs become

$$\widetilde{M}^{(n)} \sim \widetilde{M}^{(n-1)} + t_{mg}^{(n-1)};\ \widetilde{I}^{(n)} \sim \widetilde{I}^{(n-1)} + t_{ig}^{(n-1)};\ \widetilde{E}^{(n)} \sim \widetilde{E}^{(n-1)} + t_{eg}^{(n-1)}$$

which constitute $\widetilde{\mathcal{M}}^{(n)} (\equiv \{\widetilde{M}^{(n)}, \widetilde{I}^{(n)}, \widetilde{E}^{(n)}\})$.

The role of *tanmātras* $t_{mg}^{(n)}$, $t_{ig}^{(n)}$, $t_{eg}^{(n)}$ for n=2, 3, . . . , is not shown in the figure, rather all intermediate stage constructs of inner EOLs are merged into the drawing of three solid lines corresponding to the dressed mind, intellect and ego. A crossover of the three solid lines is shown for certain order of dressing, say n[th] order. The order of dressing at which the crossover takes place varies from person to person. Note that after the crossover, E still continues to be a little longer than before the crossover as compared to M and I. In fact in outward actions of EOLs, it is the ego that starts acting first compared to the mind and intellect, whereas in the inward actions the role of mind ends up first compared to that of intellect or ego. Further, in the limit when $n \to \infty$, one obtains a highly dressed micro body $\widetilde{\mathcal{M}}^{(\infty)} \equiv \{\widetilde{M}^{(\infty)}, \widetilde{I}^{(\infty)}, \widetilde{E}^{(\infty)}\}$. This perhaps becomes the source of *saṅkalpas*. In fact the constituents of $\widetilde{\mathcal{M}}^{(\infty)}$ are in the direct interaction with the causal body, C, i.e. soul, through another class of three *tanmātras* t_{ce}, t_{ci}, t_{cm} labelled with *ce, ci, cm* corresponding to SO-ego, SO-intellect and SO-mind interactions. Since ego, intellect and mind are now infinitely dressed with consciousness and also in direct contact with the pure source of consciousness SO, they sometimes also behave as the source of consciousness but an impure one. That is why, the *saṅkalpas* sometimes are the biased ones or the human virtues like expectations, thirst for worldly objects, etc. do not die that soon. Once the *saṅkalpas* originate from $\widetilde{\mathcal{M}}^{(\infty)}$ they keep busy the lower hierarchy of EOLs — dressed or even the nascent ones.

In *fig*. 8.4, in addition to the solid lines one also observes wave-like and spring-like lines or their combinations in the form of segments. While the combination in the form of segments represents the exchange of different types of *tanmātras*, the dotted, wave-like and spring-like lines respectively represent the contributions of causal, micro and gross bodies to the interaction in different domains of meditation parameter μ. Note that at low μ, the role of gross body including that of WO remains important and at moderate μ the micro-body dominates the scene whereas at high μ (intense meditation) it is all the role of causal body (or that of $\widetilde{\mathcal{M}}^{(\infty)}$) of b. This is how the Being b works between the extreme domains of SO and WO.

8.5 Conscious Actions of b on the Elements of WO

The role of consciousness in physical theories has been tactfully avoided in the past. In some cases it is either translated into the concept of probability or into the probabilistic interpretation of the phenomenon under study (as in quantum mechanics[11]), or else certain assumptions are made to avoid its explicit role at the stage of modelling the phenomenon. On the other hand, in recent years an account of consciousness in physical and biological theories has become desirable[12] in understanding several newly discovered phenomena in these disciplines. In

---

11. See, for example, Amit Goswami, "Consciousness in Quantum Physics and the Mind-Body Problem", *Journ. Mind and Behaviour* 11 (1990) 75-96; also see, H.P. Stapp, *Mind, Matter and Quantum Mechanics* (Springer, 1993); Sir John Eccles, "How the Self Controls its Brain" (Springer, 1993); Max Jammer, *The Philosophy of Quantum Mechanics* (New York: John Wiley & Sons, 1974) and Bruce Resenblum and Fred Kuttner, *Quantum Enigma: Physics Encounters Consciousness* (New York: Oxford Univ. Press, 2006), for recent reviews on the subject.

12. Roger Penrose, *Shadows of the Mind: A Search for the Missing Science of Consciousness* (Oxford University Press, 1994).

spite of the fact that consciousness manifests[13] in its varying degree in the data and its effects are realizable at the end-point of analyses of both instrumentally or manually collected data, an account of the same in the theory is, however, ignored at the cost of certain simplifying assumptions. On the other hand, in biological systems explanation and analysis of data is sought by introducing certain unknown (hidden) parameters which usually have their uncontrollable domain of variation, mainly because these systems do offer a case of "open" systems. No doubt the physical theories when applied to these open systems turn out to be inadequate but the difficulty does persist with their modification for the role of consciousness in a given phenomenon.

Having established a possible mechanism for the working(s) of inner EOLs of a conscious human Being that in turn leads to outward action in the preceding sections, here in this section we make a modest attempt to incorporate consciousness in physical theories. This we carry out through one of the fundamental principles in physics, i.e through the principle of least action or the Hamilton's principle in classical mechanics. It is true that this principle is the backbone of most physical theories; however, its viability and universality is also emphasized in Section 4.4 as the principle of minimum efforts in the context of human behaviour. The fact that both actions and the objects on which these actions are performed can have non-physical components (the components which are not describable by physical theories or detectable by physical instruments) allows us to introduce two imaginaries in mathematical terms in the respective complex domains[14] — one for the action and the other for the object on

---

13. R.S. Kaushal, "The Conscious Pendulum: A Physicist's Approach", *Indian Philosophical Quarterly* 29 (2002) 65-78.

14. Radhey Shyam Kaushal, "A Complex Domain Analysis of Actions of a Consciousness Human being", the paper presented in Int. Conf. on Advances in Mathematics: Historical Developments and Engineering Applications, held at Pant Nagar (India), 19-22 December 2007, Abstract no. 35; *Ganit Bharati* **30** (2008) pp. 99-113; *Pramana — J. Phys.* **73** (2009) pp. 287-97.

which conscious actions are performed. The space-time consciousness (STC) evolution equations so derived turn out to be rich enough to account for a variety of human actions of day-to-day life. No doubt the present method of quantification appears as toy-model but it can form a basis for many future developments in the field. In what follows, we continue with the description of methodology and a discussion of results by postponing mathematical trivialities to Appendix E.

8.6 Further Remarks on Physical and Non-physical Matter in the Universe

Physical theories explain only a limited part of the world order. As emphasized earlier at several places, the description of many phenomena in Nature definitely goes beyond the laws of physics and biology. Here we highlight again only a few cases briefly in the present context.

8.6.1 HUMAN PERCEPTION OF WORLDLY OBJECTS: SUBJECTIVE AND OBJECTIVE ASPECTS

As such an object in the universe has no existence and not even the universe itself.[15] It exists only if it is detected by an apparatus or by a living Being. Even if it is detected by an apparatus[16] then the other end of it (i.e. its realization) is again connected to a living Being, i.e. the living (human) Being is the final experiencer, realizer or perceiver of the object. Even in the living human Being, the ultimate realizer is the soul but in-between the

15. This fact is again supported by Vedānta philosophy when it emphasizes, *brahma satyam jagatamithyā*, i.e. God is real and the rest is unreal. From this one can as well extrapolate that not only God but transcends from God like consciousness is truth and the rest is the creation of truth which may not exist when the truth (creator) is withdrawn.

16. As a matter of fact "apparatus" is a measure of Nature (*jagat*) and the living Being (as a part) is that of supreme power (*Brahman*) and the measured object lies in-between. "Thus, who detects what? Or what detects what?" are the questions that need to be thought over at a deeper level but we avoid such details here.

perception passes through several other EOLs (namely B, SE, M, I and E) before its final realization.

Alternatively, it is only when the consciousness (a derivative of soul) is attached with these EOLs (or the latter are placed in the field of SO), the latter are dressed up and become ready to act as a perceiver of the outer world (or of the elements of WO). Some of these EOLs no doubt contribute in creating and perceiving the space-time aspect of realization process of the object, of course in several steps (see the preceding sections) but others do contribute to other aspects of realization which are beyond the domain of space-time, i.e. in establishing the existence of the object. For that matter the existence and even working of E, I, M, SE and B is there only in the presence of SO. Thus, not only the object itself has non-physical (extra-physical or metaphysical) aspect in it but also the action performed collectively by different EOLs on it in a coherent manner. To this effect we have already introduced the concepts of P- , EP- , and SEP- matters in (cf. Section 2.6). In the same spirit one can define here the EP (epi-physical)-action as the P(physical)-action + consciousness and the SEP (special epi-physical)-action as the P-action + consciousness + source of consciousness. In other words, physical matter becomes EP-matter after its perception by a Being in the fields of SO and WO. Not only this, the processes taking place inside a Being to this effect when realized by the Self of the same Being or as observed by another Being, also lead to the EP-action. In fact it is only a part of perception of EP-object or of EP-action which turns out to be physically describable within the framework of space-time structure of Nature; otherwise a great deal of it remains hidden, i.e. beyond the domain of space-time. The latter is definitely a part of final realization by the ultimate realizer, i.e. soul.

8.6.2 DREAMING AND IMAGINATION AS EXAMPLES OF EP-ACTIONS

In the context of mortal nature of the body, Vedic science spells out[17] that "what does not exist is unreal and the real never ceases to exist." In fact the philosophy and science of the unreal (i.e. imagination) is as important as that of the real. Indeed, space and time have both real and imaginary manifestations since events taking place in space and time have a bearing on our lives. Thus, life has both realities and imaginations. What we do is real and what we dream (imagine) is unreal. There is no one who does not dream. Thus, dreams are a part of life.[18] On the other hand, a complex number, which has a real part and an imaginary part, can be made real by adding it to or by multiplying it by its conjugate. In the same way, in the day-to-day life an imaginary fear (a negative dream) can be allayed by an imaginary hope (a positive dream) of the same weight. In the process, however, one is left with the realities of life. As mentioned earlier, consciousness in itself is a phenomenon associated with a living Being and it has several distinct features[19, 20, 21] which are missing in a "pure" physical perception of an object or an action.

As the history of quantum mechanics reveals, the quantum measurement problem translated into a physically realizable concept of probability density had bearings on similar ideas, particularly through the Born interpretation of the complex quantum wave function. In order to account for the non-physical (imaginary or unreal) aspects of both objects and actions, in the next section we shall discuss the extension of the Hamilton principle of least action to a generalized form for the case of a conscious Being (cf. Appendix E).

---

17. *Śrīmad Bhagavad-Gītā*, chapter 2, verse 16, Gorakhpur: Gita Press.

18. G.S. Tripathi, "Life Without Dream is Colourless", The Speaking Tree Column, *Times of India*, 15 May 2007.

19. G.S. Tripathi, op. cit.

20. Deepak M. Ranade, "Sever Connections Overcome Illusion", The Speaking Tree Column, *Times of India*, 30 Novermber 2007.

21. V.V. Rampal, "Universal Consciousness and Cosmic Energy", The Speaking Tree column, *Times of India*, 12 February 2007.

8.6.3 QUANTUM MEASUREMENT AS AN EXAMPLE OF EP-ACTION

Like the concept of EP-particle, a physical action combined with consciousness (or the physical action watched by a conscious observer) is termed as EP-action. Thus, the quantum measurement is an example of EP-action which is performed by a conscious observer on a microscopic P-matter particle using a physical apparatus (PA). The total Hamiltonian for this three-body system, namely particle, apparatus and the observer can be written as

$$H_{tot} = H_P + H_{PA} + H_b + H_{\text{int}}\,, \tag{8.9}$$

where H_p, H_{PA} and H_b are the Hamiltonians corresponding respectively to physical particle, physical apparatus and the human Being, b, and the interaction Hamiltonian H_{int} is given by

$$H_{\text{int}} = H_{b-P} + H_{b-PA} + H_{P-PA} + H_{b-P-PA} \tag{8.10}$$

In general, H_{tot} of (8.9) can be expressed as

$$H_{\text{tot}} = H_{\text{phys}} + H_{\text{non-phys}}\,, \tag{8.11}$$

where $H_{phys} = H_P + H_{PA} + H_{P\text{-}PA}$ is the physical part and $H_{non\text{-}phys} = H_b + H_{b\text{-}P} + H_{b\text{-}PA} + H_{b\text{-}P\text{-}PA}$, is the non-physical part of the total Hamiltonian. It may be mentioned that the effect of the non-physical part of the Hamiltonian of a quantum particle appears either in the phase of the complex quantum wave function of real variables[22] or through the hidden variables in the theory.[23] The former as such does not appear in the measured output mainly because it is tactfully eliminated while accepting the probabilistic interpretation of quantum mechanics (cf. above sub-sections). On the other hand, the hidden variable theory of David Bohm still has to find a place in modern physics. In view of the

22. See, for example, L.I. Schiff, *Quantum Mechanics*, 3rd edn. (New York: McGraw-hill, 1968); and also see citation 11 above.

23. David Bohm, *Quantum Theory* (Englewood Cliffs, New Jersey: Prentice Hall, 1951); for a recent review, see, for example, D. Bohm, B.J. Hiley, and P.N. Kaloyerou, *Phys. Reports* 144 (1987), 323.

patomic model of human Being, b, it is possible to carry out the fine-tuning of $H_{b\text{-}P}$ in (8.10) as

$$H_{b-P} = H_{B-P} + H_{SE-P} + H_{M-P} + H_{I-P} + H_{E-P} \tag{8.12}$$

where various inter-action terms of b with EOLs appear on the right-hand side. Similarly, for $H_{b\text{-}PA}$ one can write

$$H_{b-PA} = H_{B-PA} + H_{SE-PA} + H_{M-PA} + H_{I-PA} + H_{E-PA} \tag{8.13}$$

and define an extended apparatus in the spirit of von Neuman theory of quantum measurement.[24] As a matter of fact, from eqs. (8.12) and (8.13) it can be noticed that roles of some of the terms in these equations are translated into a variety of *tanmātras* while discussing the interactions taking place inside the human Being with reference to the perception of a physical object (cf. *fig*. 8.4). For further details we refer to our earlier work.[25]

8.6.4 AN ATTEMPT TO IDENTIFY THE QUANTUM OF CONSCIOUSNESS

Whenever a human Being is directly involved in the process of measurement then the first term in (8.11) will account for the pure space-time mediated interactions whereas the second term will account for other interactions beyond the space time. In the quantum domain, if H_{tot} along with its $H_{non\text{-}phys}$ piece remains Hermitian then in general, the effects of physical measurement and consciousness together will manifest through the "action," viz.

$$\exp\left[-iH_{phys}\frac{t}{\hbar} - iH_{non\text{-}phys}\frac{\mu}{g}\right]|\psi\rangle,$$

where the wave function $\psi \equiv \Gamma(\beta, s, m, i, e)$ now includes the apparatus and the human Being (or an extended apparatus[26])

24. J. von Neumann, *Mathematical Foundations of Quantum Mechanics*, (Princeton, New Jersey: Princeton University Press, 1955).

25. Radhey Shyam Kaushal, *The Philosophy of Vedānta: A Modern Scientific Perspective*, Garib Das Oriental Series 179 (Delhi: Indian Book Centre, 1994) chapters 3 and 5, Appendices A and B.

26. J. von Neumann, op. cit.

with β and s (corresponding to the EOLs B and SE) accounting for space-time and m, i and e (corresponding to EOLs, M, I and E) combinedly reflect through the meditation parameter μ. Here, while the meditation parameter μ treated on par with t, a new universal constant $g(= g/2\pi)$ is introduced in analogy with $\hbar$. The constant g can be recognized as the quantum of consciousness and its magnitude can approximately be assessed in the "3/2-rule" of Section 8.3.3 (cf. *fig*. 8.2).

8.6.5 DARK ENERGY OF PHYSICS AS A CASE FOR NONPHYSICAL MATTER IN THE UNIVERSE

As discussed in the Section 6.4, most of the Universe (96 per cent to be almost exact) is made up of dark matter and dark energy and only a small fraction (4 per cent to be almost exact) is the "normal" matter. The reasons advanced for such a huge dark energy are attributed to the origin of cosmic rays, the existence of gravitational waves and/or the mass of neutrinos, etc. Combined together these ingredients are found still insufficient to explain the existence of dark energy to such an enormity of 96 per cent. Clearly, once the physical ingredients are found insufficient then the only option would be to account for the phenomena which are outside the domain of space and time. For example, in the universe, in addition to the physical matter, there does exist non-physical matter (in the form of "bio-energy" comprising of spiritual energy of living Beings that goes undetected by physical instruments howsoever accurate they are) and the same might contribute to the stock of dark matter and dark energy.

8.7 Actions of a Conscious Human Being and their Analyses: A Mathematical Framework

The role of consciousness in classical dynamics is considered here by introducing a meditation parameter μ on par with the time variable t in the Lagrange function L. Further, the coordinate q and the velocity $p(=\dot{q})$ of the EP-matter particle now depend rather implicitly on both t and μ. We accordingly define the derivatives, $\dot{q}$ with respect to t, and $\bar{q}$ with respect to μ and write the Lagrangian as L= L(q, $\dot{q}$, $\bar{q}$, t, μ), where $\dot{q}$ = (∂q/∂t) and $\bar{q}$ = (∂q/∂μ). The action integral[27] K, now takes the form

$$K = \int_{t_1}^{t_2}\int_{\mu_1}^{\mu_2} L(q,\dot{q},\bar{q},t,\mu)d\mu\, dt \tag{8.14}$$

Here, K pertains to the action performed by a consciousness observer on the object placed at q and moving with physical velocity $\dot{q}$. The object identified with position q is also dressing up with the consciousness at a rate of $\bar{q}$. Note that K, a measure of conscious action, is a complicated quantity in the sense that it represents now the outcome of a variety of processes taking place inside the conscious (observer) Being. However, these processes become effective only when the role of μ comes into play, not only in locating the object at q but also in realizing its existence and the other details. As t and μ evolve (which is necessary not only for establishing the existence of the object in the physical universe or in the field of WO but also for realizing its existence) both outer (B and SE) and inner (M, I and E) EOLs of the Being become active. As a matter of fact the variable t is in response to the physical device (like the light ray, etc.) used to detect q and the variable μ is in response to the consciousness used to realize q by the observer. As μ increases, the self-interactions or the interactions inside the Being (cf. *fig*. 8.4) come into existence and the Being establishes other details about q in addition to its position and velocity.

Note that the trajectory of q followed with respect to t may not be the same as the one followed with respect to μ. The physical trajectory in fact could be one possibility out of a large number of possibilities which existed in the mind of the observer. However, as and when the observer focuses his consciousness (μ increases) these possibilities end up in one physical trajectory (a case of SEP-EP-P interaction to be discussed later) along with the higher-order dressings of inner EOLs (cf. Section 8.4.2).

---

27. See, for example, H. Goldstein, *Classical Mechanics* (Addison-Wesley Publishing Co., 1981), chapter 2.

Another ingredient which we are missing in writing the action integral (8.14) is the parameter responsible for efforts made by an individual in performing the action. This parameter will, however, depend on the intensity of thinking process or on the degree of concentration achieved by the individual (again on the orders of dressing of inner EOLs in the language of Section 8.4.2).

8.7.1 SPACE-TIME-CONSCIOUSNESS (STC) EVOLUTION EQUATIONS

Using the methods of calculus of variation, STC evolution equations are derived from the action integral (8.14) in Appendix E. We carry this out for the two cases, namely (i) when the Lagrangian $L(q, \dot{q}, \overline{q}, t, \mu)$ is a real (cf. Section E1) function, one obtains the STC evolution equation as

$$\frac{\partial L}{\partial q} - \frac{\partial}{\partial t}\left(\frac{\partial L}{\partial \dot{q}}\right) - \frac{\partial}{\partial \mu}\left(\frac{\partial L}{\partial \overline{q}}\right) = 0 \ , \qquad (8.15)$$

and (ii) when not only the Lagrangian $L(q, p, t, \mu)$ is complex and expressed as

$$L = L_1(q_1, p_1, q_2, p_2, t, \mu) + IL_2(q_1, p_1, q_2, p_2, t, \mu) \ , \qquad (8.16)$$

but also the coordinate $q(t, \mu)$ and the velocity $p(t, \mu)$ are complex and expressible as

$$q(t,\mu) = q_1(t) + iq_2(\mu) \ , \qquad (8.17a)$$

$$p(t,\mu) = p_1(t) + ip_2(\mu) \ , \qquad (8.17b)$$

where $p_1 = \dot{q}_1$ and $p_2 = (\partial q / \partial \mu) = \overline{q}_2$. Corresponding to L_1 and L_2 in (8.16), one can write under certain assumptions, the conscious action K of eq. (8.14) as the sum of physical and non-physical aspects of the system, viz.

$$K = K_{ph} + I\,K_{non\text{-}phy} \qquad (8.14')$$

In other words, the real parts q_1 and p_1 of q and p correspond to the case of physical reality associated with the object and the imaginary parts q_2 and p_2 are the measures of non-physical reality and in turn account for the role of consciousness in the process of realization of the given object. In spite of the fact that $I^2=i^2=-1$, we have used different "I" and "i" with the imaginary parts in eqs. (8.16) and (8.17). This is mainly because there is no reason as to why the dreaming of an object be the same as the dreaming of the action performed by it. They might belong to different imaginary planes, particularly when the environment and circumstances leave different impacts in the two situations in real life, or when the observer carries different mindsets in the two situations. In mathematical terms, we are considering different imaginaries with a complex number system and with the mapping on it (see Appendix E). As will be clear later, this is done at the cost of analyticity property of the complex function L. Moreover, since the consciousness, like time, cannot be fragmented, this non-analyticity of L in some sense becomes imperative in the present case.

For the Lagrangian (8.16) we list the results (cf. Appendix E) for the two cases, namely when "I" ≠ "i" and when "I" = "i".

Case I: when "I" ≠ "i", the STC evolution equations in component form become

$$\frac{\partial L_1}{\partial q_1}-\frac{\partial}{\partial t}\left(\frac{\partial L_1}{\partial p_1}\right)=0\ ;\quad \frac{\partial L_1}{\partial q_2}-\frac{\partial}{\partial t}\left(\frac{\partial L_1}{\partial p_2}\right)=0 \qquad \text{(8.18a, b)}$$

$$\frac{\partial L_2}{\partial q_1}-\frac{\partial}{\partial t}\left(\frac{\partial L_2}{\partial p_1}\right)=0\ ;\quad \frac{\partial L_2}{\partial q_2}-\frac{\partial}{\partial t}\left(\frac{\partial L_2}{\partial p_2}\right)=0 \qquad \text{(8.18c, d)}$$

$$\frac{\partial L_1}{\partial q_1}-\frac{\partial}{\partial \mu}\left(\frac{\partial L_1}{\partial p_1}\right)=0\ ;\quad \frac{\partial L_1}{\partial q_2}-\frac{\partial}{\partial \mu}\left(\frac{\partial L_1}{\partial p_2}\right)=0 \qquad \text{(8.18e, f)}$$

$$\frac{\partial L_2}{\partial q_1}-\frac{\partial}{\partial \mu}\left(\frac{\partial L_2}{\partial p_1}\right)=0\ ;\quad \frac{\partial L_2}{\partial q_2}-\frac{\partial}{\partial \mu}\left(\frac{\partial L_2}{\partial p_2}\right)=0 \qquad \text{(8.18g, h)}$$

Case II: when "I" = "i", the STC evolution equations in component form turn out to be

$$\frac{\partial L_1}{\partial q_1}-\frac{\partial}{\partial t}\left(\frac{\partial L_1}{\partial p_1}\right)=0\ ;\quad \frac{\partial L_2}{\partial q_1}-\frac{\partial}{\partial t}\left(\frac{\partial L_2}{\partial p_1}\right)=0 \qquad \text{(8.19a, b)}$$

$$\frac{\partial L_1}{\partial q_1} - \frac{\partial}{\partial \mu}\left(\frac{\partial L_1}{\partial p_1}\right) = 0\ ;\quad \frac{\partial L_2}{\partial q_1} - \frac{\partial}{\partial \mu}\left(\frac{\partial L_2}{\partial p_1}\right) = 0. \qquad (8.19c,\ d)$$

A comparison of equations in the sets (8.18) and (8.19) reveals that the four equations of Case II are already present in the eight equations of Case I and the remaining four equations, namely (8.18b), (8.18d), (8.18f) and (8.18h) are the outcome of non-analyticity property of L. Thus, the non-analyticity requirement of L is more informative (as it provides more equations to employ) as far as the application of these results to human behaviour is concerned. In view of our assumption, the appearance of imaginary part of L, i.e. L_2 in eqs. (8.18) and (8.19) represents the effect(s) of non-physical action (i.e. the dreaming or imagination) in the STC evolution of the system. Similarly, the terms in which the imaginary parts of q and p, namely q_2 and p_2 appear in these equations account for the non-physical aspects associated with the realization process of an element in WO. As argued in Appendix E, some of the terms in these equations have their origin purely in the domain of consciousness, some have origin purely in the domain of physics and a good number of them have origin in the domain where space, time and consciousness co-exist pair-wise or otherwise. For example, eq. (8.18a) in spite of its implicit dependence on μ describes exclusively the evolution of physical aspect and eq. (8.18h) in spite of its implicit dependence on t describes exclusively the non-physical aspect — the two extreme situations with regard to the evolution of the system. The remaining eqs. (8.18b) to (8.18g) however describe the evolution of a system in the mixed situations in which all three space, time and consciousness play their roles in certain proportions.

In what follows we discuss eq. (8.15) and each of eqs. (8.18) along with examples from human behaviour and actions in the day-to-day life:

It may be reminded that not only the location of P-matter particle at q but also the actions performed on it towards the realization of some of its features (like the charge, mass, size, shape, etc.) undergo changes with respect to both time and consciousness. In other words, the object dresses up with respect to t of "wrist watch" (termed as "t-evolution") and hence activates the outer EOLs like SE and B to perform the action and thereby making them $\widetilde{S}\widetilde{E}^{(1)}$ *and* $\widetilde{B}^{(1)}$ of eq. (8.1). On the other hand, at the same time it also dresses up with respect to consciousness (translated into μ) and activates the inner EOLs namely M, I and E (termed as "μ-evolution") and thereby making them $\widetilde{M}^{(1)}$, $\widetilde{I}^{(1)}$ *and* $\widetilde{E}^{(1)}$ of eq. (8.1). For physical aspects of a system, the variations with respect to q (termed as "q-evolution") and t while continue according to the standard Euler-Lagrange equations[28] corresponding to the given system and without accounting for the μ-evolution, for non-physical aspects, however, an account of μ-evolution is absolutely necessary. Again, the μ-evolution takes place differently from q- and t-evolutions (in view of the discussions in Section 8.4, regarding the different orders of dressing of EOLs with the consciousness). It appears that physicists who resort to account for consciousness in physical theories[29, 30] do not go beyond the first order dressing (cf. Section 8.4) of the EOLs. But the framework suggested in this chapter takes us much ahead in this direction through *trikaraṇa* rule for inner EOLs and *dvikaraṇa* rule for outer EOLs. At a crude level while this can be carried out for real (conscious) actions through the evolution eq. (8.15), a fine-tuning of the same actually manifests through a complex (conscious) action and via eqs. (8.18). Although a relative comparison of the terms in eq. (8.15) can also throw some light on non-physical aspects of an action, we concentrate here on the analysis of eq. (8.18) only.

8.7.2 ANALYSIS OF STC EVOLUTION EQUATIONS

An interesting feature of eq. (8.18) is that there is no coupling between the physical and non-physical aspect either pertaining

---

28. H. Goldstein, op. cit.

29. Amit Goswami, op. cit. in citation 11.

30. Roger Penrose, 1994, op. cit.

to object or to action. As a result a neat analysis of these equations is possible with reference to space (q)-, time (t)-, and consciousness (μ)- evolutions of the system. A summary of such conclusions arrived at from the analysis of eq. (8.18) is shown in Table 8.2 along with some hints for their application prospects. For this purpose, one should note not only the definitions of L_1, L_2, q_1, p_1, q_2 and p_2 but also the fact that q_1 and p_1 are the functions of t alone whereas q_2 and p_2 are functions of μ-alone (a feature of the definition (8.17)). Further in physical theories t always remains an external parameter, i.e. a projectile never carries a watch or clock in it, whereas here a projectile can be a living Being and could be a source of consciousness while the observer (or the measuring instrument) is already an alive one. Therefore, in picking the examples corresponding to eq. (8.18) (cf. Table 8.2) from day-to-day actions of a Being one has to be careful with regard to μ-evolution. Moreover, since the μ-evolution of both the observer and the conscious object are often equally important (and none of them can be ignored compared to the other, i.e. at times it is the case of very strong non-local effects and there is no parallel example in physical theories), the applications of eq. (8.18) hinted in Table 8.2 remain only approximate (or rather crude) in this respect. While citing the examples in Table 8.2, the μ-evolution of the conscious object (though it can also be an SEP-matter) is often kept at low pitch. From this point of view the suggested applications of eqs. (8.18f) and (8.18h), as these equations involve only the μ-evolution implicitly or explicitly, remain rather crude of a higher degree. Perhaps, a further generalization of Hamilton principle corresponding to a Lagrangian with non-local interactions in μ variable will be a better choice in accounting for the consciousness in physical theories.

Another assumption in citing the examples in Table 8.2 which a physicist will note is that we continue to search for applications to extended living (conscious) objects (often SEP-matter) whereas the theory developed here is only for point particles which in itself can perform hardly a conscious action that is realizable by

Table 8.2: Analysis of eq. (8.18) and remarks on their applications with reference to human behaviour and actions

S. No.	*Eqn. No.*	*Type of evolution involved*	*Nature of description of object*	*Nature of description of action*	*Remarks/application(s)/ Example(s)*
1.	(8.18a)	q-evol., t-evol.	Physical	Physical	Describes purely physical aspects of the system. A physical instrument collecting data on a physical object (like the time period of a pendulum or the counts of radio-active decays by an external instrument) are some examples of this case.
2.	(8.18b)	t-evol., μ-evol.	Non-Physical	Physical	Automatic recording of a stationary person performing mono-acting or a stage play, a bird or mosquito in flight but stationary.
3.	(8.18c)	q-evol., t-evol.	Physical	Non-Physical	A physical object passing through a non-physical environment, e.g. a bullet passing through a living body; a robot interacting/ performing human action, etc. Chervreul hand-held pendulum.

4.	(8.18d)	t-evol., μ-evol.	Non-Physical	Physical	Motion of a living bird projected in space.
5.	(8.18e)	q-evol., μ-evol.	Physical	Non-Physical	Space evolution of a quantum system as observed by an external observer.
6.	(8.18f)	only μ-evol.	Non-physical	Physical	An alive bird suspended from a rigid support and performing oscillations (!).
7.	(8.18g)	q-evol., μ-evol.	Physical	Non-Physical	Chevreul hand-held pendulum[31]
8.	(8.18h)	only μ-evol.	Non-Physical	Non-Physical	Describes purely non-physical aspects of the system. The only example of this case is that of a *yogī* sitting in *samādhi*. At times, the actions performed by his EOLs are beyond the domain of space and time, hence only μ-evolution.

31. H.H. Spitz and Y. Marcuard, "Chevreul's report on the mysterious oscillations of the hand-held pendulum: A French Chemists' 1833 open letter to Ampere" (translated from French), *Skeptical Inquirer* **25** (2001) pp. 35-39, no. 4. This is the magazine for Science and Reason published by the International Organization "Committee for the Scientific Investigations of Claim of the Paranormal" (CSICOP).

the external observer. No doubt the actions of living micro-organisms (like bacteria, amoeba, etc.) could be the better examples for this purpose but not for a common man. Moreover, physicists ideally identify only three varieties of motion of a rigid body, namely rotation, vibration and translation out of millions of possibilities of motion for living rigid (!) body. Thus, the examples cited in Table 8.2 remain rather crude and could offer only the test cases for a newer theory. Last but not the least important assumption made in citing these examples is in terms of closeness of the system which is not there even for physical objects because AAD and AAT-type forces due to a conscious observer always act and hence affect (in whatever little proportion it may be) the actions performed by the object. As a matter of fact the system never remains a closed one due to the presence of non-locality of highest degree in all the three q-, t- and μ-evolutions.

8.8 Different Scales of Consciousness: Roles of Mindset and Environment

The analysis of human actions discussed in the previous section in terms of q-, t- and μ-evolutions greatly depends on where the space-time recorder (STR) is placed with reference to the EOLs of a person. If it is considered inside (or imagined by) the individual (i.e. it is the part of the mindset of the performer) then the nature of the performed action in terms of quality, quantity and efficiency will be different from the one performed when the STR is an external agent, i.e. it is part of the environment. On this basis one can as well have a new classification of the performed actions. In fact in these cases consciousness of the performer works altogether at different scales. Not only this, the mindset of or the environment available for an individual also plays a dominant role in creating these scales of consciousness mainly on the basis of priorities and subsequently in affecting the nature of the performed action. Before proceeding further we briefly remark on the concepts of "mindset" and "environment" which in some sense represent the roles of micro-body and gross-body respectively in human actions.

8.8.1 MINDSET, CIRCUMSTANCES AND ENVIRONMENT

We all realize that human actions are the outcome of interplay between micro and gross-bodies of an individual and this makes their understanding rather complicated. Recall that the micro-body is defined as $\mathcal{M}\equiv\{M,I,E\}$, with its conscious versions as $\tilde{\mathcal{M}}^{(n)}$, n=1,2, . . . , ∞ and similarly the gross-body $\mathcal{G}$ as $\mathcal{G}\equiv\{SE,B,WO\}$ with its conscious version $\tilde{\mathcal{G}}^{(n)}$, n=1,2. Although the dictionary meanings of the words "circumstance" and "environment" are not very different the former word sounds a bit of subjective aspect and its setting or creation is based on external agencies indirectly, whereas the latter relates exclusively to external agencies directly. However, the realization of both comes from within an individual but with different scales of consciousness. Here, in view of the ideas developed in Section 8.4 it is not difficult to differentiate all the three, mindset, circumstance (σ) and environment (ε) at a subtle level.

While the mindset is a representation of $\mathcal{M}$ or of its dressed version $\tilde{\mathcal{M}}^{(n)}$ as a whole, i.e. for all n, all the three constituents M, I and E of $\mathcal{M}$ keep on cooking a "pudding" during the process of performing an action of priority and in this process they undergo different scales of consciousness, till the priority job is completed. Further note that $\tilde{\mathcal{M}}^{(n)}$ for $n\neq0$ contain certain components of SE and B including that of WO (cf. eqs. (8.1) to (8.8)) and this is how a feedback to the mindset comes from $\mathcal{G}$ rather repeatedly every time in an improved manner. On the other hand, for n=1, i.e. in the lowest order of dressing, we identify $\tilde{\mathcal{G}}^{(1)}$ as the environment ε which in fact provides only realization of the external surroundings, physical objects, region or conditions. The circumstance, σ, is however one step higher in terms of the scale of consciousness and we identify it with $\tilde{\mathcal{G}}^{(2)}$ since σ also accounts for certain subjective elements such as time, place, cause, manner, occasion, etc. present already in ε.

Note that since both σ and ε contain certain proportion of elements of micro-body $\mathcal{M}$, a feedback to $\mathcal{G}$ naturally comes from $\mathcal{M}$. Thus, for the success of an action a beautiful interplay between $\mathcal{M}$ and $\mathcal{G}$ is necessary and this is how it gets affected by the location of STR.

Next we translate these concepts into some functional relations which in turn can be analysed with reference to different human actions.

8.8.2 CIRCUMSTANCE-AFFECTED HUMAN ACTIONS: POSSIBILITY OF A STABLE MINDSET

While σ and ε are often imposed from outside, it is only the mindset of an individual that guides the performance of his actions towards their success. Note that M, I and E in $\mathcal{M}$ in their nascent form are just the instruments ready to be used (static mode of consciousness). Once they are in operation (dynamic mode of consciousness) either at their own or as a result of certain *saṅkalpa*s, then the workings of all the three immediately become dependent not only on space (q), time (t) and circumstance (σ) but also on the characteristic workings of each other. If the operative parts of M, I and E are translated into the corresponding variables m, i and e, then one can define the dependence of the later on q, t and σ as

$$m = m(q, t, \sigma) \,, \tag{8.20}$$

$$i = i(q, t, \sigma, m(q, t, \sigma)) \,, \tag{8.21}$$

$$e = e(q, t, \sigma, m(q, t, \sigma), i(q, t, \sigma, m(q, t, \sigma))). \tag{8.22}$$

On the other hand, the mindset $\mathcal{M} \equiv \{M, I, E\}$ now becomes an explicit function of m, i and e and it depends implicitly on q, t and σ. Thus, the mindset $\mathcal{M} = \mathcal{M}(m, i, e)$, attains an optimum domain of working not only with respect to the internal variables m, i and e but also with respect to the external variables q, t and σ. Since an individual in general has limited capacity of using M, I and E, the variations of m, i, e remain controllable whereas those of the external variables q, t and σ they remain beyond control. For the stability of the mindset $\mathcal{M}$, we shall just demand $\delta\mathcal{M}=0$ with respect to the variations in q, t, and σ. This would define an optimum domain of working of $\mathcal{M}$.

Note the sequential dependence of i on m and of e on m and i in addition to on q, t and σ of all the three m, i, e in eqs. (8.20) to (8.22). In principle, one should also have δm, δi and δe is equal to zero separately for $\delta\mathcal{M}$ to be zero, but we shall not demand this here, mainly because the consciousness keeps on dressing m, i and e separately and repeatedly which does not allow m, i and e to attain stable values. However, $\mathcal{M}$ can attain a stability and that too with respect to external variables q, t and σ. Within this framework, we derive here certain conditions which $\mathcal{M}$ has to satisfy towards its stability.

Since $\mathcal{M} = \mathcal{M}$(m, i, e), this implies

$$\delta\mathcal{M} = \frac{\partial\mathcal{M}}{\partial m}\delta m + \frac{\partial\mathcal{M}}{\partial i}\delta i + \frac{\partial\mathcal{M}}{\partial e}\delta e \tag{8.23}$$

Now from eqs. (8.20), (8.21) and (8.22) we have

$$\delta m = \frac{\partial m}{\partial q}\delta q + \frac{\partial m}{\partial t}\delta t + \frac{\partial m}{\partial \sigma}\delta\sigma \tag{8.24}$$

$$\delta i = \left(\frac{\partial i}{\partial q} + \frac{\partial i}{\partial m}.\frac{\partial m}{\partial q}\right)\delta q + \left(\frac{\partial i}{\partial t} + \frac{\partial i}{\partial m}.\frac{\partial m}{\partial t}\right)\delta t + \left(\frac{\partial i}{\partial \sigma} + \frac{\partial i}{\partial m}.\frac{\partial m}{\partial \sigma}\right)\delta\sigma \tag{8.25}$$

$$\begin{aligned}\delta e = &\left(\frac{\partial e}{\partial q} + \frac{\partial e}{\partial m}.\frac{\partial m}{\partial q} + \frac{\partial e}{\partial i}.\frac{\partial i}{\partial q} + \frac{\partial e}{\partial i}.\frac{\partial i}{\partial m}.\frac{\partial m}{\partial q}\right)\delta q \\ &+ \left(\frac{\partial e}{\partial t} + \frac{\partial e}{\partial m}.\frac{\partial m}{\partial t} + \frac{\partial e}{\partial i}.\frac{\partial i}{\partial t} + \frac{\partial e}{\partial i}.\frac{\partial i}{\partial m}.\frac{\partial m}{\partial t}\right)\delta t \\ &+ \left(\frac{\partial e}{\partial \sigma} + \frac{\partial e}{\partial m}.\frac{\partial m}{\partial \sigma} + \frac{\partial e}{\partial i}.\frac{\partial i}{\partial \sigma} + \frac{\partial e}{\partial i}.\frac{\partial i}{\partial m}.\frac{\partial m}{\partial \sigma}\right)\delta\sigma\end{aligned} \tag{8.26}$$

Next we use eqs. (8.24), (8.25) and (8.26) in eq. (8.23) and demand the vanishing of the coefficients of dq, dt and ds in the resultant expression in order to have $\delta\mathcal{M} = 0$. This would yield the following set of three equations,

$$\frac{\partial \mathcal{M}}{\partial m}\cdot\frac{\partial m}{\partial q}+\frac{\partial \mathcal{M}}{\partial i}\left(\frac{\partial i}{\partial t}+\frac{\partial i}{\partial m}\cdot\frac{\partial m}{\partial q}\right)+\frac{\partial \mathcal{M}}{\partial e}\left(\frac{\partial e}{\partial q}+\frac{\partial e}{\partial m}\cdot\frac{\partial m}{\partial q}+\frac{\partial e}{\partial i}\cdot\frac{\partial i}{\partial q}+\frac{\partial e}{\partial i}\cdot\frac{\partial i}{\partial m}\cdot\frac{\partial m}{\partial q}\right)=0, \quad (8.27a)$$

$$\frac{\partial \mathcal{M}}{\partial m}\cdot\frac{\partial m}{\partial t}+\frac{\partial \mathcal{M}}{\partial i}\left(\frac{\partial i}{\partial t}+\frac{\partial i}{\partial m}\cdot\frac{\partial m}{\partial t}\right)+\frac{\partial \mathcal{M}}{\partial e}\left(\frac{\partial e}{\partial t}+\frac{\partial e}{\partial m}\cdot\frac{\partial m}{\partial t}+\frac{\partial e}{\partial i}\cdot\frac{\partial i}{\partial t}+\frac{\partial e}{\partial i}\cdot\frac{\partial i}{\partial m}\cdot\frac{\partial m}{\partial t}\right)=0, \quad (8.27b)$$

$$\frac{\partial \mathcal{M}}{\partial m}\cdot\frac{\partial m}{\partial \sigma}+\frac{\partial \mathcal{M}}{\partial i}\left(\frac{\partial i}{\partial \sigma}+\frac{\partial i}{\partial m}\cdot\frac{\partial m}{\partial \sigma}\right)+\frac{\partial \mathcal{M}}{\partial e}\left(\frac{\partial e}{\partial \sigma}+\frac{\partial e}{\partial m}\cdot\frac{\partial m}{\partial \sigma}+\frac{\partial e}{\partial i}\cdot\frac{\partial i}{\partial \sigma}+\frac{\partial e}{\partial i}\cdot\frac{\partial i}{\partial m}\cdot\frac{\partial m}{\partial \sigma}\right)=0 \quad (8.27c)$$

In principle, the solution of these simultaneous equations for $\partial\mathcal{M}/\partial m$, $\partial\mathcal{M}/\partial i$ and $\partial\mathcal{M}/\partial e$ in terms of m, i, e, can be obtained in the form of three coupled partial differential equations whose integration with appropriate initial conditions would provide the function $\mathcal{M}_0$(m, i, e) which defines the optimum mindset. In practice it is going to be a difficult task; therefore, we shall demonstrate the use of eqs. (8.27) to some specific human actions where some of the variables are absent and this will make life simple. However, a general condition for the existence of an optimum mindset can be derived as follows: For this purpose we write eqs. (27a) to (27c) in the form

$$a_1x+(b_1+ca_1)y+(d_1+fa_1+gb_1+gca_1)z=0, \quad (8.28a)$$

$$a_2x+(b_2+ca_2)y+(d_2+fa_2+gb_2+gca_2)z=0, \quad (8.28b)$$

$$a_3x+(b_3+ca_3)y+(d_3+fa_3+gb_3+gca_3)z=0, \quad (8.28c)$$

where the variables x, y, z are identified as

$$x=\left(\frac{\partial \mathcal{M}}{\partial m}\right), y=\left(\frac{\partial \mathcal{M}}{\partial i}\right), z=\left(\frac{\partial \mathcal{M}}{\partial e}\right), \text{ and } a_1=\left(\frac{\partial m}{\partial q}\right), a_2=\left(\frac{\partial m}{\partial t}\right), a_3=\left(\frac{\partial m}{\partial \sigma}\right)$$

$$b_1=\left(\frac{\partial i}{\partial q}\right), b_2=\left(\frac{\partial i}{\partial t}\right), b_3=\left(\frac{\partial i}{\partial \sigma}\right); \; d_1=\left(\frac{\partial e}{\partial q}\right), d_2=\left(\frac{\partial e}{\partial t}\right), d_3=\left(\frac{\partial e}{\partial \sigma}\right);$$

$$c=\left(\frac{\partial i}{\partial m}\right), f=\left(\frac{\partial e}{\partial m}\right), g=\left(\frac{\partial e}{\partial i}\right)$$

Further note the condition for the existence of non-zero solutions of these simultaneous algebraic equations that the determinant of the coefficients in eq. (8.28) must vanish, viz.

$$\begin{vmatrix} a_1 & (b_1 + ca_1) & (d_1 + fa_1 + gb_1 + gca_1) \\ a_2 & (b_2 + ca_2) & (d_2 + fa_2 + gb_2 + gca_2) \\ a_3 & (b_3 + ca_3) & (d_3 + fa_3 + gb_3 + gca_3) \end{vmatrix} = 0 \,, \tag{8.29}$$

which on simplification leads to a simpler version as

$$\begin{vmatrix} a_1 & b_1 & d_1 \\ a_2 & b_2 & d_2 \\ a_3 & b_3 & d_3 \end{vmatrix} = 0 \quad \text{or} \tag{8.30}$$

$$\text{or } a_1(b_2d_3 - b_3d_2) - b_1(a_2d_3 - a_3d_2) + d_1(a_2b_3 - a_3b_2) = 0 \tag{8.30a}$$

The condition (8.30a) in original notations takes the form

$$\frac{\partial m}{\partial q}\left(\frac{\partial i}{\partial t}\cdot\frac{\partial e}{\partial \sigma} - \frac{\partial i}{\partial \sigma}\frac{\partial e}{\partial t}\right) - \frac{\partial i}{\partial q}\left(\frac{\partial m}{\partial t}\frac{\partial e}{\partial \sigma} - \frac{\partial m}{\partial \sigma}\frac{\partial e}{\partial t}\right) + \frac{\partial e}{\partial q}\left(\frac{\partial m}{\partial t}\frac{\partial i}{\partial \sigma} - \frac{\partial m}{\partial \sigma}\frac{\partial i}{\partial t}\right) = 0. \tag{8.31}$$

This requirement in fact restricts infinitely many choices in which the mind, intellect and ego depend on space, time and circumstance to a particular choice which in turn supplies a feedback for the optimum mindset in the form of the solution of eqs. (8.28a) to (8.28c) for $(\partial \mathcal{M}/\partial m)$, $(\partial \mathcal{M}/\partial i)$, $(\partial \mathcal{M}/\partial e)$. Reduction of eq. (8.29) to a simpler version eq. (8.30) implies the self and mutual cancellation of a number of intermediate processes taking place inside the human Being before the mindset with regard to a particular action is made. Such an observation in fact, supports the Vedānta philosophy of *guṇa guṇeṣu vartantu* (cf. Chapter 2 verses 2.4 and 2.5).

8.9 Slow Growth and Fast Decay Model of the Mindset

The mindset $\mathcal{M}$ of a person while it is a function of m, i and e, also depends implicitly on space, time and circumstances. It plays a crucial role in the successful performance of an action. The conditions for the occurrence of an optimum $\mathcal{M}$ are discussed in the previous section. As our experiences reveal, it takes some time for the mindset to locate an appropriate environment in which it can effectively work towards the success of an action. In other words, the growth of $\mathcal{M}$ with respect to consciousness is rather slow since its constituents keep on dressing up (or becoming more and more upgraded in terms of understanding) repeatedly with consciousness until $\mathcal{M}$ attains a crucial value which immediately starts working towards the performance of an action, i.e. it undergoes a fast decay. In order to understand this phenomenon better here we make use of an already available mathematical framework of a Lienard system.[32] In particular, we shall study the evolution of the mindset with consciousness in an altogether different manner from that discussed in Section 8.4.

For this purpose, we define the derivatives (denoted by over bars) of the mindset $\mathcal{M}$ with respect to the meditation parameter, m (i.e. $\overline{\mathcal{M}} = (d\mathcal{M} / \partial\mu)$, $\overline{\overline{\mathcal{M}}} = (d^2\mathcal{M} / \partial\mu^2)$ (μ here in fact accounts for a cumulative effect of the variables m, i and e) and assume that the evolution of $\mathcal{M}$ with consciousness is described in general by the Lienard equation,

$$\overline{\overline{\mathcal{M}}} + f(\mathcal{M})\overline{\mathcal{M}} + g(\mathcal{M}) = 0, \tag{8.32}$$

where the functions f($\mathcal{M}$) and g($\mathcal{M}$) in general satisfy certain conditions,[33] or in particular eq. (8.32) assumes a simpler version and becomes the Van del Pol equation, viz.

$$\overline{\overline{\mathcal{M}}} + \in(\mathcal{M}^2 - 1)\overline{\mathcal{M}} + \mathcal{M} = 0. \tag{8.33}$$

Eq. (8.33) describes a relaxation-oscillation system corresponding to a slow build-up and a fast discharge of consciousness with regard to a particular action. In fact the values of the positive parameter $\in$ in eq. (8.33) play a crucial role with regard to the stability of $\mathcal{M}$ when studied as a function of μ.

In the present context while the consciousness is constantly

32. See, for example, R.S. Kaushal and D. Parashar, *Advanced Methods of Mathematical Physics*, 2nd edn. (New Delhi: Narosa Pub. House and London: Alpha Science, 2008), chapter 8.

33. R.S. Kaushal and D. Parashar, op. cit.

pouring into the system, the mindset $\mathcal{M}$ oscillates between two of its values (say $\mathcal{M}_1$ and $\mathcal{M}_2$) and with two periodic values of the meditation parameter μ, say μ_s and μ_F. During μ_s, $\mathcal{M}$ slowly attains the (higher) value $\mathcal{M}_2$ (i.e. $\mathcal{M}$ undergoes a kind of relaxation) and during μ_F it decays (decreases) rather fast to the (lower) value $\mathcal{M}_1$. This process with varying (or oscillating) $\mathcal{M}$ continues until the role of damping term (i.e. $\bar{\mathcal{M}}$-term in eq. (8.33)) in conjunction with the value of the parameter $\in$ becomes crucial. Finally, for some critical values of $\in$, μ_s and μ_F a stability in the system (in the form of "limit cycle") is achieved and at this stage $\mathcal{M}$ is fit for the success of an action. With regard to the application of these constructs in human behaviour, recall the roles of encouragement and depression (or frustration) in the evolution of the mindset and subsequently in the success of an action. While encouragement can be considered as an analogue of positive damping (i.e. $\bar{\mathcal{M}}$ is positive), depression (or frustration), on the other hand, it plays the role of negative damping (i.e. $\bar{\mathcal{M}}$ is negative). Now it is not difficult to study the stability of $\mathcal{M}$ in terms of the formation of a limit cycle.[34]

8.10 A Classification of Non-physical Interactions

Although the efforts in this chapter have been to investigate SEP-P interactions, the fact is that the EOLs, other than SO, act as EP-matter and that too in the presence of SO. On the other hand, the external P-matter with respect to an individual when watched by the same or different person also acts as an EP-matter. Thus, the whole problem now reduces to the study of the non-physical interactions produced either by two EP-matter particles or by the same P-matter particle but illuminated (or dressed) by different consciousness. It may be reminded here that the consciousness broadly speaking is of two categories — relative and absolute. While absolute consciousness is a direct attribute of SO, relative consciousness manifests through different EOLs or the body parts once they are dressed up by the presence of SO. In all, there arise four possibilities of non-physical interactions between EP-matter

34. R.S. Kaushal and D. Parashar, op. cit.

particles corresponding to EP-EP, EP-E′P, EP-EP′ and EP-E′P′. Interactions are non-physical in the sense that they could be of AAT- or AADT-type in addition to the AAD-type. Before elaborating on these interactions we discuss below the mechanism which takes place in converting the P-matter of WO into EP-matter in the field of SO, or the manner in which the absolute consciousness divides itself into its relative category.

The consciousness which converts (or dresses) the P-matter of WO into the EP-matter in the field of SO, in fact, is a collective and cumulative effect of conscious inner (except SO) and outer EOLs. As argued earlier, this happens in several stages of dressing of EOLs with consciousness. With regard to an understanding of interactions, we restrict here only to the two initial stages for the sake of simplicity. In the first step, all EOLs get illuminated (or dressed up) and themselves become EP-matter, i.e. E, I, M, SE and B now become $\widetilde{E}$, $\widetilde{I}$, $\widetilde{M}$, $\widetilde{S}\widetilde{E}$ and $\widetilde{B}$ as a result of *pañcīkaraṇa* rule. The latter in turn enable the detection of P-matter. Then in the second stage, these epi- (or dressed-) EOLs interact with the external P-matter and correspondingly form $\widetilde{E}$P, $\widetilde{I}$P, $\widetilde{M}$P, $\widetilde{S}\widetilde{E}$P and $\widetilde{B}$P out of the same P-matter particle. These new epi-matter states do not act instantly (of course, this depends on the nature of P-matter object) but follow a sequence[35] for this purpose. The

35. In Vedanta philosophy the prevailing analogous concept is that of the sequence of seer and seen followed from outside to inside in the sense that for the object first SE become seer, then for SE , M becomes seer, and then for M, SO becomes ultimate seer with the help of I and E. All this happens when EOLs are dressed with consciousness and the same has been discussed in the previous chapters. In this case the experience of an external object is gained sequentially, viz. B→SE→M→I→E→SO. An alternative to this process is the experience of an object on the basis of imagination, i.e. from inside to outside. This becomes possible when the knowledge (or the experience) about the external object is already stored in E or, in general, in $\mathcal{M}$ on the basis of experiences about the object in the "past". In Vedānta philosophy, this word "past" might continue even to previous birth(s) of the Being and the dreaming (or imagination) in fact is said to be the outcome of such past experiences.

experience about $\tilde{S}\tilde{E}P$ (or $\tilde{B}P$) now first noticed by $\tilde{M}$ as $\tilde{M}\tilde{S}\tilde{E}P$ (or $\tilde{M}\tilde{B}P$) and if necessity arises (again depending on the nature of P-matter) then it passes through $\tilde{I}$ and $\tilde{E}$ as $\tilde{I}\tilde{S}\tilde{E}P$ (or $\tilde{I}\tilde{B}\tilde{P}$) and $\tilde{E}\tilde{S}\tilde{E}P$ (or $\tilde{E}\tilde{B}\tilde{P}$), respectively before its final realization by SO.

Now we remark on the non-physical interactions arising from the presence of two such objects. In a way it is a kind of three-body interactions, but the third (or the other) body remains only a spectator after illuminating the objects by its consciousness. In some sense these interactions lie in the domain of $\tilde{\mathcal{G}}^{(2)}$.

EP-EP interaction: This could be the case of self-interaction of a P-matter particle placed in the realm of the same (but relative) consciousness. Alternatively, two identical P-matter particles interacting and "looked at" by the same observer also constitute the example of this case. In this case though the observer may be the same the relative consciousness emanating from different body-parts could be different. For example, different perceptions can be derived by touching the same P-matter particle first by finger and later by thumb or vice versa.

EP-E′P interaction: The same P-matter particle but illuminated by different sources of consciousness (or perceived by different mindsets) clearly constitute the example of this case. The same object could be watched by different observers or by the same observer but at different space-time points and the circumstances as well.

EP-EP′ interaction: This is the case of two different P-matter particles interacting and at the same time illuminated by the same source of consciousness. In other words, the interaction is noticed by the same person or by two persons having the same order of dressing of their inner EOLs. It is rather impossible to find two persons who ideally have the same mindsets, therefore the first situation is applicable.

EP-E′P′ interaction: This is a very general case of two different P-matter particles interacting and illuminated by two distinct (and not connected) sources of consciousness. Such a situation can be created by two isolated observers or by the same observer but provided with different mindsets in terms of the dressing of its constituents or in terms of development of their EOLs.

8.11 Puruṣa, Prakṛti and the Universality of Sexual Processes

In this section we present another aspect of interaction between the human Being and physical world. As mentioned earlier, the cosmic consciousness (and its localized version SO in a Being) and five cosmic elements (*PM*s) are the synonyms of *puruṣa* and *prakṛti* of Vedānta philosophy. Not only this, a grand world order is maintained by the *puruṣa, prakṛti* and their interactions in general. One aspect of this interaction is the creation of *jīva* (Being) — human or non-human. This creation takes place through a sexual process and the latter is universal in the sense that it is always present as a part of the world order but its modes and methods change for different species. In fact according to some thinkers, sex and sexual processes are the main cause of existence of universe or the world order maintained in it. Although for a common man the concept of God (*puruṣa*) or the related experiences keep on changing with the development of his FOUs the fact is that he cannot ignore observing Nature (*prakṛti*) or deriving the related experiences from it. In fact these experiences for him are always there and everywhere since the time of his birth and until his death.

In view of the ideas developed so far in the preceding chapters, it is not difficult to define God (or the *puruṣa* of Vedānta philosophy) for a scientific mind. As a matter of fact the "ultimate cause" of dynamism in Nature can be termed as God. On the other end, there also exists an absolute "statism" in Nature which could be the manifestation of inertia in Nature. There exists a spectrum of interactions between these two extreme realities. These interactions are of varying nature in terms of their physical and non-physical aspects. Although physicists and biologists have been able to extract only a few varieties of these interactions in the "man-made" laboratory, the fact is that the existence and experiences of other vast classes of interactions cannot be denied in the "God-made" laboratory of Nature, i.e. in the realm of *PMs*. The end-point of one class of such interactions is the sex and sexual processes which lead to reproduction of all Beings. Needless to say that various and peculiar are the ways of performing such processes in different species.

Although the "cause and effect principle" is in the background of all physical processes in general, there exists a unique cause corresponding to a process that has roots again in some physical interaction which is translated into a particular choice of force-law out of a plethora of choices. One can say that the unique force-law found to explain the underlying natural phenomenon is the manifestation of *puruṣa* of Vedānta philosophy whereas the objects between which this force-law acts are the part of *prakṛti*. (In the language of field theory of physics it is the field-particle or *puruṣa–prakṛti* duality that maintains the world order in physical domain.) In other words, a generalized version of the *puruṣa–prakṛti* marriage is responsible for the maintenance of world order. This fact is clearly emphasized by Lord Kṛṣṇa in *SMBG*[36] when he says,

mama yonir mahad brahma tasmina garbhaṁ dadhāmyahaṁ ।
sambhavaḥ sarvabhūtānāṁ tato bhavati bhārata. — 14.3 (8.34)

sarvayoniṣu kaunteya mūrtayaḥ sambhavanti yāḥ ।
tāsāṁ brahma mahadyoniraham bījapradaḥ pitā. — 14.4 (8.35)

My *prakṛti* or Nature in her primordial, undeveloped state is the womb of all creatures; in that I place the seed (of consciousness). The birth of all Beings follows from this combination of matter and spirit. O descendent of Bharata.

The universal fact of motherhood of *prakṛti* is further emphasized by the Lord in the second verse when he says,

Of all the bodies that take birth from different wombs, this

36. *Śrīmad Bhagavad-Gītā*, chapter 14, verses 3 and 4, Gorakhpur: Gita Press.

> primordial matter is the mother and I am the procreating father, O son of Kuntī.

Modern researchers have shown that females have better power of expression through sense organs, body parts and body actions than their male counterparts, and so is the case with the present cosmic male and female, i.e. with the *puruṣa* and *prakṛti*. The Nature (*prakṛti*) expresses itself in a wonderful style and variety of ways which force one to become curious to know about its working (i.e. the role of a scientist). The role of *puruṣa* is in fact hidden (in the form of interactions) but it is always present and without its role *prakṛti* (Nature) also cannot work, i.e. a kind of dynamism at different levels cannot be brought into the system. On the other hand, *puruṣa* without *prakṛti* cannot do anything as far as the maintenance of world order is concerned. Thus, the complementary roles of *puruṣa* and *prakṛti* are there not only in the maintenance of world order but also in the existence of this universe as a whole. The super cause of this dynamism in Nature can be termed as "God" or "super power."

8.12 Concluding Discussion

In view of the fact that subjects like modern physics and modern biology now deal with several phenomena whose theoretical understanding would require the introduction of a new variable which is an attribute of consciousness of a Being, the present chapter is devoted to investigate some such aspects of consciousness with an eye on their quantitative applications. In fact the consciousness emanating from a living Being is a phenomenon in itself. No doubt an account of consciousness in the theory leads to non-physical interactions (in the sense that they are no more mere space-time mediated interactions). A modest attempt is made in this chapter to explore different facets of the phenomenon of consciousness with regard to human actions and experiences. To this effect, several new concepts and models are suggested here, perhaps for the first time, which may be of immediate help in any kind of quantification of consciousness. Of course, the patomic model of human Being has always remained in the background of all these developments.

After having discussed some intricately interwoven roles of space, time and consciousness in human actions and experiences, the possibility of a (3/2)-rule with regard to the manifestation of consciousness through different body parts is proposed as a first step towards the quantification of consciousness. The static and dynamic modes of consciousness are then discussed, which, in turn, become responsible for active and passive roles of EOLs in human actions. In analogy with the *pañcīkaraṇa* rule well known for *PM*s in Vedic sciences (cf. Appendix D), a new *pañcīkaraṇa* rule for EOLs is suggested here (cf. Section 8.4). As offshoots of this new *pañcīkaraṇa* rule a *trikaraṇa* rule for inner EOLs (M, I and E) and a *dvikaraṇa* rule for outer EOLs (SE and B) are suggested. The latter help in producing highly dressed micro and gross bodies with consciousness and the same in turn act as refined instruments in the perception process of a P-matter particle. Also, these dressed $\mathcal{M}$ and $\mathcal{G}$ help in analysing the interactions which take place inside the human Being before the actual performance of an action. Several new *tanmātras* responsible for these interactions are defined in the process and they provide some sort of fine-tuning of the known classical *tanmātras* of Vedānta philosophy.

As a second step towards the quantification of consciousness, the Hamilton's principle of least action of classical mechanics is generalized to the extent that it now accommodates the consciousness through the meditation variable μ introduced in the Lagrangian and treated on par with the time variable t. The extremization of the action-integral so constructed gives rise to STC evolution equations as an analogue of Euler-Lagrange equations. With a view to accounting for the non-physical components associated with both the object and the action performed on it, the STC evolution equations are also derived using a complex action integral with a Lagrangian as a function of complex coordinate and velocity. While the real parts of these complex quantities correspond to physical aspects of the system, the imaginary parts, on the other hand, are expected to account for the non-physical aspects of a process and human action. In fact such a prescription leads to a rich system of STC evolution equations and the same in turn are capable of accounting for a fine explanation of several human actions and experiences (cf. Section 8.7).

The repeated use of *trikaraṇa* rule for inner EOLs suggests that consciousness in human actions appears on different scales and thereby defines a mindset, $\mathcal{M}$ (m, i, e), of variable nature. Since m, i and e are the functions of space (q), time (t) and circumstances (σ), therefore, an active mindset also becomes a function of space, time and circumstances. In this context, the conditions for the occurrence of an optimum mindset towards the success of an action are derived in mathematical terms. As a matter of fact towards the performance of an action first a slow build-up of mindset takes place and then it decays rather fast as a function of μ variable. This fact is modelled through a non-linear Van der Pol type equation (cf. Section 8.9). The study of solutions of this latter non-linear equation can again throw light on obtaining a stable mindset in a certain parametric domain.

Although the studies in this chapter are focused on SEP-P interaction the mechanism discussed in Section 8.10 suggests that it all reduces to four types of non-physical interactions between the EP-matter particles. An interesting example of SEP-P interaction is the sex and sexual processes. These processes are common to all species of living Beings and are constantly taking place (of course only modes are different) towards the maintenance of world order. The universality of these processes is well supported by Vedānta philosophy in Section 8.11 in terms of *puruṣa-prakṛti* interaction.

A few remarks about the order of dressing of micro-body (cf. Section 8.4) and the meditation parameter, μ, (cf. Sections 8.4 and 8.5) are necessary here. While the repeated use of *dvikaraṇa* rule for outer EOLs already gives equal weightage to the contributions of both B and SE in higher orders, the repeated use of *trikaraṇa* rule for inner EOLs, however, has a tendency to generate equal contributions of M, I and E in higher orders (cf. Table 8.1). This is what actually happens for a person sitting in meditation or undergoing a thought process. Initially, any one out of M, I, E dominates the scene (depending upon the circumstances or the external environment with reference to a particular object) and later when they are repeatedly dressed according to the *trikaraṇa* rule, i.e. the meditation becomes deeper and deeper, their roles with reference to the given external object become comparable (cf. Table 8.1). In other words, the dressings of higher and higher orders make them more and more active to work in the sense that M undergoes much deeper feelings, I brings in the best of the decisions or the discriminatory powers, and E supplies all the past experiences possible and this is how the inner EOLs succeed in providing the best towards the performance of an action. Note that in different quantitative approaches followed in this chapter, the meditation parameter μ is used as a representative of consciousness. In some sense it is fully justified because first of all only a conscious person will give a thought prior to the performance of an action, and once he starts thinking within given circumstances (σ), then his thinking (or meditation) will continue to search "the best" out of the given σ with the help of M, I and E. For this search of "the best" he will freely use not only his inner EOLs but also their level of development attained till then. Thus, the infinite sequence of dressings will finally give rise to an optimum mindset function $\mathcal{M} = \mathcal{M}(\text{m, i, e})$. This is how the variable μ collectively accounts for the consciousness manifesting through M, I and E in terms of the variables m, i and e respectively. For this reason only $\mathcal{M}$ as a function of μ alone is considered in the Van der Pol model (cf. Section 8.9).

As an example of interactions inside the human Being, next look at *fig*. 1.2 and its discussion given in Section 1.7. This is the case of AI-type interaction in general, and of SEP-P interaction in particular. For both the situations discussed there, namely when pizza piece is in the hand of the boy or when it is lying on a table and the boy is still planning to eat it, the processes taking place inside the boy can be analysed in terms of orders of dressing of his M, I and E with consciousness. Of course, the level of development of FOUs of the boy will play a crucial role in the success of the action. Although there are plenty of examples from human behaviour where the interactions inside the Being are affecting his outer actions a few of them are worth citing for a scientific mind and they are (i) the case of a Chevreul hand-held pendulum[37] in which varying mindset reflects in the time period, or (ii) the time period also gets affected for the case of a swinging lady suspended from a rigid support. In either case the effect of consciousness present in the system will be reflected.

All Beings have divinity in them. It predominates more in human Being. Human Being is not only a special epi-physical (SEP) matter like any other Being but it has something further special which makes it a unique species and that is, it has the capacity of self-awareness.[38] Commonly it is thought (as also argued earlier) that it is the faculty of reasoning that sets us apart from other living Beings. But it is not so since the reasoning alone can-not teach us anything new. In fact the distinguishing feature of humans lies in our capacity of self-awareness. Other living creatures may have ability to perform a greater variety of tasks or may have developed superior sensibilities in certain areas; but we alone have the capacity to look at ourselves and be aware of ourselves. This makes the understanding of fundamental processes, on which the human perception, actions and reactions, experiences and the behaviour are based, more complicated. Perhaps the situation may be somewhat simple

---

37. H.H. Spitz and Y. Marcuard, op. cit.

38. S.H. Venkatramani, "Self-awareness Makes us a Unique Species", The Speaking Tree Column, *Times of India*, 10 January 2008.

with non-human Beings. We shall return to some of these discussions in Chapter 10. We can attain knowledge, but what is unique about us is that we can also get to know as to how we could attain that knowledge like the RAM-ROM case with the computer (cf. Section 6.5).

No doubt the use of elements of Vedānta philosophy through patomic model (cf. Appendix A) has offered an explanation of several intricate processes pertaining to human actions and behaviour, but the perfection of this explanation still remains questionable. It is not because of the tools of Vedic science but due to the limitations of the author. As a matter of fact, we could not account here for several interesting aspects.

For example, for the interactions between a physically and/or mentally challenged (PMC) person or of a non-human with the physical world. In some sense this will fall under the case of a "fractured" patomic model as they both deviate from the perfect creation like (normal) human Being. Whether it is the case of a PMC person or a non-human with certain minimum inner EOLs (like, M), both types of Beings perceive the physical world differently and it again depends on the missing inner and/or outer EOLs and the development of existing FOUs in an individual. In case of a PMC person it also matters whether the person is challenged since birth or during an accident after birth and that too at which stage of the lifespan. In the latter case, however, there remains some possibility of development of his FOUs which improves the quality of his perception of the physical world. Note that these perceptions of or the interactions with physical world could be further different for a person who is (i) physically challenged (PC) in terms of senses of knowledge (SEKs) or in terms of organs responsible for actions (SEAs), or is (ii) mentally challenged (MC) in terms of his decision-making faculty (I) or his memory faculty (E). Similarly, non-humans have different perceptions of the world depending upon the EOLs they are equipped with. We shall return to some of these details in Chapter 10.

All through this chapter no doubt a basis for several new ideas, concepts and models is discussed and often examples are cited to this effect, but the fact is that some of these developments could not be pursued up to their end-points. Perhaps future studies can take care of these aspects along with some more applications of these ideas. The interesting point to be noted here is that the fine-tuning of the earlier crude patomic model (cf. Appendix A) has definitely provided a basis for explanation of many human actions and experiences.

9

Interactions Among Human Beings

THE interaction of a human Being with an external (inanimate) object and also its impact on human actions and behaviour are investigated in the previous chapter. In this chapter we continue our studies to the case when the external object is also a conscious human Being; or else when a human Being is interacting with a group (finite or infinite) of conscious persons. In either situation we assume that the (conscious) observer is not a part of the interacting system. Of course, certain analogies from physics will be helpful for this purpose but the fact is that the physical theories themselves work under some simplifying assumptions (cf. chapters 1 and 6). In particular, "physics interactions" are just space-time mediated whereas here the "human interactions" are more complex and their description will go much beyond the space-time structure of Nature. Our efforts will be to provide a basis for quantification of these human interactions within the framework of patomic model.

As a matter of fact, true "physics interactions" are the ones recorded by an ideally non-interacting apparatus; otherwise the interactions of the apparatus with the system under study are bound to affect the observations, particularly when the system is a microscopic one. On the other hand, if this apparatus happened to be a human Being (as is the case with direct measurement or that with quantum measurement) then the observations will contain relatively more errors and the same can be eliminated by statistical methods or by repeating the experiment. However, if a human Being is recording the interaction between other two or among more human Beings, then it is going to be a very complex situation. In what follows, we shall neglect the interactions of the recorder human Being and assume that he remains only a spectator of the interacting system. Though this assumption is not justified in the present context, it is a reasonable choice for any kind of quantification of interactions among Beings.

After carrying out surveys of many-body interactions in physics and many-human Being interactions in a society, we cite certain cases of two- and many-human Being interactions from Vedic literature in Section 9.3. From Section 9.4 onward we continue with our efforts of quantification of interactions among human Beings within the framework of patomic model which in some sense started in the previous chapter. The case of two-human Beings is analysed in great detail in Section 9.5 by citing certain specific examples from day-to-day life which in fact form the basis of a society. With somewhat less emphasis, the case of interactions among three and four human Beings is discussed in Section 9.6. The possibility of a new kind of socialization is highlighted in Section 9.7 by borrowing certain analogies from physics and using the framework of patomic model. Finally, concluding remarks are made in Section 9.8.

9.1 A Brief Survey of Many-Body Interactions in Physics

In physics there exists a hierarchy of many-body systems at different levels and scales. Starting with the system of galaxies and stars in the universe, it comes down to molecules of gas in a container, then to atoms in a crystal, to a collection of electrons in a metal or in an atom, and then to the case of nucleons in a nucleus which also constitute a many-body system. The most fine many-body system discussed by physicists is the concept of field and particle in the language of field theory. As such it is very difficult to deal exactly with or to understand completely a many-body system in terms of its interacting constituents. Often approximate methods are explored and employed for studying the many-body systems of different scales. These approximations could be either in terms of modelling the arrangement of constituents in the system or in terms of the mathematization of the underlying forces between the constituents to start with. In fact it is the basic two-body force which becomes the basis for generating the many-body forces, either pair-wise or otherwise. However, the study of this "otherwise" part of the force still remains a problem of research even today, in spite of the fact that the three-body problem with an inverse square law of force is solved to a fair degree of accuracy (e.g. the problem of sun-earth-moon).

Since the inverse square law of force is long-range, the effect of four- or higher-body forces can be easily neglected. However, this is not the case with the nuclear force which is a short range one and hence three- or higher-body forces become as important as the two-body one. Moreover, there is already a problem of finding a suitable (as is the case with the Coulomb force between charged particles or the gravitation force between heavenly bodies) law of force between nucleons. In fact many such choices to the two-body force between nucleons have led to many models of the nucleus; often there is a model to explain a particular property of the nucleus.

Among other approaches to tackle the many-body problems in physics are: (i) By considering, in the first approximation, the motion of an individual constituent in an average potential generated as a result of many body forces and then correcting the results for the effect of two- and higher-body forces, rather in an approximate manner at the second stage of approximation. This approach has been very successful in nuclear physics. (ii) By considering the dynamics of an interacting many-body system through statistical methods (e.g. Fermi-Dirac or Bose-Einstein statistics for the collection of electrons or of photons). In this case also, in the lowest approximation, the system is considered as non-interacting and the dynamism of the system is translated into the arrangement of constituents on the basis of their properties; and then at the next stage the corrections due to two- and higher-body interactions are incorporated through a state-function (called partition-function). In spite of the fact that both these approaches are successful in their respective domains with reference to experiments, yet there does not exist a unified approach to handle the many-body systems in physics rather exactly.

As a matter of fact, as a result of many-body interactions in a many-body system several new features like correlations, collective behaviour, co-operative phenomenon, etc. appear which do not find explanation in a non-interacting many-body system. While correlations to some extent can be understood in terms of two-body forces, for other features however an explanation is sought in terms of three- and higher-body forces. Sometimes the models for this purpose are formulated on the basis of theories of fluid dynamics.

9.2 A Survey of Many-Being Interactions: Socialization

It has been observed that there exists a sign of love and affection, co-operation and co-ordination as well as efforts for the co-existence among the members of a particular species of living Beings. On the other hand, negatives of this systematics are also observed among these members as and when there is a question of their survival. Further, for a given species although there may be variations in these systematics with respect to space, time and environment, by and large this kind of socialization is universal for all species of living Beings in the sense that at times different species also follow these systematics.

While the follow-up of the above systematics by the members of a given species is understandable as they are the present generation fruits of the same (genetic) tree but how about the follow-up of these systematics by a mixture of different species? No doubt a kind of natural law and the external circumstances force them to co-exist and co-operate but the fact is that all living Beings have at least certain EOLs (like SO, B and SE) in common. Although at the level of finer details while B and SE could also be different, it is the commonality of the EOL SO among all living Beings that brings them together and the same manifests through all of them in a variety of ways. Since each living Being is a part of cosmic consciousness, this forms the basis of all causes of socialization. Of course, the degree of socialization varies not only among different species but also among the sub-groups of the same species. Here, we continue our studies on two broad classes of living Beings, namely on human and non-human Beings. While the studies of the former are pursued in this chapter, that of the latter are postponed to the next chapter.

It may be mentioned that with respect to the age of a person, his fronts of socialization increase in terms of relationship, citizenship, professionalism, religion and the like. In what follows we briefly review as to how one develops socialization on different fronts as he becomes older and older. In general, it has been observed that the FOUs of a person develop with age and accordingly different fronts of socialization (or the kind of bonds of society) slowly emerge and come into existence.

9.2.1 INTERACTIONS DURING CHILDHOOD

While a newly born baby has come with his *prārabdha* (an essence of *karmas* of previous birth(s)), he interacts with his mother for his survival. As he grows he starts interacting with his father and other family members and later with his friends (that might include non-human pets as well) of the same age group. Note that first these interactions mostly are at the level of B and soon after his learning of the "mother-tongue" (which need not be a formal verbal language or script) he starts reacting and interacting through SE not only with humans and non-humans but also with Nature. While all this continues in the "school" of his family, at the same time his FOUs start developing in a particular way in the sense that family traditions are inculcated in him at the level of M and I. Since E is still not very active till this time M and I also function "linearly" and this is the reason for the innocence and simplicity built in the child's behaviour in general. As E is not fully developed by this time, the child has the tendency to forget and ignore the effects of many of the interactions temporarily or permanently. While *prārabdha* also plays a role in this case, some of the *saṁskāra*s (tendencies) in the child are going to a stay throughout life.

At the next stage when the child is admitted to a formal school or college, he is exposed to a variety of personalities for interactions. During the schooling, the FOUs (including E) of the child start working exponentially with time and they are trained in various ways for digesting the preliminaries of the existing world order. By this time the child along with his contemporary friends becomes prepared to survive properly in this world. If somehow the training of formal school is missing for him, then the training of his "family school" continues and works for his survival in a specific way and without many options. Even in this case he has opportunity to learn many lessons from the interactions with society of which he himself becomes a part and these lessons supply a feedback for further development of his FOUs. In summary, the child learns at a fast rate from the circumstances in which he is left and starts behaving accordingly.

9.2.2 INTERACTIONS DURING ADULTHOOD

Once the child becomes an adult, his socialization increases. Besides the educational (if attached to a centre of higher learning) two more fronts of his interaction open and these are the extended domain of interaction at the family level through his marriage and a new front of interaction for the sake of livelihood in future. Note that by now family *saṁskāra*s become more or less static and remain only in the background. The marriage front, however, offers only limited personalities to interact with, but of sensitive nature in the sense that they matter a lot in maintaining peace at home and at work. When the married person has a child, then no doubt history repeats for the child as per his father or mother but for the latter it is an altogether new experience in terms of interactions with the child at every stage of his growth. This experience in terms of interactions becomes even richer when the parents have more than one child.

The livelihood front, on the other hand, brings in countless personalities for interaction of the adult. In fact the individual adult becomes a nodal point of many and sometimes diverging fronts of interaction with various organizations and societies. Now, he automatically becomes an important member of the society in the same way as he was the important member of the family during his childhood. At every stage and point of time his FOUs keep on enriching in terms of experiences and the same in turn also supply a feedback to his EOLs for further improving the lifestyle or behaviour. This is the period in one's lifetime when all the EOLs are most active and the person is capable of leaving certain impact on the society or the footprints on the sands of time in whatever form it can be.

9.2.3 INTERACTIONS DURING MIDDLE AGE

During the adulthood the interactions of an individual with other persons reach a peak mainly because of the maximum activity of his EOLs at this point of time. Then comes the period of middle-age in which the already developed interactions are just maintained with a possibility of certain new interactions with third generation whether it is at home or at work. With the experiences becoming richer and richer with time, the behaviour of the person accordingly becomes more refined. As a result, a middle-age person develops a natural tendency to share and express himself through these experiences now and then, and again at home and at work. This sometimes further enhances his domain of interactions with other persons. If one subtracts the "himself" part from these experiences, then a good fraction of these experiences can be noticed as universal in the sense that they are not only free from caste, colour, creed or country but are also from the boundaries of time. This is the starting point of the "wisdom of old persons" which continues in the old age as well, of course with further refinements.

During the middle age both inner and outer EOLs in general remain equally active. In some cases, however, B and SE start showing the symptoms of decay.

9.2.4 INTERACTIONS DURING OLD AGE

During the old age while the inner EOLs namely M, I and E remain equally active as they do in the middle age, outer EOLs, B and SE start decaying. As a result, the interactions with other persons, which once achieved the peak during adulthood and a constant level during the middle age, however start decreasing because of the limitations on the workings of body parts and also of senses of knowledge and action. On the other hand, if the person has been a true observer of his conscious and serious actions during earlier stages of life, then his experiences, gained so far out of the interactions with other persons, now indeed become the "wisdom of old persons." They not only become the source of inspiration to the new generation but sometime they become the role models for the society as a whole.

9.3 Cases of Two- and Many-Being Interactions in Vedic Literature

Ancient Indian seers had established certain norms for a peaceful living and a happy co-existence of human Beings in a society or in a country. These norms in fact are defined with a view to establishing the moral, ethical and social values first in an individual and then in a society as a whole. Starting with Upaniṣads, the details of these norms are repeatedly cited in Saṁhitās, Smṛtis, *Rāmāyaṇa*, *Mahābhārata* and in several other sacred texts. In other scriptures like *Pañcatantra*, *Hitopadeśa*, *Mitralābha*, etc. the importance of these norms is emphasized through stories involving birds and animals. Lord Rāma in *Rāmāyaṇa* and Lord Kṛṣṇa in *Mahābhārata* also appear as reviver, ideal follower, ideal establisher and inculcator of these norms which disappeared from society at different points of time.

Although these norms originate basically from the philosophy of an individual (or from the science of Self as described in Vedānta) at the next stage they revolve around the natural and canonical interactions that are found to exist between two specific individuals like child and mother, son and father, husband and wife, two ideal friends, teacher and taught (one), etc. As a matter of fact these are a few cases in which the one-to-one interaction originates from the innermost existence (and that is the Soul) and it is hardly affected by the presence of other interactions in the family or in the society. In this way many morals are made available to an individual to follow, as mentioned in Chapter 5, from the sacred scriptures for his better living and a fruitful interaction with society. Here we cite a couple of cases to this effect from the Vedic literature mainly as examples of two- and many-Being interactions.

Recall the verse (5.1) of Chapter 5 which basically is a prayer-couplet, however, it aims at the quality of interaction that would exist ideally between the teacher (one) and the taught (one or many). The Verse offers the highest degree of moral in a sequential manner from the level of outer EOLs to that of inner EOLs in the sense that first there should be a peaceful co-existence and peaceful survival of the teacher and the taught and then there should be the best of co-ordination in the duties of both and the best output of this co-ordination through the best intellectual interactions by way of not hating each other. All this has to proceed in a peaceful manner.

In another context, Arjuna in *SMBG* cites[1] some of these unique cases of one-to-one interactions to emphasize the quality of his prayer to Lord Kṛṣṇa to ignore his sins and misbehaviour which he might have committed prior to realizing the Cosmic existence of Lord Kṛṣṇa through the verse:

tasmāt praṇamya praṇidhāya kāyaṁ ।
prasādaye tvāmahamīsamīdyam ।
piteva putrasya sakheva sakhyuḥ ।
priyaḥ priyāyārhasi devasoḍum ॥ — 11.44 (9.1)

1. *Śrīmad Bhagavad-Gītā*, chapter 11, verse 44.

> O Lord, laying my body at Your feet and bowing low, I seek to propitiate You, the ruler of all and worthy of all praise. It behoves You to condone my fault even as a father condones the fault of his son, a friend that of his friend and the loving husband that of his beloved consort.

In fact there is an infinite scope of interaction (may be sweet or sour) between the members of these unique pairs of human Beings. The two-Being interaction have also been the theme of many literary works in different languages.

As mentioned before, Ṛṣi Yājñavalkya, while convincing his wife Matreyī about his proceeding on *saṁnyāsa* in *Bṛhadāraṇyaka Upaniṣad,* again uses these examples to explain as to why a mother loves his child, father loves his son or a wife loves her husband and so on. The *ṛṣi* supplies the reason to this kind of intimacy again in terms of the interaction that appears at the level of soul and the same is often missing from the interactions between any other two human Beings.

The cases can also be traced easily when three or more persons in a family or society also appear to maintain similar degree of intimacy as in the above two-Being cases. But by and large in such cases the love and affection are generally for vested interests or for a kind of business and the same ends up at the level of intellect or ego. Selfless love, which is free from any kind of boundaries, is hardly ever seen in such cases except in the case of mother-child interaction.

9.4 Interactions Among Human Beings: An Attempt Towards Quantification

It is a common experience that when a single person is left in the field of *PM*s or in general that of WO he alone feels and realizes the interaction with them first through B and SE and later through M, I and E depending on the development of his FOUs. However, when two or more than two persons are present in a given environment then, in addition to the individual's feeling and realization, there is also a tendency for sharing these feelings and realizations with other persons about the same WO.

If the sharing-person(s) are strange to each other (i.e. they are not biased or do not have any prejudice) then normally the same sequence of interactions follows; otherwise the interactions can start at any subtle level and the same depends on the development of FOUs of the sharing persons. Although the interactions initiate at a fundamental level through EOLs (bare case), the presence of *PM*s in the form of environment just dresses them up (dressed case). This enables the interactions to become more effective and the same leads to a success of the outward action.

With a view to quantifying these interactions we employ here the patomic model of human Being in the spirit of our earlier work.[2] Within this framework it becomes possible to discuss the nature and subtlety of these interactions. Recall that these interactions in general are beyond the domain of space-time but in addition to the physical content like the contact and AAD-type forces, they now also have non-physical content like the AAT- and AADT-type forces.

9.5 Interactions Between Human Beings

9.5.1 A NEW CLASS OF TANMĀTRAS IN b-b INTERACTION

Consider two human being b_1 and b_2, each of them is described in terms of gross, micro and causal bodies (cf. reduced version of patomic model in chapter 1), viz.

$$b_1 \equiv \{\mathcal{C}_1, \mathcal{M}_1, \mathcal{G}_1\}\ ,\ \mathrm{b}_2 \equiv \{\mathcal{C}_2\ \mathcal{M}_2, \mathcal{G}_2\}$$

Now they are placed within the range (!) of interaction. In fact the concept of range here is a bit ambiguous. Unlike the physical forces the range here is not defined in the space-time domain; rather it is characterized by the meditation parameter μ, e.g. the persons sitting next to each other in a train or a bus may not interact for hours or even days unless the environment forces them to do so. On the other hand, the persons far apart (distance-wise) can interact with each other either through the

2. Radhey Shyam Kaushal, *The Philosophy of the Vedanta: A Modern Scientific Perspective*, Garib Das Oriental Series 179 (Delhi: Indian Book Centre, 1994), chapter 6.

thought process or through the material means like phone calls, etc. Similar is the picture with time variable. Sitting persons together may or may not go in the past or future; or else they can as well share their experiences of infinite past or infinite future (though rare but it might include their past or future births provided they are capable enough) depending on the development of their FOUs. In the former case while M, I of $\mathcal{M}$ play the important role, it is E of $\mathcal{M}$ which plays the role in the latter case. As a whole the process is very complicated.

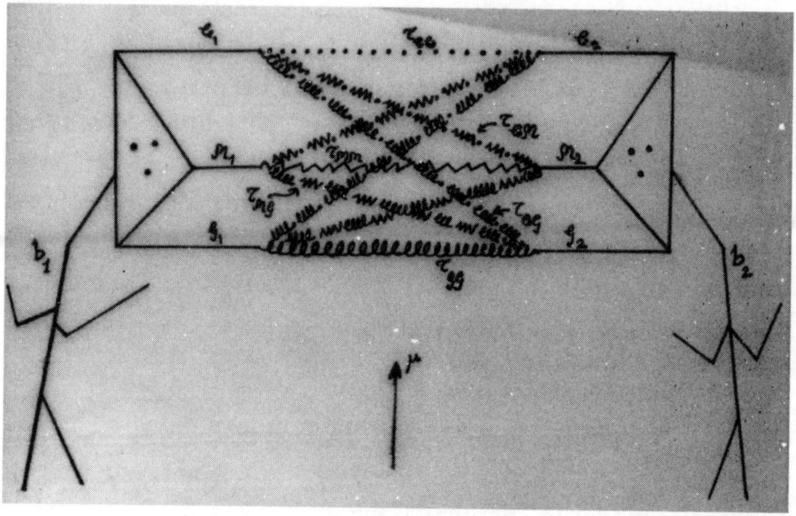

fig. 9.1: Interactions between human Beings.

In *fig.* 9.1 the interactions between b_1 and b_2 are shown within the framework of reduced version of patomic model with upward direction of μ. While the meditation parameters μ_1 and μ_2 corresponding to individuals b_1 and b_2 already exist separately, μ here is with reference to the observer (author!). Before proceeding further a few points need to be re-emphasized here:

(i) Since $\mathcal{C}_1$ and $\mathcal{C}_2$ merely represent the quantized versions of the same cosmic consciousness field, for any interaction whatsoever between b_1 and b_2, the $\mathcal{C}_1$ or $\mathcal{C}_2$ or the combination thereof would provide only the background for the interaction.

(ii) Note that subsets $\{\mathcal{M}_1,\mathcal{G}_1\}$ or separately $\mathcal{M}_1$ and $\mathcal{G}_1$ of b_1 and $\{\mathcal{M}_2,\mathcal{G}_2\}$ or separately $\mathcal{M}_2$ and $\mathcal{G}_2$ of b_2 are active only in the presence of $\mathcal{C}_1$ and $\mathcal{C}_2$, respectively.

(iii) In view of (i) and (ii) above, for the interaction of $\mathcal{M}_1$ with $\mathcal{M}_2$ or with $\mathcal{G}_2$, or of $\mathcal{G}_1$ with $\mathcal{M}_2$ or with $\mathcal{G}_2$ (or vice versa) $\mathcal{C}_1$ and $\mathcal{C}_2$ separately remain in the background. Similarly, for the interaction of $\mathcal{G}_1$ with $\mathcal{G}_2$ (or of $\mathcal{G}_2$ with $\mathcal{G}_1$), $\mathcal{M}_1$ (or $\mathcal{M}_2$ in the reverse case) remains in the background (cf. seer-seen sequence).

(iv) Note that each $\mathcal{C}_i$, $\mathcal{M}_i$, $\mathcal{G}_i$ (for i=1,2) is again a set in itself and as such for i=1, they often will be in different frequencies (moods or mindsets) as compared to that for i=2.

In general there exist nine quanta (*tanmātras*) of interaction between b_1 and b_2, namely namely $\tau_{\mathcal{C}1\,\mathcal{C}2}$, $\tau_{\mathcal{C}1\,\mathcal{M}2}$, $\tau_{\mathcal{C}1\,\mathcal{G}2}$, $\tau_{\mathcal{M}1\,\mathcal{C}2}$, $\tau_{\mathcal{M}1\,\mathcal{M}2}$, $\tau_{\mathcal{M}1\,\mathcal{G}2}$, $\tau_{\mathcal{G}1\,\mathcal{C}2}$, $\tau_{\mathcal{G}1\,\mathcal{M}2}$, and $\tau_{\mathcal{G}1\,\mathcal{G}2}$. Further, the universality of $\mathcal{C}_1$ and $\mathcal{C}_2$ implies that $\tau_{\mathcal{C}1\,\mathcal{C}2} = \tau_{\mathcal{C}2\,\mathcal{C}1} = \tau_{\mathcal{C}\,\mathcal{C}}$. In view of (iv) and because of the peculiar features of the cosmic consciousness field in which the concept of forward and backward processes is irrelevant, it is reasonable to assume

$$\tau_{\mathcal{M}_1\mathcal{C}_2} - \tau_{\mathcal{C}_1\mathcal{M}_2} = \tau_{\mathcal{C}\mathcal{M}}\;;\; \tau_{\mathcal{G}_1\mathcal{C}_2} = \tau_{\mathcal{C}_1\mathcal{G}_1} = \tau_{\mathcal{C}\mathcal{G}}\;;\; \tau_{\mathcal{M}_1\mathcal{M}_2} = \tau_{\mathcal{M}_2\mathcal{M}_1} = \tau_{\mathcal{M}\mathcal{M}}\;;$$
$$\tau_{\mathcal{G}_2\mathcal{M}_1} = \tau_{\mathcal{G}_1\mathcal{M}_2} = \tau_{\mathcal{G}\mathcal{M}}\;;\; \tau_{\mathcal{G}_1\mathcal{G}_2} = \tau_{\mathcal{G}_2\mathcal{G}_1} = \tau_{\mathcal{G}\mathcal{G}}. \tag{9.2}$$

Such symmetry considerations thus imply only six quanta, namely $\tau_{\mathcal{C}\mathcal{C}}$, $\tau_{\mathcal{C}\mathcal{M}}$, $\tau_{\mathcal{C}\mathcal{G}}$, $\tau_{\mathcal{M}\mathcal{M}}$, $\tau_{\mathcal{M}\mathcal{G}}$, $\tau_{\mathcal{G}\mathcal{G}}$ for b-b interaction. Out of these six, $\tau_{\mathcal{C}\mathcal{C}}$ (denoted by dotted line in the figure) will not contribute in view of the universality of soul. Thus, there remain only five *tanmātras* to account for the b-b interaction at the level of reduced version of patomic model. While $\tau_{\mathcal{G}\mathcal{G}}$ and $\tau_{\mathcal{M}\mathcal{M}}$ are shown by spring-like and wave-like lines in the figure, $\tau_{\mathcal{C}\mathcal{M}}$, $\tau_{\mathcal{C}\mathcal{G}}$ and $\tau_{\mathcal{M}\mathcal{G}}$ are respectively shown by 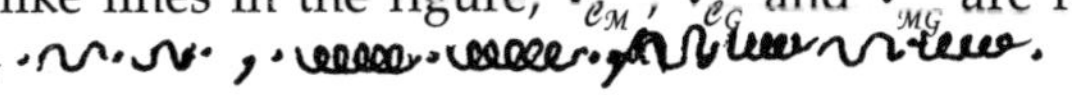

With regard to the description of b-b interaction in terms of these five *tanmātras*, not only the values of μ_1 and μ_2 parameters associated with each Being plays the important role but also the role of μ associated with the observer in terms of the development of his FOUs becomes important. While $\tau_{\mathcal{CC}}$ may correspond to *turīya* state of either of the Beings, $\tau_{\mathcal{CM}}$ or $\tau_{\mathcal{CG}}$ correspond to the stage when the micro- or gross-form of b_1 is in direct communion with the SO of b_2 or vice versa. As can be seen from the figure they correspond to different values of μ. As a matter of fact it is the relative consciousness manifesting through M, I and E and finally through SE and B of the one Being that is responsible for the interaction with the other Being. Alternatively, the conscious mind of the one Being is capable of activating the different EOLs of the other Being. In fact the mindsets of b_1 and b_2 as a function of their individual μ_1 and μ_2 play a crucial role in the whole process of interaction.

In the b-b interaction, it is the $\tau_{\mathcal{GG}}$-type component which lies within the purview of physical and biological theories; otherwise as μ increases any or all non-physical components $\tau_{\mathcal{MG}}$, $\tau_{\mathcal{MM}}$, $\tau_{\mathcal{CG}}$, $\tau_{\mathcal{CM}}$ can come into existence as a result of fine-tuning of the interaction and also in the order of their subtlety. In Table 9.1, we elaborate on these fine-tuned processes that take place at the levels of individual EOLs of each Being.

9.5.2 FINE-TUNING OF b-b INTERACTION

Next we use the finer details of $\mathcal{G}$, $\mathcal{M}$ and C as $\mathcal{G}$ ≡{B, SE}, $\mathcal{M}$ ≡{M, I, E} and C ≡{SO} to analyse the "reaction" (or the interaction process)

$$b_1 + b_2 \underset{\leftarrow}{\overset{\rightarrow}{}} b_1' + b_2' + \tau_{b_1 b_2}, \tag{9.3}$$

where b'_1 and b'_2 are the enlightened version of b_1 and b_2 after the interaction(s), and the *tanmātras* $\tau_{b_1b_2}$ satisfies $\tau_{b_1b_2} = \tau_{b_2b_1}$ as argued earlier (cf. eq. (9.2)). Here the system in general evolves with respect to space, time and consciousness variables and the latter is translated into the meditation parameter μ. However, we proceed here with the evolution of the system with respect to μ only since the scales of space-time and non-space-time mediated interactions are quite different. Moreover, the reaction (9.3) is just a symbolic representation of the process as far as the physics content of the reactants and the products is concerned.

In Table 9.1, we list the fine-tuned versions of various quanta of exchange of awareness (consciousness) between b_1 and b_2. Corresponding to the five *tanmātras* established above at the level of reduced patomic model, namely $\tau_{\mathcal{GG}}$, $\tau_{\mathcal{GM}}$, $\tau_{\mathcal{Ge}}$, $\tau_{\mathcal{MM}}$ and $\tau_{\mathcal{Me}}$, in all we have twenty *tanmātras* at the subtle level each of which, in fact, accounts for a new-type of interaction between b_1 and b_2 at a deeper level and hence is responsible for a specific type of fundamental process during the exchanges between b_1 and b_2. Note that as these exchanges are between bare EOLs (not dressed with environment) of b_1 and b_2, the examples cited in Table 9.1 are accommodated only approximately in the scheme of classification or they suggest the cases of ideal interactions as far as real life is concerned. While circumstances and environment need to be taken care of for the cases of real life (cf. next section), the occurrence of ideal cases can also be traced in the screen play or on a dais of dramatic acting. In fact in a particular case when the role of B or of *SE* in either b_1 or in b_2 is absent, then the exchanges take place during processes of dreaming or imagination. As a matter of fact, corresponding to each subtle *tanmātra* the nature of interaction between b_1 and b_2 is being identified in certain cases in Table 9.1 and accordingly its role is pointed out in certain cases.

The meanings of various subtle *tanmatras* are further elaborated through the Feynman-like diagrams of particle physics in *fig*. 9.2. Possible exchanges of awareness between b_1 and b_2 are shown in *figs*. 9.2(a)-9.2(e) keeping in mind the symmetries of eq. (9.2). Further note that in *figs*. 9.2(c) and 9.2(e), the choice of the point SO on the dotted line is arbitrary. It could be anywhere firstly because of the all-pervading property of SO and secondly, for a person who is in this domain; the meditation parameter also attains constancy. It may be mentioned that in all these figures the evolution of the system takes place with respect to increasing μ_1 and μ_2 (and perhaps (!) with μ as well).

9.5.3 HYPERFINE-TUNING OF b-b INTERACTION

Further fine tuning of the interaction between b_1 and b_2 discussed above in Table 9.1 is also possible because of the fact that each of the EOLs of a person comes in more than one variety

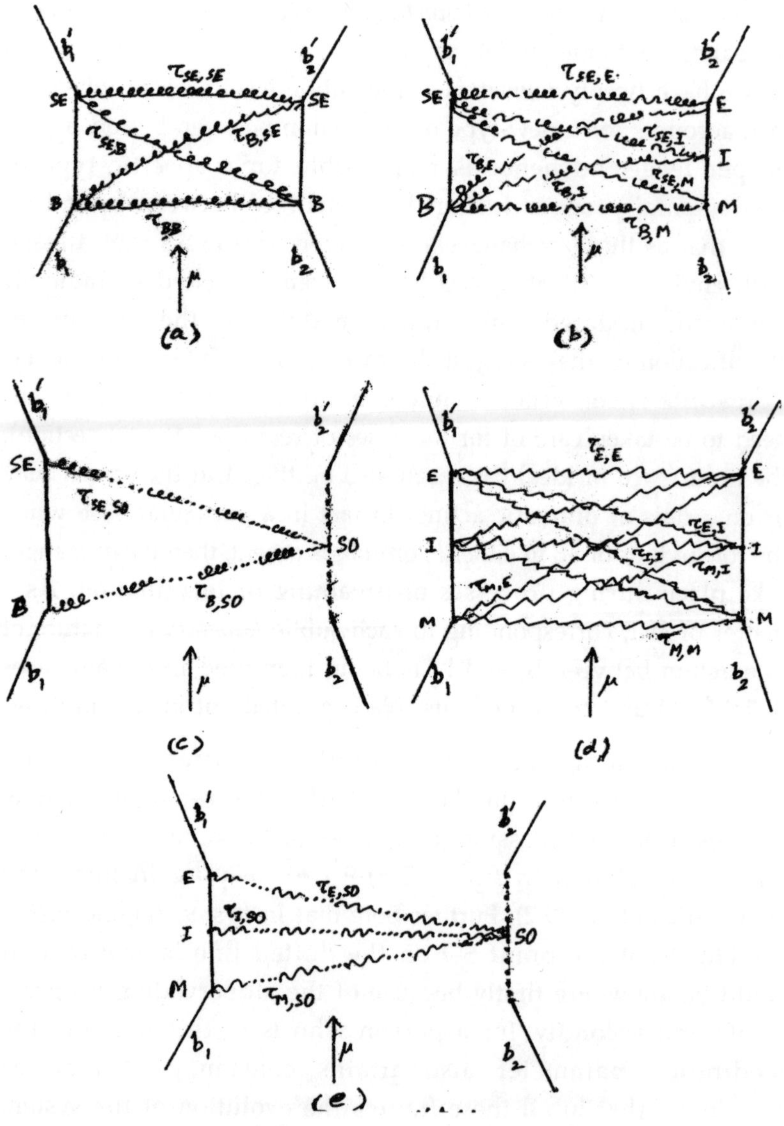

fig. 9.2: Fine-tuning of b-b interactions mediated by
(a) $\tau_{\mathcal{GG}}$, *(b)* $\tau_{\mathcal{GM}}$, *(c)* $\tau_{\mathcal{GC}}$, *(d)* $\tau_{\mathcal{MM}}$, *and (e)* $\tau_{\mathcal{MC}}$.

Table 9.1: Quanta of exchange of awareness (consciousness) between human Beings b_1 and b_2 ($\tau_{b_1b_2}$) and their role at different levels of subtlety in b-b interactions

S. No.	*Quantum of consciousness exchange*	*Fine-tuning of the exchange*	*Nature of interaction: Remarks and examples*
1.	$\tau_{\mathcal{GG}}$	$\tau_{B,B}$	Body-body interaction without prejudiecs; certain instances in the wrestling of two wrestlers, meeting of husband and wife or of two drunkards.
		$\tau_{B,SE}$	Body-senses (of knowledge and actions) interactions without prejudices; many examples in a family in day-to-day life, like kissing, blessings, etc.
		$\tau_{SE,SE}$	Senses-senses (of knowledge and action) inter-action without prejudices; many examples, like shaking hands, interacting through eyes, etc.
2.	$\tau_{\mathcal{GM}}$	$\tau_{B,M}$	Body-mind interactions without the roles of I, E or SE (only emotions); many examples, but ideal one is that of mother-baby or at times of husband-wife interactions.
		$\tau_{B,I}$	Body-intellect interaction without the role of M, E or SE; a scientific inner analysing the body of a person or of a patient in dream or in imagination.
		$\tau_{B,E}$	Body-ego (memory) interaction without the roles of M, I or SE; Imaginary verbal duel or anger of a person over the other.

		$\tau_{SE,M}$	Senses (of knowledge and action)-mind interaction; a person inducing the emotions in the other, through his SEs mono-acting of mother-baby as viewed by a viewer.
		$\tau_{SE,I}$	Senses (of knowledge and action)-intellect interaction: A person initiating the analysing power in the other through his SEs, mono-acting of jokers or dialogue as viewed by a viewer.
		$\tau_{SE,E}$	Senses (of knowledge and action)-ego (memory) interaction: A person inducing the memory aspect in the other through his SEs; mono-acting of a historical event as viewed by a viewer.
3.	$\tau_{\mathcal{G}e}$	$\tau_{B,SO}$	Body-soul interaction: A person in *samādhi* receiving the salutation of another person.
		$\tau_{SE,SO}$	Senses (of knowledge and action)-soul interaction: A person in *samādhi* enjoying the offered prayer by his devotee.
4.	$\tau_{\mathcal{MM}}$	$\tau_{M,M}$	Mind-mind interaction: Imagination of or dreaming the emotional exchanges between two persons like weeping of a lady as she watches the other weeping lady.
		$\tau_{M,I}$	Mind-intellect interaction: Imagination as if the emotions of one person are analysed by the other, as in screen play or in drama.

		$\tau_{M,E}$	Mind-ego (memory) interaction: Imagination that the emotions of one person are inducing the joy or anger in the other.
		$\tau_{I,I}$	Intellect-intellect interaction: Imagination of or dreaming the intellectural exchanges between two persons.
		$\tau_{I,E}$	Intellect-ego (memory) interaction: Imagination of analysis by one person of the anger or joy of the other.
		$\tau_{E,E}$	Ego (memory)-ego(memory) interaction: Imagining or dreaming the exchange of memory-mines between two persons.
5.	$\tau_{\mathcal{ME}}$	$\tau_{M,SO}$	Mind-soul interaction: A person in *samādhi* noticing the emotions of the other.
		$\tau_{I,SO}$	Intellect-soul interaction: A person in *samādhi* noticing the decisions of the other.
		$\tau_{E,SO}$	Ego(memory)-soul interaction: A person in *Samādhi* noticing the anger or joy of the other.

or component except the SO. For example, the biological body, B, of a person itself has various inner and outer organs and each of them is capable of interacting with those of the other person, similarly, the senses of knowledge and action, SE, again are ten in number which either separately or jointly have very high interacting-capacity with those of the other person; the different stages of mind, M (like its conscious or subconscious states or the ones discussed in the previous chapter in terms of its dressings with consciousness) can again interact with those of the other person; intellect, I, could also be in active or passive role towards the b-b interaction, and finally the ego, E, also has its variety of stages for the interaction between b_1 and b_2. In particular, we elaborate below the hyperfine tuning of E as an example.

If a person has some prejudices against the other it is all due to the storage of certain past memories in the faculty, E, and this accordingly materializes the interaction between b_1 and b_2. A person feels joy or becomes angry as a result of his interaction with the other person depending on the good or bad memories stored already in E. In fact the storm of anger (or of joy for that matter) has three stages: First in the form of seed at the level of micro-body. If one is very alert then he can feel the coming of this storm and becomes a little silent to treat it properly. The second stage is when the anger has taken possession. Then it is almost impossible to push the force back. As a matter of fact one is so much possessed that "he" cannot be there to control it. It may be only for a single moment, but one loses himself in it. Anger envelopes in such a way that one does something for which he has to repent later, but one is helpless by this time. Then there is a third stage when the anger has gone and the person becomes aware of himself. Then he repents, tries to find excuses for why he became angry, rationalizes it, tries to go to the other party (person) towards whom he directed his anger. Note that during the first two stages when there is a loss of great deal of memory only a limited aspect of it however becomes sharpened and acts outwardly. The situation becomes more alarming when the EOLs of both b_1 and b_2 are in resonance.

Thus, there could be further large variety of quanta of exchanges of awareness possible between b_1 and b_2. Though we have tried to identify only a few of them above but the fact is that there is a continuous spectrum of exchanges and at times it becomes difficult to attribute the nature of interaction to a particular quantum. The interesting part is that there is a wonderful co-ordination (which often goes unnoticed) among different EOLs of each human Being when they are interacting.

9.5.4 DRESSING-UP OF b-b INTERACTION: THE EFFECT OF ENVIRONMENT

What has been discussed above is the b-b interaction generating basically from the bare EOLs of b_1 and b_2. These interactions (or their measure in the form of associated *tanmātras*) get dressed up in the presence of WO in general or of *PM*s in particular. In fact the external environment may consist of two aspects, namely the presence of kith and kin (or a third person) and/or the *PM*s. In either case the b-b interaction gets modified (dressed up) and enriches the awareness of each of b_1 and b_2 and hence affects their interaction.

The dressing up of external *tanmātras*, namely τ_{ea}, τ_w, τ_a, τ_f and τ_{et}, associated with the interaction of a human Being with *PM*s (cf. Appendix D), is already discussed in the previous chapter. However, the presence not only of *PM*s but also of a third Being (human or non-human), if that happens to a relative, a pet or even a stranger, accordingly affects the b-b- interaction. Although the latter forms the case of three-Being interactions (which we shall take up in the next section), as long as the third Being remains a spectator the b-b interaction will only be marginally affected. Thus, in the presence of environment all the five *tanmātras*, namely $\tau_{\mathcal{GG}}$, $\tau_{\mathcal{GM}}$, $\tau_{\mathcal{GC}}$, $\tau_{\mathcal{MM}}$, $\tau_{\mathcal{MC}}$ get dressed up to become $\tilde{\tau}_{\mathcal{GG}}, \tilde{\tau}_{\mathcal{GM}}, \tilde{\tau}_{\mathcal{GC}}, \tilde{\tau}_{\mathcal{MM}}, \tilde{\tau}_{\mathcal{MC}}$. Note that the "dressing" here means enriching the quota of sharing between b_1 and b_2 or enriching the FOUs of each of b_1 and b_2.

Dressing up of b-b interaction, in fact, is a two-step process:

First each of b_1 and b_2 gets enriched by the presence of WO through $\tilde{\tau}_{ea}, \tilde{\tau}_{w}, \tilde{\tau}_{a}, \tilde{\tau}_{f}, \tilde{\tau}_{et}$, and then the enriched FOUs of b_1 and b_2 mutually interact via $\tilde{\tau}_{\mathcal{GG}}, \tilde{\tau}_{\mathcal{GM}}, \tilde{\tau}_{\mathcal{GC}}, \tilde{\tau}_{\mathcal{MM}}, \tilde{\tau}_{\mathcal{MC}}$ or in the language of Section 8, via $\tau_{\tilde{\mathcal{G}}\tilde{\mathcal{G}}}, \tau_{\tilde{\mathcal{G}}\tilde{\mathcal{M}}}, \tau_{\tilde{\mathcal{G}}C}, \tau_{\tilde{\mathcal{M}}\tilde{\mathcal{M}}}, \tau_{\tilde{\mathcal{M}}C}$. In other words, the mindsets of b_1 and b_2 namely $\mathcal{M}_1(m_1, i_1, e_1)$ and $\mathcal{M}_2(m_2, i_2, e_2)$ now become $\mathcal{M}_1(m_1, i_1, e_1; \sigma)$ and $\mathcal{M}_2(m_2, i_2, e_2; \sigma)$ respectively (cf. Sections 8.8 and 8.9).

It may be mentioned that the bare *tanmātras* whether they are τ_i's (with i= ea, w, a, f, et) or τ_{ij}'s (with i, j=b_1, b_2) could be more or less the same for all human Beings but the dressed ones $\tilde{\tau}_i$*'s or* $\tilde{\tau}_{ij}$*'s* may differ from individual to individual or for pair to pair of human Beings. This is mainly because the EOLs of each of us react with the environment differently even if it may appear to be the same at the B and SE levels but it is definitely different at the levels of M, I and E. If one also accounts for such differences (which at times are very crucial) then the assumption expressed through eq. (9.2) breaks down, i.e. $\tilde{\tau}_{b_1 b_2}$ is no more equal to $\tilde{\tau}_{b_2 b_1}$.

Vedānta philosophy in general emphasizes[3] 23 points (or rather vertices) of interaction associated with each of b_1 and b_2 and these are: five senses of knowledge, five senses of action, five sense objects of senses of knowledge, namely smell, taste, sight, sound and touch corresponding to nose, tongue, eyes, ear and skin, five *PM*s, mind, intellect and ego. Thus, in all there could be 23 × 23 = 529 quanta of exchanges of awareness which are possible between b_1 and b_2. However, under certain simplifying assumptions they are reduced to twenty only as in Table 9.1. Of course, some of these vertices (or causes) contribute towards environment and circumstances. But, if necessity arises to explain certain intricate aspects of human behaviour at a deeper level, then all 529 quanta of exchanges of awareness between b_1 and b_2 can be exploited at the next level of fine-tuning. However, the role of *PM*s is already accounted for in the above process of dressing up of *tanmātras*.

3. Radhey Shyam Kaushal, 1994, op. cit.

9.5.5 b-b INTERACTIONS IN REAL-LIFE: APPLICATIONAL ASPECTS

Here we attempt to find an explanation of various actions involving two human Beings in terms of the fundamental processes discussed above. As a matter of fact, in spite of listing a large number of actions as examples of different types of interactions in Table 9.1 not many of them appear in real life. Often a superposition of two or more than two of these processes in any of the real life exchanges between the two persons takes place. This is mainly because here, unlike physical sciences, the co-ordination and correlations among the workings of various EOLs with regard to the success of an action are so strong that the concept of fundamentality attached with the process appears as a misnomer. Moreover, intricately interwoven nature of these processes while further supports this feeling, this is perhaps also a reason for objective scientists not to tread into this domain and to avoid tactfully the handling of the same in a phenomenon. The present scheme however offers a systematics within which the human actions can be analysed at their most subtle level. In fact in the process of analysing the real life actions it is not only the superposition of these subtle b-b interactions but also the effects of environment which need to be taken care of. In what follows we discuss some typical applications of these concepts of b-b interaction to some real life cases including the ones highlighted in Section 1.7. Before proceeding further it is worthwhile to recall the terminology "inside out" (ISO) and "outside out" (OSO) with regard to EOLs of a human Being. In fact unlike the atomic model of matter, in the patomic model of human Being these are the WO, B, SE EOLs which are readily available to interact with and their participation corresponds to ISO case whereas that of the SO, E, I and M EOLs corresponds to OSO case and their participation generally appears at a later stage.

(a) Husband-wife interactions: Only an ideal couple offers a typical case of b-b interaction in which all the exchanges outlined either in *figs*. 9.1 and 9.2 or in Table 9.1 are possible, of course at different space-time points and also over a period of time. In some sense we are now in a position to find an answer to Einstein's query posed in the beginning of Chapter 6, namely, "what is the physics and chemistry of the first love?". We elaborate here on this "physics and chemistry" of love on the basis of the systematics developed above for the b-b interaction. Also, recall the universality of sexual processes, discussed in Section 8.11 and are necessary for the maintenance of world order. The words "husband" and "wife" can be considered as synonyms of "male" and "female" respectively for different living Beings. As a matter of fact it is the male-female interaction in which the maximum exchanges, discussed in *figs*. 9.1 and 9.2 take place starting from the OSO situation to the ISO situation or the vice versa in the particular case. As a matter of fact the first love starts at the level of SO (i.e. OSO case) in its purest form. By the time it comes down to the level of B and WO (i.e. ISO case), it all gets polluted by the interplay of exchanges at the level of SE, M, I and E. However, a link is always maintained in terms of exchanges at the level of SO in case of an ideal couple.

According to a mythological story of the East, God created man and woman together not as two Beings but as a single entity — they were joined in one body. But then there were conflicts. The woman wanted to go to the East and the man was not willing to do so. Or, the man was ready to do something and the woman wanted to rest. They complained and God separated their bodies. Since then, every man is searching for his woman, and every woman is searching for her man. Now it is such a big crowd that it is very difficult to find your woman or man. The myth says that if you can find, everything fits; you can again become one. But it is very difficult to find. According to a modern Indian saint, Osho, there are ways to find a woman, because woman is not outside. There are only parallel similarities outside. What happens when one falls in love with a woman? Somehow the outside woman fulfils your inner woman's image, may not be 100 per cent, but enough to fall in love. What happens when one falls in love with a man? Something inside you clicks and says, "Yes, this is the man, the right man."

It is not that woman finds all the pros and cons about the man and then she decides or she compares the man with all other men in the world, then she decides. Something (!) happens out of the blue. Suddenly she sees that this is the man (or the woman for a man) whom she (he) was waiting for. In other words, she carries an image of man, he also carries an image of woman inside. In fact you are both and you go on looking outside. Nobody is going to fit 100 per cent, because the woman you find outside has her own image about you and you have your own image. It is very difficult to fit with each other. So marriages are always on rocks, and people, by and by, learn how to carry on peacefully.

This story and its interpretation by Osho provide[4] a good moral and an important essence relevant to the society. Also, there seems to exist a plausible answer in it to Einstein's query about the first love but this is with regard to love-marriages. The situation is however, marginally different with regard to arranged marriages. Actually, in the former case, the b-b interaction starts immediately at the level of SO, then sequentially continues through E, I and M over a period of time; each of the man and of the woman analysing the case in terms of all pros and cons on the basis of their past experiences (memory) and slowly becoming emotionally attached, and finally ending up with the interactions first at the SE level and then at the B level. Ideally, since both the man and the woman have been the parts of the same SO (as per above story) and so are their micro-bodies, certain matching frequencies between the workings of EOLs E, I and M of one with those of the other person are expected. However, in practice it may not be so, but there should be continued efforts to attain such a limit. If the matching becomes impossible, then marriages break down.

4. See, for example, Osho, "Transfer Heat to Light with Inner Alchemy", The Speaking Tree Column, *Times of India*, 3 March 2007, and the reference cited therein.

In the arranged marriages and for conscious pair of man and woman, the b-b interactions start at the level of M, continues through I and E by way of imagination to which the feedback comes as a result of listening from elderly persons, reading the newspaper or by meeting each other. Of course, the SO-level interaction also starts simultaneously but temporarily. At times, the help of the science of astrology (cf. Appendix D) is also sought in searching a suitable match. In the life of an ideal couple, occasions also come when the full dynamics of b-b interaction (that includes all the twenty exchanges of Table 9.1) comes into existence, i.e. during the conceiving by woman or during the enjoyment by both.

Moments also come in the life of husband and wife when the interactions are highly confined to the levels of B and SE in the field of WO. For example, in *fig*. 9.3 (courtesy, *Times of India*, 10 October 2007) the exchanges taking place between husband and wife are unhealthy and they might result into an angry relationship, which is full of stress, anxiety of hostility, etc. and the same can lead to a heart disease.

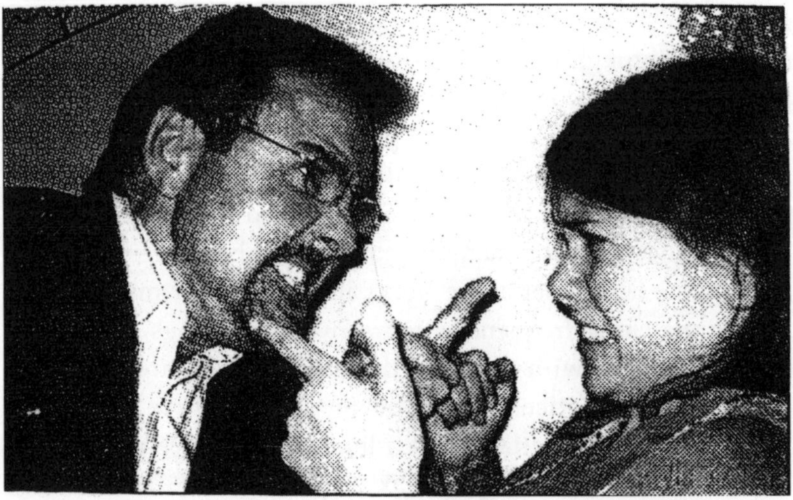

fig. 9.3: At times, unhealthy exchanges between husband and wife also take place at the levels of B and SE in the field of WO.

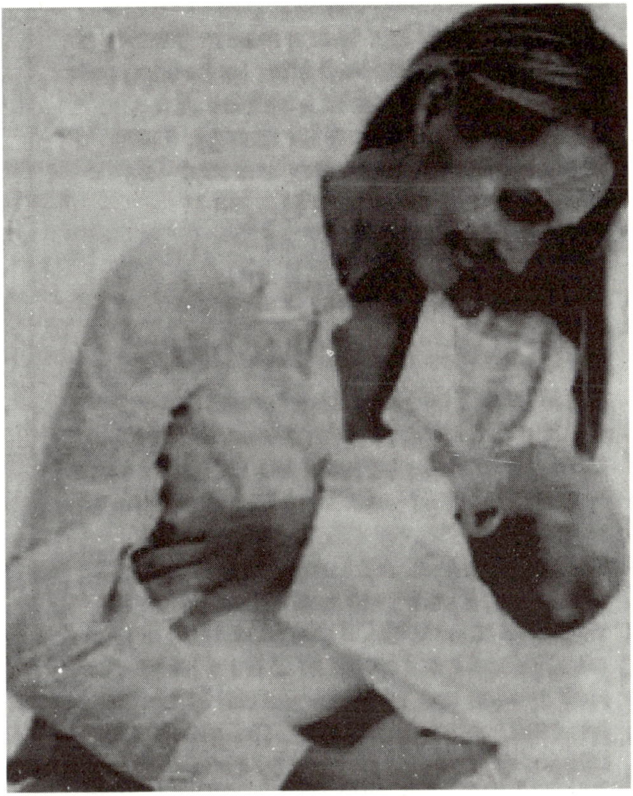

fig. 9.4: A unidirectional mother-baby interaction is unique in the world.

(b) Mother-baby interactions: Whether a baby is in the womb or has taken birth, in either case, the mother-baby interaction starts taking place at the level of SO and why should it not be? After all it is the same SO of mother which is now just partitioned into two Beings. Only because of this peculiar nature, the mother-baby interaction is unique in this world and there is no parallel to it. Also, this interaction is mostly unidirectional since all the EOLs of the baby are not yet developed except for a few like SE and B. As can be noticed from *fig*. 9.4, the mother is "emptying" her heart in the process of breast-feeding to her crying baby. The interactions start at the level of M, i.e. with emotions, often keeping aside the interactions at levels of I and E. In fact M-level interactions are so strong that they are hardly affected by the presence of other Beings or from the environment. This aspect of mother-baby love is universal — true for most of the living Beings. Physics and chemistry of the mother-baby interaction can be noticed from *fig*. 9.4 in which $\tau_{B,SO}$, $\tau_{B,M}$, $\tau_{B,SE}$, $\tau_{B,B}$ and several other interactions can be seen at the same time.

(c) Mother-child and father-child interactions: When the baby grows up, some of his EOLs, like B and SE develop and start enriching themselves from the worldly objects particularly from the environment and from the one-sided interactions of mother. At this stage, the EOLs, I and E of the mother also start showing their role as far as her interaction with the child is concerned. This is in addition to the roles of her EOLs, M, B and SE. Now the child has enough time to interact not only with others but also with environment including pets. As a result, the scope of his interaction with mother in a reciprocate manner increases and thereby diluting the unidirectional character of the interaction with mother.

At this stage father-child interaction along with several other family interactions also come into existence. However, if father has enough time for the family, the mother-child and father-child interactions can be considered on par except that mother's interactions are dominated by emotions.

The above three categories of b-b interactions are the ones in which an individual does not have much choice except for choosing the life-partner; otherwise the naturality in these interactions reflects at every stage and they are basically the emotion-dominated ones. Now we discuss another three categories of b-b interactions in which the individual's choice plays a role and they are intellect-dominated interactions.

(d) Friend-friend interactions: Before discussing the exchanges in the friend-friend interactions we highlight certain norms which are essential for an ideal friendship. Generally, the friendship is for vested interests and as and when these interests are met, the friendship dies. However, there are cases of ideal friendship in the history and also in modern times. It is said that the friendship continues longer if it is extended to a "like-minded" person. The "like-minded" means that there exists a compatibility not only at the level of micro-body but also on certain factors in the gross-body. Other norms, which can be fixed for an ideal friendship, are (i) compatibility of views and mindsets of the two persons, (ii) certain degree of sacrifice and forbearance from both sides, and (iii) a clear understanding with each other. As a matter of fact a lot has been said in Indian scriptures (see, for example, the epic *Rāmāyaṇa*) about ideal friends. In some sense, in friend-friend interaction all these exchanges are there which are necessary for an ideal couple of husband and wife except for the fact that certain exchanges at the soul level are missing in the present case. The close binding between the friends through $\tau_{\mathcal{GG}}$ and $\tau_{\mathcal{MM}}$ in an ideal case can serve as an example of a diatomic molecule in physics.

(e) Teacher-taught interactions: Like ideal friends, a lot has also been said in Indian scriptures about an ideal teacher and an ideal disciple. Still for a meaningful interaction between the two it is worthwhile to highlight a few analogies from physics. (i) In the class room, the teacher and taught are like "transmitter" and "receiver" (of radio signals) with certain matching frequency ranges. Although the exchanges of *fig*. 9.1, in the present case, are by and large unidirectional (i.e. from teacher to taught, as is the case with the mother-child interactions) but certain prerequisites in terms of competence of both teacher and taught (may be in a particular domain) are essential for a meaningful transmission in that domain. During the teacher-taught interaction, clearly there is an exchange of quanta at the level of micro-body and also at the level of SE, however by suppressing the B-level interactions. While emotions remain in the background of the teacher, the I and E dominate the teacher-taught exchanges. Again there are certain norms to maintain a meaningful unidirectional flow of energy. In particular, (i) a disciple should have faith and confidence in the teacher in order to act as a best receiver. (ii) According to the second law of thermodynamics, the energy flows from source to sink and the opposite is prohibited. The same is the case here, a teacher should act as a source (or a person at higher potential) by way of developing his FOUs up to the mark and the student as a sink (or a person at a lower potential) by suppressing his egoism, so that there is a meaningful flow of energy from source to sink.

(f) Boss-subordinate interactions or the interactions between business partners: Boss-subordinate interaction is a special case of employer-employee interaction and is a very delicate one as

fig. 9.5: In spite of working with the boss in the office, a smart subordinate always finds time to interact with him at the level of micro-body, particularly when the subordinate knows his worth.

far as the source of livelihood of employee is concerned. While both the boss and the subordinate work within certain set of rules, yet the human component comes in the way from either side but at the secondary stage. In appearance they both work in an isolated manner but the fact is that they interact at the level of micro-body. Command of the boss gives a direction to the subordinate to work so that a defined output can be seen in the stipulated time. The exchanges are unidirectional as far as their official component is concerned; however, they could be both ways with regard to human component. In either situation the exchanges are full of prejudices and bias in most cases.

An interesting aspect of boss-subordinate interactions is displayed in *fig.* 9.5 (courtesy, *Times of India*). A clever subordinate knows his worth and expects of the manager to know it too. So how does a manager deal with the subordinate or vice versa, is beautifully demonstrated in this figure.

With regard to the interactions between business partners, they are not unidirectional, instead there is some sort of balance separately between official and human components of exchanges; if not, then the partnership breaks down.

(g) Description of b-b interactions in Examples of Section 1.7: *Figs.* 1.3(a)-1.3(d) represent some typical cases of b-b interactions from real life. In the interaction between two girls in *fig.* 1.3(a), there may not be $\tau_{B,B}$-exchange but $\tau_{B,SE}$, $\tau_{SE,SE}$, $\tau_{M,SE}$, $\tau_{M,M}$, $\tau_{I,SE}$, $\tau_{I,M}$, $\tau_{I,I}$ interactions dominate the exchanges while the girls are discussing their dress code, perhaps using a book. In *fig.* 1.3(b), while the two persons are enjoying the scratching of each other's body, the exchanges are involved at the levels of both gross- and micro-bodies. Here, in addition to $\tau_{B,SE}$, $\tau_{SE,SE}$, $\tau_{M,SE}$, $\tau_{M,M}$, $\tau_{I,SE}$, $\tau_{I,M}$ and $\tau_{I,I}$, $\tau_{B,B}$ also makes their scratching enjoyable. Note that the enjoyment also involves an element of SO through $\tau_{M,SO}$ (cf. Table 9.1). *Figs.* 1.3(c) and 1.3(d) appear to deal with exchanges between two persons as of highest and lowest orders in the domains of $\tau_{\mathcal{MM}}$, $\tau_{\mathcal{GG}}$, $\tau_{\mathcal{GM}}$. While the two ladies in *fig.* 1.3(c) are prepared for the ultimate, the two persons in *fig.* 1.3(d) have already achieved the ultimate in terms of blows.

9.6 Interactions among Three and More Human Beings

In physical theories of many-body systems, after accounting for the pair-wise two-body forces very little is left for the account of three- and higher-body interactions as their effects are found to be small (perhaps not in nuclear physics). However, in view of the nature of forces there are ways to account for the effects arising from such forces using certain mathematical tools. In case of Beings in general and the human Beings in particular it is not so; three or more Being interactions could be as important as the two-Being ones and they often dominate the outcome. This is because in this case in addition to the contact and AAD-type forces, AAT- and AADT-type components are also active in the interaction. As a matter of fact it is the mind, M, present in an individual and forms a bridge between other inner EOLs and the outer ones that initially brings in the role of other type of interactions[5] in a group of human Beings. We discuss and analyse some of these features for the case of three human Beings and generalize the results later for systems of many human Beings.

9.6.1 CASE OF THREE HUMAN BEINGS

We first demonstrate here as to how the mind M, initiates the interactions in a group of three human Beings. Recall that it is the presence of SO (or of self-awareness or of the source of consciousness) in a human Being that makes him an SEP-matter from the EP- or P-matter existing already inside b. Let b_1, b_2, b_3 be the three human Beings characterized by

$$b_1 \equiv \{SO, E_1, I_1, M_1, SE_1, B_1\};\ b_2 \equiv \{SO, E_2, I_2, M_2, SE_2, B_2\};\ b_3 \equiv \{SO, E_3, I_3, M_3, SE_3, B_3\}$$

where E_j, I_j, M_j, SE_j, B_j, for j=1, 2, 3 are various EOLs present in b_j. Note that the EOL, SO, is the same in all the three because of its cosmic character and the same offers a basis for their interaction. However, other EOLs are shown to be different and in general they are different in all human Beings for not totally independent reasons, namely (i) each Being has different *saṁskāra*s (tendencies) generated out of his *prārabdha, sañcita,* and *kriyamāṇa* components of actions, (ii) each has varying development of his FOUs, and lastly (iii) each is affected differently by Nature-generated three

5. Radhey Shyam Kaushal, 1994, op. cit.

guṇas (or lives in different circumstances and environment). In principle, one should analyse the b-b-b interaction with these reasons in mind but it has been found that it is the EOL, M, while acting as a bridge between $\mathcal{M}$ and $\mathcal{G}$ of an individual, also plays a dominant role in these interactions. Not only this, to whichever SE, the mind M is attached, the same SE controls I of that person and accordingly his behaviour gets affected. This is what Lord Kṛṣṇa has emphasized in *SMBG*[6]

yatato hyapi kaunteya puruṣasya vipaścitaḥ ।
indriyāṇi pramāthīni haranti prasabhaṁ manaḥ ॥ — 2.60 (9.4)

Turbulent by nature, the senses even of a wise man who is practising self-control, forcibly carry away his mind, Arjuna.

As mentioned in the case of b-b interaction, the bare exchanges between the EOLs of two individuals take place only under ideal situations; otherwise in real life it is the superposition of different exchanges (*tanmātras*) that takes place, or the dressed version of *tanmātras* with consciousness and/or environment is considered to explain even a simplest action of the two persons. Exactly same is the situation with b-b-b interaction and essentially this is what has been in the background in suggesting the three reasons given above.

Thus, while the M at the one end is attached to SE and B, it however affects I accordingly on the other for an individual. In general, the mindsets $\mathcal{M}_j$(m, i, e) with j=1, 2, 3 for the three persons get affected and become $\mathcal{M}_j$(m, i, e; σ) by the presence of the same circumstances, σ for each. As before, for the b-b case, if we consider 23 vertices of each individual to interact with, then the possible number of exchanges turn out to be (1/2)(46 × 69) = 1587 and it is a tedious task to account for these many exchanges. Therefore, we resort to work in terms of the mindsets, $\mathcal{M}_1$, $\mathcal{M}_2$, $\mathcal{M}_3$ of the three persons and each as a function of the four variables m, i, e, and σ respectively representing the

6. *Śrīmad Bhagavad-Gītā*, chapter 2, verse 60.

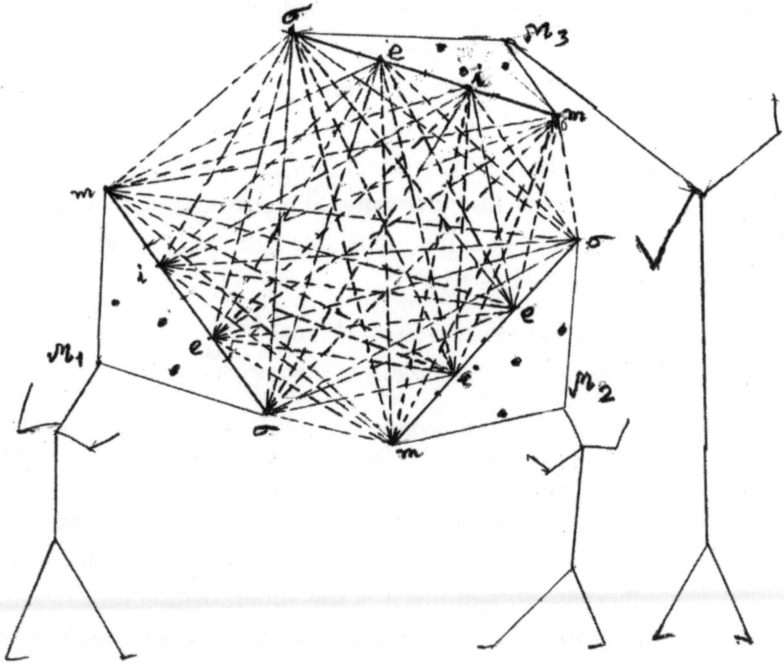

fig. 9.6: Possible 48 pairwise exchanges among the three mindsets M_1, M_2, M_3.

attributes of mind, intellect, ego and circumstances with reference to the individual. Even with four variables there are (1/2)(8 × 12) = 48 exchanges possible shown in *fig*. 9.6. Again there are two categories of exchanges pair-wise, i.e. $\tau_{b_j . b_k}$-type which we have counted above and the three-Being-type, namely $\tau_{b_j b_k b_l}$ with j, k, l=1, 2, 3.

However, we shall not account for the $\tau_{b_j b_k b_l}$-type interactions as they normally take place when the pair-wise interactions satisfy certain conditions like "reflexivity, symmetry and transitivity relations. In mathematical terms, one can say that $\tau_{b_j b_k b_l}$ type interactions occur when the elements $\tau_{b_j b_k}$ of a set of 48 candidates ideally satisfy:

(i) Reflexivity: $\tau_{b_j b_k} \mathbb{R} \tau_{b_j b_k}$ for all $\tau_{b_j b_k}$ in the set

(ii) Symmetry: If $\tau_{b_j b_k} \mathbb{R} \tau_{b_j b_{k'}}$, then $\tau_{b_{j'} b_{k'}} \mathbb{R} \tau_{b_j b_k}$.

(iii) Transitivity: If $\tau_{b_j b_k} \mathbb{R} \tau_{b_{j'} b_{k'}}$ and $\tau_{b_{j'} b_{k'}} \mathbb{R} \tau_{b_{j''} b_{k''}}$, then $\tau_{b_j b_k} \mathbb{R} \tau_{b_{j''} b_{k''}}$.

In other words, these 3-Being-type interactions take place on the ground of 2-Being type ones and they generally come into play instantaneously and rarely by cool thought and memory processes. Of course, 3-Being type interactions also take place prior to the above pair-wise relations are established. Note that in the notation $\tau_{b_j b_k}$ while each b can be (m, i, e, σ), j and k are allowed to take three values (j, k): (1, 2), (1, 3), (2, 3) and this makes 4×4×3=48 elements in the set. This means, while EOLs of one person are allowed to interact with that of the other person, their mutual (internal) interactions are not counted. Further if we do not assume $\tau_{b_j b_k} = \tau_{b_k b_j}$ (which may not be true in general as all the persons do not have the same development of FOUs), then the set will consist of 96 elements.

Next we present a broad classification of b-b-b interaction depending upon the mood of an individual. Recall that each person can be in any of the three modes while interacting with the other, namely SEP-mode (with an alert self-awareness), EP-mode (conscious but without self-sense) and P-mode (unconscious or may be dead). For a meaningful b-b or b-b-b interaction, the last mode is ruled out. Therefore, for b_1-b_2 case we have EP-EP, SEP-EP, SEP-SEP varieties of interactions whereas for the b_1-b_2-b_3 case, the following choices naturally emerge:

(I) *EP-EP-EP type interaction*: when all the three persons are in light moods.

(II) *SEP-EP-EP type interaction*: when b_1 is in serious mood and b_2 and b_3 are in light moods.

(III) *SEP-SEP-EP type interaction*: when b_1 and b_2 are in serious moods and b_3 is in light mood.

(IV) *SEP-SEP-SEP type interaction*: when all the three persons are in serious moods.

Now we analyse some typical examples of b-b-b interaction within the above framework.

(a) Husband (b_1), wife (b_2) and the third person (b_3) interaction: In general man and woman have different body structures and different working domains and as such interact only in a limited domain. Marriage is a kind of bond between a man and a woman and after which they become intimate, and start interacting to the extent that their interactions, in an ideal situation, become example of a complete b-b interaction, as mentioned before. Now, if a third person whether a man or woman enters in their personal life then these rigid bonds of marriage become rather loose. Conversely, in true sense one can say that this happens when the marriage bonds, in spite of all efforts, could not remain rigid and a woman in case of husband and a man in case of wife easily become available in the form of source of attraction at a certain level. Very often this happens because of selfish motives involved or for temporary enjoyments but the main reason is that there has been a loss of faith and confidence between the husband and wife or lack of understanding and clarity between them at the same time.

All this becomes very serious when the SEP-SEP-EP type b_1-b_2-b_3 interaction tries to become SEP-SEP-SEP type one. Further, the nature of interaction dynamics depends on whether b_3 is a man or a woman. If it is a man, then b_2-b_3 exchanges will increase at the cost of b_1-b_2 exchanges and again at the levels of all the three gross, micro and causal bodies. On the other hand, if b_3 is a woman then b_1-b_3 exchanges will increase at the cost of b_1-b_2 exchanges. Since b_1, b_2 interactions are supposed to start from the level of causal body, it is very difficult to find an equilibrium (may be possible in some rare cases) in the exchanges among b_1-b_2 and b_3, particularly when all the three are present in given circumstances. Also, the $\tau_{b_j b_k b_\ell}$-type interactions will start dominating the scene in the latter case.

(b) Mother (b_1), father (b_2) and the child (b_3) interaction: Recall that both b_1-b_3 and b_2-b_3 interactions by and large are unidirectional as the FOUs of b_3 are not yet fully developed. While the interactions of b_1 and b_3 are emotion-dominated, those of b_2 and b_3 are intellect (guidance) dominated, in general. However, both these interactions help in developing the FOUs of b_3 but in a limited domain unless a fourth Being (b_4), i.e. a teacher comes in the life of b_3. The exchanges from b_3 side are normally B and SE dominated ones and the category of the b-b-b interaction is of SEP-SEP-EP type unless the child is of serious nature.

(c) The case of a trio of friends: As mentioned before, ideally the friendship between friends can continue at all the three levels, namely at gross, micro and causal levels and the same can be extended to third and more persons provided the latter have the same level of development of their FOUs. For a trio to become friends, initially the $\tau_{b_j b_k b_\ell}$-type interactions start at the gross and micro levels and soon they convert into pair-wise b-b interactions and subsequently a kind of equilibrium is established among various exchanges. Once the equilibrium or the understanding grows up among b_1, b_2 and b_3, then $\tau_{b_j b_k b_\ell}$-type interactions again come into play in addition to the $\tau_{b_j b_k}$-type ones towards the success of an action performed by the trio. A true friendship of the trio continues longer, if all the variables m, i, e and σ in the mindsets of the trio are allowed to vary freely towards the attainment of an equilibrium among the exchanges.

(d) The case of a trio of business-partners: equilibria at different levels: Like the trio of true friends, the trio of business-partners also maintains equilibrium but at different levels, depending on the nature of business-sharing. Self-interests of each person in the trio and that too for certain material and monetary gains dominate the b-b and b-b-b exchanges and there exists a setting or equilibrium behind each material gain. Mindsets of the trio are also tuned to this kind of limited exchanges; normally they are full of bias and prejudices.

(e) Some other examples of mixed category: Many examples of b-b, b-b-b and b-b-b-b interactions can be traced in the day-to-day life and at home, at office and in the society. The same can be analysed easily within the above framework. A few of them are (i) husband-wife and a parent-in-law; (ii) mother-daughter and the son-in-law, (iii) boss-subordinate and a peon, (iv) landlord, tenant and the agent, etc. Regarding the two-Being case, the daughter-in-law and mother-in-law interactions are worldwide known particularly when they are living under the same roof. A typical case of 4-Being interactions is shown in *fig.* 9.7. In this figure, while b_1 and b_2 appear to be spectators, b_3 and b_4 are in direct confrontation, of course, with certain prejudices as are indicated by the body actions of b_3 and b_4. The phrase in the inset indicates that b_1, b_2, b_4 have been the part of certain 3-Being system with limited exchanges among them. In this cartoon, the Prime Minister, Dr Manmohan Singh (b_1) alongwith (Congress) Party president, Smt. Sonia Gandhi (b_2) is watching the reaction of the health minister (b_4) when the misdeeds of the latter are exposed by the law expert T.N. Sheshan (b_3).

fig. 9.7: A typical case of four Being interactions. (Courtesy: *Times of India*, 11 May 2008)

9.6.2 DIFFERENT EQUILIBRIA VERSUS ORDERS OF DRESSING OF EOLs OF INTERACTING MEMBERS

Here we look for an answer to the question as to why the husband-wife or the friend-friend interaction in ideal cases is more intense than any other. While we have been using the phrase "development of FOUs" of the participating individual in the interaction, it is more plausible to talk of the same in terms of the dressings of EOLs with consciousness of that individual. As a matter of fact each interacting member in a two- or three-Being system continues to enrich his FOUs by way of dressing the EOLs with consciousness and environment as well. To this effect, both inner and outer EOLs undergo different orders of dressings according to the *trikaraṇa* and *dvikaraṇa* rules respectively which are discussed in Section 8.4.2. In case of an ideal husband-wife couple, these dressings are of the highest order (except for the case of God-devotee interactions) which in turn form the basis for their intimacy and the same in due course of time are translated into their mutual faith and confidence and subsequently into their strong bonds — whatever odds persist. The same is the case with the duo of true friends. However, the orders of dressing of the EOLs in this case remain rather low compared to the case of husband and wife.

When the question of equilibrium among exchanges comes, in principle, it should be settled and resettled at every stage of dressings of EOLs as it is very much essential for the maintenance of continued and prolonged relations. Thus, in addition to the equilibria at gross, micro and causal body levels, this new class of equilibria at the dressing levels of FOUs is equally important for the success of an action performed by the duo, trio or quadra of human Beings.

9.7 Case of Many-Being Interactions: A New Description of Socialization

The formation of groups and subgroups of persons in a society can be analysed on the basis of development of FOUs of an individual. This is what one actually observes in a society, particularly in the Indian context the concept of four major castes perhaps was originated on this very basis. For example, those who developed their FOUs to the highest level in the domain of thinking constituted one caste called "brāhmaṇa" (the intellectual category who guided the society), the second who were with somewhat less developed FOUs constituted another caste called "kṣatriya" (the fighter category) who ruled the society, then the next one is "vaiśya" (business category) and lastly the "śūdra" (manually serving category) who had not developed their FOUs sufficiently. The persons of these four castes were assigned duties in the society accordingly. This was a kind of broad classification of persons with so many exceptions that existed; otherwise, at present, in real life there exists a wide spectrum of persons who have varying developments of their FOUs and forming somewhat stronger groups, subgroups, unions, associations, cults, etc.

We have seen that the magnitude of complexity of interaction among human Beings increases with increasing number of interacting members. No doubt, for these many-Being systems, the starting b-b interaction, in its general form, still remains in the background but at the same time the environment and circumstances demand many-Being interactions to be equally important. Social and ecological sciences are full of such examples of many-Being systems. In fact in physics few-body approaches fail to describe several features of a many-body system and hence statistical approaches are adopted for this purpose; the same is the case here. The knowledge of b-b, or b-b-b interactions cannot be extrapolated to a system of many-Beings in a straightforward manner. As a matter of fact, the many-Being features that evolve are co-existence, co-operation, co-ordination and the like and the same at a higher level are more pronounced than for a pure physical system. In social and ecological sciences, one uses statistical methods to describe many-Being systems but with limited predictive power, mainly because the constituents of the system here are not the inanimate objects but they are (i) living Beings, (ii) having will-power and self-sense, and (iii) have sensitive dependence on the environment provided, or in general they are the open systems. Secondly, the statistical laws derived using an inanimate dice can feed better only to a system of inanimate objects in physics, but not in the present case. As mentioned earlier, the probabilistic approaches are also the manifestations of human ignorance or of the limitations of the measuring instrument, as far as the understanding of a phenomenon in totality is concerned.

Keeping these difficulties in mind, we suggest here a new style of description of a collection of human Beings (which in turn form a society particularly when this collection is in action) within the framework of patomic model. In some sense we plan to use the core-valence type model used in the physics of atoms and nuclei.

9.7.1 CORE-VALENCE PICTURE IN PATOMIC MODEL AND ITS APPLICATIONS

When a many-body system (like an atom consisting of electrons or a nucleus consisting of nucleons) in physics interacts with the surroundings (like an external field) or with another many-body system, then the so-called weakly bound particle(s) in the outer periphery of the system (an electron in the case of atom or a nucleon in the case of nucleus), termed as "valence" particle, participate actively in the interaction after leaving behind the remaining part, the so-called "core" which is considered more or less as inert during the interaction. No doubt, all this is a modelling game which has a basis in the specific nature of the constituents (as they are the Fermi particles) but the interesting aspect of this is that such a picture works and explains a variety of data in both atomic and nuclear physics. This kind of valence-sharing, while found successful in describing higher composites in case of atoms (like diatomic or polyatomic molecules) or in chemical compounds, its role however remains non-transparent in case of nuclei. Further, such a picture also explains excited states of both the systems within their respective mathematical frameworks and has also been employed to many-atom or many-nucleus systems but with a limited success.

Here, we attempt to employ such a core-valence picture in patomic model of human Beings mainly on the basis of analogy. The points of difference to be noted here are that (i) the excited particles here are the EOLs, which are going to be different in each excitation, and (ii) the core left behind after the excitation does not remain inert as such but in general it becomes more and more active than before in each excitation. There are a few exceptions (those who know the "art of living" (cf. Section 4.3)) to this observation where the core can still remain inert but the excitations continue. To be more specific, the picture in the patomic model is as follows:

Unlike atoms and nuclei where the particle(s) in the outer periphery participate first in a reaction or in a two-body interaction (a case of "outside out" (OSO)), the situation is just opposite in the patomic model; it is the case of "inside out" (ISO), in which the EOL B, deep inside and close to WO in the schematic picture (cf. *fig*. 2.1), first comes out to interact with, provided the mind is in the passive state. Therefore, the actions at the B-level can be considered as the lowest excitations. However, B is not isolated but the set of senses of knowledge and action are attached to it, then in the next stage these are the senses of action (SEA), hands, feet, etc. and later the senses of knowledge (SEK) eye, ear, etc. that immediately join B to perform an action. During all this period when M, I and E are still working through the passive mode of consciousness (a departure from the conventional core-valence picture), at the next stage of excitation its active mode through M, I and E also starts manifesting. At any stage, the remaining core(s) do not remain inert; rather they prepare the ground for the next stage of excitation. The excitation that started with B, continued through those of SEA, SEK, M and I leaving behind certain impact every time in E. For a conscious person, these different stages of outward excitations increasing accordingly the orders of dressing of his remaining EOLs with consciousness, can be realized from the b-b interactions shown in *fig*s. 1.3 to 1.6. As a matter of fact here (unlike atoms and nuclei) the excitation (synonym of exchanges) could be in either way first ISO type and later OSO type or vice versa. In *fig*. 1.4 it is from ISO type to OSO type whereas in *fig*. 1.5 it is going to be from OSO type to ISO type, and in *fig*. 1.6 it appears to be a mixture of both.

Next comes the formation of groups and subgroups in a society on the basis of the above prescription. As a matter of fact whichever EOL (or EOLs) work(s) through the active mode of consciousness, the same dominates the actions of the person in the space-time domain by leaving others in the passive mode. When persons with such a specific personality come together, they join hands to form a group, a union, an association, even a caste or a clan. Then there turns out to be some common minimum programme in their daily routine that brings them closer, in spite of the fact that they might have some differences on other fronts of manifestation of consciousness through EOLS, though at a low pitch. Here we list certain groups formed in the society on the basis of such an affinity among the persons and also with reference to their common working domain. Even if there is a common working domain, the motivation and the tools used for the purpose by some of them are different. This will lead to the formation of subgroups among a group. Note that the expertise of a person plays an important role here; the professionals like potter, carpenter, blacksmith, goldsmith, etc. are the examples of subgroups. This is a kind of natural group formation and is different from the type of groups formed in the presence of external pressures or the agent as is the case with administrative, security, police, or defence fora, meant for the maintenance of law and order in the society. With regard to the latter situation it may be reminded here that whether it is a physical many-body system or a many-human Being system, it becomes an ordered one as and when the external forces dominate; otherwise the system becomes disordered or chaotic (i.e. when the internal forces dominate over the external ones). Here, however, we restrict our discussion to the first category of group formation.

(a) Groups on the basis of sharing at B- and SEA-level: The groups of wrestlers or manual labourers are the befitting examples of this category. In society there are both skilled and non-skilled workers. While the actions of a non-skilled worker are dominated by B and SEA, his other EOLs work under the passive mode of consciousness. Ideally, his capability of performing an action is defined to this extent only, whether he is a house-help, a factory worker, or a building-construction labour. A skilled worker, on the other hand, no doubt can perform the same set of actions as of the non-skilled one but he also uses some of his other EOLs in the active mode of consciousness and that brings in him some sort of creativity and guiding capacity in his deeds. This limited creativeness in his actions again in fact is the result of his devotion in developing some of his FOUs over a period of time and the same contributes to his expertise in that limited domain.

(b) Groups on the basis of sharing at SEK-level : Groups and subgroups formed in a society on the basis of exchanges at the SEK-level are plenty. Each sense of knowledge (such as ear, eye, nose, tongue, skin) separately or jointly with other SEKs or in conjunction with B and/or SEA is capable of creating an expertise in a human Being. As a matter of fact, a great deal of network of human actions can be attributed to the role of senses of knowledge in conjunction with M, I and E at the inner level and with B and SEA at the outer level. In society one can find all sorts of examples of groups and subgroups resulting from various permutations and combinations of inner and outer EOLs with a possible fulcrum-like role of SEKs in the middle either of one or more than one SEKs. Not only this, different orders of dressing of the participating M, I and E (or their levels of development) in these permutations and combinations lead to the formation of different subgroups. As we argued in the previous chapter, while there is a limited scope for the dressing of EOLs of non-skilled workers, skilled workers however appear with a variety of expertise in a society and consequently constitute a large number of subgroups. For example, a subgroup of persons in a society formed on the basis of exchanges through s^{th} SEK and having their dressed EOLs as $\widetilde{B}$, $\widetilde{S}\widetilde{E}\widetilde{A}$, $\widetilde{S}\widetilde{E}\widetilde{K}$, $\widetilde{M}^{(\ell)}$, $\widetilde{I}^{(m)}$, $\widetilde{E}^{(n)}$ can be expressed in its very general form as

$$G_{\ell mn}^{(r)(s)} \equiv \{\widetilde{B}, \widetilde{S}\widetilde{E}\widetilde{A}_{(r)}, \widetilde{S}\widetilde{E}\widetilde{K}_{(s)}, \widetilde{M}^{(\ell)}, \widetilde{I}^{(m)}, \widetilde{E}^{(n)}\}, \qquad (9.5)$$

where r denotes either individual SEA like hands, feet, power of speech, copulatory organs or their certain combination and similarly s denotes either individual SEK such as ear, eye, nose, tongue, skin or their certain combination, and l, m, n=0, 1, 2, ... ∞ correspond to different orders of dressing of M, I and E respectively with l, m, n = 0 corresponding to the nascent EOLs (or the ones without tilde).

Note that (i) the case of semi-skilled workers can also be accommodated in this scheme of construction of subgroups in a society; (ii) these constructions are on the basis of actions performed by an individual towards his livelihood or professionalism, and however do not pertain to his personal life; (iii) a subgroup of super-specialists can be defined with reasonably high values of integers l, m, and n, though with varying expertise, and (iv) in the limiting case when anyone of l, m and n or all the three tend to infinity, the person becomes "seer" of the corresponding profession rather than working manually and acts as a guide of his profession with so many creative ideas. For example, take the case of a singer or a teacher which corresponds to $G_{\ell mn}^{(\textit{power of speech} +),\, (\textit{tongue} +)}$. Here the plus sign in superscript indicates the involvement of other SEAs and SEKs but at a secondary level.

9.7.2 ONE-TO-MANY HUMAN BEINGS AND MANY-TO-ONE HUMAN BEING INTERACTIONS: A SAHA-LIKE IONIZATION FORMULA FOR A SYSTEM OF EXCITED HUMAN BEINGS

A detailed study of ionization of gases by thermal excitation was carried out by M.N. Saha about eighty years ago.[7] In particular, the question as to what happens when a gaseous mass consisting of atoms is heated to very high temperatures was discussed by Saha. To this effect, a formula for computing the fraction of the number of (r+1)-times ionized to r-times ionized atoms was derived in terms of pressure, temperature and internal energy of the system. Here we use an analogy in

7. M.N. Saha and B.N. Srivastava, *A Treatise on Heat* (Allahabad: The Indian Press Pvt. Ltd., rpt. edn. (1972), and 1st edn. (1931)); also see M.N. Saha and Rai, Proc. Nat. Aca. Sc. 4, 319; B.N. Srivastava, *Proc. Roy. Soc. Lond.* 175 (1940) 26.

which the gaseous mass containing many atoms is replaced with a system of human Beings. Such a system when exposed to a lecture either by a teacher (a person who has developed his FOUs to a higher level), a politician (a person who has certain ideas to convey to masses), or by a spiritual leader, then each member of the system undergoes a kind of excitation (or a transformation) at different levels (depending upon the initial development of his FOUs). As a matter of fact whatever may be the nature of theme of the lecture by the "transmitter," the members of the "receiving system" undergo some sort of imposed collective thinking (or meditation) like the atoms of the gas when exposed to the same very high temperature, get excited to different energy levels. In the same way, the members of the "receiving system" get excited from different initial to different final states of their EOLs and this leads to a further development of their FOUs. As a matter of fact each member, in general, will react differently to the same lecture and digest the theme differently, depending on his receiving capacity or on the evolution of his mindset till then. Naturally, some persons will derive the inspiration to work at the level of B, some at the level of SEA, some at the level of SEK, some at the level of M, and so on while listening or exposed to the same lecture in the given circumstances.

We use here Saha's prescription to compute the evolution (excitation) of a single EOL as a result of imposition of such a collective thinking represented by a collective meditation parameter μ_c (on par with the external temperature in Saha's theory). Let α be the fraction defined as $\alpha = N_+/N_0$, where N_+ is the number of beneficiaries in terms of evolution of their any one EOL and N_0 be the number of persons initially ready to undergo such an experience at a given space-time, then it can be shown[8] that

8. For a recent application of the Saha formula in quark-gluon plasma see, R.S. Kaushal, "A Model for Quark-gluon Plasma with Pentaquark Baryons and Tetraquark Mesons", *Ind. Journ. Phys.* 82 (2008) 891-906 #7, July issue, and the references therein.

$$\alpha(\mu_c,\sigma) = -\phi(\mu_c,\sigma) + [\phi^2 (\mu_c,\sigma) + 2\phi(\mu_c,\sigma)]^{1/2} \tag{9.6}$$

$$\text{with } \phi(\mu_c,\sigma) = \left(\frac{\mu_c}{\mu_c^0}\right)^{3/2} e^{-\chi_s^\sigma/\mu_c}. \tag{9.7}$$

Here χ_s^σ is the measure of negative efforts (in appropriate units consistent with μ_c) made by an individual in the given circumstances σ to achieve the s-th level in the patomic model (in the spirit of ISO case) and μ_c^0 is the measure of initial mindset of the "transmitter" prevailing and derived by judging the nature of the gathering. The behaviour of the fraction of beneficiaries in the audience is shown in *fig.* 9.8 as a function of the collective meditation parameter, μ_c (in the units of μ_c^0) for three typical values of χ_s^σ, namely solid, dashed and dotted curves correspond to χ_s^σ = 0.1, 1.0 and 10.0 respectively in the units of μ_c^0. In general α increases with μ_c and then slowly attains the value unity rather asymptotically. Note that for a given μ_c, α is large for small values of χ_s^σ, meaning thereby that if μ_c is compatible with μ of the

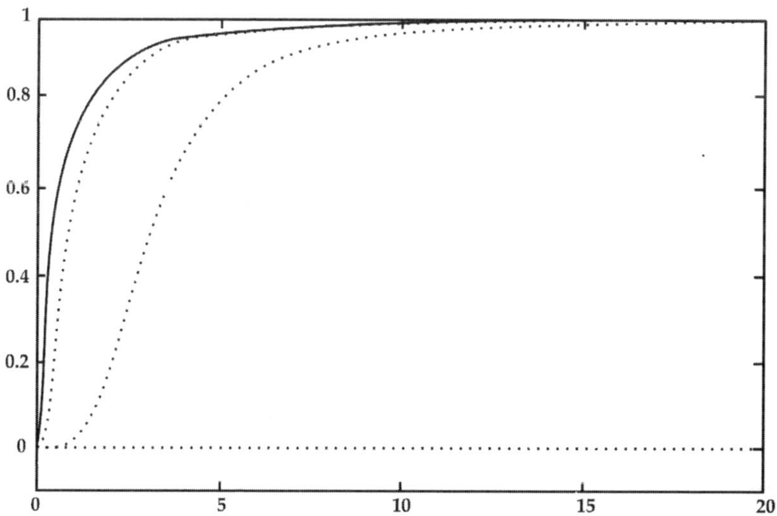

fig. 9.8: Behaviour of the fraction of beneficiaries in the audience as a function of the collective meditation parameter, μ_c, for different efforts of the individual. Solid, dashed and dotted curves respectively correspond to X_s=0.1, 1.0 and 10.0 in the units of μ_c.

individual in the gathering (or if there is a matching of mindsets of the transmitter and the receiver) then most beneficiaries are those who have never made an effort (or negative effort) in the past but now they are conscious to learn or to gain from the given transmitter. The limiting value of α as unity is an ideal situation and the same is hardly attained by a group of audience, but for those who have small χ_s^{σ}, such a limit is achieved rather quickly.

For example, when evaluated it is found that different students learn differently from the same teacher in the class, members of public meeting gather different ideas about the politician and the theme of his speech, or devotees undergo different experiences after attending a meditation class and so on. Thus, using Saha's prescription it is not difficult to have a feel for the number of beneficiaries in a gathering at least for a single excitation (although it is not an easy task to identify whether the excitation is single (unique) or multiple in the framework of patomic model; perhaps the same is easier for the atomic systems). It may be mentioned that Saha's prescription also contains certain elements of statistics (Maxwell-Boltzmann type) in it.

Now we return to the case of many-to-one human Being interaction, i.e. when a teacher in the class, a political leader in the masses, or a spiritual leader in the meditation class, etc. is showered with questions and queries from the audience at the same time. If this conversation is one-to-one then the life is simple for the speaker; otherwise the speaker becomes puzzled, because the quality of questions posed is not only different scale-wise (scales in the sense of different levels of EOLs) but also varies over a wide range for which, particularly, the newly "designed speaker" is not readily prepared to answer. At times, the combined system (speaker plus audience) takes an ugly scene or becomes a chaotic one because each individual in the audience or in the gathering has different mindset and works in different circumstances to start with. Imagine the scene when a truck driver is caught by the public after an accident on the road by his truck.

In the one-to-many human Being interaction case μ_c varies smoothly and systematically as it is mostly decided in advance by the speaker whereas in the present many-to-one human Being case μ_c varies randomly and at times on different scales. In fact in the latter case μ_c is some arbitrary combination of μ's of individuals and hence becomes a very complicated variable. Many examples to this effect can be cited from the day-to-day life but we refrain ourselves from going into such details here.

9.8 Concluding Discussion

With a view to understanding the nature and other finer details of interactions among human Beings, the framework of patomic model is employed in this chapter. Several analogies from many-body theories in physics are frequently used for this purpose. After summarizing certain aspects of studies of many-body systems in physics and the interactions of an individual in a family or society, the quantification of the latter is attempted in Section 9.4 onward. It may be mentioned that since the two-human Being interactions form the basis of several aspects of human personality and behaviour (in the same way as the two-body forces do in the study of many-body systems in physics) they are investigated here in detail. While at a lower level it is found that five *tanmātras* (quanta of interactions) define the broad classes of exchanges between two persons, their numbers become twenty or more if the fine- or hyperfine-tuning of these interactions is carried out at higher levels. As a result, the existing scheme becomes capable of accommodating a large number of exchanges between two persons (cf. Table 9.1). With regard to applications of these studies several typical cases of two-Being interactions from a family and society are discussed. The case of husband-wife exchanges sets the example of a perfect interaction between two persons. The scheme with possible modifications is also employed to analyse the cases of three- and four-human Being interactions. As a matter of fact the nature of these exchanges is found to have sensitive dependence on the circumstances given and hence this accordingly affects the behaviour of members in the system individually or collectively.

With regard to many-human Being interactions, the present studies suggest a new way of socializing and the same in fact persists in society. The core-valence picture of interaction in a many-object system, while appears to be a useful tool for such studies in atomic physics, its viability is however limited in the patomic model of human Being. Still several interesting implications of the model are shown with regard to formation of groups and subgroups in a society. An important aspect investigated here for many-Being systems is through the use of Saha-like ionization formula for the excitations of members in a system. By way of introducing a collective meditation parameter, μ_c, on par with the temperature in Saha theory, attempts are made to study one-to-many human Beings and many-to-one human Being interactions. In this case, while a detailed study of the roles of circumstances and of efforts in the computation of EOL-ionization fraction need to be pursued, the results for single EOL ionization are found encouraging here in the sense that they conform to several day-to-day human experiences.

What has been attempted in this chapter is the quantification of interactions among human Beings by way of borrowing certain concepts and analogies from physics. To this effect, for the purpose of analysis, we have picked up only a few out of a sea of phenomena which prevail in human behaviour and experiences and pertain to many-human Being systems. No doubt, the human component brings in many complexities in the methodology of physics when employed in the present context, but the fact is that the use of patomic model of human Being has been able to overcome a good deal of them, particularly when the tuning of its constituents, i.e. of both inner and outer EOLs is carried out at the highest level. It is noticed that even within this framework, few-person interactions can be better analysed than many-person interactions as is the case in physics. Although there is a better possibility of mathematization of exchanges between two persons than for the many-person case, we have however avoided the same here. However, the viability of certain concepts and models of physics is demonstrated for the many-person case. It may be interesting to pursue these ideas further and to check the predictive power of the patomic model; of course by way of identifying certain ingredients of the latter with physics-like quantities as it is done for the many-person case in Section 9.7 by using collective meditation parameter for the temperature.

Finally, we remark on some salient features of many-person interactions that might act as a guide for future studies:

(i) Note that difference between the two situations in which one-to-many person interactions are discussed (cf. Sections 9.2 and 9.7.2). No doubt in both the cases the purpose is the same as to enhance the development of FOUs but in Sect. 9.2 this happens for an individual whereas in Section 9.7.2 it goes for a group of persons. Secondly, in the former case the FOUs of an individual develop in parts, at different space-time points and in different circumstances whereas in the latter case they all are externally fixed and there are chances of uniform development of FOUs of an individual in the group.

(ii) Reversibility of Exchanges: In certain cases in physics the exchanges (or the interactions) between objects show symmetry with respect to the space and time, so-called parity and time-reversal invariance. Here, however, this is not the case in general; only in rare cases one can think of such a possibility of complete reversibility of exchanges between human Beings, particularly when these exchanges take place with respect to nascent EOLs of each individual and that is rare. Normally, EOLs are dressed with the consciousness comprising of space, time and circumstances. This in fact leads to different orders of dressing not only of each EOL but also to the development of

FOUs of each individual. The same is the case when we consider the exchanges among three and more persons.

(iii) Personality influence: Personality of a person cannot influence inanimate objects except for the appearance of some physical forces. It can however influence humans and non-humans and accordingly the nature of interactions gets affected. The personality of a person is basically a collective phenomenon that originates out of the mindset of an individual to which the contribution comes from the interactions inside the conscious human Being. In fact at the end-point of dressings of EOLs, this mindset appears again in the space-time domain. If the influenced object is a human Being then the exchanges between the interacting personalities are richer and could be both ways as compared to the case when the influenced object is a non-human Being. The exchanges in the latter case are mostly unidirectional. Thus, the personality also matters in one-to-many persons and many-to-one person interactions.

(iv) Secrets of nurturing beautiful relationship: Because most of us have not explored life in its full depth and dimension, as a result we feel some sort of incompleteness within and seek partnership with another life. This is how the relationships are initiated and developed. The relationship itself is a complex process because there are too many expectations from the other Being (the exchanges of $\tau_{M,E}$-type in Table 9.1 dominate). This involves somewhat deeper roles of M, I and E of an individual at every stage of development of relationship. At times, these expectations become the source of conflict between the partners, particularly when they are not fulfilled.

Fundamentally, one seeks a relationship because he wants to be happy, joyful; or one is trying to use the other person as a source of his happiness. As a matter of fact in the process of establishing relationship you are trying to squeeze happiness out of somebody and that somebody is trying to squeeze happiness out of you and this is going to be very painful. Indeed, just shifting of life from the pursuit of happiness to an expression of joyfulness can lead to what is needed for a beautiful and prolonged relationship. This becomes possible by way of minimizing the expectations from the other Being.

(v) Judging people by reading minds: This is an interesting phenomenon that basically emerges out of the b-b interaction. People think that by knowing other people, or by reading their minds, they can be effective in the world. But this is not true. Contrarily, if one knows himself, he can become very effective. No doubt, one can read other's mind because he himself also has mind, but the point is that by doing so he falls into the trap of good and bad and this changes his mindset. Once such a mindset is carried by an individual, then there is a natural tendency of downward transitions of the Being in the patomic model. The way out is to remain unattached to these goodness and badness of others and try to find time to know himself (as the police or inquiry personnels do); otherwise, at times, the misunderstanding is so deeply ingrained that people are being used and the things are being loved, whereas it should have been the other way round, i.e. the things were made to be used and people to be loved. One should accept the fact as it is, in the spirit of differentiating the situations of b-b interactions and the interactions of a human Being with physical world. It has been seen in the day-to-day life that people can divorce the relationship but not their money. Peculiar are the ways of life (!).

(vi) Why living with people is so difficult?: While it is perhaps easier to live with birds and animals, the most difficult thing to do is to live in peace and harmony with people. Why is living with people a problem? The answer is simple — we have too many expectations of them. As mentioned in (iv) above, the expectations and the desire of their fulfilment, are the main cause of conflict with a person or with a group of persons. Again the exchanges of $\tau_{\mathcal{M},\mathcal{M}}$-type (cf. *fig*. 9.1 and Table 9.1) play a dominant role in these processes. If I expect something of another, that person may also expect something of me. Furthermore, I am unable to fulfil my own expectations of myself — I want to do so many things, but unable to do them. Thus, I feel disappointed and frustrated with myself, and aggrieved or upset with others when they fail to satisfy my expectations. Thus, the message, as in point (v), is that one should accept the fact as it is. Then if a change is necessary, try to make that change, but do not insist on it. Always try to give "freedom" "and "space" to other people.

(vii) At a certain level of hierarchy in the science of Self, while consciousness becomes the creator of space, time and circumstances (particularly when b performs downward transitions towards WO in the patomic model), at another level it however dresses up the EOLs of an individual with space, time and circumstances and thereby enriching his FOUs with a possibility that b becomes capable of performing upward transitions towards SO. It is this latter process that is supposed to dominate during the exchanges among human Beings ideally; but in practice the things are made different.

(viii) One has to be cautious while applying the methodology of physics to a system of human Beings. By any standard, the groups and subgroups of interacting persons cannot be considered as closed systems — a basis for the viability of physical theories. Therefore, a judicious selection of tools of physics is necessary for the present purposes.

10

Interactions Involving Non-human Beings

SINCE time immemorial, human Beings have never lived in isolation from other living species on this planet whether it has been his living or the working place. With regard to their survival they have been interacting with each other in various forms. Though there has been interdependence between the two, humans however have depended more on non-humans than the other way round. While this had been the case prior to the machine-age, the co-existence of humans and non-humans can be found even today in many parts of the planet.

As a matter of fact, not only animals and birds but also at times other creatures have been the source and means of livelihood for humans. Certain categories of the former are the domestic, caged or the pets with which humans frequently have interactions. On the other hand, if a conscious person notices existence (at a physical or mental level) of a non-human, may be in close vicinity or at a far off distance, in either situation his actions and behaviour get affected. Though the study of animal behaviour *vis-à-vis* humans is a subject in itself, in this chapter however we aim at highlighting some of the fundamental processes resulting from the interactions between a human Being and non-humans. No doubt, our arguments and discussions based on patomic model will be quite general, but for non-humans our examples will be limited to the cases of pets, domestic animals and some other non-humans.

To start with, first we briefly discuss a spiritual link between humans and non-humans and then introduce the concept of a fractured patomic model in Section 10.3 mainly to accommodate the cases of non-humans and the physically and mentally challenged (PMC) persons. Then we discuss limitations of evolution of EOLs and the development of FOUs in these cases in Section 10.4. Section 10.5 is devoted to categorize the non-humans in the present context. Cases of interactions between a normal person and a PMC person and that between a human Being and non-humans are discussed, respectively in Sections 10.6 and 10.7. Several interesting features of the last category of interaction are further explored in Section 10.8 in view of several real-life examples from the animal world. Finally, concluding remarks are made in Section 10.9.

10.1 A Spiritual Link between Humans and Non-humans

Since Beings are just manifestations of the same source of cosmic consciousness, each of them has all the attributes of the source, though in varying proportions and degrees. As the consciousness — an attribute of SO — manifests differently through different body parts of a Being (sometimes depends on the number of biological cells present in that body part), similar is the case with different living Beings. In fact, the same cosmic consciousness manifests through different Beings differently. These are the space and time introduced as illusory media to ensure the delusion of separateness in the varieties of creation; otherwise they all have a common link through their origin from the same source. As is the case with humans, i.e. for consciousness to experience itself, a state of duality had to be induced to resolve the dichotomy of the perceiver and the perceived; all creations (Beings) in the same way can be thought of as an induced illusion of duality to enable the cosmic source to experience itself.

There is another aspect of separateness of Being, namely the ego. The illusion of a Being built-in already as the doer and the centre of universe, manifests as ego. Ego, in fact, serves initially as a tool for self-preservation of a Being but later, as it crystallizes, it totally envelopes the consciousness and that prevents the Being from realizing his true nature. Thus, among several points of difference between humans and non-humans (which we shall list below) one is that humans have the quality of repenting, analysing and improving their deeds but not most of the non-humans. In a nut-shell, Deepak Ranade emphasizes[1] that, "The purpose of creation was for the source to experience itself. Creation is like democracy: Made of the source, by the source and for the source." This is what happens during self-awareness (or during self-realization or in the state of unperceiving) — a quality of humans.

Self-awareness is unique to humans, which is not there in most non-humans. For example, a cat before a mirror does not know that it is looking at its own reflection. It thinks that there is another cat in front of it. But a baby by the age of two realizes that he is seeing his own image in a mirror. In fact this self-awareness makes us compare our happiness/sorrow levels with those of people we know well, like friends, relatives, colleagues, etc.

In this context Himani Dalmia[2] carries out a survey of Hindu mythology, works of various poets and writers to look for the reasons of and the justifications for the common link that exists between humans and non-humans. According to Dalmia, animals occupy a spiritual space that seems to originate in the feelings of companionship, affinity and kinship. Not only this, some birds and animals are given highly sacred place in the Hindu mythology in the sense that each deity uses them in one form or the other to carry out his assignment, in most cases as a vehicle. As a matter of fact, uncomplicated or less complicated nature of these species in philosophical terms perhaps is the reason for their use by humans.

---

1. Deepak Ranade, "The Democratic Nature of All Creation", The Speaking Tree Column, *Times of India*, 26 March 2008; "The Human Species is so Special", The Speaking Tree Column, *Times of India*, 23 April 2008.

2. Himani Dalmia, "Spiritual Link Between Human and Animals", The Speaking Tree Column, *Times of India*, 29 March 2008.

10.2 Why the Human Species is so Special?

Out of the broad biological classification of species as animals and plants, the sub-classes of humans and non-humans fall under the same head of animals. Non-humans are further divided into those who share the human's habitat (inquilines) and those who are wild or do not share the human's habitat (non-inquilines). Here, however, our studies will pertain mainly to the first category so far as the use of the term "non-human" is concerned, particularly the interactions of humans with mammals, birds or caged animals will be highlighted. In biological terms, humans have several distinct features from non-humans, namely humans are psychozoans (responsible for emotions), carry larger frontal lobe per unit body mass, deepest sulci and highest gyrci compared to non-humans so as to increase surface area and in turn the neuron density in the peripheral region of the brain, an opposable thumb in the hand that can be juxtaposed on any finger, etc.

With regard to humans as a unique species, the neurosurgeon Deepak Ramade brings out[3] further details of these points more in a philosophical spirit. The same can be listed as follows:

(i) Humans are bestowed with frontal lobe (i.e. the extensions of the brain that insinuate between the eyebrows and hairline), which also cleave us our immediate ancestors, the apes. Frontal lobes are the seat of abstraction, intellect and empower us with qualities like imagination, and conceptual thought.

(ii) Primitive nervous system of humans is designed to enable them to perceive and interact with the environment, successive evolutionary improvements in the system served to increase the speed and complexity of the response, although as a reaction to the

3. Deepak Ranade, op. cit.

environment. However, with frontal lobes appearing, humans could engage them in abstraction, e.g. philosophy, poetry and culture and the likes and some intangibles that the human brain can delve into. At the same time, this added faculty — the power to use this creative imagination — also becomes a tool to promote imaginary fears, such as the fear of the unknown, the concept of destiny, suspicion, anxiety and an entire spectrum of "imaginary" fears and angst.

(iii) According to Ranade, "Abstraction has given boon to humans to comprehend the 'inner' world. It is unlikely that other species would query 'who am I' or 'why has this creation been made?' These are doubts that can arise only as an extrapolation of thought-process beyond the travails of daily mundane living." Further, ". . . this heightened ability of imagination and comprehension was made available for human mind to fathom itself." These features are human-specific, perhaps not possessed by any other species. Moreover, we are just given these additional tools to utilize, but we are not the creator of these tools.

Since animals and birds miss many of these ingredients in their body-structure in biological terms and in their way of life, in philosophical terms, they have been used by humans for their survival and livelihood. At times, poets and writers used them as metaphors in their works to emphasize and narrate worldly wisdom, polity, morality, etc. through stories involving them (as in *Pañcatantra* or in other texts). Scientists, on the other hand, have been using them in experiments to test and verify their new researches, which otherwise become difficult to carry out on humans.

10.3 Deviations from the Perfect Creation of God (i.e. Human Being): Fractured Patomic Model

As mentioned earlier (cf. Section 8.12), the human Being in an ideal and perfect creation of God. There exist a large number of species in Nature which deviate from this perfect creation in terms of certain missing or undeveloped EOLs in them. While there are cases of physically and/or mentally challenged (PMC) individuals even among the human Beings, varieties of non-humans do exist in Nature with these characteristics. As a result, not only their actions and subsequently the behaviour in the field of WO become different but they also undergo different types of exchanges when interacting with a perfect human Being. Here, within the framework of a so-called "fractured patomic model," we shall try to analyse the interactions of this category of human as well as of non-human Beings with a perfect human.

Further note the difference between the PMC category of humans and the non-humans as far as their interaction with a human Being is concerned. As a matter of fact, in the former case the FOUs do exist and are capable of fully developing as in the case of a perfect human Being, but the missing EOL(s) block the development of FOUs and subsequently affects the actions of the person concerned. However, the characteristic features specific to a perfect human (cf. Sections 10.1 and 10.2) remain intact for the case of PMC category of humans. On the other hand, with non-humans this is not the case; because of the lack of development of frontal lobe in non-humans the psychozoan is generally missing. In PMC category of humans, certain EOLs are missing either since birth or as a result of an accident at a certain point of time in the life of an individual. In the former situation the development of FOUs remains rather minimum (including zero) whereas it attains some reasonable finite limit in the latter situation. Again the development of FOUs in these two situations depends on the fact whether an inner EOL is missing in an individual or an outer one.

While modern medical science has provided a great relief to those who suffer from the missing of outer EOLs (sometimes by transplantation of organs responsible for action, SEAs, or by way of attaching appropriate sensor(s) to the respective missing

SEKs), it has not been very successful in curing the patients suffering from the deficiency of inner EOLs like M, I and E. In fact in a PMC person there may be deficiency of any number out of 13 EOLs (namely M, I and E in the inner domain, and 5 SEKs namely eyes, ears, nose, tongue, skin and another 5 SEAs namely hands, feet, power of speech, copulatory organ, anus in the outer domain). Not only this, at least one of the sensors out of 5 SEKs has also to be there to respond for this purpose. Further note that larger the number of missing EOLs, lesser is the chance of survival of a PMC person. Medical science can, of course, be helpful only in some selective situations and that too to a certain limited extent, but by and large the PMC person has to suffer and accordingly his actions and behaviour get affected.

If we assume that in addition to mind at least any one of the five SEKs is also present in a PMC person for any meaningful interaction with a perfect person, then there turn out to be very large varieties of PMC persons as a result of different permutations and combinations of five SEKs and five SEAs and the remaining inner EOLs I and E. Of course, the chances of survival of a PMC person in many of these categories are negligibly small. We refrain ourselves from going into these details here and shall remark on the interactions of a perfect human with only a few selective types of PMC persons. However, for non-humans a detailed classification will be presented on this basis in Section 10.5.

10.4 Evolution of EOLs and the Development of FOUs in Non-humans

Before investigating the nature of interaction between a human Being and non-humans it is worthwhile to survey the evolution of EOLs in non-humans and subsequently the development of FOUs which has taken place in them. It is true that in the history of evolution, the human species at present is the most developed one and has a very fine and balanced body structure in biological terms, particularly with regard to the working of heart, brain, nervous system, neural network, etc. These features perhaps have given birth to a most developed (cf. Section 10.2) psychozoan in humans and as a result they have been able to command over other species for their survival and lifestyle. Within the framework of patomic model, while SO, B and the WO as well (by way of supplying environment) and may be some of the SEAs are common to other living Beings, the difference with humans arises at two fronts, firstly in terms of the existence of some or all the remaining EOLs (like E, I, M, and SEKs) in a non-human and secondly, if they exist, then in terms of their development over a period of time in the history of evolution. As a matter of fact these two points are crucial as far as the nature of interaction of a human with non-humans is concerned. The species simply having SO, B and SEAs and left in the field of WO will not be able to respond to humans. For them, the presence of a human (or for that matter of any other Being) will go un-noticed. The interactions (exchanges) will be strictly unidirectional, as if this is the case of interaction of a human with an inanimate object (cf. Chapter 8). Even the presence of some or all of SEAs in the species will not matter in this case.

For a meaningful interaction at least some of the sensors of SEKs in the non-human Being must be present. Although the interaction of a human with a non-human (who is an imperfect creation) will depend upon the number of EOLs present in the latter, for a systematic study it is worthwhile to classify the non-humans in general on this ground. Note that for this purpose, the discriminating parameters left in all are eight in number, namely E, I, M and the sensors of eyes, ears, nose, tongue and skin. In order that some of the sensors of SEKs present in a non-human have to work in response to a human action on them, at least one of the inner EOLs, i.e. M with appropriate sensitiveness (in terms of the orders of its dressing with consciousness) has to be present. Not only this, as non-humans at times are selective in their actions towards defence, survival, hunger and thirst, a certain degree of decision-making power, i.e. intellect I, has also to be present in them. At times, since non-humans also show the symptoms of memory in their actions and behaviour, therefore a certain degree of faculty of memory, i.e. E (which occasionally takes the form of gross ego) has to be present in them. In spite of all these possibilities in a non-human, a particular non-human Being may not be equipped with all of them at the same time particularly at the present point of time in its history of evolution. Thus, different non-humans are equipped with different number of EOLs and accordingly the interaction of a human with them gets affected.

In what follows, we present a classification of non-humans who are capable of interacting with humans, by keeping in mind that a non-human manages to have at least one SEK and M, in addition to SO, B and may be some SEAs, for a meaningful interaction.

10.5 A Classification of Non-humans Capable of Interacting with Human Being

For a systematic study it is necessary to classify the non-humans within the framework of fractured patomic model. This is carried out by way of retaining some minimum number of EOLs in the non-human species so that its interaction with a human becomes meaningful or noticeable. In a compact form we can express the different classes of non-human species in terms of a modified notation for the mindset $\mathcal{M}(m, i, c; \sigma)$ of Chapter 8 as $\mathcal{M}^{(jklrs)}(m, i, e; \sigma)$ and its n-times dressed version as $\mathcal{M}^{(n)\,(jklrs)}(m, i, e; \sigma)$. Here, while $\mathcal{M}$ remains a function of m, i, e and σ attributes respectively of the roles of M, I, E and the environment — a creation out of WO, it is also labelled with superscripts j, k, l, r and s. These five superscripts respectively correspond to the five sensors of SEKs namely eyes (j), ears (k), nose (l), tongue (r) and skin (s), some of which are possibly present in the given species. Further, in this notation, the variables m, i, e (except σ) and the superscripts j, k, l, r, and s are considered to take discrete values 0 and 1 only which correspond respectively to the absence or the presence of a particular EOL in the given non-human species.

For example, $\mathcal{M}^{(n)\ (11111)}$ (1, 1, 1; σ) represents the n-th order dressed mindset of a perfect human Being in which all the EOLs are present. Similarly, $\mathcal{M}^{(n)\ (00000)}$ (0, 0, 0; σ) represents the n-th order dressed mindset of a species consisting only of SO, B and SEAs in the field of WO. In other words, such a species has no mindset at all. This is perhaps the simplest (!) creation of God. Next come the situations in between these two extreme cases; namely take the case of $\mathcal{M}^{(n)\ (01000)}$ (1, 0, 0; σ) which represents species having n-th order dressed mind as an inner EOL and conscious ear(s) or any other similar device as a sensor in the domain of outer EOLs. Note that m=1 is considered for all the cases since the existence of the EOL, M, in a species is a must for any kind of meaningful interaction with it via the available sensors of SEKs. Moreover, the basic need to fulfil the desire of thirst or hunger of a non-human will bring in the role of M in the behaviour of species. Now onward and also in Table 10.1 we drop the tilde (~) and the superscript (n) on $\mathcal{M}$ unless a discussion on the dressing of $\mathcal{M}$ is required. With these prescriptions, in all we have 92 varieties of non-humans, out of which 90 varieties are listed in Table 10.1. The two cases corresponding to $\mathcal{M}^{(11111)}$ (1, 0, 1; σ) and $\mathcal{M}^{(11111)}$ (1, 1, 0; σ) are not shown in the table. Entries in this Table as 0 and 1 in various columns respectively represent the absence or the presence of that particular EOL in the species and accordingly its interaction with a person gets affected. Thirty distinct cases corresponding to i=e=0 and m=1 and with various possibilities of j, k, l, r and s are listed in this table and for the rest 60 cases when i=m=1, e=0 and i=m=e=1, note that the given thirty entries for various possibilities of j, k, l, r and s can be repeated in both the cases. Though it remains for the biologists to identify these species in Nature and accordingly draw certain conclusions about the systematics of their behaviour, in the last column of Table 10.1, however we only make a few remarks about the concerned non-human species mainly due to the limitations of the author. In the next section, we shall take up some representative but familiar cases to analyse the interaction of a human with non-human Beings within this framework.

Table 10.1: Classification of non-humans within the framework of a fractured patomic model and on the basis of their interacting capacity with a human Being. Entries 0 and 1 in various columns indicate the absence or the presence of that particular EOL in the given species or in its mindset denoted by $\mathcal{M}^{(jklrs)}$ (m, i, e;σ).

	Inner EOLs			*Five SEKs*					
Sr. No.	*Ego (E) (e)*	*Intel-lect (I) (i)*	*Mind (M) (m)*	*Eye(s) (j)*	*Ear(s) (k)*	*Nose (l)*	*Tongue (r)*	*Skin (s)*	*Characteristics of species/Remarks*
1.	0	0	1	1	0	0	0	0	Emotions exist; sensitive only to optical category of sensors
2.	0	0	1	0	1	0	0	0	Emotions exist; sensitive only to sound-like sensors
3.	0	0	1	0	0	1	0	0	Emotions exist; sensitive only to smell-like sensors
4.	0	0	1	0	0	0	1	0	Emotions exist; sensitive only to taste-like sensors
5.	0	0	1	0	0	0	0	1	Emotions exist; sensitive only to touch-like sensors
6.	0	0	1	1	1	0	0	0	Emotions exist; sensitive to both optical and sound like sensors

7.	0	0	1	0	1	1	0	0	Emotions exist; sensitive to both sound and smell-like sensors
8.	0	0	1	0	0	1	1	0	Emotions exist; sensitive to both smell- and taste-like sensors
9.	0	0	1	0	0	0	1	1	Emotions exist; sensitive to both taste- and touch-like sensors
10.	0	0	1	1	0	1	0	0	Emotions exist; sensitive to both optical and smell-like sensors
11.	0	0	1	1	0	0	1	0	Emotions exist; sensitive to both optical and taste-like sensors
12.	0	0	1	1	0	0	0	1	Emotions exist; sensitive to both optical and touch-like sensors
13.	0	0	1	0	1	0	1	0	Emotions exist; sensitive to both sound- and taste-like sensors
14.	0	0	1	0	1	0	0	1	Emotions exist; sensitive to both sound- and touch-like sensors
15.	0	0	1	0	0	1	0	1	Emotions exist; sensitive to both smell- and touch-like sensors
16.	0	0	1	1	1	1	0	0	Emotions exist; sensitive to optical, sound and smell-like sensors

17.	0	0	1	0	1	1	1	0	Emotions exist; sensitive to sound, smell and taste-like sensors
18.	0	0	1	0	0	1	1	1	Emotions exist; sensitive to smell, taste and touch-like sensors
19.	0	0	1	1	0	0	1	1	Emotions exist; sensitive to optical, taste and touch-like sensors
20.	0	0	1	1	1	0	0	1	Emotions exist; sensitive to optical, sound and touch-like sensors
21.	0	0	1	0	1	0	1	1	Emotions exist; sensitive to sound, taste and touch-like sensors
22.	0	0	1	0	1	1	0	1	Emotions exist; sensitive to sound, smell and touch-like sensors
23.	0	0	1	1	0	1	0	1	Emotions exist; sensitive to optical, smell and touch-like sensors
24.	0	0	1	1	0	1	1	0	Emotions exist; sensitive to optical, smell and taste-like sensors
25.	0	0	1	1	1	0	1	0	Emotions exist; sensitive to optical, sound and taste-like sensors
26.	0	0	1	0	1	1	1	1	Emotions exist; sensitive to all five (except optical-like) sensors

27.	0	0	1	1	0	1	1	1	Emotions exist; sensitive to all five (except sound-like) sensors
28.	0	0	1	1	1	0	1	1	Emotions exist; sensitive to all five (except smell-like) sensors
29.	0	0	1	1	1	1	0	1	Emotions exist; sensitive to all five (except taste-like) sensors
30.	0	0	1	1	1	1	1	0	Emotions exist; sensitive to all five (except touch-like) sensors
31-60	0	1	1						Emotions and decision taking capacities exist; with repetition of above 30 possibilities for j, k, l, r and s sensors.
61-90	1	1	1						Emotions and decision taking capacities and memory exist; with repetition of above 30 possibilities for j, k, l, rand s sensors.

With regard to the above classification of non-human species the following remarks are in order:

(i) Out of these 92 varieties of non-human species, further large number of sub-varieties of these species can be generated by considering different orders of dressing with consciousness separately of both their inner EOLs M, I, and E and outer EOLs eyes, ears, nose, tongue and skin, whichever of them exist in that original species. This will accommodate a large number of non-human members in a particular species known for their certain specific characteristic features. In fact it has been found that certain members in a species have their EOLs more intense than other members of the same species.

(ii) If one goes with the same, i.e. one unit of consciousness attached with the SO of each Being (cf. *fig*. 8.2), then this one unit, in the present case, will divide into lesser number of organs and EOLs compared to that for humans. Therefore, the fraction of consciousness attached with an EOL for a non-human (particularly in its dynamic mode) turns out much larger than for a human; of course, it depends on the number of existing EOLs in the non-human species. Perhaps for this reason many non-human species are found to have their EOLs (whichever they have) extra-sensitive or extra-conscious as compared to a normal human Being.

(iii) This classification is based on dissimilarities rather than on similarities unlike the case in biosciences.

10.6 Interaction of a Human Being with Physically and Mentally Challenged (PMC) Persons

In many respects the interactions of a human Being with a PMC person are much richer than with non-humans. The reason is that in most PMC persons EOLs exist and to this extent they are part of the biological body which is not the case with non-humans. The only difficulty with the EOLs of a PMC person is that some of them are not operative for one reason or the other and modern science has become advanced either to make them operative or to replace them by artificial substitutes. Of course, such repairing makes the person in general or that repaired organ or limb in particular functional and thereby improving his actions and behaviour. Further, the non-existence or non-functionality of inner EOLs (i.e. M, I and E) in a PMC person is of more serious nature than that of the outer EOLs as far as the biological cure of the system is concerned. In other words, mentally challenged (that also includes the deficiencies in the EOLs I and E) persons, in spite of having their outer EOLs in perfect order, display more abnormality in their actions and behaviour as compared to those who are physically challenged. While a great success in recent times has been achieved in curing the latter situation, the same is not the case in treating the former situation.

For example, if all the three EOLs M, I and E in a PMC person are non-existent and non-operative, he cannot survive for a reasonable period of time because he will not be able to express the desire of hunger or thirst. It is a different matter that at the time of his birth some of the cosmic elements (cf. Appendix D) come to his rescue but only temporarily. Practically, he becomes a dead person. Therefore, a certain element of the EOL, I and most of the element of M need to be present in a PMC person. Partly, for this reason we have chosen m=1 all throughout in Table 10.1 for the classification of non-humans. Here we separately analyse the actions and behaviour of mentally and physically challenged persons.

10.6.1 INTERACTIONS WITH A MENTALLY CHALLENGED (MC) PERSON

In spite of the fact that some or all of the outer EOLs in a mentally challenged (MC) person are present, his interactions with a normal human Being are highly restricted and the number of exchanges very much depends on whether only the EOL M is present, or both M and I are present or all the three M, I and E are present. The last case combined with the absence of an outer

EOL falls under the category of a physically challenged (PC) person that we shall discuss later.

(a) Case when both I and E are absent in an MC person: In this case a good percentage of exchanges will be unidirectional as the MC person will not be able to respond much to the normal human Being in spite of the latter being equipped with all the five sensors. No doubt, the MC person might have emotions and feelings but may fail even to have cognizance of the other human Being; then what to say of having a proper communication with the latter? The cognizance and/or discrimination are the attributes of I and E and the same are absent in the MC person. The only thing is that the MC person can dare to express himself through body actions or the actions of SEKs and SEAs. Even for his hunger and thirst the MC person has to be taken care of by the other person since the former is not able to communicate properly. The EOLs, B, SEAs and SEKs of MC person will of course work but without his notice (note that the process of "noticing" itself lies in the domains of I and E). In fact the situation becomes very much similar to the case of a normal person who has "slipped" into coma. In the spirit of Table 9.1, mostly $\tau_{\mathcal{G}\mathcal{G}}$-type exchanges, namely $\tau_{B,B}$, $\tau_{B,SE}$ and $\tau_{SE,SE}$ and some others like $\tau_{B,M}$, $\tau_{SE,M}$, $\tau_{B,SO}$, $\tau_{SE,SO}$, $\tau_{M,M}$ will dominate and the rest like $\tau_{B,I}$, $\tau_{B,E}$, $\tau_{SE,I}$, $\tau_{SE,E}$, $\tau_{M,I}$, $\tau_{M,E}$ will be unidirectional. As a result, the interacting human Being will be able to extract information about the MC person from the actions of his B, SEAs and SEKs.

(b) Case when only E is absent in an MC person: The MC person of this category can communicate and interact better with a human Being than that in the previous case (a). Except for the memory aspect in the actions of the MC person everything else could be normal, as far as the exchanges with the interacting human Being are concerned. MC person can express emotion, he can feel, decide, discriminate and at times can recognize (or else can go only in the recent past). The possible exchanges that can take place are $\tau_{B,B}$, $\tau_{B,SE}$, $\tau_{SE,SE}$, $\tau_{B,M}$,

$\tau_{B,I}$, $\tau_{SE,M}$, $\tau_{SE,I}$, $\tau_{M,M}$, $\tau_{I,M}$, $\tau_{I,I}$, and the rest will be unidirectional. As a result, the interacting person will be able to extract information from the MC person through the actions of his B, SEAs and SEKs but in a more logical and consistent manner than that of the MC person of case (a) above.

(c) Interactions among mentally challenged persons: Interactions among MC persons are quite interesting from the point of a normal person. As a matter of fact two MC persons whether of category (a) or (b) or one from each category can also interact in view of their basic needs of hunger and thirst and also their preconceived and often ill-conceived notions. For this purpose, the most effective way of their mutual communication is the body language which they develop on their own, or through the actions of SEAs and/or SEKs depending upon the missing EOLs in either of them. While we refrain ourselves from going into these details here, the fact is that in either situation the exchanges between MC persons are highly restricted and mostly unidirectional. As a result, there are maximum chances of misunderstanding between each other and often the purpose of communication is lost. When there are more than two MC persons present at the same space-time point then for a normal person the whole situation (gathering) appears to be chaotic or dramatic. However, the MC persons of the same category can have somewhat better interaction or communication.

10.6.2 INTERACTIONS WITH A PHYSICALLY CHALLENGED (PC) PERSON

A physically challenged person might suffer from the deficiency of an organ in B or any one or more of five SEAs and/or five SEKs. As a result the exchanges with the interacting person accordingly get affected and in general they fall in the domain of exchanges $\tau_{\mathcal{GG}}$, $\tau_{\mathcal{GM}}$ and $\tau_{\mathcal{GC}}$. While some of the sub-classes of these exchanges (cf. Table 9.1) could be unidirectional, the others namely $\tau_{\mathcal{MM}}$, $\tau_{\mathcal{MC}}$ could be both ways depending on the mindsets of the interacting persons and the circumstances given. In particular we consider the following cases:

(a) Interactions with an SEA-challenged person: While everything else remains normal (except for some psychological feel) with an SEA-challenged person, his actions pertaining to the missing SEAs get affected. It has been found that other organs at times are automatically trained to perform the actions of the missing organ(s) in one form or the other, even though not with the same efficiency as the original organ(s) if they could have been present. For example, a hand can be used for a foot or vice versa, mouth can be used for hand (or for the job of fingers) but not vice versa, etc. Even the left-over portion of a broken arm is found to perform certain actions of a complete arm. Somehow the PC person is able to manage life. In some cases, these alternative substitutes for the missing SEAs are found to work so efficiently that one is amazed to the extent that the person interacting with the SEA-challenged person remains unaware of any difference in actions at the mental level, while there remains a difference in actions at the physical level. Moreover, the replacement of such missing organs by the artificial ones has also become possible in recent times and at times the latter one are found to work with great success.

(b) Interactions with an SEK-challenged person: Unlike the case (a) above for an SEA-challenged person, other SEKs for an SEK-challenged person do not directly substitute for the actions of a missing sensor in him. However, it has been found that a certain fraction (maybe small) of the job of the missing SEK is definitely shared by other existing SEKs in an indirect manner in the sense that they become extra sensitive to an external response as compared to that for a normal person. For example, for a blind person ears for sound, nose for smell, tongue for taste, skin for touch become extra-sensitive while eyes for sight do not work. It is only to this extent that other SEKs can work for the missing SEK; otherwise modern researchers have been quite successful in providing any kind of external aid or in repairing the defective sensor. Similarly, for a deaf person the SEKs other than ears become extra-sensitive. Note that while the missing of a particular sensor leads to extra-sensitivity of other existing SEKs, this definitely curtails the working of certain SEAs as well in more than one way. With regard to the restriction on exchanges with an interacting person, not only those which are related to the missing SEK but also the ones pertaining to certain existing SEAs get affected.

(c) Interactions among PC persons: An interesting case of a blind person and a lame person: Whether it is an SEA-challenged or an SEK-challenged person, in either case the disability in terms of an organ or a sensor never comes in the way as far as one's career-advancement is concerned. It is the will-power of an individual that works. Often such persons perform better than a normal person, of course only in a limited domain of actions. They not only take the task as a challenge but have enough time to devote to it since their other involvements in worldly objects automatically get curtailed. Not only the persons of different SEA-challenged categories or of different SEK-challenged categories find common domain of interaction among themselves but there also exists a domain of inter-category interactions. One can find many examples to this effect in day-to-day life. When inter-category challenged persons interact, then it all appears a dramatic scene to a normal person, but in reality the interacting PC persons get benefited from these exchanges which in fact turn out to be highly complex. These exchanges definitely result in a more positive output than the output of those of a similar group of MC persons of the previous section.

At this point, it is worthwhile to cite a story of friendship between a blind person and a lame person from the text for Indian children. The story will throw light on how the circumstances enhance the domain of exchanges between two different categories of PC persons.

There was flood in a village in which two friends — one of them was blind and the other was lame — lived along with other villagers. When the flood was at peak, then to save themselves people started moving to safer places and everybody was bothered about himself or about his belongings. There was no one who could take care of the blind and the lame persons. Then both friends — the blind one and the lame one came in contact and made a pledge. The pledge was that the lame will sit on the shoulders of the blind and the blind will move to a safer place on the instructions and guidance of the lame who had normal eyesight. This is what they did and ultimately succeeded in reaching the safe place.

It is quite clear that a unique class of exchanges between the blind and the lame particularly of the type $\tau_{\mathcal{MM}}, \tau_{\mathcal{MC}}, \tau_{\mathcal{GG}}$ must have taken place and the same has led to a success in their collective efforts. This is how the circumstances activate the mindset and hence enhance the exchanges between interacting persons.

10.7 Interaction of a Human Being with Non-humans: A Quantitative Analysis

In this section we analyse the possible exchanges τ_{b_1,b_2} that can take place between a human Being (patomic model), b_1 and a non-human b_2 of different category (fractured patomic model) in terms of sensors alone. While fine-tuning of the analysis is always possible for non-humans with other varying EOLs, for simplicity however we broadly analyse the cases in which non-humans are equipped only with different number of sensors (SEKs) and ignore the roles of SEAs in the interaction if at all it is there in a particular species. Recall that these are the SEKs which in conjunction with M constitute the important component of the whole perception process in an individual and later play a role in the interactions with other Being. Further, a non-human may not always have exactly the same SEKs or SEAs as a human but their analogues are found to exist for the same purpose. No doubt, most of the species do have SEAs in one form or the other yet their modes and the ways of functioning are ambiguous and different for different species. Also, an account of such variations in the world of non-humans becomes a tedious task. This might curtail certain exchanges of $\tau_{B,B}$- and $\tau_{B,SE}$-categories (cf. Table 9.1). Biologists of course have been doing this job at a fine level but that too for limited classes of species.

Thus, here we go ahead with the assumption that the interacting non-human species can adopt any mode to express itself of what its sensors have sensed (or perceived) out of the presence of the interacting human Being in the vicinity. Note that as the number of sensors (SEKs) increase in the species with all three inner EOLs, the non-human starts attaining the ideal case of a human Being as far as its actions, behaviour and subsequently its interaction with an interacting human Being is concerned.

In order to understand the exchanges, τ_{b_1,b_2} between a human b_1 and the non-human $\bar{b}_2$ of Table 10.1, we have to re-analyse the exchanges listed in Table 9.1 for the case of two human Beings. Here we shall look only for those exchanges which could be both ways, i.e. those which are not unidirectional. An account only of such exchanges can in fact lead to some meaningful interactions between b_1 and $\bar{b}_2$. The domain of such exchanges however increases as the number of sensors in a non-human with all the three inner EOLS, increases. Although such an analysis was desirable in the previous section for the interactions with a PMC person, here it is a must as one would like to identify the human-friendly non-human species in Nature out of the huge list in Table 10.1. Since the non-human $\bar{b}_2$ follows a fractured patomic model, all the fine-tuned twenty exchanges of Table 9.1 are not possible at the same time and for a given species. Even if a non-human species has all the four (maximum) sensors along with three inner EOLs, its FOUs may not be developed to the same extent as for a human, mainly because the former lacks the basic characteristics of self-awareness. Therefore, most of the exchanges between b_1 and $\bar{b}_2$ while remain unidirectional, the question of exchanges like $\tau_{E,E}$, $\tau_{I,I}$, $\tau_{M,M}$ does not arise. As a result, while a nonhuman species close to perfection can use I and E judiciously in the interactions with physical world (for its survival and in its behaviour) in isolation, the same is not there, when it comes to sharing his decisions, experiences and emotions with a human or with another non-human (may be of the same species).

In order to have these interactions effective, perhaps a language for expression comes in the way and the same is missing. Even if such a language is there, then its compatibility with a human or with another non-human remains questionable. Of course, some persons (trainers) who happen to live with such non-humans for some time are able to derive certain language from their behaviour either in terms of body actions or through the functions of SEKs and SEAs. In fact only the outer EOLs like B, SEAs, SEKs of the non-human are found to play an important role in sharing his decisions, experiences and emotions with an expert human trainer. Thus, while complete set of EOLs in a human is ready to interact, only a few EOLs in a non-human participate in the interaction. On this basis, an effective and meaningful b_1-$\bar{b}_2$ interaction turns out to be of $\tau_{\mathcal{GG}}$-type in Table 9.1 and the same can be expressed as $\tau_{\mathcal{GG}} = \{\tau_{B,B}, \tau_{B,SE}, \tau_{SE,SE}\}$, where $\tau_{B,SE}$ and $\tau_{SE,SE}$ now split as $\tau_{B,SE} = \{\tau_{B,SEA}, \tau_{B,SEK}\}$, and $\tau_{SE,SE} = \{\tau_{SEA,SEA}, \tau_{SEA,SEKp}, \tau_{SEKp,SEKq}, \tau_{SEKq,SEA}\}$, respectively with the subscripts p and q defined before in Table 10.1 as p, q = eyes, ears, nose, tongue, skin. Now it is not difficult to identify the exchanges possible in the interactions with non-humans having different number of sensors. For example, for non-humans with one sensor the effective exchanges are seven, namely, $\tau_{B/B}$, $\tau_{B/SEA}$, $\tau_{B/SEKp}$, $\tau_{SEA/SEA}$, $\tau_{SEA/SEKp}$, $\tau_{SEKp/SEKq}$, $\tau_{SEKq/SEA}$, where p= q = any one out of eyes, ears, nose, tongue and skin. Similarly, for non-humans with 2, 3 and 4 sensors both p and q stand for the same numbers – two, three and four and are the number of items to be picked up out of the set {eyes, ears, nose, tongue and skin}. As a result, the number of possible exchanges becomes 11, 15 and 19 for non-humans with 2, 3 and 4 sensors respectively. Here, we have not accounted for the cross-sensor exchanges like $\tau_{SEKp,SEKq}$ — type with p≠q, which appears to be a reasonable assumption for certain class of species having some nascent EOLs like SEKs; otherwise once the existing inner EOLs of a non-human become intense (highly dressed with consciousness), as may be the case with some other species, then not only these cross-sensor exchanges but also $\tau_{\mathcal{GM}}$ and $\tau_{\mathcal{MM}}$ in some cases become important.

Further, the relative importance of these cross-sensor or other exchanges will depend again on whether the non-human is equipped with I or E or with both in addition to M. We refrain ourselves from going into these details here.

10.8 Non-humans with Human Qualities and Human-Non-human Interactions

In spite of the fact that non-humans follow a fractured patomic model some of their species (cf. Table 10.1) possess human-like qualities, particularly the species which are close to perfection in the arrow of time. All this depends on the existence of self-awareness and inner EOLs in that particular species and their corresponding roles in two distinct aspects. Firstly, in the day-to-day actions of members of that species towards the survival, and secondly, in the interactions of these members with a human and other non-humans including their own race. Once their existence in whatever proportion is evidenced, then the fundamental processes leading to their actions and behaviour could be the same, to some extent, as for a human except for a modification due to the missing EOL. Even if a non-human has similar experiences as a human, he is not able to express it to other species because of a missing language code. The members of such an advanced non-human species, no doubt, may have their own code to share among themselves, but such a code is definitely missing with reference to other species. Such a code is of course derived empirically by the (human) trainers only after their association with the members of such a given non-human species for a considerable period of time.

In recent times several systematic studies on this front have been carried out. Researchers have found the existence of several human-like qualities like self-awareness, memory, decision-making capacity, emotions, etc. in some "close to perfection" non-humans (cf. Table 10.1). Here, we cite some examples of non-humans depicting these interesting features in their behaviour and then comment on the nature of human-non-human and non-human-non-human interactions through some selective examples to this effect.

10.8.1 EVIDENCE OF SELF-AWARENESS IN SOME NON-HUMAN SPECIES

Recently, researchers around the world are beginning to provide evidence that animals cannot only learn and remember through instinct but that some species may also possess a degree of self-awareness, i.e. they may be capable of thinking about their thoughts and knowing that they know. It was earlier believed that the characteristics of self-awareness — the ability to distinguish oneself from others or the ability to monitor one's own thought — existed only in humans, chimpanzees and to a limited extent in dolphins. Jane Goodall, after her detailed study on chimpanzee's social and family life arrived at[4] the fact that these hominid cousins of humans do experience a whole gamut of conscious behaviour similar to a human. Normally, the evidence for the existence of self-awareness is sought in the data collected on the behaviour of an animal who is made to stand in front of a mirror — so-called "mirror test." Also, a lot of pet owners (or trainers) believe that their cats or canaries respond to situation like peoples do.

Results similar to the great ape-chimpanzee are also found with elephants. An elephant also exhibited[5] the symptoms of self-recognition or self-awareness when the experiment was performed by using a mirror of 8×8 ft^2. The animal was allowed to see her image when a cross "×" was painted above her eye. The elephant could not see the mark (painted, perhaps, when she was in sleep) except in her reflection and she repeatedly used her trunk to touch the painted mark "×". This act of hers could not be noticed when the mark "×" of the same smell and texture was painted at the back of her head.

4. As cited by Mukul Sharma, "Ape and Awareness", *Times of India*, 1 Novermber 2006.

5. "Elephants are Self-aware, Shows Mirror Test" The World of Mouth Column, *Times of India*, 1 Novermber 2006.

In spite of these clean evidences of self-awareness in some non-humans one can raise several doubts on the way in which the conclusions about self-awareness are drawn from these experiments. However, many animal experts are found unanimous on the fact that some of the animals do have a concept of self which in turn indicates an ability to monitor one's own thought — a definition of self-awareness.

10.8.2 STARTLING EVIDENCES OF EXISTENCE OF INNER EOLS IN SOME NON-HUMAN SPECIES

Some non-human species in Nature, at times, exhibit certain interesting phenomena in their actions and behaviour which forces one to believe that non-humans do possess memory, decision-making capacity and/or emotions which respectively are the attributes of inner EOLs, E, I and M. To this effect, several systematic studies have been carried out in recent years on different non-human species. We list below a few of such cases:

(a) Emotion aspect: There are increasing evidences that animals feel joy, grief, jealousy though they may not be in the same way and proportion as humans do. Several non-human species exhibit emotions in their actions and behaviour. According to a recent reporting,[6] (i) Gorilla mother is found to carry even the dead body of her baby — shows affection and affinity to the child; (i) dogs and cats are seen to become "depressed" not only on the death of their children but also on the loss of their human companions, and (iii) monkeys too become emotional, at times they enjoy giving to or sharing with others.

According to ethologist, Marc Bekoff of University of Colorado and a primatologist Jane Goodall,

> If we feel jealousy, then dogs and wolves and elephants and chimpanzees feel jealousy. Animal emotions are not necessarily identical to ours but there is no reason to think they should be. Their hearts, stomachs and brains also differ from ours, but it does

6. "Feel Factor: Emotions not Just for Humans" a Reporting by John-Paul Flintoff, Times Trends column, *Times of India*, 25 August 2008.

> not stop us from saying that they have hearts, stomachs and brains. There is a dog joy and chimpanzee joy and pig joy, and dog grief and chimpanzee grief and pig grief.

Thus, many non-humans do have feel factor, emotion, it is only the way of expressing the same that is different or its proportion varies from species to species.

(b) Decision taking aspect: Monkeys and apes share many traits that are similar to humans. For this reason monkeys are used in laboratory testing because they have psychological and physiological similarity with humans. Behaviour of a particular class of monkeys indicates that they do have decision taking capacity. For example, capuchin monkeys are found to share food spontaneously in both nature and captivity, and commonly sit next to each other while eating. Monkeys or for that matter dogs and elephants seem to care for their masters or for the welfare of those they know.

Baboons are known to use their brains in many ways similar to a human.[7] Some studies about their behaviour have revealed that (i) baboons carefully keep track of their transient relationships, and (ii) their mind affords to have an excellent grasp of the dynamics of society.

(c) Memory aspect: Experiments have revealed that several birds like pigeon and crow, and pets like dog and elephant have excellent memories. For example, a common pigeon has astonishingly good long-term memories. In tests it has been found that a single bird can memorize as large as 1200 pictures at a time. Researchers have found[8] that despite clear physical differences between birds and other animals, there are important similarities in the way their memories work, i.e. the processes that drive the way we store and retrieve memories appear to be

---

7. "Baboon use Their Brains to Socialize", A Reporting by Nicholas Wade in *Times of India*, 10 October 2007.

8. "Birds are No Bird-brains, Claim Scientists", World of Mouth Column, *Times of India*, 8 November 2006.

largely the same throughout the animal world. Similar experiments performed on baboons show that baboon can memorize as large as 5000 pictures.

Crows and their relatives — among them ravens, magpies and jays — are well known for their intelligence and for their ability to recognize individual human faces. Also, the degree with which the elephants are able to classify people has not been known before in any animal.

As these are evidences of inner EOLs in some non-humans, there are also evidences of very intense or extra-sensitive outer EOLs like some of the SEKs. To this effect, studies have shown that elephants can literally smell danger. Not only this, the animal can sniff out whether the person in the vicinity is a friend or foe. As indicators of natural calamity like earth quake, dogs erupted in wild howling and barking hours before the quake struck. Mice and snakes skittered around crazily in the open. Horses and cows kicked at their stable walls.

Next we highlight the roles of these inner and outer EOLs of a non-human in the interactions with a human or with another non-human through some specific example.

10.8.3. SOME REPRESENTATIVE EXAMPLES OF INTERACTION BETWEEN A HUMAN AND NON-HUMANS

Since the human intelligence has always overcome the intelligence of any other non-human, the former has been able to have a control over non-inquilines class of non-humans as well, as one can see in circus or in other public shows. In this case non-humans are trained to work under pressure and fear. Then other places where one can notice such human-non-human interaction are zoos, where caged animals are forced to live and behave conveniently. Experts in animal behaviour of a particular category can also be found among the managers of bird or wild-life sanctuaries or among the tribes living in forest. We however will not go into such discussions. Also, there are numerous examples of interaction of a human being with inquiline class of non-humans but again we discuss only a couple of cases below, where the interactions originate more in a natural manner. This is mainly to give some glimpses of the fundamental processes taking place during these interactions within the framework of fractured patomic model .

(a) Example of *fig.* 1.5 — a child (b_1) trying to feed a caged bird ($\bar{b}_2$): This is the case of an interaction between a person whose FOUs are not fully developed and a bird (non-human) who is caged for one reason or the other and appears to be hungry. As the child himself feels hunger, he also thinks that the bird will also be hungry. Then he tries to offer a bread piece or a cake to the bird without realizing whether the bird needs it or not. On the other hand, while the bird is already in captivity it is afraid of any harm from the child behind his offer, whereas child appears to be innocent and has clean intentions. Therefore, the exchanges between the bird and the child are unidirectional as long as the child and his actions are new to the bird. However, if it happens to be a routine matter for the child to feed the bird at appropriate timings, then the bird comes forward to catch the cake using its beak. In this case the exchanges by and large are of $\tau_{M,M}$, $\tau_{M,SEA}$, $\tau_{SEA,SEA}$, $\tau_{SEA,SEK}$-type. Not only this the bird eats the cake affectionately, feels satisfaction and in that case the child draws joy out of this action of his. The exchanges in the latter case become both ways.

Instead of child, suppose there is a matured person available to feed the bird. Then, the developed FOUs of the person will make the job of feeding the bird easy in the sense that the person understands the mindset of the bird or the bird also understands the person through his body actions and behaviour and accordingly prepares itself to eat. Such exchanges again are both ways.

(b) A rare of the rarest example of interaction between a person and an animal (cf. *fig.* 10.1): In the previous chapter the mother-child interaction was ranked next to the complete husband-wife interaction as far as the richness and the intensity of exchanges between two persons is concerned. Here, we discuss a rare but extended version of the case of mother-child interaction. In *fig.* 10.1, a mother while providing breast food to her child, she is allowing the sharing of the same also by a fawn (the young deer) at the same time. This is really a unique picture photographed by Himanshu Vyas. With regard to this unparallel case, the lensman Vyas had heard about an orphan fawn being looked after by a Bishnoi woman near his hometown Jodhpur. At the mud dwelling, he noticed the fawn playing with her children. When hungry, the mother breastfed both the fawn and her baby girl simultaneously.

*fig.*10.1: A rare example of mother-baby-fawn interaction (courtesy: *Hindustan Times*, 4 April 2008). The mother breast feeds both her baby-girl and the fawn at the same time.

In some sense this is the case of three-Being interaction in which the mother (b_1), feeds her child (b_2) and the fawn ($\bar{b}_3$). While there is every chance, maybe small in proportion, of the three-Being $\tau_{b_1 b_2 \bar{b}_3}$-type interactions, the pair-wise interactions not only like $\tau_{b_1b_2}, \tau_{b_2\bar{b}_3}, \tau_{b_1\bar{b}_3}$ but also their exchanges $\tau_{b_2b_1}, \tau_{\bar{b}_3b_2}, \tau_{\bar{b}_3b_1}$ are bound to be there. Now it is a different thing at which level these exchanges take place. If we identify b_1 = {SO , E_1, I_1, M_1, $\mathcal{G}_1$}, b_2 ={SO , E_2, I_2, M_2, $\mathcal{G}_2$}, $\bar{b}_3$ = {SO , E_3, I_3, M_3, $\mathcal{G}_3$} with $\mathcal{G}_1$ = {SEK_1, SEA_1, B_1}, $\mathcal{G}_2$ = {SEK_2, SEA_2, B_2}, $\mathcal{G}_3$ = {SEK_3, SEA_3, B_3} then some possible exchanges in appearance are $\tau_{\mathcal{M}_1\mathcal{M}_2\mathcal{M}_3}, \tau_{\mathcal{M}_1\mathcal{M}_2\mathcal{G}_3}, \tau_{\mathcal{M}_1\mathcal{G}_2\mathcal{M}_3}, \tau_{\mathcal{G}_1\mathcal{M}_1\mathcal{M}_2}, \tau_{\mathcal{M}_1\mathcal{G}_2\mathcal{G}_3}\,\tau_{\mathcal{G}_1\mathcal{M}_2\mathcal{G}_3}, \tau_{\mathcal{G}_1\mathcal{G}_2\mathcal{M}_3}$, of $\tau_{b_1b_2\bar{b}_3}$-type in addition to some occasional ones as $\tau_{I_1\mathcal{M}_2\mathcal{M}_3}, \tau_{I_1\mathcal{G}_2\mathcal{M}_3}, \tau_{I_1\mathcal{G}_2\mathcal{G}_3}, \tau_{I_1\mathcal{M}_2\mathcal{G}_3}$, etc. On the other hand, the varieties of pair-wise $\tau_{b_1b_2}, \tau_{b_1\bar{b}_3}, \tau_{b_2\bar{b}_3}$ and their exchanges are plenty in number as the mother-child, mother-fawn, and fawn-child live together and share so many things in isolation during their routine. The difference one should note from the case of three-human Being interactions (cf. Section 9.6.1) here is that fawn follows a fractured patomic model and the child still does not have her FOUs in a fully developed stage. That is why a large number of $\tau_{b_ib_j}$-type exchanges are suppressed as compared to the ones discussed in *fig*. 9.6 or of $\tau_{b_ib_jb_k}$-type.

10.8.4 SOME REPRESENTATIVE EXAMPLES OF INTERACTIONS BETWEEN NON-HUMANS

It has been found that two different non-human species, which normally do not see each other eye-to-eye, interact affectionately when the member of one is young and that of the other is old but female, i.e. they are of mother-baby-like age groups. This is perhaps the reason the mother member already has her developed FOUs and is full of sentiments, emotions and affection which she wants to shower on any young member who need not be of the same species but should be an innocent and does not have its developed FOUs, so that the exchanges remain unidirectional. Contrary to this, this interesting feature of interaction is not present to the same extent when (i) the young member becomes old and interacts with the same old female member of other species, or when (ii) the young member of a species interacts with an old male member of other species. In some sense this shows the universality of motherhood or of mother-baby interactions and at times it is independent of species. To this effect, while one example is already discussed above in Sections 10.8.3(b), we list here a few more cases from among nonhuman members.

(a) The case of adopted tiger cubs by a mother dog: As shown in *fig*. 10.2, a mother dog is showering her emotions and affection on tiger cubs. While the exchanges $\tau_{\mathcal{M}_1\mathcal{M}_2}$, $\tau_{SEK_1SEK_2}$, $\tau_{SEK_1SEA_2}$, $\tau_{SEA_1SEA_2}$, for some of the senses of knowledge and action, could be both ways, the rest by and large appear to be unidirectional. Once again this example conforms to the universality of motherhood.

fig. 10.2: Dogged tiger cubs. A mother dog is showering her emotions and affection on tiger cubs (courtesy, *Times of India*, 1 August 2008).

(b) Friendship between a three-month-old tiger cub and an Alsatian puppy: As shown in *fig*. 10.3, a three-month-old tiger cub plays with an Alsatian puppy of the same age group. This is an example of universality of friendship during the childhood, which at a later stage becomes rare when the members become old and particularly between the species who do not see each other eye-to-eye. In fact during the childhood the members of different species are innocent and their FOUs are not developed to the extent that they can realize the realities of life. In this case, the possible exchanges, $\tau_{b_1b_2}$, appear to be of $\tau_{\mathcal{M}_1\mathcal{M}_2}$, $\tau_{\mathcal{M}_1 SEK_2}$, $\tau_{\mathcal{M}_1 SEA_2}$, $\tau_{SEK_1SEK_2}$, $\tau_{SEK_1SEA_2}$, $\tau_{SEA_1SEA_2}$ - type and they are both ways.

(c) Leopard nurtures baboon after killing its mother: This is a unique example of its own type and in some sense it is rare of the rarest case of interaction between non-humans and that too of different species who do not see each other eye-to-eye. Note that baboons are arch enemies of the leopard but in this case, as shown in *fig.* 10.4, young female member of one species

fig. 10.3: Friendship between a three-month-old tiger cub and an Alsatian puppy (courtesy, *Times of India*, 14 August 2008).

once again showers emotions and affection on a baby-member of another species and that too after killing its mother. Such maternal instincts towards one-day-old baby baboon generated spontaneously in the female leopard, indicate the existence of highly sensitive (or developed) inner EOLs in a non-human like leopard. The real story behind the picture, as described by Dereck

Joubert[9] a film-maker who followed the female leopard for three-and-a-half years in Botswana, is as follows:

A young female leopard kills the mother (primate) baboon, but then from the bedraggled pelt of her kill crawls a tiny infant — a one-day-old baboon. In that moment this young leopard forgets that she is a hunter, and starts nurturing the baby baboon as if it were her own cub. This did not happen all of a sudden. In fact after killing the mother, the young leopard paused for a moment, apparently not knowing what to do. Then she gently

fig. 10.4 : Mother Nature! A leopard mother nurtures infant baboon after killing its mother (Courtesy, *Times of India*).

picked the baby in her mouth, holding it by the scruff of its neck and carrying the infant up a tree to keep it safe.

The exchanges in this example are of very fine degree and no doubt are unidirectional but it appears that the inner voice to take care of the infant baboon after killing its mother must

9. "Leopard Nurtures Baboon After Killing Its Mother", World of Mouth Column, *Times of India*, 16 December 2006.

have come from the innermost existence in the female leopard. The exchanges do include the roles of SO, E, I and M in view of Section 10.1.

(d) Dynamics of exchanges in the prey-predator problem: Whether it is a human Being hunting an animal or an animal hunting another animal, the underlying dynamics of exchanges between prey and predator are more or less the same except for some prejudices or intentions on the part of the human hunter. It is a rare case when the prey is killed only for the sake of killing or for satisfying the ego of predator; otherwise there are always certain intentions in the mind of predator. If the hunter is a human Being he will generally kill the animal for two reasons, either for his survival in terms of his own or of his family food or for earning money out of it. Note that animal hunters hunt only for the first purpose unless they are used by another human Being for the second purpose. Again the dynamics in this latter case becomes more complicated and we refrain ourselves from going into these details here. Further, the mindsets and accordingly the actions and behavior of the predator in the two situations become different with regard to quality and quantity of meat of the prey and other selections as well. On the other hand, on the part of prey there remain two possibilities of mindset depending on whether the prey is moving freely or it is caged. If the prey is in captivity or is caged, it has to surrender to master to die. All exchanges in this case remain finally unidirectional since the predator has full freedom in his actions.

If however the prey is capable of moving freely or has a scope to escape, then some of the exchanges could be both ways but still dominated on the side of predator. Again the expertise (or the development of FOUs) built in both prey and predator along with the circumstances also become crucial in a quick killing. While the prey tries to escape cleverly, the predator also tries to kill the prey cleverly using his full expertise. This is how the "predator and prey" system works in competition not only within the laws of jungle but also of (human) society. Theory of games like "hide and seek" can also be used for further studies of this phenomenon.

Look at the situation in *fig*. 10.5 where Siberian tiger is trying to hunt for the chicken who is capable of having only small flights. While the tiger seems to be fully concentrating on the prey, the mindset of chicken, on the other hand, is divided into two parts — one for looking for a safer place and other for keeping track of the dynamics of the hunter tiger. In the latter case the exchanges could be both ways as long as the chicken is not within the reach of the tiger. In another case in *fig*. 10.6 two tigers are trying to hunt the same chicken. It has very little chance to escape because the chicken now has to use his limited

fig. 10.5: A Siberian tiger tries to catch a chicken.

energy and safety measures against both the tigers. Thus, he has to spend more energy on the back than on the front in terms of two- and possibly three-Being exchanges as compared to the case in *fig*. 10.5. As a result he will be tired soon and surrender to the tiger.

fig. 10.6: The Siberian tigers try to catch a chicken (Courtesy: *Times of India*).

(e) A joyful interaction between two white tigers: As shown in *fig*. 10.7, two white tigers are in a playful mood. They seem to share a lot at both physical and mental levels or at the level of

fig. 10.7: Royal fun; two white tiger cubs in a playful mood (Courtesy: *Times of India*).

the joyful mood of tigers it appears that the animals have their own language to share the experiences when they interact. In terms of exchanges, this example of interaction between two non-human Beings is worth comparable with that between the two human Beings as in *fig.* 1.3(d).

(f) An intresting case of human, non-human and EP-matter Interaction: As a last example of this section, we consider here an interesting case of interaction among a human (lady, b_1), a non-human (buffalo, $\bar{b}_2$) and an EP-matter (a mobile phone) as

fig. 10.8: An interesting case of human, non-human and EP-matter interaction (Courtesy: *Times of India*, 7 November, 2009).

shown in fig. 10.8. The lady while taking milk out of buffalo is also talking on the phone. This is the case of three-body (b_1-$\bar{b}_2$-EP) interaction, particularly that of SEP_1-SEP_2-EP type (cf. Section 9.6) in which SEP_2 is describable by fractured patomic model. Unless buffalo also enjoys the music or conversation on the mobile, the interactions remain pair wise. While buffalo is physiologically/biochemically prepared to give milk, the lady is mentally prepared to draw the milk and starts taking the milk. This enriches the exchanges between b_1-$\bar{b}_2$. All of a sudden incoming phone disturbs the setting and the number of exchanges between b_1-$\bar{b}_2$, which were initially of $\tau_{\mathcal{G}_1\mathcal{M}_2}$, $\tau_{\mathcal{M}_1\mathcal{G}_2}$, $\tau_{\mathcal{G}_1\mathcal{G}_2}$ type, are now shared by $\bar{b}_2$-EP interaction. The latter are basically of $\tau_{\mathcal{M}_2\mathcal{M}_3}$, $\tau_{\mathcal{M}_2\mathcal{G}_3}$, $\tau_{\mathcal{G}_2\mathcal{M}_3}$, $\tau_{\mathcal{G}_2\mathcal{G}_3}$ type. Note that the mobile phone, though is an EP-matter but also represents a copy of living Being in the sense that on the other end of it the transmiter is a living Being. This living Being on the other end, while affecting the mind set of b_1, also affects that of its own. In such a situation the interactions between b_1-$\bar{b}_2$ become unidirectional.

10.9 Concluding Discussions

At the outset, after showing a spiritual link between humans and non-humans, several special qualities which a human Being possesses over a non-human are emphasized both in philosophical and biological terms. For the description of behaviour of Beings who are devoid of some or many of these special features associated with a human, the concept of fractured patomic model is introduced in Section 10.3. Then the evolutions of EOLs and the development of FOUs in non-humans is discussed within this new framework. This framework is further employed in suggesting a new classification scheme for non-humans. In all there turn out to be 92 varieties of non-humans with nascent EOLs. However, if one accounts for different orders of dressing of EOLs with consciousness in the light of *trikaraṇ* and *dvikaraṇ* rules (cf. Section 8.4.2) and with all possible permutations and combinations of EOLs, then this number of species can be made as large as the one highlighted in Vedic sciences, namely 8.4 million or as the one speculated in modern biological sciences.

We have also analysed the possible interactions of a normal person with physically and mentally challenged persons within the framework of fractured patomic model. So many intricacies in the interaction are shown to exist as compared to the case of normal humans. In the same spirit, the interactions of a human Being with non-humans, the interactions among the members of the same non-human species, and among the members of different non-human species are discussed in detail. To this effect, several representative examples of real-life situation from among the non-humans are analysed in the respective contexts, mainly from the animal kingdom.

In continuation of Chapter 9, we have attempted here to analyse the fundamental processes responsible for actions and behaviour of PMC persons as well as of some selective non-human species. No doubt a human Being is gifted with so many specialties by Nature but many phenomena involving non-humans (some of them are cited in Section 10.8) reveal that some non-humans also do have these specialties (like the question of self-awareness, emotions, decision-making power, memory, etc.) even though in varying proportions. The only difference is that it is not "all in one" rather scattered differently among different species. It may be mentioned that in the form of evolution of inner EOLs like E, I and M these specific features are found to exist in certain non-humans and the latter use them freely for their own survival. Their role (particularly in a combined manner) however becomes less pronounced during the interaction of these non-humans with a human or with the members of other non-human species unlike the case with humans.

Moreover, a particular non-human species has its own rules of the game to act and has its own dynamics of interaction among its members which may appear to be "foreign" for an outsider whether he is a human or a member of any other non-human species. Then arises the question of code of communication or of language used by them and that perhaps is best known to the members of the corresponding non-human species. For that matter, this is also true with several tribes on this planet itself. Theoretically, there could possibly be as many codes or languages as the number of species, but only those species which have a better developed set of their inner EOLs, like apes, baboons, etc. are able to observe perhaps such a code. This becomes evident from the kind of safety measures that certain non-humans take with regard to their survival or livelihood; otherwise it appears that most of the non-human species are born only for the sake of dying in author's opinion.

It has been found that members of some non-human species in Nature, when they are in a group, show certain peculiarities in their collective behaviour. At times, such of their actions become the example to be followed by the mob of humans. For example, human can learn from ants about the way to deal with traffic congestion and exiting large venues after concerts or sporting events. They move in an orderly fashion, and never panic, even when there is danger or congestion. Studies have shown that ants organize their freeways so that ants bearing loads are in the middle of the freeway — all going in one direction and the ants that are unloaded are on both sides of the middle row. Next, we cite the case of birds when they stay in tune with times. As a matter of fact, studies have shown that the birds are not "pre-programmed" to sing their songs — rather birds listen closely to their tune to keep their song's notes perfect. Also, bird songs are so distinctive they are often used by ornithologists to identity individual bird. Song-birds do not start out life as virtuosos; they often begin by "babbling" random pitches and then advance to sing sophisticated tunes with the help of a tutor. Once they develop their own particular melody, they use it to announce territorial claims or to attract a mate. The slight variations in the song identify one bird from another, so birds take great pains to preserve their unique tune throughout life.

Part III
Predictive Power and Future Prospects

11

Fundamental vs. Physio-Biochemical Processes Their Roles in Human Behaviour

CREATIVITY in a human Being is the symptom of evolution of human race. It is basically an exploration of the invisible and this invisible could be in the domain of STCG or beyond this domain. While the objective sciences in terms of four fundamental interactions are taking care of the invisible in the domain of STCG, the science of Self deals with the quest of invisible beyond STCG in terms of some more additional interactions discussed in the previous chapters. It may be mentioned that the studies of physio- or bio-chemical processes in conjunction with brain, body and nervous system (BBNS) are still in their infancy with regard to the explanation of human behaviour and actions. The fundamental processes of Vedic science discussed and surveyed in previous chapters, on the other hand, offer a full-fledged scheme of explanation of the same.

In this chapter we once again address the question of fundamentality and the interdependence (if it is there) of the above two categories of processes, namely, the ones discussed so far in Chapters 8-10 and the ones arising as a result of physio- or bio-chemical reactions inside the human body. For this purpose, we shall compare and contrast various aspects of these two working zones inside the human Being. Although it is yet to be established by researchers that the two working zones, namely the "mind over matter" and the "matter over mind," have some overlap or are interdependent, it has now become clear that both are equally responsible for the success of an action performed by a human Being.

First we analyse the question of "mind over matter" or of "matter over mind" in the maintenance of world order. Then, in Section 11.2 we discuss some modern researches carried out in search of the so-called "God-Centre" or the centre of consciousness in the human body. Psychologists in collaboration with neuroscientists are also trying to look for the origin of thought and its impact on human actions. Some glimpses of such studies are given in Section 11.3. In Section 11.4, we discuss briefly the theoretical concept of thought transmission technology in modern biophysics and the efforts made to verify this concept in experiments. Finally, concluding remarks are made in Section 11.5.

11.1 The Question of "Mind over Matter" or "Matter over Mind" in the Maintenance of World Order

While Western thinkers are puzzled and still do not have definite answer to this question, the Vedic science (as discussed in Chapter 4) since time immemorial has been advocating in support of the phrase "mind over matter" by arguing *Brahman* as the witness (root cause) of working of "Nature" at the Cosmic scale and the same in each of us, in its quantized version as SO, becomes the witness of all our actions. On the other hand, since many of us (including certain category of scientists as well) do not want to tread into the zone beyond STCG, the philosophy of "matter over mind" prevails more in society. To support this fact, scientific experiments are already going on in recent times to establish the existence of the philosophical entities like M, I, E and SO (inner EOLs) inside the body or to explore their distinctive roles in human/non-human actions.

In this venture, not only the biochemists, biophysicists, physiologists including the brain and neuroscientists but also psychologists and parapsychologists (cf. Appendix F) jointly or independently are making efforts. No doubt, if they succeed in identifying these inner EOLS in isolation (which in some sense appears to be an impossible task since a living Being is a highly complicated (non-physical) open system unlike any other physical open system even for which the existing physical laws are inadequate) then this will correspond to the fact "matter over mind" and thereby the behaviour of a living Being will become completely controllable by a machine. Conceptually, this appears to be an interesting challenge before a scientist but the unfortunate part associated with these studies is that the probes, devices, detectors, sensors, etc. used for this purpose are the ones whose working is based on the principles derived mostly in the domain of electromagnetic interactions or in general in the domain of STCG. Then the question is as to how a STCG-based detector (probe or sensor) can detect or describe completely a phenomenon of non-STCG domain involving nonphysical interactions. In fact only a partial detection, description, or study is possible. Alternatively, if they start using living Beings as probes or detector, then in view of the highly composite structure of the Being (cf. patomic model) it is going again to be a difficult task from the point of view of analysis of the data since other additional interactions also manifest in the data. Perhaps for this reason statistical methods are used to analyse the data collected on a group of individuals by psychologists. In such studies the intrinsic characteristics of individuals are diluted and the conclusions thereby drawn may be relevant to a group behaviour rather than to an individual's behaviour. However, the fundamental processes discussed in the preceding chapters can also form a basis of such studies using the core-valence picture (cf. Section 9.7.1) of the individual.

According to a famous Indian saying, "whatever food one eats, so becomes his mind." This supports the phrase "matter over mind." In this phrase the word "mind" is further generalized as "as is the mind, so are the thoughts; as are the thoughts, so are the *karmas* (actions); as are the *karmas*, so are the fruits (of *karma*)" and one enjoys these fruits of his own actions performed towards his basic needs including that of food. Thus, the cycle is complete in its own way and supports the phrase "matter over mind." The message which one can carry from this saying is that he should have a balanced (ideal) diet to start with at the one end and a *sāttvika* (or a highly refined) intellect with a maximum distinctive power on the other to have a success in the action. No doubt, the completion of this cycle requires the human body to undergo a large number of biochemical, physiological and neuronal processes to produce the fruit(s) of an action; however, all this happens when the person is alive or conscious or there is "something" inside the body that ultimately remains a witness to all these processes directly or indirectly. As a matter of fact in Vedic science the existence of both mind and matter is attributed to the same field of consciousness that originates from the source SO. While the mind (or in general the mindset comprising of M, I and E) is enlightened more with SO (*Brahman*), the matter, on the other hand, belongs to the domain of *PM*s as an integral part of Nature. The individual mind refers to the individual consciousness whereas the external matter can be considered as an attribute of cosmic consciousness.

11.2 "God-Centre" Hypothesis and its Search in Modern Science

11.2.1 BRAIN AND CONSCIOUSNESS

While scientists in recent times have started believing in the phenomenon of consciousness[1] and its role in certain physical processes and human behaviour, they appear to be ignorant about the way(s) in which it manifests through EOLs or even about the arrangement of inner EOLs in a Being like in a patomic model. To this effect without bothering much about the finer details of philosophical entities like M, I and E which are perceived in a Being (as a cause) even at the conceptual level, they are looking for their end-product (as an effect) in the data. In fact with a view to identifying the source(s) of happiness, sorrow, memory, intelligence, emotions and several other

1. See, for example, Roger Penrose, *Shadows of Mind: A Search for the Missing Science of Consciousness* (Oxford: Oxford University Press, 1994).

qualities in an alive Being (human or non-human) scientific researches in the fields of brain functioning and neurodynamics have been going on in the spirit of "matter over mind." As these are the characteristics of a conscious (human) Being, the studies, in general, are focused towards the search of a centre of consciousness (termed as "God-centre") in the body. Though some of these studies are already discussed in Chapter 6, here, however, we highlight a few more cases in the present context. Before proceeding further we narrate certain facts about the human brain.

In the human body brain perhaps is the most important and complicated organ. It consists of some 100 billion cells organized into discrete processing systems which have highly non-linear functioning. Though each cell (called neuron) acts like a computer chip, the brain is far more complex than any modern computer. Brain is able to derive meanings of words. Unlike computer, the brain wires and rewires itself using the mechanisms of specificity and plasticity.[2] While the plasticity is responsible for the interface between the word and the brain, it underlines learning and memory of events. Modules of brain networks are considered as the substratum of mind and electrical spikes as the language of brain. The time interval between two successive spikes is very small. Essences of life like memory, intelligence or in general consciousness are the products of such a complex networking of the brain. With respect to modern computers the working of brain can be understood as follows:

In the brain's wiring, space is at a premium, and is more tightly packed than even the most condensed computer architecture. One cubic centimetre of human brain tissue which would fill a thimble, contain 50 million neurons; several hundred miles of axons — the wires over which neurons send signals; and close to a trillion synapses — the connection between neurons. Note that the memory capacity in this volume is

2. Mriganker Sur, "Brains, Computers and Intelligence", Lecture delivered at INSA, New Delhi, 16 December 2008.

potentially immense. Since neural basis of memory is not yet completely understood, one can guess that one movable synapse could store one byte (8 bits) of memory. That thimble would then contain 1000 gigabytes (1 terabyte) of information. A thousand thimblefuls make up the whole brain, giving us a million gigabytes (a petabyte) of information. To put this in perspective, the entire archived contents of the internet fill just 3 petabytes. What a wonderful creation of God! A brain success is not just measured by its ability to process information in precisely repeatable ways; instead it has evolved to guide behaviours that allow us to survive and reproduce, which often requires fast responses to complex situations. As a result, we constantly make approximations and find "good enough" solutions. This leads to mistakes and biases.

11.2.2 SEARCH FOR THE CENTRE OF CONSCIOUSNESS

The neurosurgeon, Deepak Ranade makes[3, 4] a beautiful survey of recent studies on the search for the centre of consciousness inside a Being. Note that all sensory perceptions reach nerve centres that are specific for particular sensory modality. On the other hand, the brain's neurons are differentiated on the basis of their execution of specific functions. During this process of execution, the Being-specific qualities like memory, intelligence or the consciousness in general are considered to emerge while the attempts to localize precisely the centre of consciousness have failed. To this effect, an experiment on a caged mouse is worth mentioning:

Experiment: An electrode was implanted in the brain adjacent to the pleasure centre of a caged mouse. When a lever was pressed, a small current would stimulate the locus of neurons and the mouse experienced a sensation of pleasure. When the

3. Deepak Ranade, "Is Realization Nothing More Than a Chemical Reaction", The Speaking Tree Column, *Times of India*, 5 March 2009.
4. Deepak Ranade, "Search for the Centre of Consciousness", The Speaking Tree Column, *Times of India*, 10 April 2007.

mouse realized that pressing the lever was the case of wonderful sensation, he endeavoured to keep pressing the lever tirelessly till he died of exhaustion.

From this experiment one concludes that happiness is just a matter of neurotransmission stimulating specific areas resulting in momentary gratification — a chemical reaction in the brain.

Intellect classifies and analyses the events. It also compares the event with its database (i.e. memory) and accordingly delivers a threat or non-threat verdict which, in turn, makes the subject interact with the environment. This interaction is primordial in Nature and in-built for survival. The categorization of reality into sub-groups such as pleasant or unpleasant, endeavouring only pleasant situations to prevail causes unhappiness. In medical terms, when there is a threat perception, there is rise in heart-beat rate, blood pressure, and blood sugar which keeps the individual in a state of combat with typical responses: fight, fright or flight. According to Ranade, if the threat perception apparatus keeps getting stimulated too frequently, then the body, instead of shifting gears, often compensates by raising these parameters permanently. This causes hypertension and stress and the same in turn results into diabetes. On the other hand, in the enlightened state, what changes is not the environment but *the perception of the environment*. In this case while the consciousness is just awareness, it is non-judgemental or with no reaction or without any classification; it is just a witness to what happens at the lower strata. In fact when perception eliminates all fragmentation, then one becomes conscious or aware and he no longer gets exhausted — like the mouse did in the above experiment.

11.2.3 REALIZATION AS A CHEMICAL REACTION AND THE "GOD-CENTRE" IS A PRODUCT

It may be mentioned that belief systems, behavioural traits and even temperament with reference to an individual are considered as the effect of *conditioning* that occurs due to the development of certain specific neural networks. Even the search of God-Centre is related to this kind of conditioning as can be noticed from the following experiment:

Experiment: According to a researcher when a person was subjected to a pain stimulus before and after being shown the picture of a deity he had faith in, his tolerance to pain was found significantly better after than it was before seeing the picture. Such was the increase in the level of tolerance — the result of conditioning. Would such a premise imply that a similar outcome was possible if the patient was shown the picture of a mountain? The answer, of course, is in the negative unless the patient had been conditioned to believe that mountains are also the object of devotion (as is the case with "Goverdhan Hill" in north India).

Does it mean that whichever deity the patient believes in, the final locus of God in the brain remains the same except for some particular developments in the neuronal networks? Alternatively, a person could experience calm, bliss, even ecstasy as a result of stimulation of the God-Centre. Would this imply that all spiritually advanced souls have, over a period of time, been able to devise an intrinsic mechanism to stimulate the God-Centre? Or, are all spiritually advanced masters just those who, by repeated practice, develop the God-Centre further so that it can be stimulated at will? In fact even today many examples of persons can be found corresponding to this latter situation. This shows that the realization merely reduces to a neuro-chemical phenomenon or reaction and there do exist some tangible parameters for either localization or verification of God-Centre.

With regard to mediation in this framework, it is just a process that converts all eccentric thought processes into a concentric pattern with the God-Centre as the epicentre. All thoughts pertaining to mundane activities may be eccentric in nature and the corresponding pattern could be a deterrent to stimulating the God-Centre. In this context there also exists a concept of two hemispheres — dominant and non-dominant. Most explanations given by realized masters seem to defy all logic that belongs to the domain of dominant hemisphere whereas the non-dominant hemisphere concerns with intuitive and non-analytical networks.[5] The God-Centre perhaps resides in the non-dominant hemisphere and the realization could affect a state of awareness that transcends the baseline neuronal activity of just being conscious. In fact the advent of functional imaging techniques like the magnetic resonance imaging (MRI) can be helpful in the verification of God-Centre hypothesis.[6] In the same vein one can understand the "happiness" as the consequence of perceptive modalities giving a positive feedback via established neuronal circuits.[7] For a discussion of some of these concepts in the language of patomic model we refer to Section 13.1.

11.3 Search for a Theory of Thought, Mind and Action in Cognitive Psychology

While Vedic sciences have been advocating consciousness and its role in human actions from time immemorial, in cognitive psychology the role of consciousness in thought processes was considered in 1975 by G. Mandler.[8] The concept was abandoned for some time in American psychology but only recently[9] this concept is revived in understanding the relationship between "information processing" and cognition. The main reason for this was that the introspective methods erred in assuming that consciousness could be made the datum of psychology. Also,

---

5. In fact in the language of patomic model these dominant and non-dominant hemispheres are the highly dressed versions of I and M, respectively corresponding to conscious intellect and subconscious mind. (cf. Chapter 8).

6. Deepak Ranade, 2007, op. cit.

7. Deepak Ranade, 2007, op. cit.

8. G. Mandler, "Consciousness: Respectable, Useful and Probably Necessary", in *Information Processing and Cognition*, Proc. Loyola Symposium, ed. R.L. Solso (Hillside, New Jersey: Lawrence Erlbaum Associate, Inc., 1975) pp. 229-54.

9. G. Mandler, *Consciousness Recovered: Psychological Functions and Origins of Conscious Thoughts* (Amsterdam: John Benjamin, 2002).

there appear individual differences in narrating subjective experiences. Plurality of consciousness manifesting in various actions of a person also come on the way in these studies. As a matter of fact these are generally the difficulties with a theory that is developed out of data or that with the so-called empirical science. Contrarily, the well-built theories in science (like the field theory in physics) originate at a much deeper level maybe out of modelling at a finer but fundamental level or out of certain plausible postulates again at the fundamental level. As is clear from preceding chapters, this aspect, to some extent, is now taken care of by the patomic model of Vedic science as far as the role of consciousness in behaviourism is concerned.

Recently, Glicksohn and Lipperman-Kreda,[10] following the Mandler approach[11] discuss a relationship among time, thought and consciousness in terms of state of consciousness and a newly-coined word "reflective awareness." Mandler adopted a constructivistic approach to the study of duration, meditation and consciousness by way of introducing the notion of a conscious "frame" available to consciousness that itself is considered as a flow. The normal form of consciousness is the flow; however, when the flow of consciousness stops, a frame enters into consciousness and that gives an experience which is different from consciousness. Given that the flow of frames is radically altered, one would expect a similar and unusual change in the duration of experiences. Mandler finally succeeded in tying together an "information processing" (i.e. the content and rate of flow of the frames) with changes in both consciousness and consciousness coupled with a change in the experienced duration. Though the theory has several ambiguities yet it prevailed for some time.

10. See, for example, J. Glicksohn and S. Lipperman-Kreda, "Time, Thought and Consciousness", *The Journal of Mind and Behaviour* 28 (2007) 289-306.

11. G. Mandler, 2002, op. cit.

With regard to definition of consciousness in cognitive psychology various concepts have been advanced in the literature.[12] Glicksohn and Lipperman-Kreda for this purpose use an analogy between the construct of a state of consciousness and that of a level of cognition. This analogy, in fact, is in conformity with the so-called "orthogenetic principle of development" of Werner.[13] According to this principle, "whenever development occurs it proceeds from a state of relative globosity and lack of differentiation to a state of increasing differentiation, articulation and hierarchic integration." In this context Werner further talks of "inner circumstances" which are nothing but a shift in consciousness. In fact just as one can envisage different forms of consciousness constituting its different states, in the same way one can identify different forms of thinking constituting qualitatively different modes of expression and comprehension that are linked to these forms.

These sketchy concepts of consciousness in cognitive science become however easy to comprehend in terms of patomic model. In this case, E in conjunction with I and M and in the presence of SO (i.e. consciousness) contributes to the thinking and feeling processes or in general to the process of perception as a whole. Within this framework, while the mindset $\mathcal{M}$ evolves with μ (the meditation parameter), or the FOUs of the individual develop, the reflective awareness increases and its impact is to enhance the orders of dressing of inner EOLs (cf. Chapter 8) that defines the state of consciousness or of its variants.

At this point it is worthwhile to differentiate between meditation and concentration. Meditation is in fact a quality of spiritual domain of a human Being that automatically comes

12. See, for example, T. Natsoulas, "The Concept of Consciousness: The General State Meaning", *Journ. for the Theo. of Soc. Behaviour* 29 (1999) 59-87, and the references therein.

13. H. Werner, "The Concept of Development from a Comparative and Organismic Point of View", in *Developmental Processes: Heinz Werner's Selected Writings* (New York: International Univ. Press, 1978) vol. 1, pp. 107-30.

into action as a derivative from SO and often without any motive. On the other hand, concentration concerns the controlling of functioning of outer EOLs with the help of inner EOLs. That gives a direction to the outer EOLs in achieving a materialistic (vested) goal in WO. Seed of concentration grows in the domain of WO whereas that of meditation grows in the domain of SO. However, it is the same consciousness which works in both the domains and dresses repeatedly the corresponding EOLs. In fact it is the role of ego E that offers a boundary line for reflection of awareness in the process of perception of elements of WO on the one hand, and simultaneously it defines a state of consciousness or the order of dressings of EOLs on the other.

11.4 Some Remarks on the Theoretical Concept of Thought Transmission Technology

Recall that the electromagnetic signals are used in various types of brain studies. If this radiation happens to be more intense than necessary, then it may be hazardous. Therefore, in recent studies the electromagnetic radiation is used only in a responsive manner and this restricts its use in the thought transmission technology[14] in strict accordance with certain ethical guidelines. Why only in the brain studies, this equally applies to all other studies in biophysics as far as the use of electromagnetic radiation is concerned.

The theoretical concept of thought transmission technology has been designed to overcome the limitations of traditional methods for broadcasting information, such as radio and television. Also, mobile telephone facilities once available to some selected persons and that too in emergencies can also be replaced. While this concept shows the theoretical feasibility of thought transmission, it is partially based on the perceptibility of microwaves. The concept deals with methods and apparatuses for thought transmission via electromagnetic waves whereby

---

14. See, for example, B. Nolting, *Methods in Modern Biophysics* (Springer-verlag, Berlin-Heidelberg, 2004) chapter 11.

the receiving person does not need any electronic device for the reception.

According to this concept, the thought transmission is performed by sending focused low energy modulated electromagnetic waves into the organism of the receiving person in such a way that it changes the probability of certain thoughts. In one category of methods and apparatuses of the concept, the steps followed are: (a) electrical signal of voices are stored in a computer, (b) the computer then translates the signals into the sequence of electrical pulses (with the help of tables or neural networks) of which the envelope correlates with the intensity course of voices, (c) a maser (microwave amplification of stimulated emission of radiation) beam is then modulated with obtained sequence of pulses, and finally (d) the beam is aimed at the receiving person and an intensity is chosen which is just below the intensity that can be perceived consciously. In another category of methods and pieces of apparatus of the concept, the sequence of steps followed is delineated below: (a) Firstly, a large number of correlations between acoustical stimuli and reactions (or thoughts) is measured, (b) next the set of correlation is picked up by the computer to generate a sequence of stimuli which would cause a particular reaction of the thought with high probability, (c) the sequence is then modulated onto a focused beam of electromagnetic energy, (d) the beam is then sent to a receiving person at a subliminal or perceivable intensity and duration, and finally (e) the reactions of the person are monitored with millimetre wave cameras after adjusting the intensity appropriately.

Some possible applications of this technology are in the following contexts: (i) to support the communication with persons buried by rubble after an earthquake, (ii) for unobtrusive transmissions of information to security personnels, (iii) to support important persons delivering lecture in public, (iv) to sensitize persons regarding important topics in emergency situations, e.g. by sending warning, and to protect the population from catastrophic events, (v) to support essential learning and re-learning when other methods are not applicable, and (vi) for the therapy and prophylaxis of certain pathological limitations and stress situation and some others like, and (vii) in combination with detective methods for thought reading on consenting people to contribute to the understanding of function of the human brain.

Before highlighting some potential applications of the above theoretical concepts, the technology can be described as follows. In fact according to the theoretical concept, remote thought transmission is based on the use of a directional radio. In contrast to a common directional radio, the electromagnetic beam is directly coupled into the organism of the receiving person, e.g. the head, big cerebral cortex, inner ear, auditory nerves, or other nerves. Depending on the type of signal modulated onto the electromagnetic beam, this coupling causes an intended change of the thoughts of the receiving person. Normally, this change of thoughts is only statistically effective, e.g. the probability of certain thoughts is increased or decreased in a predictable way. However, in some cases the change may be a deterministic one. At times, the thought transmission is suitable for combination with observations by millimetre wave cameras and microwave-based voice transmission in which the conscious audibility of modulated microwave energy is used. For this purpose, the choices of the carrier wave frequencies (which are normally in the range 100 MHz-100 GHz) and that of the radiation (which are normally the maser, say the free-electron or the semiconductor dipole one) are important.

With regard to practical aspects of the above concepts, several potential applications are discussed in the literature.[15] In particular, both an automated and small hand-held devices are used for the purpose of thought transmission. We refrain ourselves from going into these details here. Note that within

15. B. Nolting, op. cit.

the framework of patomic model it is rather a misnomer to call these techniques as the thought transmission techniques. Instead it is the mindset of the individual combined with the given environment that transmits between the two space-time points. Even this environment is the outcome of a scientific circumstantial evidence (SCE).

11.5 Concluding Discussion

In this chapter we have attempted to explore relative success of the two methods dealing with fundamental processes responsible for human behaviour and actions. One is that described in Vedic science through patomic model and the other is that advocated by modern brain studies and cognitive psychology. It appears that modern science and cognitive psychology of the West have to go a long way to describe the human behaviour and experiences in totality. Note that an experience never needs any experiment since it cannot be reproduced at will and under specified conditions. It is strictly a subjective phenomenon. Further the knowledge in the subjects of physiology, biophysics and biochemistry, neurodynamics and brain studies, etc. when combined together still remains insufficient in this regard. As a result, the search for a God-Centre in the context of modern science remains a far cry. On the other hand, keeping the developments in previous chapters in mind, there already exists a treasure in Vedic science for such descriptions.

Despite the fact that both "mind over matter" and "matter over mind" jointly form a cycle towards the survival of a human Being in the field of WO, the former phrase however dominates over the latter in the spirit of "intelligent design" in the context of Darwinian theory. While looking for a basis of the process of realization (cf. Section 11.2.3), the processes like thinking, or feeling (cf. Section 11.3) in modern science as the products of biochemical reactions or of neural networks or the likes, still do not have a satisfactory and complete answer towards their origin. It is only a partial answer available and that too often is phenomenon-based. A general framework in modern science in this regard does not exist even today. In cognitive psychology of the West each author propounds his own concept and framework for consciousness without actually touching the root of the problem. Often it is a jargon of words that does not lead to a unified understanding and description of different consciousness-manifesting phenomena as is the case in the objective science of the West.

In fact all this is amazing and appears interesting as to how the consciousness works in the body of a living Being — whether we understand its working or not, that is immaterial. In modern biology viruses are considered at the borderline of living and non-living things. As a matter of fact a virus has a very simple composition. It has a protein sheath inside which there is a strand of DNA. A virus shows some properties of living organisms. However, unlike other organisms, they show some properties that are akin to non-living things. They can undergo crystallization and in that form, survive for billions of years. They can survive at very high temperatures, freezing cold and ultra-violet radiation in space vacuum and in crystalline form. Such theories can perhaps explain the origin of life but not the "working of life."

12

Behavioural and Allied Sciences Strategy for Testing the Theory

In earlier chapters, what we have analysed and discussed is only one aspect of science of the Self with reference to an individual. In particular, the processes lying in the domains of $\mathcal{G}$, $\mathcal{M}$, $\mathcal{G} \cup \mathcal{M}$ and $\mathcal{G} \cap \mathcal{M}$ (as the domains of working of $\mathcal{G}$ and $\mathcal{M}$ are not sharply defined) are emphasized. Two additional aspects not much emphasized earlier and need further elaboration are (a) to extend the viability of this science of Self to a collection of individuals, i.e to a society, and (b) to look for details of processes taking place exclusively in the domains of $\mathcal{M}$, $\mathcal{C}$, $\mathcal{M} \cup \mathcal{C}$ and $\mathcal{M} \cap \mathcal{C}$. With regard to the aspect (a) although some sketchy and passing remarks are made earlier here and there and a basis for understanding the processes is suggested in Sections 9.6 and 9.7 in the light of some analogies, yet in this chapter, we plan to provide some applications of these ideas to more practical situations in a focused manner. With regard to the aspect (b) a basis of spirituality will be eventually established in the second half of this chapter within the framework of patomic model and further discussions on this aspect will be continued in the next chapter.

12.1 The Question of "Predictive Power" of the Theory

Recall the predictive power and the outcome of developments of the theory of fundamental processes in physical science (cf. Preface and Chapter 1). Such deeper studies by scientists suggested (i) a changed outlook towards the structure of matter and about the associated physical processes and interactions, (ii) a clarity to certain phenomena whose explanations were ambiguous and the occurrence otherwise was attributed to supernatural powers and thereby creating many myths and dogmas in the society; for example, *PM*s were considered as gods, like sun-god, fire-god, etc. and finally (iii) a controlled use of natural resources, so that a balance in Nature is maintained at all costs towards the survival of human race. The aspect (iii) of these developments pertains to the predictive power as well as the limitations of these theories. Exactly the same is the case with the fundamental processes discussed in the preceding chapters mainly with regard to the actions and behaviour of an individual. In spite of a certain degree of arbitrariness involved in identifying the contents in the patomic model, an understanding of these processes will definitely provide (i) a changed outlook towards the understanding of human behaviour, (ii) a sensible reason for any abnormality noticed in one's behaviour, in particular with reference to the exotic phenomena (cf. Appendix F), and finally (iii) a regulated and controlled use of one's physical, mental and spiritual energies through SPP and SNP towards the success of an action or in general towards mottos in life.

We all have experienced that a regulated and controlled life-style produces positive definite fruits of actions. However, following such a lifestyle is like going upstream in a river as EOLs are forced to work against their normal flow, i.e. towards the worldly objects. In this case, they have to be trained accordingly and this pinches the individual at least in the initial stages. Contrarily, a follow-up of an irregular and uncontrolled lifestyle provides only the so-called negative fruits of one's actions that are full of uncertainties and normally prolongs the completion of an action. In either case there are certain elements in the behaviour which can be predicted in the light of present studies of fundamental processes, particularly by a conscious observer. While the individual himself can also act as a conscious observer (provided he spares time and undergoes the process of introspection), an outsider with better developed FOUs and who is constantly watching the behaviour of the person is by far the most suitable for making such predictions. In either situation a sequential role of EOLs towards the performance of an action becomes important in the analysis. Thus, at times an explicit prediction about one's behaviour becomes possible to a fair degree of accuracy in the present case.

12.2 Humanities and Social Sciences as Laboratories for Testing the Theory

Whether these are the hard or soft disciplines of knowledge, in either case wherever the human component is involved, the theory discussed in the preceding chapters is going to provide a better understanding of the concerned phenomenon. This involvement can range over the entire gamut of human actions performed by both inner and/or outer EOLs or of human interactions with other humans, non-humans and physical world. Here, while we overview the applications discussed earlier, we also briefly pinpoint some additional applications of the theory in different disciplines.

12.2.1 PHILOSOPHY AND PSYCHOLOGY

In a true sense philosophy is not a subject in itself. It is an exercise of the finest degree done by the EOL, I, through its dressed and highly dressed versions with regard to (i) how a particular discipline of knowledge originates, develops or progresses; once it is developed then, (ii) what the limitation on its development are, and (iii) what trends it is going to set with regard to the understanding of the Nature or the human values, or how much "pure knowledge" component is contained in its development. Recall that the dressed and highly dressed versions of I do include the roles of M and E and other outer EOLs (cf. Section 8.4.2). An expert with such an I (called philosopher) is while able to explore the above aspects in one or more than one disciplines in a critical manner, at times he is also capable of using his EOLs in search of absolute reality in Nature, of course with an eye on the universality of human values. What has been investigated in previous chapters is in fact the science of philosophy (cf. Section 1.4) and not the philosophy itself. Within this framework many philosophies of different cultures can be accommodated or analysed.

Exactly the same is the role of the EOL, M, in constituting the subject of psychology. In this case, the EOL, M (and its dressed and highly dressed versions) of an expert (conscious observer) is consistently used to study and analyse the actions performed by inner EOLs and the processes taking place in the psychic domain of a common man. Normally, in this case, the rules of the game are first derived either from the experiences of a super expert in an intuitive manner or are extracted from the data collected on a group of persons in an empirical or a statistical manner. Here the mental domain of an individual is explored on the basis of these collected data. In fact the source of data is the experimental investigation of choice and decision processes — a combination of the roles of M and I and their dressed versions, prevailing in the behaviour of an individual. Further, quantitative studies are carried out in terms of the models so designed.

The picture of a human Being presented in previous chapters, i.e. the patomic model with appropriate dynamics of interactions of EOLs inside (cf. Section 8.4.3), however, allows one to derive the underlying laws of psychology[1] or to verify the existing ones, in a rigorous manner. In this connection it is worth citing an empirical model proposed by the author[2] with regard to a common experience, namely "to perform a time-bound act, the

---

1. In this connection, several empirical laws concerning the rote memory, habit strength, sensory discriminating capacity, etc. are derived. For many of such empirical laws, see for example, J.P. Chaplin and T.S. Krawiec, *Systems and Theories of Psychology*, (New York: Holt, Reinhart and Winston, Inc., 1968), chapters 6 and 14.

2. Radhey Shayam Kaushal, "Patomic Model of Human Being in the Context of Modern Science", Ph.D. Thesis (unpublished), University of Delhi, 1998 chapter 8, Also see *Structural Analogies in Understanding Nature* (New Delhi; Anamaya Publisher, 2003), chapter 3.

left-over time sharpens the mind in terms of the degree of concentration (i.e. the meditation parameter μ) or the efficiency."

In Chapter 8 and in Appendix E, the meditation parameter μ is considered as separate and independent variable from time t, of course at par with t, and that may be true with certain processes beyond the domain of $\mathcal{G}$. In the above experience, however, the concentration or meditation μ is a function of time variable t itself. The experience involves a sequence of processes mostly taking place in the overlapping domain of $\mathcal{G}$ and $\mathcal{M}$. Further, we have considered[3] the rate of increase of μ at any time t as inversely proportional to the time left to complete the task, i.e. $(d\mu/dt) \propto (1/(t_0-t))$, where t_0 is the allotted time for the task. This implies the relation

$$\mu(t) = \mu_0 - \lambda \ln\left(1 - \frac{t}{t_0}\right)$$

where μ_0 and λ are positive constants. For $t \ll t_0$, the above equation reduces to

$$\mu(t) \simeq \mu_0 + \lambda t / t_0$$

This explains how the time sharpens the mind towards the completion of a task. Here, the effect of circumstances and environment will be taken care of by the constants μ_0, t_0, and λ. Like this, there are several other phenomena in the overlapping domain of $\mathcal{M}$. and $\mathcal{G}$ that can be modelled in a similar way. For example, one can study (i) how the concentration of a student affects the grasp of a subject in the class room, (ii) what roles the memory, concentration and decision of a student play in attempting the questions in a question paper in the examination hall, or (iii) how quickly one recovers from a tragedy or setback towards his normal life, etc.

Note that the modern psychology mostly revolves around the experimental study of choice and decision processes prevailing in an individual, but the fact is that there is a huge

3. Radhey Shayam Kaushal, 2003, op. cit.

class of psychic phenomena — exotic or otherwise (cf. Appendix F), whose study in totality requires the roles of EOLs, M, I and E on equal footing. In fact in the subjects of philosophy and psychology one studies the EOLs, M, I and E for M, I and E using again the EOLs, M, I and E (cf. K-effect, Appendix F). Further, with regard to active and passive components of a philosophy (cf. Chapter 1), it is the active (or dynamic) component of the Vedānta philosophy that is highlighted in the preceding chapters with reference to the performance of an action.

12.2.2 SOCIAL SCIENCE: THE SCIENCE OF MANY-BEING SYSTEMS

Note that many-Being systems can arise for both humans and non-humans and at different occasions during their daily mundane living. Again in the behaviour of both — many-human and many-non-human Being systems, certain commonalities and systematics can be observed when they are exposed to the same external environment or undergo the same circumstantial conditions. It is the presence of the EOL, I, in humans that makes a lot of difference when it comes to their behavioural studies. In general, the systems of non-humans show more regularities as compared to those of humans mainly because the reasoning capability of the latter, in fact, creates several differences in their individual behaviours and hence at times leads to a chaotic nature of the system.

To elaborate further, all humans in a collection when exposed to the same environment do not react in the same manner since they all in general have different levels of developments of their FOUs. Though the environment is the same, it generates different mindsets in each individual in the collection and accordingly the individual reacts and that at times is responsible for an irregular behaviour of the system. On the other hand, for a many-non-human Being system this is not the case; for most of the species the reasoning capacity either remains at low pitch or it is absent, particularly when it is compared with a human Being who at times also happens to be their master.

In physical theories one frequently applies the knowledge of one-, two- or in general few-body systems to the study of many-body systems and the idea works well to a fair degree of accuracy, except for some collective effects that are produced and depend on the nature of forces involved. Although some applications of this category are already highlighted (cf. Sections 9.2, 9.6 and 9.7), in general the idea does not work for the reason listed above. In view of the concepts of inside-out and outside-out in the patomic model, the analogy seems to offer a reasonable effectiveness of the ideas with regard to the description of many-human Being systems, but only for the system exposed to a particular environment. The fact is that the human dynamics is very complicated and totally different from the space-time mediated dynamics of physics. The role of this difference manifests more in a many-human Being system than that in a many-non-human Being system. Note that in addition to AAD-type and contact-type forces, these are the AAT-type and AADT-type interactions with which the interacting participants are now equipped and the latter dominate among humans (cf. Chapter 9).

In fact each individual (as a conscious person) may carry with him the past memories and experiences, the future ambitions and aspirations and/or the dreams to fulfil the desires at different space-time points in the world. All this makes his meditation parameter μ a complicated function of space and time. When such a person with his so-developed FOUs interacts with another human, non-human or with external physical world, naturally the interactions (and so are the fundamental processes) are going to be equally complex. However, the life is simple in case of interactions with the physical world (cf. Chapter 8), less simple in case of interactions with non-humans (fractured patomic model, cf. Chapter 10) and is least simple in case of interactions with humans.

Now consider the collection of such interacting humans, particularly when such a system is placed in an external environment or in the so-created circumstances. The latter affects the basic qualities of a many-human system as far as the end-point of these interactions, i.e. the bahaviour of the system as a whole, to an external observer is concerned. In what follows, we briefly demonstrate through examples as to how the behaviour of a given many- human or non-human system gets affected when exposed to different environments and/or is put in different circumstances.

12.2.3 ORDER AND CHAOS IN THE BEHAVIOUR OF MANY-BEING SYSTEMS: DIFFERENT STAGES OF STABILITY

In the context of statistical physics, it is well known that a many-body system becomes ordered when the external forces dominate and its chances of becoming disordered (chaotic) are more when the internal forces start overcoming the external forces. To some extent, this observation holds equally true for many-Being systems, particularly for many-non-human systems. Let us reanalyze the interacting vertices present in a member of the many-Being system. In addition to the EOLS, B, SE, M, I, E and their dressed and varyingly highly dressed versions present in different individuals, there is also a fixed mindset $\mathcal{M}$ (m, i, e; q, t) associated with each individual. Depending upon the development of the FOUs of each individual, his mindset evolves with respect to the meditation parameter μ which in turn is also a function of space and time or in general of environment and circumstances. Note that in non-humans the role of the EOL, I, remains at low pitch.

When such a member of a many-Being system interacts with other members of the same system, the resulting interactions are of different orders/categories ranging from the gross-body level to the causal-body level. This generates an overall collective mindset, $\mathcal{M}_c$(m_c, i_c, e_c; q, t) of the system which now is a function of collective variables, like collective emotion, collective wisdom, and collective ego in addition to that of normal space and time variables that are responsible for creating the given environment and/or circumstances and thereby affecting the behaviour of the system. For such a system of living Beings, there also arises a collective meditation (consciousness) parameter μ_c with respect to which the function $\mathcal{M}_c$ (m_c, i_c, e_c; q, t) evolves and attains certain optimum (stable) values as and when a rapport among the interacting constituents of different levels settles, for example, at the level of B (when the system is left in the same physical conditions), SE (when the same sense-objects like food, water, sun, accommodation, etc. are made available to the members of the system), M (when the system is subject to the same, for example, joy or sorrow), I (when the system is forced to take a unanimous or collective decision), and E (when the system is forced to speak out or bear the same experiences). All this happens when the many-Being system is forced to live in the same, but strong man- or god-made environment or under intense man- or god-created circumstances. Note that even the slightest but serious protest against the given conditions or circumstances by an individual at any stage of stability, is sufficient to affect and to bring the system into disorderliness. In the extreme case, however, when the protests are there from among several members of the system (who themselves have varying levels of development of their FOUs), then the behaviour of the many-Being system turns into a chaotic one.

It may be remarked that an ordered many-Being system achieves the success in an action generally by following the SPP whereas a disordered (or chaotic) one lacks in achieving such a success since the tendency of the system is to follow SNP in the form of protests. Even in the disordered case, orderliness appears at a lower level when the protests by like minds against the given conditions (or the existing external controller) come together and form subgroups of reasonable size. However, such a move weakens the very existence of the system unless a cure is sought by the external agent. If the external forcing agent happens to be a local man-made device, then the EOLs M, I and E of individuals become biased towards the protests and collectively oppose at times mainly to satisfy their collective ego. Further, if the external forcing (commanding) agent happens to be a human

Being then it is necessary for him to have his FOUs at highly developed level, may be in a limited domain, to maintain the orderliness of the system. Note that a variety of phenomena related to many-Being systems can be investigated by way of carrying out a mathematical analysis of the function $\mathcal{M}_c$ (m_c, i_c, e_c; q, t) in terms of collective variables equally for many-human and many-non-human systems, but we avoid going into such details here. Of course, when it comes to an actual description of the behaviour of a system, then one also needs to account for the gender of the members. In fact the behaviour could be different when the members of the system are of the same (male or female) gender or are of different (mixed) genders. Note that such differences arise mainly in a restricted peripheral domain of very wide spectrum of interactions among the members, namely in the domains of B and SE and possibly of M; otherwise the behaviour of the system under the given conditions by and large remains gender independent.

Next we analyse the behaviour of some representative many-Being systems of day-to-day life subject to different conditions and circumstances.

12.3 Analysis of Some Many-Being Systems of Day-to-Day Life

12.3.1 MANY-CHILD SYSTEM: A CASE OF DEVELOPING FOUs

In this case each member of the system always and everywhere has and maintains a limited development of his FOUs as compared to the external agent. Members, in fact, are forced to become the part of the system mainly for an overall development of their FOUs so that they can become good citizens. Whether it is a many-boy or many-girl system, it undergoes the same training and whomsoever, even with little experience, can act as external agent and controller of the system. Further, whether it is a prayer assembly or class-room studies or an assembly at home everywhere the system in general appears as ordered as long as the teacher or any other external agent is present. The system by and large works under pressure and fear which in turn constitute the environment.

As a child grows up and is promoted to higher and higher classes, his FOUs also develop and slowly the difference in the developments of his FOUs and that of external agent in general becomes less and less. As a result the chances of disorderliness of the system increase. At this stage, an expert needs to be appointed as a teacher or external agent so that the difference in the developments of FOUs may be there even in a limited domain. Such a difference is essential for imparting good knowledge.

Before proceeding further it may be remarked here that for the success of an action by the system, often there are two types of external agents, namely local and non-local, responsible for creating the conditions and circumstances. In philosophical terms, one can think of a third external agent as well and that is global agent or God that inspires one and all to work individually or collectively. While the local external agent has to be present with the many-Being system physically, the non-local (or for that matter global) agents can work even from "remote," i.e. with a changed mindset of each member of the system. Some examples of non-local external agents are the commands or the rules of the game as suggested or prescribed by political, religious, cultural, or academic fora, etc. within which the many-Being system is broadly supposed to work. In the above example of many-student system however the local external agent is sufficient and the members (or their mindsets) are at times not aware of the non-local external agent that guides the running of the institution and sometimes the quality of teachings.

12.3.2 MANY-ADULT SYSTEM: A CASE FOR SETTLING OBJECTIVE(S) IN LIFE

Consider a system whose members are adult and coming from different backgrounds (or with different developments of their FOUs). Such members assemble for a purpose decided by a non-local external agent. For example, we analyse the working of three categories of systems, namely (i) assembly of workers of a trade union, (ii) group of defence trainees or a trained army battalion in action, and (iii) assembly of politically, religiously, culturally, or academically motivated persons. In all the three cases the members are biased a priori and motivated by both local and non-local external agents. In spite of the fact that all members have their FOUs sufficiently developed, their mindsets are conditioned, temporarily or permanently, is a different matter. In case of category (i) the members protest collectively normally for their needs on the initiative of the local external agent. The system remains ordered only in a limited domain of interactions among the members. On the other hand, in category (ii) the defence trainees undergo a learning process with the help of an expert external agent on the face value; otherwise the members have already conditioned their mindsets to achieve certain higher objective. Similarly, when a trained army battalion is in action against the attack by an enemy, the system is highly ordered (and in fact it has to be) to achieve the success of its action. In this latter case, all lower-level interactions inside a member are highly suppressed or controlled with a view to achieving the success and on the initiative of both local and non-local agents. Many-adult systems in category (iii) also behave in the same manner as the second system in category (ii) except for the fact that members are now motivated differently by different local and non-local external agents.

12.3.3 MANY-OLD PERSON SYSTEM: A CASE OF DEVELOPED FOUs AND RIPENED EXPERIENCES

Consider an assembly of old (particularly of retired) persons. They all have highly developed FOUs (perhaps the highest possible for each member in his lifetime) and experiences of their life. To this extent, members do not need any longer local or non-local external agent for their guidance since many of them do not have any desire or capacity to learn further. They analyse the world or world order on the basis of what they have gathered so far in their lifetime. Many of them enjoy sharing the discussions on the ideas/themes which originate out of the domains of $\mathcal{G}$ or at the most of $\mathcal{G} \cup \mathcal{M}$ or $\mathcal{M}$ in an individual. However, one can always find some members in all such gatherings who have the tendency to think beyond these domains, namely in the domain of $\mathcal{M} \cup \mathcal{C}$ or $\mathcal{C}$. While many such members are inspired by the global external agent (God) at this stage of life, they also feel satisfied if an external local agent (possibly with better developed FOUs) comes and shares with them in these domains. It has been found that all members become united on this front. This means that old persons develop the habit of detaching themselves from worldly objects in certain corner of their faculties.

Unlike the systems discussed in above sub-sections, this system by and large does not have collective vested interest and to some extent it remains unbiased a priori. In spite of the fact that members have different but sufficiently developed FOUs, their eagerness to listen to something beyond WO, i.e. in the realms of $\mathcal{M} \cup \mathcal{C}$ and $\mathcal{C}$ or spirituality, remains.

12.3.4 MANY-WOMAN SYSTEM: A CASE OF DEVELOPED FOUs BUT WITH A WEAKNESS FOR SHOWING OFF BEAUTY

For the system consisting of old ladies, the behaviour remains more or less the same as for the many-old person system. However, with the system of young ladies (unlike the case of many-adult system), members here have a tendency to confine to the interactions of domain $\mathcal{G}$ or at the most of $\mathcal{G} \cup \mathcal{M}$. In particular, in addition to the interactions of B-level, the interactions at the levels of SEA and SEK also dominate the dynamics of the system. The behaviour of the system also depends on whether the local or non-local external agent is a male or female. As a matter of fact, despite the fact that members may be having sufficiently developed FOUs, most of the members of the system have a natural tendency to show themselves as more beautiful than any other member and this often distracts the mind of members and accordingly affects the working of the collective mindset of the system and hence the behaviour of the system as a whole. However, once the members overcome this weakness, then the many-woman system is capable of showing wonders and is perhaps able to perform better than the corresponding many-adult system, of course under the given conditions and circumstances.

12.3.5 MANY-NON-HUMAN BEING SYSTEM: A CASE OF DOMINATING ORDERED BEHAVIOUR

Among non-human Beings we have two broad classes (cf. Section 10.2), namely inquilines and non-inquilines. In these two classes there are further sub-classes and the behaviour of each such system varies from one sub-class to another under given conditions, of course with certain systematics in common. Except for systems constituted by pet, for all other systems whose members are of the same species, there exists a code of conduct among members and also the local and non-local external agents to control the behaviour of the system. In case of homogeneous systems (whose members are of the same species) it has been found that the system by and large remains ordered for any kind of variation in conditions and circumstances. Induction even of a single member of other species however allows the system to behave in a chaotic manner.

12.4 Remarks on Some Other Classes of Many-Being Systems in Nature

What we have tried to identify above in Section 12.3 are certain specific many-Being systems with finite members and ideal external conditions that exist in the man-made society; otherwise in the "god-made" society of Nature there are varieties of such systems that consist of humans, non-humans and both, and survive under certain "god-made" external conditions and circumstances. With a view to studying certain aspects of behaviour of such systems, the following remarks are in order: Firstly, these systems can be considered as heterogeneous, i.e. their members can belong to different species, different age groups and the like. Secondly, these systems can have countable infinite members since at times it may be difficult to keep track of all the members and their locations and they may not be subjected to the same external conditions, which are necessary for the survival of members. Thirdly, certain many-Being systems can evolve and become extinct with respect to both space and time (for example, recall the famous prey-predator problem discussed in Section 10.8.4(d), particularly with respect to wolves and dogs, dogs and cats, cats and rats, foxes and rabbits, etc.). In the last case, however, there arises a situation of inter-system interactions in addition to the intra-system ones and one studies the overall behaviour of one system which matters a lot in its existence *vis-à-vis* that of the other system. In fact a basis for the analysis of behaviour of such interacting systems *vis-à-vis* external conditions does exist in the present framework. However, we restrict ourselves from going into further details here.

12.5 Religion, Dharma and Spirituality

In order that a society or a many-human system remains an ordered system certain rules of the game working among the members are floated from time to time by the local, non-local and/or global (!) external agents. One such set of the rules of the game, which perhaps provides an ordered system of the highest degree and capable of continuing this feature for centuries, pertains to the personal life of members, and at times it is called religion in a restricted sense. While the word "religion" spells out only a limited mode of working in an individual's lifestyle with reference to a particular ideology and belief, the Sanskrit word *dharma*, on the other hand, stands for a very wide spectrum of positive definite or the best possible actions needed to be performed by an individual at given space-time points and circumstances. Note that a religion (or its synonym "cult") generally originates with an individual external agent who may as well be a reviver of universal values that may have existed prior to him but have been lost in the sands of time. For (*sanātana*) *dharma*, however, there is no space-time bound originator or propounder; it is just the adoption of an ordered lifestyle with a freedom and tendency to follow up SPP over SNP at all space-time points and circumstances.

Religious teachings provide us with a difference between good and bad so that one can live a peaceful life, of course with a constraint of belief or faith in the background. *Dharma*, on the other hand, goes one step ahead to tell us as to how we can live beyond the domain of good and bad and attain an *eternal pleasure* (cf. Chapter 13) with reference to inculcating the "universal values" in an individual and in the society as a whole. This is the domain of spirituality characterized here by $\mathcal{M} \cup C$ and C. Thus, *dharma* is capable of accommodating several religions along with a unique (and perhaps universal) path to be followed by an individual towards his salvation (cf. Chapter 13).

Next, we just have a glance on what some other people have to say on faith, religion, *dharma* and spirituality:

> Faith is an act of a finite (human) Being who is grasped by the infinite (God). — Paul Tillich

> Without faith, hope and trust, there is no promise for future, and without a promising future, life has no direction and no justification. — Adlin Sinclair

> Religion is for those who are scared of hell, spirituality is for those who have been there. — Bonnie Raitt

In what follows, we present a famous example of *dharma* from Vedic science.

12.5.1 PĀTAÑJALA YOGA AS AN EXAMPLE OF (SANĀTANA) DHARMA

Look at the systematics as derived by ancient Indian seers, for example by Patañjali out of the mundane living of an individual. What a wonderful discretization of continuous spectrum of all human actions which one can think of performing individually or collectively for a positive pursuit had been suggested by Pātañjala. In a nut-shell, this discretization (cf. Chapter 2) of actions consists of *eight* main components: (i) *yama*, (ii) *niyama*, (iii) *āsanas*, (iv) *prāṇāyāma*, (v) *pratyāhāra*, (vi) *dhāraṇā*, (vii) *dhyāna*, and (viii) *samādhi*, and their further divisions and sub-divisions.[4] Since a lot of specialized literature is available[5] on the subject, we will not go into further details here except for making some general remarks in the present context. (a) Note that a variety of models of religion can be created just out of the first three components alone, since the underlying fundamental processes under these heads mainly belong to the domains of $\mathcal{G}$ and $\mathcal{G} \cup \mathcal{M}$. (b) While the components (iii)-(vi) are meant to keep oneself physically and mentally fit (in fact, such a fitness is a prerequisite for attaining peace and subsequently for achieving the highest in life), the components (vi)-(viii) in some sense constitute the domain of spirituality and the underlying processes belonging to the domains of $\mathcal{M} \cup \mathcal{C}$ and $\mathcal{C}$. (c) Note that the processes originating out of the components (i) and (ii) have sensitive dependence on space, time and circumstances, whereas those originating out of the components (iii)-(v) have somewhat mild dependence on space, time and circumstances; however, the ones originating out of the components (vi)-(viii) do not depend on space, time and circumstances at all. They perhaps originated with the human race and will perhaps continue and come to an end with the human race. For the fact that there is a scope of

4. For example, the five divisions of *yama* are: nonviolence (*ahiṁsā*), truth (*satya*), continence (*brahmacarya*), non-stealing (*asteya*), want of accumulation of wealth with the sense of meum (*aparigṛha*) and the five divisions of *niyama* are: purity (*śauca*), contentment (*santoṣa*), austerity (*tapa*), self-study (*svādhyāya*), faith in God. Similar classifications do exist for *āsanas*, *prāṇāyāma*, *dhāraṇā*, *dhyāna* and *samādhi*. These eight components constitute the so-called *Aṣṭāṅga Yoga* of Patañjali or termed as *Rāja-Yoga* in Vedic science. This is a distinct class of Yoga in the sense that it provides a step-by-step development of one's mindset. Further, the first five components constitute the so-called *bahiraṅga-yoga* and the last three the *antaraṅga-yoga*.

5. See, for example, Swami Vivekananda, *The Yoga-Sūtras of Patañjali*, Delhi: Motilal Banarsidass, Swami Kriyananda (J. Donald Walters), *The Art and Science of Rāja Yoga: Fourteen Steps to Higher Awareness* (based on the Teachings of Paramhamsa Yogananda), Delhi: Motilal Banarsidass.

discussion of these last category of processes and that too at the finest possible level in Vedic science, the corresponding way of life is termed as *sanātana* (free from the beginning and the end) *dharma*. (d) Note that it is the mindset of a conscious person that evolves and subsequently his FOUs develop when the actions of an individual are transformed from the domain of one component to that of another. For example, when the mindset of a person works in the domain of spirituality, his actions sometimes become examples for others and may be a trend-setter as well. This is mainly because the actions of the person and his experiences in this domain now become universal — free from the boundary of space and time. (e) Why only an individual, a group of human Beings through its collective mindset $\mathcal{M}_c$, can also be benefited by such a transformation of actions as one proceeds from component (i) to component (viii); of course this depends on individual's or collective efforts in view of the minimum effort principle (cf. Section 4.4).

12.5.2 SPIRITUALITY AND THE QUESTION OF "UNIVERSAL VALUES"

In what has been said above in this section, we have tried to identify the domain of spirituality in the Eastern and Western ways of thinking. As it is also clear from the saying of Bonnie Raitt above, spirituality is over and above the psychic domain of an individual in which one moves around the pair of opposite like good and bad, pleasure and pain, etc. Although the domain of spirituality is not independent of $\mathcal{M}$ it is definitely independent of the actions of $\mathcal{M}$ to some extent. In fact $\mathcal{M}$ and $\mathcal{C}$ and their dressed and highly dressed versions constitute this domain. For further details we shall return in Chapter 13.

Spiritual counsel is usually given to persons after they have reached the supposed age of discretion, i.e. when they can make up their mind as to which set of values they will follow. Unfortunately, only a few persons ever develop such discretion and most of us in fact go by the values imbibed during childhood. In childhood and mostly in the class rooms, what one gathers in modern times are scientific thoughts which themselves have limitations and speak only a partial truth in Nature, and a variety of systems of belief, which also do not have an objective validity.

What is missing in the curriculum is the inculcation of true or universal values in children; for example, the depth of qualities like co-operation, positive thinking, kindness and other eternal values which are essential for a truly productive life. In fact true values are not only subjective but they are based on a Universal experience that goes with a "spiritual" person. No doubt there is a lack of such persons in the teaching community associated with the formal education; however, inculcation of such values in children will be possible if the following steps are followed: Firstly, there should be a course on spirituality and spiritual values in the curriculum. Secondly, the teachers with appropriate spiritual experience should be available to teach this course. Thirdly, an appropriate atmosphere should be provided to impart these values by a spiritual person. Once the students become truly aware of these values, their mindset will definitely rank them higher than even the modern scientific thoughts.

It may be mentioned that while India in ancient times was leading the world on this front of education, however, now it is not able to follow the system. With regard to the importance of spiritual knowledge in life, Lord Kṛṣṇa in *SMBG* clearly emphasizes[6]

> *adhyātma jñāna nityatvaṁ tatvajñānārtha darśanam* ।
> *etaj-jñānamiti proktam ajñānaṁ yadato-anyathā* ॥ — 13.11 (12.1)

> Fixity in self-knowledge (spirituality), observing everywhere the object of true knowledge (i.e. God); all this is declared to be knowledge (wisdom); what is contrary to this is called ignorance.

We shall return to some of these details in the next chapter.

---

6. *Śrīmad Bhagavad-Gītā*, chapter 13, verse 11, Gorakhpur: Gita Press.

12.5.3 SPIRITUAL PERSON AND HIS WAY OF LIFE

About a spiritual person or its synonym the "man of perfection" or the "man of wisdom" we have already discussed earlier in Section 4.3.1. Here, however we make some additional remarks about his way of life, specific to the domain of spirituality. A spiritual person is in no way different from an ordinary person as far as his day-to-day life is concerned. It is only the development of his FOUs or the evolution of his mindset as a function of thinking and practice, that makes him different from others. No doubt such personalities are rare in a society; if they are there, they may appear to be strange to the new generation or may find it difficult to survive in a society full of values of spatio-temporal nature. For the sake of establishing universal values, it becomes the responsibility of local or non-local external agents to induct or create spiritual persons in a society.

With regard to the qualities and symptoms of a spiritual person, a lot has been given in *SMBG*. Here, however, we highlight only a few of these characteristics of a spiritual person. Lord Kṛṣṇa defines such a person through[7]

adveṣṭa sarvabhūtānāṁ maitraḥ karuṇa eva ca ।
nirmamo nirahaṅkāraḥ samaduḥkha sukhaḥ kṣamī ॥ — 12.13 (12.2)

santuṣṭah satatam yogī yatātma dṛḍha niścayaḥ ।
mayyarpita manobuddhir yo madbhaktaḥ sa me priyaḥ ॥ — 12.14 (12.3)

He who is free from malice towards all Beings, who is friendly as well as compassionate, who has no feeling of envy and is free from egoism, to whom pleasure and pain are alike and who is forgiving by nature, who is ever content and mentally united to Me (God), who has subdued his body, mind and senses and has a firm resolve, who has surrendered his mind and intellect to Me — that devotee of mine is dear to Me.

The Lord continues further such a description of spiritual person in the next five verses as

7. *Śrīmad Bhagavad-Gītā*, chapter 12, verses 13-19, Gorakhpur: Gita Press.

yasmānnodvijate loko lokānnodvijate ca yaḥ ।
harṣāmarṣa bhayodvegairmukto yaḥ sa ca me priyaḥ ॥ — 12.15 (12.4)

anapekṣaḥ śucirdakṣa udāsīno gatavyathaḥ ।
sarvārambha parityāgi yo madbhaktaḥ sa me priyaḥ ॥ — 12.16 (12.5)

He who is not a source of annoyance to the world, and who never feels offended with the world, who is free from delight and anger, perturbation and fear. He who craves for nothing, who is both internally and externally pure, is clear and impartial, and has risen above all distractions, who renounces the feeling of doer-ship in all undertakings, that devotee is dear to Me.

Further,

yona hraṣyati na dveṣṭi na śocati na kāṅkṣati ।
śubhāśubha parityāgi bhaktimān yah sa me priyaḥ ॥ — 12.17 (12.6)

samaḥ śatrau ca mitre ca tathā mānāpamānayoḥ ।
śītoṣṇa sukhaduḥkheṣu samaḥ saṅga vivarjitaḥ ॥ — 12.18 (12.7)

He who neither rejoices nor hates, nor grieves, nor desires, who renounces both good and evil and is full of devotion to me. He who is alike to friend and foe, and likewise to honour and ignominy, who is alike to heat and cold, pleasure and pain etc., and is free from attachment.

Finally, the Lord advises to renounce the most difficult aspect of human life, i.e. praise, by the spiritual person through,

tulya nindāstutirmaunī santuṣṭo yena kenacit ।
aniketaḥ sthiramatir bhaktimān me priyo naraḥ ॥ — 12.19 (12.8)

He who takes praise and reproach alike, who is given to contemplation and content with whatever comes unasked for, without attachment to home, fixed in mind and full of devotion to me, that man is dear to Me (God).

Further description of such a person can be found in verses 22-25 of Chapter 14 in *SMBG*.

In the above verses, the Lord has described the entire spectrum of human qualities along with their opposites which need to be present in a spiritual person. While some of these qualities belong to psychic domain, which perhaps are not difficult to achieve, the rest, of course, define an ideal spiritual person. When the Lord says that such a person is "dear to Me"; there is no harm if this phrase be interpreted as the "near to Me," in view of the fact that an ideal spiritual person is very close to the state of salvation, i.e. capable and fit to merge into "infinity." Even the presence of a nearly ideal spiritual person in a society can be helpful to the latter.

12.6 Concluding Discussion

With a view to exploring strategy for testing the theory discussed in the preceding chapters with reference to an individual to the case of many-Being systems, several practical applications of the theory are highlighted in this chapter and in the context of behavioural and allied sciences. As far as the predictive power of the ideas is concerned, it is in no way less than that of certain physical theories. The ideas developed here not only suggest an alternative way of analysing the data in psychology but also the convergence of various philosophies into the one that belongs to the domain of spirituality. The social science is discussed as the science of many-Being systems. In this regard, the behaviour of some particular many-human and many-non-human systems with finite number of members *vis-à-vis* the role of local, non-local and/or global external agents is analysed, though within the framework of patomic model. It may be mentioned that even the induction of one member of different species into the system can make the system chaotic and at times it can happen irrespective of the roles of external agents and circumstances.

Sanātana Dharma — a creation out of Vedic science is shown to account for both religion — a restricted but commonly adopted way of life on the one end, and spirituality — a global and unique way of life, on the other. It is argued that while the science of spirituality and the associated universal values need a place in modern society, there still exists dearth of persons with appropriate spiritual training and experience. To this effect, some symptoms of such a person from *SMBG* are cited which may help in identifying such persons in society.

In Sections 12.3 and 12.4 we have limited our discussions and analyses mainly to many-Being systems with finite members which in some sense are homogeneous systems that exist in human society; otherwise in Nature (on our planet earth itself) one can find varieties of heterogeneous many-Being systems with (countably) infinite members whose studies may provide still interesting observations to verify the ideas advanced here.

QUALITY OF CREATIVITY IN ACTIONS OF A HUMAN BEING

It may be mentioned that the creativity in actions of a human Being is an expression of inner evolution of FOUs of an individual that originates from different domains of $\mathcal{G}$, $\mathcal{G} \cup \mathcal{M}$, $\mathcal{M}$, $\mathcal{M} \cup C$ and C. In fact creative thinking is an infinite movement of thought that covers the entire spectrum of EOLs and their actions, starting from WO and B and finally to E and SO. Varieties of experiences gathered by the Being b during this coverage, contribute differently to creativity as far as its merit and its expression in space time is concerned. In some sense there is a close connection between the quality of creativity and the quality of success of actions performed by the Being b pertaining to achieving a goal. For example, the experiences originating out of the domains of $\mathcal{G}$, $\mathcal{G} \cup \mathcal{M}$, $\mathcal{M}$ may not give rise to creativity of the same finer order as compared to the ones originating from the domains of $\mathcal{M}$, $\mathcal{M} \cup C$, C in terms of spatio-temporal values. While the values associated with the former situation are generally bound by space and time, the ones associated with the latter are generally universal. It is this spirit in which the discussions in Section 12.5.2 are carried out.

As a matter of fact the thinking remains creative as long as the movement of thought is infinite and free; otherwise it is influenced by the circumstances. In this regard J. Krishnamurti clearly emphasizes,[8]

8. Jiddu Krishnamurti, "Creative Thinking is Infinite Movement of thought", The Speaking Tree, *Times of India*, 27 May 2009.

> That is, creative thinking ceases when the mind is crippled by adjustment through influences or when it functions with the background of a tradition which it has not understood, or from a fixed point, like an animal tied to a post. So long as this limitation, this adjustment exists, there cannot be creative thinking, intelligence which alone is freedom.

Whether it is thinking or creative thinking, in either case the practice of self-discipline is a must. At times, even this practice does not bring about creative thinking. Ultimately, the peace of mind derived by following certain systematics of positive pursuits pays in this regard. Lord Kṛṣṇa in *SMBG* beautifully summarizes this fact in the verse[9]

> *śreyo hi jñānam abhyāsāj-jñānād dhyānaṁ viśiṣyate* ।
> *dhyānāt karmaphala tyāgas tyāgācchāntiranantaraṁ* ॥ — 12.12

(12.9)

> Knowledge is better than practice (carried on without proper insight, i.e. *parokṣa Jñāna*), meditation (i.e. *dhyāna*) is superior to knowledge, and renunciation of the fruit of action (i.e. *tyāga*) is even superior to meditation; for peace immediately follows from renunciation.

9. *Śrīmad Bhagavad-Gītā*, chapter 12, verse 12, Gorakhpur: Gita Press.

13

Theory of Fundamental Processes, So What Next for Peace and Eternal Pleasure: Self-Realization

WHAT we see around us in the form of scientific and industrial development is the outcome of fundamental processes studied in the domain of objective sciences and that too in the STCG domain. Some of these gains can be recounted as follows: (i) The biggest gain is the satisfaction of a scientist by knowing about how the Nature works, of course only in the STCG domain, (ii) these studies have made the survival of human Being on this planet comfortable and in some sense luxurious by way of contraction of space and time in terms of daily needs and communication, etc. and (iii) these studies make the scientist further curious to know more and more about the smallest as well as the biggest in the universe and investigating the finer and finer details of the matter in-between, of course again within the domain of STCC and other limitations of physical laws (cf. Chapter 6). No doubt human FOUs are now becoming more creative and innovative — a symptom of growth in the evolution of human race, but the fact is that this growth remains one-sided or partial unless a similar evolution continues simultaneously in the spiritual domain or at the level of inner EOLs, with reference to attaining peace and later on eternal pleasure or joy. Needless to say, the existing objective science can hardly provide anything on this front unless it opens its doors beyond STCG domain.

The types of fundamental processes discussed in previous chapters are also not the final solution of the problem; their studies offer only a step in this direction in the same way as the objective scientists, even after identifying the fundamental processes in the STCG domain in Nature, are looking for a theory of everything. The contents of the present chapter mostly remain in the domain of spirituality defined in Chapter 12.

Here, we suggest certain ways and means to an individual to go beyond the previously discussed fundamental processes so that he can at least aspire for further higher goals in life. To start with, we elaborate on the process of Self-realization. Then in Section 13.2 we define the stages of peace and eternal pleasure as the milestones in this process of Self-realization. These milestones in fact should be the main goals in the life of a truth seeker. In search of the "ultimate" or "actual doer" of an action, we once again invoke in Section 13.3 the self-consistent theory of action (cf. Section 4.3.2) and discuss the role of deities in this regard. As a matter of fact the achievement of the stages of peace and eternal pleasure depends on certain combination of environment and circumstances, the so-called scientific circumstantial evidence (SCE) or in its generalized version as *saṁyoga*. We elaborate on these concepts in Section 13.4. While SCE will define the parameter σ introduced earlier in the definition of mindset $\mathcal{M}$(m, i, e; σ), the answer to the question as to how knowledge overcomes one's ignorance will also be discussed in this section. Even the process of self-realization has limitations as far as achieving the last stage of *mokṣa* or salvation by an individual is concerned. Such concluding remarks will be made finally in Section 13.5.

13.1 What is Self-Realization?

13.1.1 THE SELF AND THE NON-SELF

Most of the fundamental processes discussed in the previous chapters are inspired by the interactions of $\mathcal{M}$ and $\mathcal{G}$ but do occur in the presence of SO, i.e. SO acts as an important spectator of functions performed by the constituents of $\mathcal{M}$ and $\mathcal{G}$. This is one category of fundamental processes. Now we introduce another rather fine category of such processes. For this purpose, we define a new composite $\mathcal{B} = \mathcal{M} \cup \mathcal{G}$, as the union of sets $\mathcal{G}$ and $\mathcal{M}$, and treat $\mathcal{B}$ as a separate entity altogether from SO in spite of the fact that SO through consciousness still remains a spectator not only of all constituents of $\mathcal{M}$ and $\mathcal{G}$ (or in general of $\mathcal{B}$) but also of their constituents. Recall that SO is the cause of SEP-matter and $\mathcal{B}$ is the example of an EP-matter. A feel for such a concept by an individual is the start of his entering the domain of spirituality. The main hindrance in attaining such a state of feel by a person arises from his own EOL E in the form of "I-ism" or "me-ism" while the feel of "my-ism" and "mine-ism" clearly indicates the separateness of SO from $\mathcal{B}$. In fact it is the ego E that plays the important (and some time crucial) role among the exchanges between $\mathcal{B}$ and SO. The art of elimination of E from among these exchanges while forms part of *ātmajñāna* (cf. verses (4.2) and (4.1)), is also a first step in the direction of attaining salvation (*mokṣa*). Here, E acts at a very fine level and causes the bondage of $\mathcal{B}$ and SO. Alternatively, if one learns the art of noticing the working of $\mathcal{B}$ (i.e. non-Self) as distinct and separate from that of SO (i.e. Self), in spite that the latter is deeply involved in all functions of $\mathcal{B}$, then this is the state of "true knowledge" or *ātmajñāna* (or the knowledge of Self) (cf. Section 4.1). The knowledge of everything else except this is termed as relative knowledge or just *jñāna* or at times as ignorance in relative terms in Vedic science that can provide only temporal (worldly) pleasure or at the most peace but not the eternal pleasure. If one can develop such a habit of noticing distinct roles of the Self and the non-Self in all his actions forever, then he becomes qualified for salvation. Though attaining such a state is a difficult task, after a long practice (in some cases it might take several human births) a stage comes when SO, in its purest form, is liberated and becomes capable of merging into the field of cosmic consciousness from where it originally started its journey, possibly with certain seeds of actions (SOAs) of previous births in it — a kind of impurity in SO.

Earlier, we have discussed (cf. Sections 3.5 and 7.3.3) mind-body interactions at the overlapping front of $\mathcal{M}$ and $\mathcal{G}$, now in the same vein one can develop the dynamics of exchanges between SO and $\mathcal{B}$ (i.e. between the Self and the non-Self). In this dynamics, it is the ego E that plays a dominant role all throughout. While the equilibriums attained in the former case provide satisfaction, happiness, peace, etc. at different stages, in the latter case, however, they guide an individual towards eternal pleasure, even though in steps. Such a dynamics is beautifully described in Vedic science[1] and we shall return to some of these concepts later.

13.1.2 REALIZATION AND SELF-REALIZATION

With a view to searching the "God-Centre" or the centre of consciousness inside the human body, the realization is discussed as a physiochemical process in Section 11.2.3. Definitely, the process of realization is much more complex than is discussed there in the spirit of objective science. In the present context, the process of realization of an element in WO ends up at the level of $\mathcal{B}$; of course it proceeds in the presence of consciousness — an attribute of SO, as the dressed M, I and E (cf. Chapter 8) play a role in it. For a scientist, the object to be realized belongs to the domain of outer world with reference to his inner EOLs. In particular, for him the observation process of a phenomenon ends up at the level of M. However, from the point of view of Vedic science there exists[2] a sequence of the seers and the seen,

1. As an important source of Vedic science, see for example, *Shri Yogavashishtha Bhasa* (Hindi) Pt. I and II, Tej Kumar Depot (Pvt) Ltd, Trilok Nath Road, Lucknow, 2003, and for other detailed works on the subject, see the citations in the next chapter.

2. See, for example *Vākya Sudhā* by Paramhans Yoganand, Belan Ganj, Agra; verse 1, viz. *rūpaṁ dr̥śyaṁ locanaṁ drak tādrasyaṁ draṣṭamānasaṁ, draṣyādivratiyaḥ sākṣī drageva na tu draṣyate*. That is, eyes are the seer of shape; mind is the seer of eyes ; soul (*sākṣī*) is the seer of mind, which is a particular state of the intellect. There is no seer of the (ultimate) soul. The same sequence holds for other senses of knowledge as well.

as WO(→B)→SEK→M(→I)→E(→SO). Here, no doubt the ultimate seer (i.e. the realizer) is SO through consciousness but basically it is E and the bracketed EOLs that have indirect roles to play in the process of realization.

But this is not the end of the story. The above type of realization is generally true with an extrovert person but for those who are introvert, wish to enter the domain of spirituality, and are desirous to know about the "ultimate," the object of realization becomes SO (i.e. Self) itself instead of $\mathcal{B}$ or its constituents including WO. What actually happens in this case is, the composite $\mathcal{B}$ plays a dual role as far as the mechanism of self-realization is concerned. While $\mathcal{B}$ does some sort of filtering of the fruits of action (FOAs) performed by a conscious individual on the interface of his $\mathcal{M}$ and $\mathcal{G}$ using again I and E to bear the same, it also germinates new seeds of action (SOAs) using M, I and E by way of dressing up itself with consciousness repeatedly, i.e. by remaining in the vicinity of SO. Note that these SOAs produce SPP if $\mathcal{B}$ is in the vicinity of SO and produce SNP if they are in the vicinity of WO and SEK. In what follows, we shall elaborate further on these roles of $\mathcal{B}$. While a scientist ends up at the realization, only a spiritualist, on the other hand, goes further for the realization of his Self, so-called Self-realization. For the latter, $\mathcal{B}$ is not only already enlightened by the presence of SO, but SO itself becomes the object of realization in the sense that his thinking and views about world order become quite different. Such a person notices the omnipresence of the same SO in all living Beings at every stage. These are a few symptoms of a self-realized person or of a man of perfection (cf. Section 4.1).

13.2 Exchanges in the Domain of Spirituality: The Composites $\mathcal{B}$ and $\mathcal{C}$

13.2.1 SEEDS AND FRUITS OF ACTION

Earlier, in Section 8.4 we have discussed the interactions inside the human Being, mainly between $\mathcal{G}$ and $\mathcal{M}$ and identified the causal body $\mathcal{C}$ with SO alone. But the fact is that SO (i.e. the Self) is the purest form of the innermost existence and $\mathcal{C}$ is a composite of SO and some dressed elements of $\mathcal{M}$ viz. $\mathcal{C}$ = {SO, some dressed elements of $\mathcal{M}$}, where the non-self $\mathcal{B}$ is already defined as $\mathcal{B}=\mathcal{M} \cup \mathcal{G}$. In fact whichever element of $\mathcal{M}$ (out of M, I and E) is highly dressed with the consciousness produces the corresponding *bhāva* or seed of action (SOA) in the non-Self, $\mathcal{B}$. The germination of this seed is guided by SPP and/or SNP for which the mindset of the individual is trained. While SPP produces the fruits of action (FOAs) in the domain of spirituality, SNP however produces fruits of action in the worldly domain. As a result the actions performed by EOLs can be in the visible form in the domain of WO and/or they can be in the invisible form in the domain of SO. The ones which are in the domain of SO are combined with SO to constitute $\mathcal{C}$ and thereby cause bondages of $\mathcal{B}$ with SO in the present as well as in future births.

On the other hand, FOAs of previous birth(s) are also enjoyed by b in the present birth. Note that all this is possible only with the human Being who has the freedom to germinate new SOAs in this birth itself, while enjoying the fruits (however good or bad in relative terms) of the seeds germinated in the previous birth(s). Further, it is the causal body that carries the FOAs (and at times SOAs as well) to the next life after death. In fact if $\mathcal{B}$ and SO are already detached in this life by suppressing or eliminating ego to its extreme limit, then there is nothing to be carried by SO and the latter, in its purest form now becomes fit to attain *mokṣa*. Such a mechanism does not go with non-humans who can only enjoy the fruits of deeds of their earlier birth(s) but cannot germinate new seeds at appropriate level to produce actions either in the present or in future birth(s), mainly because they lack in certain EOLs like a judicious intellect I. In what follows we discuss how the ego E plays a crucial role in the wide spectrum of functions of EOLs, particularly in realizing the Self SO and the non-Self $\mathcal{B}$ as the two distinct entities. Such a realization in some sense becomes the first step in the direction of *mokṣa*.

13.2.2 EXPRESSION AND SUPPRESSION OF EGO E IN THE FUNDAMENTAL PROCESSES

In Jainism and Vedic science the role of *ahaṁkāra* (a version of ego E) is discussed at great length. Here, however, we make a few pertinent observations on its role in human actions.

In Sanskrit language ego (E) means *ahaṁkāra* (=*ahaṁ*+*kāra*) implying the assumption that "I am the doer," i.e. an action which is rich with *ahaṁ* or "I-ism." This "I-ism" starts at the level of WO and continues through B, SEA, SEK, M, I and finally until SO. "I-ism" or "me-ism" is a kind of wrong belief carried by an individual by way of identifying the Self with the non-Self, i.e. SO by $\mathscr{B}$. But that is not true. This wrong belief has to be replaced with the right belief, i.e. by way of realizing SO and $\mathscr{B}$ as two distinct entities, of course, bound by the so-called "false" ego. While this wrong belief goes unnoticed to an individual, its replacement by right belief becomes rather impossible for him alone because the bondage between $\mathscr{B}$ and SO via ego is very strong and subtle. This becomes possible if the ego is highly suppressed or eliminated so as to enable SO and $\mathscr{B}$ to become free. At this stage, one normally needs guidance or *ātmajñāna* by an expert (so-called "Satguru" in the Indian context). Once such knowledge is achieved by a person, his attitude towards life and the lifestyle changes completely. In real sense, there does exist scarcity of such experts everywhere and at all times.

While the role of gross form of E ends up at the level of $\mathscr{B}$, its role at subtle level, however, continues beyond, i.e. up to the domain of SO. The suppression of this subtle form of E is really a difficult task; it expresses itself in a variety of ways. That expression and subsequent involvement of E becomes the root cause of all bondages in this world. For example, this subtle form of E prepares a ground in the individual to react to the respect and disrespect given to him, the fear and fearlessness developed in him, the fruits of right and wrong deeds done by him, the attachment and detachment created by him to worldly objects, etc. Other expressions of E generally are through desire, anger, greed, pride etc. shown by the person. A man of perfection (cf. Chapter 2), however, develops a habit to keep himself above all these pairs of opposites[3] by way of suppressing the subtle form of E.

In a fundamental process (attributed basically to functions of EOLs towards the success of an action) the EOL E appears in several incarnations in different domains of $\mathcal{G}$, $\mathcal{M}$ and $\mathcal{C}$, depending initially upon the nature of the seed and thought of action. (Note that the seed or *bhāva* is a certain combination of dressed E and M, and similarly the thought or *vicāra* is a certain combination of dressed E and I). Further, while the nature of seed and thought is responsible for the fruits of action at the end-point, it is derived from the systematics of pursuits (whether it is SPP or SNP) followed by the individual. These are the fruits of deeds of previous births and the new seeds germinated in this birth of the person that collectively force the person to follow either SPP or SNP or their certain combination. Also, the following of this systematics is a function of space, time and circumstances. Even the spatio-temporal durations for which a given systematics remains effective in the behaviour of the person, at times appears to be predecided. In any case, once the follow-up of systematics starts appearing in the actions of a person, then the fruits of actions are bound to be there in the respective domains. Throughout this game of EOLs, the ego E or its different dressed versions $\tilde{E}$, $\tilde{\tilde{E}}$, . . . $\tilde{E}^{(n)}$ (cf. Chapter 8) play crucial roles visibly or invisibly.

13.2.3 PEACE AND ETERNAL PLEASURE AS MOTTOS OF LIFE

Expression and suppression of ego E in the entire spectrum of fundamental processes have to be such that certain milestones

3. In fact keeping oneself above all the pairs of opposites is a step in the direction of spirituality. Such a habit, if developed, not only helps the person in realizing $\mathcal{B}$ and SO as two distinct entities but also converts him to become a "man of perfection" or a *yogī* in the limiting case, and it becomes possible only after a considerable practice. For the symptoms of such a person see, for example, *SMBG*, chapter 12, verses 17-19, or the Section 12.5.3.

like pleasure, satisfaction, peace, eternal pleasure, etc. in the journey of b have to be achieved. Out of these milestones peace, as the net outcome of equilibrium of interactions (cf. Section 8.4.3) within the non-Self $\mathcal{B}$, and eternal pleasure, as the resultant of a "particular" equilibrium of interactions between $\mathcal{B}$ and $\mathcal{C}$, are important and, in fact, they should be the mottos in one's life. In some sense, the former is the result of expression of E in various actions in the domains of $\mathcal{G}$ and $\mathcal{M}$, whereas the latter is the result of suppression of E in the domain of $\mathcal{C}$. While we postpone some of these discussions to the next chapter, one thing is clear that the achieving of these milestones depends on various factors, like (i) one's own efforts, (ii) the development of his FOUs in terms of knowledge and subsequently on the quality and quantity of knowledge, and (iii) *Saṁyoga* translated as scientific circumstantial evidence (SCE). In fact the discussion of factor (iii) will be continued in Section 13.4 and note that the factor (i) does not go without factors (ii).

As a matter of fact, unless one makes efforts nothing can be achieved in this life. Now the question is, the efforts for what? As an answer to this question, we have already discussed in detail, in Sections 4.4 and 4.5, and the same is however not independent from factor (ii). Although the spirit of factor (ii) is also discussed there in Section 4.1 yet we add a few more pertinent remarks here.

It may be mentioned that not only the human Beings but all Beings in general are born with some minimum knowledge enabling their survival. However, as mentioned before, human species is specific as far as the achieving of further knowledge is concerned. With regard to quantity of knowledge different disciplines have been developed in modern times by and large corresponding to each EOL and its functioning. This knowledge corresponding to each EOL can broadly be classified as (a) peripheral (observation-based) and (b) basic (based on the underlying theory or philosophy of working). Even in the second aspect of knowledge there are varieties of ideas which inspire and provide explanation to factor (i). However, out of the entire gamut of theories the ones which connect and lead to spirituality are generally appreciated by wise persons.

13.3 The Question of "Actual Doer" of Actions: The Role of Deities

Many intricacies involved in performing an action by an individual using his EOLs are already discussed in Chapter 4 within the framework of patomic model. Note that the *saṅkalpa*s discussed there are basically the *bhāva* or the seeds of action — a concept used in the previous section. The mechanism of germination of an SOA, its growing with the help of various EOLs and finally its giving rise to FOAs, particularly after following a systematics of pursuits are beautifully described in Vedic science. No doubt, the whole mechanism works in a self-consistent manner (cf. Section 4.3.2) but the fact is that the ego E comes in the way in associating the doer-ship of the action with "I-ism." Note that for an action performed in the domain of $\mathcal{G}$ and accordingly the fruits are obtained, it is the mind M that has given birth to *saṅkalpa*s, then it is the intellect I that has given proper direction towards the success of the action, next is the memory and experience — certain aspects of E, that in turn, have provided the quality of success of the action following the appropriate systematics of pursuits. In spite of all this there remains the "I-ism" aspect of E that claims the doer-ship of the action and this is the root cause of bondage between $\mathcal{B}$ and SO. For many of us this bondage appears in the form of pairs of opposites, like pain and pleasure, sorrow and joy, fear and fearlessness, attachment and detachment, failure and success, etc. and the same are not only carried out deep inside $\mathcal{B}$ (in terms of higher order of dressing of EOLs with consciousness) but also leave an impact on $\mathcal{C}$ and are thereby responsible for the exchanges between $\mathcal{B}$ and SO. Then comes the "art of suppressing" E or "I-ism" which, in turn, will liberate SO in the limiting case.

Now the question is, who is the "actual doer" of an action in this whole self-consistent and self-contained process? Obviously, the answer is "none." It is the "true knowledge" (*ātmajñāna*) that guides the individual at every step, provided that individual is a conscious seeker (cf. verses (4.1) to (4.6)). Next question is how to achieve this true knowledge — either by a human guide who himself has attained the best and the highest possible in the domain of spirituality, i.e. a *satguru* or else one should wait for the appropriate birth and time in the cycle of rebirths and life spans, provided the person continues his efforts and goes on improving them in each successive birth. The unfortunate part is that many of us know this art of living but really find it difficult to follow in the midst of this mundane living and with so many odds.

It is a common practice that if one surrenders himself totally before "someone," then that "someone" is expected to take care of all liabilities of the person who surrenders, provided the "someone" is capable enough for this purpose. It does not mean that the surrendering person becomes weak or handicapped by doing so, rather he draws power by remaining in the shadow of that "someone" and as and when the person is in trouble physically or mentally, he approaches the "someone." By doing so the person passes a peaceful life — a motto of life. How would be the life of the person in the absence of that "someone"; it will continue except for the fact that the person now might feel more insecure and worried. Note that such an insecurity or worry could also have been there if the surrendering person knows the limitations of the "someone" but those will be at somewhat lower level. Exactly the same is the role of a deity in one's life. If the deity is not all capable but has limitations, then a devotee gets peace only on a limited front.

Now comes the question of faith and belief. It is the degree of faith or of belief that makes the deity all powerful or limitless. In this respect, the form or the nature of deity is immaterial. In scientific terms, this, in fact, becomes the case of conditioning the mindset or developing certain specific neuronal networks (cf. Section 11.2.3 and the experiment discussed there). This is not the end of the story rather the role of scientific circumstantial evidence or of *saṁyoga* also appears in this whole process (cf. Section 13.4).

As a matter of fact, the devotee is benefited from deity only up to certain extent. Then, after a great devotion a stage comes when the devotee becomes capable of developing his FOUs sufficiently so that he himself starts feeling as a part of deity as far as the omnipotence of the deity is concerned. This stage of devotee is worth comparing with a true knower, i.e. *ātmajñānī*.

13.4 "Saṁyoga" and Scientific Circumstantial Evidences (SCEs)

13.4.1 THE PARAMETER σ IN THE MINDSET-FUNCTION AND ITS NEW ROLE

In Section 8.8, we have elaborated on the meanings of the words circumstances and environment and discussed their effect on the working of the mindset of an individual. While circumstances (σ) appear out of dynamics in the domain of $\mathcal{M}$, the environment (ε) is the result of dynamics in the domain of $\mathcal{G}$. However, at times it is found that actions (and so are their fruits) get drastically affected by another hidden and uncontrollable factor which can be attributed to deeds performed in previous birth(s) and the fruits of which are carried over to the present birth through $\mathcal{C}$, i.e. the *prārabdha* as discussed earlier. In other words, at times certain situations occur all of a sudden without anticipating or they were not the part of the planning but they do occur. Such situations are accounted for by a factor f and they do affect the actions and the fruits thereof. Thus, the parameter σ used in earlier chapters needs to be redefined in a generalized sense as Σ and the same in fact will now include circumstances, environment and a factor (f) assumed to be responsible for the FOAs of previous birth(s)). They collectively constitute the so-called *saṁyoga* (denoted by Σ). The role of this factor particularly becomes important and realizable in the processes involving highly dressed inner EOLs and where the roles arising out of a careful accounting of other factors like σ and ε becomes inadequate towards the success (or failure) of an action. Therefore, for the fundamental processes taking place in the overlapping region of $\mathcal{M}$ and C the parameter Σ instead of σ need to be used where $\Sigma=\Sigma(\varepsilon, \sigma, f)$ with all the three ε, σ and f are the functions of space, time and meditation μ. In some sense Σ offers a scientific circumstantial evidence (SCE) in the presence of which an action is performed. (Scientific in the sense that all possible physical, mental and spiritual conditions under which an action proceeds, are thought over and that too in a logical manner and in the spirit of verses (2.4) and (2.5)).

As a matter of fact, an account of ε, σ and f is linked not only with the orders of dressing of individual's EOLs (through μ) but also with the development of his FOUs. For example, in the context of a common man it is found that the role of the factors appears in reverse order as his FOUs are not sufficiently developed, i.e. he will immediately attribute the success (or failure) to f, then after a little thought he will attribute to σ or even much later to ε. Thus, as knowledge becomes more and more refined the understanding of world order changes.

13.4.2 "KNOWLEDGE" CAN OVERCOME "IGNORANCE" LIKE PEELING OF COVERS OF AN ONION

Dressing of EOLs with consciousness is tantamount to (i) increase in the meditation parameter, μ, (ii) development of FOUs, (iii) enhancement of knowledge (in quality and quantity) over ignorance, and (iv) thereby providing finer and finer experiences and consequently resulting in a refined behaviour. While the discussion of other points can be found elsewhere in the previous chapters, the point (iii) needs an elaboration here.

Note that the absence of knowledge is ignorance and the quality of knowledge also matters in the success of an action. In view of the discussion in Section 4.1.1 (cf. verse (4.2)) knowledge of the Self is supreme and the Self appears like the innermost part of an onion. The different layers of the onion can be considered as different layers of ignorance and the peeling of them one by one as one proceeds from outside to inside, is equivalent to saying that knowledge of Self becomes finer and finer. While the outer layers may correspond to the worldly knowledge pertaining to the domain of $\mathcal{G}$ or its constituent, the next set of layers can be considered as corresponding to the domain of $\mathcal{M}$ and finally the inner layers correspond to the knowledge of the domain of $\mathcal{C}$ or spirituality. Even if one goes on peeling the layers of an onion one does not find a core inside, it is all the same; in the same way as one searches for the soul inside the human Being but never finds it. However, one feels it because the "whole" Being exists and works only because of it in the same way as onion exists even without any attracting core inside. Thus, the onion is like the non-Self $\mathcal{B}$ and the entity that allows its existence and its layers is like SO — the Self. With regard to the quality of knowledge we shall remark further in Chapter 14.

13.4.3 ROLE OF SCEs IN THE ENTIRE SPECTRUM OF ACTIONS

As representative examples, we discuss below some situations in which the actions and the fruits of actions thereof are largely affected by *saṁyoga*. This happens mainly in the overlapping domains of (a) $\mathcal{G}$ and $\mathcal{M}$, (b) $\mathcal{M}$ and $\mathcal{C}$, and (c) of all the three $\mathcal{G}$, $\mathcal{M}$ and $\mathcal{C}$. These are the roles of the factor f or in general of Σ in the form of fate, destiny, luck, God's desire, etc. which produce different FOAs from the ones expected, in spite of providing the same (!) efforts at the input level and the physical and/or mental conditions. As a matter of fact, the role of these factors though significant is definitely beyond one's own control as far as the success of an action is concerned. Therefore, one should rely more on the remaining part of Σ during the proceedings of an action.

(a) Actions in the overlapping domain of $\mathcal{G}$ and $\mathcal{M}$: All the students sitting in the same class room, taught by the same teacher and provided with the same environment, do not achieve the same success in the examination mainly because their efforts made at the mental level and their attitudes towards the same goal are different. Not only the deeds of this birth but also of previous birth(s) are responsible in producing different results (fruits of action) for them. The difference is noticed even between twins in this regard, then what to say of real sisters or brothers born at different space-time points.

(b) Actions in the overlapping domain of $\mathcal{M}$ and $\mathcal{C}$: Each teacher, when given the same topic to teach, teaches differently while other physical conditions are kept the same. This is because each of them has developed his FOUs differently in terms of experience, grasp, and expertise in the subject. This can again be related to the deeds and efforts made by the teacher in this and previous birth(s) in understanding the subject matter.

(c) Actions in the overlapping domains of $\mathcal{G}$, $\mathcal{M}$ and $\mathcal{C}$ pair-wise and otherwise: In this case the observer maintains a constant watch on the entire activities of the person whose $\mathcal{G}$, $\mathcal{M}$ and $\mathcal{C}$ are going to interact themselves with reference to certain actions(s). For the warden of a hostel, for an in-charge of an orphan home or for a manager of an *āśrama* or the likes, the behaviour of residents who otherwise are living under the same physical conditions, is found to be different. In fact in this case the same given physical conditions are perceived differently and accordingly different experiences are gathered in constituting $\mathcal{C}$ over a period of time.

13.5 Concluding Discussion

While the dynamics of exchanges between $\mathcal{G}$ and $\mathcal{M}$ in terms of their constituents is discussed earlier (cf. Section 8.4.3), in this chapter an attempt is made to give some glimpses of dynamics of rather subtle interactions between $\mathcal{M}$ and $\mathcal{C}$. Recall that these types of dynamics are described with respect to the meditation variable μ alone instead of the time variable as used in physical theories (cf. Appendix E). The ideas presented in this chapter in some sense show the path to those truth seekers who are desirous of entering into the domain of spirituality. Moreover, the spirituality is going to be the talk of the day as it is capable enough to impart the universal values in the society (cf. Section 12.2).

After introducing the concepts of the Self (SO) and the non-Self ($\mathcal{B}$), the phenomenon of Self-realization is explained. These concepts of Self and non-Self then help in describing the dynamics of interactions in the domain of spirituality. These interactions are mediated mainly through the ego E at subtle level. While the expressions of E following SNP are responsible for the strong binding of $\mathcal{B}$ and SO, its suppression following SPP, however, provides a path to *mokṣa* by way of dissociating SO from $\mathcal{B}$. No doubt, peace for a person whose acts are confined to the domain of $\mathcal{B}$, and eternal pleasure or joy for a person who is desirous to attain *mokṣa* be the motto of life, a "man of perfection" however manages both despite his involvement in this world. While the concept of *guṇa guṇeṣu vartantu* of *SMBG* (cf. verse (2.5) and Section 4.3.2) for a conscious seeker defines an "actual doer" in the domain of spirituality, however, needs a generalization in the form of *saṁyoga*, as the role of hidden and unmanageable factor f in Σ becomes important. (Note that a part of f is attributed to *prārabdha*). Further, as the variable μ takes higher and higher values, the quality of knowledge improves by way of progressively breaking the layers of ignorance on SO (cf. Section 13.4.2).

A few remarks about the processes of introspection, realization and Self-realization in the present context are in order. In introspection a highly dressed intellect ($\tilde{I}^{(n)}$) analyses the actions performed by the inner and outer EOLs of a person and identifies the faults or shortcomings in actions in the light of the pursuits followed (SNP or SPP). In realization, however, a person digests and stores the knowledge about an object or a process taking place in the domain of $\mathcal{G}$ and/or $\mathcal{M}$ using highly dressed mind ($\tilde{M}^{(n)}$) intellect ($\tilde{I}^{(n)}$) and ego ($\tilde{E}^{(n)}$) irrespective of the nature of pursuit. In fact the value of n (i.e. the order of dressing) required for this purpose could be different not only for different EOLs but also for different individuals and accordingly defines a degree of introspection or of realization. While this dressing of EOLs in the higher order, particularly that of inner ones, continues, they constantly draw consciousness from the source SO for this purpose. A stage comes when the highly dressed non-Self $\mathcal{B}$, i.e. $\tilde{\mathcal{B}}^{(n)}$ in the limit $n \to \infty$ and ego $E \to 0$ starts behaving like SO — the source of consciousness itself. This is the true state of Self-realization; otherwise for any arbitrary but finite value of n, the Self-realization remains essentially partial and provides only a stage of satisfaction (cf. next chapter) but not the stage for *mokṣa*.

Recall that it is the ego E that does not allow the separation of $\mathcal{B}$ from SO. The more one endeavours to attain *mokṣa*, the sense of separateness only gets reinforced. Finally a comment on the subtlety of E is necessary. A proud and status-conscious person, full of vanity, demands exclusive treatment and such a person goes on throwing his weight and tantrums around. The person becomes egocentric and this may cause a variety of aberrations in his behaviour and character as he is likely to follow the SNP. It is under such conditions that ego becomes a trait which earns unfavourable views and is decried. But the same trait, employed gainfully (i.e. following the SPP), urges a person to do his best, to appreciate even the humblest of professions and he wins. A subtle interplay of ego also appears when one describes his experiences.

14

Summary, Conclusions and Future Prospects

14.1 Summary and Concluding Remarks

WITH a hope that philosophy can be taught in the class room in the same way as physical sciences, the ideas in the preceding chapters are developed in a specific style so that they become suggestive in further developing a quantitative approach to understand a phenomenon in the entire gamut of human experiences and behaviour. It is for a reader to judge the merit of this modest approach which, in some sense, is based on Vedāntic thinking. In essence, the efforts have been to quantify the philosophy of *karma* (the theory of human actions) as described in Vedic sciences with reference to an individual. What has been investigated in previous chapters is in fact the science of philosophy (cf. Section 1.4) and not the philosophy as such. Within this framework many philosophies of the world can be accommodated and analysed.

After providing some basics of Western and Eastern thoughts in this context (of course, within the limitations of the author) the role of concepts and facts which at times dominate the behaviour of a conscious person, is emphasized. The limitations of modern science in describing some of these aspects of human behaviour are repeatedly pointed out at different places and in different contexts in the book (cf. Chapters 2 to 6). In Part II (cf. Chapters 7 to 10) the workability of the tools of Vedic sciences reviewed in Part I, is demonstrated by way of providing certain relevant mathematical frameworks for different phenomena in human behaviour in general and for those appearing in the day-to-day life of an individual in particular. In fact there have been efforts to quantify the interactions among humans and among some selective non-human species within a unified but specific framework. This in turn provides explanations of various phenomena that take place in the behaviour of different interacting species. The viability of the present approach from the point of view of its further applications and its possible links with modern scientific researches on this front, are discussed in Part III (cf. Chapters 11-13). For readers who may be interested in details of certain ideas that could not be elaborated in the text, six Appendices given may prove useful for this purpose.

Since the concluding remarks made in various chapters earlier pertain mainly to the contents of the corresponding chapters, this perhaps will not suffice as far as the main message of the book is concerned. Therefore, in this chapter we highlight further some more tenets of Vedāntic thoughts in the light of verses (4.1) to (4.3). As a matter of fact, from the stone-age to the present scientific age there always existed some persons in a society who had thought and still think about the existences of the world and its habitat after lifting themselves above the daily mundane living, or who acted and continue to act as the friend, philosopher and guide of society. This thinking brings in them a kind of curiosity to know about themselves and about the working of Nature or the Universe as a whole (or, they are *jijñāsu* or truth seeker in the language of *SMBG*). In this endeavour, as the history of science reveals, a great deal of discoveries are focused around making an easy access to livelihood, survival and a comfortable/luxurious life. However, there exists only a little percentage of advancements of knowledge pertaining to the search of ultimate truth/reality in Nature. This ultimate truth could be about the knowledge of the Self or about the working of Nature, or about their interplay; however, all this knowledge finally merges into one in the limit.

Further efforts have been made to look for certain minimal number of principles on which the science of Self or of Nature works. In modern times, no doubt there have been considerable progress in exploring the philosophy of (objective) science from this point of view, but similar efforts have been missing on the front of (subjective) science of Self. If the latter becomes available, this will further add to a better life of human race on this planet. The present book is an effort in this direction; particularly the viability of a Vedāntic framework in terms of EOLs and their functions is emphasized all through in this regard. While the demonstration of this viability is not yet complete as far as the quantification of various concepts and phenomena in human behaviour is concerned, whatever (little) is demonstrated in this book can be taken as a guide for future studies. There appears to be a need to employ better mathematical tools to explore and explain further intricacies involved in human behaviour and actions.

Here, we once again remark on the categorization of quality of knowledge and highlight in brief its successes in the subjective and objective domains of human actions. This in turn will motivate better the future applications of the present framework and ideas.

14.2 Science of Eternal Pleasure: Knowledge Pertaining to Three Stages of Satisfaction

As we have seen, there do exist certain fundamental processes behind every action performed by an individual in the domains of gross, micro and causal bodies. One can easily categorize and objectify the efforts made by an individual towards the success of an action in the three stages corresponding to gross, micro and casual bodies. These three stages, namely *worldly pleasure* at the level of gross body $\mathcal{G}$≡{WO, B, SE}, *peace* at the level of micro-body $\mathcal{M}$≡{M, I, E}, and *ātmānanda* at the level of soul or of casual-body $\mathcal{C}$≡{SO}, while form the part of *eternal pleasure* (*mokṣa* or salvation) the knowledge of ways and means to attain these stages constitutes the *science of eternal pleasure*. In fact these three stages define the best and perhaps the highest objective in one's life out of the actions he performs in the three corresponding domains and this accordingly provides satisfaction to him or defines the purpose of life to him. Worldly *pleasure*, *peace* and *ātmānanda*, in fact are the different aspects of the same eternal pleasure (see *fig*. 14.1) which one draws (or realizes) in stages as the fruits of his actions or efforts. As a matter of fact, for a conscious person his actions or efforts are directed to achieve these aspects of eternal pleasure in one way or the other, maybe step by step, as they define the "best" in each domain of action.

Also, these stages of satisfaction are linked with the three components of a religion,[1] namely practice (*karmakāṇḍa*), methodology (*upāsanā*) and knowledge (*jñāna*) by way of identifying one's own actions in the three realms. One draws worldly pleasure by performing the best in the domain of practical life or in a society; one draws peace adopting the best of methodology towards the performance of an action; and it is the knowledge component of a religion that assists in drawing the *ātmānanda*. Finally, over and above all of them is the knowledge of Self that leads to eternal pleasure (salvation). In view of such an identification of components of a religion, all religions can be analysed in this common scientific framework and as a result their conflict with a scientific thinking will minimize.[2]

Next comes the question of efforts *vis-à-vis* the degree of achievement and the duration for which these objectives by an individual are being achieved as a result of his efforts. In fact in the mundane living of an individual these aspects go side by side but only temporarily. Except the *yogī* category of persons, for all the rest the attainment of these aspects remains temporary and space-bound. Only a *yogī* enjoys the eternal pleasure or joy in a true sense. Also, the degree of achievement of these aspects of satisfaction as such is not quantifiable. For a common man while it remains mostly subjective — full of expectations and desires, in the objective domain however once again it depends on space, time and circumstances. No doubt the degree of

1. Radhey Shyam Kaushal, *The Philosophy of the Vedanta: A Modern Scientific Perspective*, Delhi: India Book Centre, 1994, chapter 6.

2. Radhey Shyam Kaushal, 1994, op. cit.

achievement of these aspects also depends on the development of one's FOUs and accordingly on the preparation of his mindset, but sooner or later everyone wishes to achieve such states of stability or equilibrium in some or in all domains of functions of EOLs; otherwise for him the whole purpose of life will be lost. In other words, it is necessary for the survival of the individual who is constantly making efforts for any of these objectives; otherwise for him a state of suicide or collapse does not remain distant at any point of time.

Although many centres of spiritual learning in the world are propagating the messages in this respect, we briefly remark here on how the achievement of these objectives of life becomes easier to an individual, particularly after having a feel for the knowledge of the fundamental processes involved behind each of his actions from the preceding chapters.

14.3 Mundane Living and Achieving the Stages of Satisfaction by an Individual

First we highlight once again the stages of knowledge and then discuss their role in achieving the stages of satisfaction or finally the eternal pleasure.

14.3.1 STAGES OF KNOWLEDGE: FROM OBJECTIVE WORLD TO SUBJECTIVE AWARENESS

Note that Vedic science emphasizes on two broad classes of knowledge. (a) the knowledge of the manifest, and (b) the knowledge of the unmanifest. As a matter of fact the knowledge of the unmanifest is as rich as (or perhaps more than) the knowledge of the manifest about which the entire gamut of disciplines of modern science focuses. On the other hand, the knowledge of manifest is a stepping stone towards enhancing awareness.

Recently, Deepak Ranade[3] has nicely summarized the stages of knowledge which, while conforming to tenets of Vedic science

3. Deepak Ranade, "Stages of Knowledge for Becoming Aware", *Times of India*, Speaking Tree Column, 17 December 2007.

through patomic model in some sense, also appear to appeal to a scientific mind. In particular, his remarks on the obstacles coming in the way of attaining these stages by an individual are interesting and logical. Being a neurosurgeon, Ranade starts analysing the knowledge pertaining to objective (physical or external) world at the level of brain in the spirit of Chapter 11 and then discusses in stages the categories of knowledge pertaining to different EOLs including B and SE. Corresponding to the roles of inner and outer EOLs in attaining knowledge about the visible and invisible in Nature, we categorize the stages of knowledge into four possibilities, namely (a) knowledge of the manifest by the manifest, (b) knowledge of the unmanifest by the manifest, (c) knowledge of the manifest by the unmanifest and (d) knowledge of the unmanifest by the un-manifest. As a matter of fact the inner EOLs, M, I, E and also SO, remain unmanifest as far as the scientific instruments for their detection are concerned. These four possibilities happen to coincide with the four categories of persons in this world as discussed in Chapter 1 and also elsewhere,[4] on the basis of development of their FOUs, namely common man, scientist, philosopher, and *yogī*, respectively.

(a) Knowledge of the manifest by the manifest: This happens with a common man who is not able to realize "invisible" beyond "visible" in the field of WO and hardly uses his inner EOLs for this purpose. Such a person has his own view about the world order and attains the knowledge accordingly.

(b) Knowledge of the unmanifest by the manifest: Before the development of inner EOLs or of the FOUs in general, an individual starts attaining this aspect of knowledge immediately after birth. While a great deal of knowledge of the manifest in recent times has become quantifiable in scientific terms, yet a considerable amount of it needs to be perceived in a subjective manner. In the words of Ranade, "science is essentially related to spatio-temporal grid. It is seemingly restrained by the confines

4. Radhey Shyam Kaushal, *Structural Analogies in Understanding Nature*, New Delhi: Anamaya Publishers, 2003, chapter 1.

of cause and effect. Any theory has to be reinforced by experimental verification and then ratified by adding the attributes of repeatability and predictability, mediated by measurable parameter, which again are slaves of tangibles governed by the senses." With regard to the analysis of data so collected in objective science, let us see how the brain functions in the words of Ranade, "the brain is ever endeavouring to learn, comprehend and understand. It is being flooded with information that it processes at astonishing speed. Processing data implies prioritizing the data and assigning meaning to it. Interpretation of data requires a highly developed intellect. Data is ubiquitous. Right from the radio waves emitted by celestial bodies from a few million light years away, to the feel of our clothing against our bodies, we are being bombarded by data." Besides this (mechanical) working by the machinery or by the tools of outer EOLs, there is subjective component involved at each stage in the process of learning about the world order, i.e. the "realization" which in certain proportion exists in all the four stages of knowledge. In this respect, Ranade continues,[5] however, only in terms of the EOL, intellect, alone as

> sense organs can navigate the intellect only within the "waters" of the tangible. Once it touches the shores of the intangible the sense organs are powerless. The realms of the intangible may be delved into only by awareness which is supra-sensory and out of the spatio-temporal Cartesian grid (STCG). The reason why this aspect of knowledge is termed as "realization" implies knowledge which already exists but which we are unaware of. The knowledge of the form shifts focus to awareness. Awareness is independent of subject-object bifurcation. Reasoning, deduction and investigation are meaningless tools which only obfuscate.

However, the roles of other EOLs, like M and E are equally important in this subjective domain of learning.

As emphasized earlier (cf. Chapter 3), the understanding of Nature in modern science is generally not permitted to cross

5. Deepak Ranade, op. cit.

the border of STCG. But that should not be the case; rather the role of inner EOLs (i.e. of inner unmanifest) needs to be incorporated in a complete analysis of the data taken in the field of WO. This is what a "perfect scientist" needs to do and the same will fulfil his quest for understanding the complete truth prevailing in Nature.

(c) Knowledge of the manifest by the unmanifest: This stage of knowledge generally goes with the philosopher category of persons in the sense that they make use of their fully developed inner EOLs to understand a limited domain of WO, i.e. the outer manifest. Again, Ranade[6] puts these ideas in an effective form,

> The knowledge of the manifest is a stepping stone to enhancing awareness. By knowing what you are not, you get to know what you are. If you cannot fathom the manifest, then you cannot even dream the unmanifest. The journey to realization involves travelling over a diverse terrain. Each distinct terrain requires commensurate vehicle. The vehicle of reason used to traverse the *terra firma* of tangibility needs to be abandoned when one has to take to the aerial journey of enhanced awareness.

This describes another dimension of development of FOUs.

(d) Knowledge of the unmanifest by the unmanifest: Whether it is the unmanifest of the outer world or of the inner EOLs of a "receiver," none of these can stand on its own. For understanding both, first the understanding of manifest of the outer world and then that of the outer EOLs becomes a prerequisite. In other words, the knowledge of the unmanifest by the unmanifest is the case corresponding to knowing complete outer world by a complete and (ideally) "perfect" receiver. This kind of knowledge is definitely beyond the subject-object domain and perhaps the highest one, hopefully possessed by a *yogī* category of persons in order to attain salvation.

---

6. Deepak Ranade, op. cit.

14.3.2 STAGES OF SATISFACTION VERSUS STAGES OF KNOWLEDGE

Satisfaction is a subjective concept which one feels but cannot be quantified. Even its four stages mentioned above are not sharply defined and so are the stages of knowledge. Knowledge in any form is always useful in performing an action, particularly when it concerns the positive pursuits (cf. Section 4.4) in life. Knowledge is necessary but not sufficient in achieving success in the fruits of an action whether the action belongs to the domain of WO or of SO (i.e. the domain of spirituality) or in the domains of other EOLs between these extremes. In performing journey from the domain of WO to that of SO, the conscious Being b (cf. patomic model) undergoes different stages of development of his FOUs in the light of knowledge he receives from the external agencies or he realizes within.

Although there may be exceptions, by and large each of us starts receiving knowledge since birth, first with the developments of B and SE and later that of M and I and the same keeps on storing in E for a conscious person. All this is in addition to the one which one gets out of *prārabdha*. Accordingly, one achieves worldly pleasure first, then peace and later *ātmānanda*. Note that these stages of satisfaction, once achieved, are the functions of space, time and circumstances. Also, the duration for which any one, two or all the three are realized within remains finite. It is only after a long practice and patience for a considerable period of time (which again depends on the ways and means an individual follows or is trained for with regard to the art of living), some or all the three stages become time-independent or eternal for an individual. When such a state of mind of an individual continues beyond the spatio-temporal domain, then he becomes fit for the eternal pleasure or salvation, and he(!), in fact, enjoys(!) the same(!). (Exclamatory signs here after the words "he", "enjoys" and "same" require special attention as the author has yet to pass through such a state.) As a matter of fact, who enjoys what? When all this inside and outside is the same — cosmic consciousness — an absolute Reality.

At this point it is worthwhile to recall once again the stages described in *fig*. 4.1 in the path of a conscious person who is trying to achieve the highest. In fact even a common man can raise himself to the state of highest perfection by following the steps described there.

It may be mentioned that the man of perfection or truly liberated soul of *fig*. 4.1 or cosmic consciousness or eternal pleasure are the synonyms of the absolute reality in Nature. Not only in the actions performed by EOLs but also in the dynamics of EOLs itself this absolute reality manifests at every stage, of course in varying proportions in terms of its so-called subjective and objective components. At the end-point, the former provides peace to an individual. In this case the Being has the tendency to remain in the domain of SO by way of

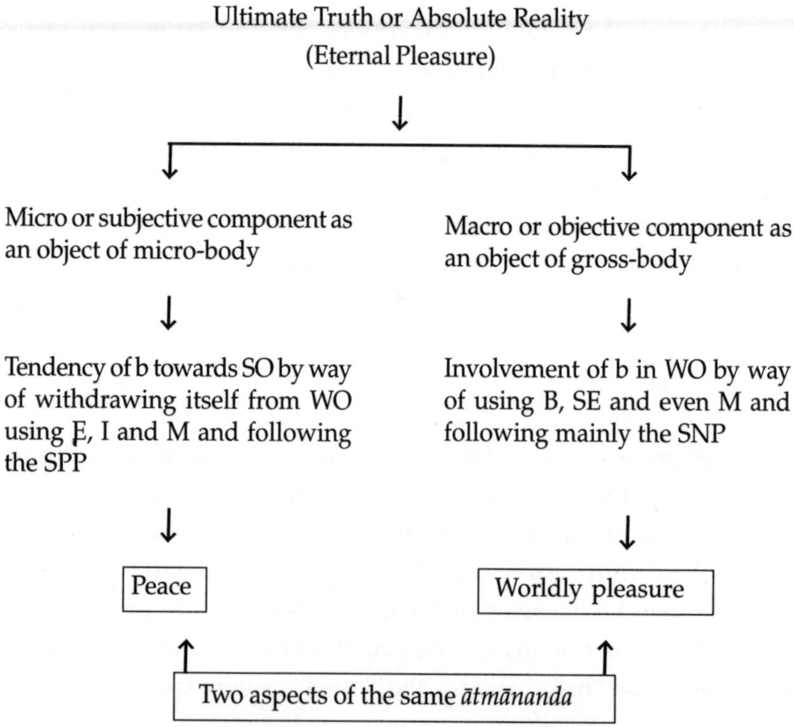

fig. 14.1: Eternal pleasure and its manifestation through peace, worldly pleasure and *ātmānanda*.

withdrawing itself from WO and following the SPP (cf. Section 4.4). On the other hand, the objective component of the absolute reality keeps on providing worldly pleasure to an individual at different levels and stages by way of involvement of b in the WO through B, SE and even M and mainly after following the SNP. Schematically, these two end-points of the actions of EOLs, namely peace and worldly pleasure are shown in *fig*. 14.1 as the two aspects of the same stage of satisfaction, i.e. *ātmānanda*. Note that the two aspects have different but related spatio-temporal existence.

14.4 Future Prospects

What we have explored in the present work concerns the identification of certain EOLs in a human Being and their role in the dynamics of human actions. As far as the attempts to quantify the Vedic science are concerned, the main motivation behind this package, only a ground-level work has been done here. A further fine-tuning of various aspects of this kind of modelling and the associated analytical methods, missing so far from the point of view of a modern scientific mind, is necessary, particularly in view of the available sub-categories or sub-classifications of EOLs and their roles in human actions. Of course, some of them have already been accommodated in the present scheme of study by way of considering different orders of dressing of EOLs with consciousness (cf. *dvikaraṇa, trikaraṇa* and *pañcīkaraṇa* rules in Chapters 8 and 9).

No doubt, various verses of *SMBG* or of Upaniṣads constitute the so-called Vedic science and describe the purest of the pure knowledge of the Self but when the question of their applications in the behavioural domain comes, an analogy[7] is worth citing here. That is, as the concepts of pure mathematics like the abstract system, groups, vector spaces, fields, etc. and the derived theorems of geometry have very wide applications in the fields of applied mathematics, physical sciences and engineering the same is the case of verses of *SMBG* and of Upaniṣads in the day-

7. Radhey Shyam Kaushal, 2003, op. cit.

to-day behavioural domain of a human Being. Thus, the concepts discussed and analysed in the book can have very wide applications and these verses can have different meanings depending on the circumstances. From this point of view, we briefly highlight below certain fronts of growing knowledge where the present scheme of study can be continued and which lead to some viable applications in the day-to-day life.

14.4.1 ON THE FRONT OF QUANTIFICATION

What we have provided in this book is a kind of flow chart of (working) machinery responsible for the fundamental processes that take place inside a (human) Being during his performance of an action in the outer world. But this is not sufficient since the human actions constituting his behaviour are more intriguing, intricate and subtle than the ones visualized by the author in different contexts here for the purposes of quantification. Therefore, further fine-tuning of the models and the processes discussed in this work is necessary. In addition to several other improvements discussed in various chapters, the role of *PM*s (cf. Appendix D), in particular (i) in patomic model and the associated EOLs through *tanmātra*s and (ii) in mechanisms responsible for interactions with physical world and also with other Beings need to be quantified appropriately so as to make the science of astrology more precise.

In some contexts, although we have discussed the fine-tuning of EOLs in terms of dressings with consciousness (ef. *dvikaraṇa, trikaraṇa* and *pañcīkaraṇa* rules, Chapter 8) the fact is that the discussion of such a fine-tuning at a deeper level has been avoided. However, Vedic sciences (or for that matter say Jainism) are rich enough in providing the information for such a fine-tuning not only on EOLs but also on their interactions with outer world. Even delicate acts of an individual could not be touched upon and the same need to be accommodated in the present scheme. For example, in the inner domain besides the existence of *mahātattva* and/or *citta*, several varieties of M, I and

E are discussed.[8, 9, 10, 11] Similarly, in the outer domain sub-varieties of SE (besides SEA and SEK) and of B (in terms of inner biological organs) in different environments of WO are known. Inclusion of such aspects will perhaps make the present framework more useful and viable.

Certain glimpses of the use of modern mathematics in some contexts in Chapters 8 and 9 are given but the fact is that there is a need to use full-fledged mathematical tools for further quantification of the underlying philosophy. It is quite possible that the existing mathematical tools may not suffice for this purpose and newer tools have to be discovered because the underlying processes depart heavily from the conventional physical ones in terms of non-centrality, anharmonicity, non-linearity, closeness of the system, complexity, etc. The present framework will however act as a basis for further such developments. In the author's opinion, such studies will definitely bring in a better predictive power of the present framework as far as the studies of human behaviour are concerned.

14.4.2 ON THE FRONT OF ANALYSIS

At present times there is a huge accumulation of data in human and animal psychologies and also in social sciences. Study of this data is generally carried out using an analysis based on models that are derived empirically, and different models are found to work well in different domains of studies. The application of the framework suggested in this work will

---

8. *Vivekacūḍāmaṇi*, Śrī Ādiśaṅkarācārya Racit, tr. in Hindi by Muni Lal, Gorakhpur: Gita Press, 1966.
9. *Śvetāśvataropaniṣad*, Gorakhpur: Gita Press, 1962.
10. *Isadi Nau Upaniṣad*, tr. in Hindi by Harikrishna Das Goyanka, Gorakhpur: Gita Press, 1994.
11. *Vedānta-Darśana (Brahmasūtra)*, Śrīmanmaharṣi Vedvyāsa Praṇīta, tr. in Hindi by Harikrishna Das Goyanka, Gorakhpur: Gita Press, 1999.

definitely be a step in the direction of studying such data at a more fundamental level. In fact the patomic model along with associated processes can form a basis of all such studies. This will be a step in the direction of developing a unified theory in humanities and social sciences in the same way as we have for physical science.

Another rather important aspect of application of the present scheme of study could be in maintaining records of individuals regarding their character, efficiency, hobbies, habits, etc. The ingredients of the patomic model in conjunction with the basics of fundamental processes discussed in terms of *tanmātra*s can suggest some parameters for the categorization of these records and qualities of a human/non-human Being. Not only the maintenance of records, even character analysis of an individual can easily be carried out in this framework.

14.4.3 ON THE FRONT OF APPLICATIONS

In the above case, if the analysis of an individual's character or behaviour is carried out by another individual, then the role of subjectivity involved can be minimized to a certain degree. This is possible by way of defining the roles of SPP and SNP (cf. Chapter, 4) in advance and one can maintain a graph for the evolution of the mindset of an individual, mainly for police records.

If an individual or a student is told about this science of Self (or about the sequence of events as they are bound to follow one after the other in life) at appropriate age/time in a systematic and scientific manner, there is every possibility of his attaining peace or coming out of a stage of depression or stress, if he is undergoing one. As a matter of fact these ideas are also advocated from the dais of different religious forums but only in a fragmented manner and generally with the bias of a cult. How would it be if such a scientific analysis of human behaviour be included in the class room curriculum of students of different standards?

Appendices

Appendix A

Patomic Model of Human Being[†]

A1. Introduction

NOWADAYS, while the attempts are being made to establish every discipline of knowledge — no matter whether it belongs to scientific or non-scientific studies — on the scientific reasoning, there is no reason why philosophy should be left untouched from this kind of foundation. In fact to the present-day human mind such an abstract discipline would easily be understandable if the scientific reasonings are available as its basis. Here a philosophical atom-type model of the human being is proposed, which may fulfil this requirement to some extent. Although this model is based on the underlying ideas of the Hindu philosophy it is very well compatible, conceivable and at par with the philosophies of other races of the world, because the reasoning is somewhat scientific in nature. Furthermore, this model is also expected to throw some light on the domains of physics and philosophy.

By bringing philosophy to the level of science we are not doing justice to the former because it has not only accommodated the latter, rather it is also the originator. Apparently, there is no disadvantage in the use of science to understand philosophy better. In a recent article Professor J.V. Narlikar has emphasized[1] the importance of science and of scientific equipments like pelletron — a nuclear particle accelerator in serving the Arts

† This is a revised version of an article published in *Journal of Scientific and Industrial Research* (New Delhi) **49** (1990), 578-83.

1. J.V. Narlikar, "Past Perfection: Science in the Service of Arts", *The Times of India*, 10 February 2004, p. 16.

better. The aim of this article is not to touch the open and challenging questions which are generally put before a philosopher, but to provide a tool by which the understanding of the difficult philosophical ideas to a scientific mind could be made easily comprehensible.

A2. Atom-type Model of the Human Being

While going through the studies of the structure of matter in physical sciences one comes across the atomic model. This model, through the inverse square law of forces, not only works at the microscopic level but its validity in the form of the law of gravitation is well known for the motion of heavenly bodies. This fact is rather very well in accordance with *yadā piṇḍe tadā brahmāṇḍe* (whatever is true at human-body level, is true at cosmic level too), the longstanding idea of the Hindu philosophy.[2] Furthermore, the validity of this law is also noticed in recent time[3] at the level of elementary particle physics. According to the atomic model of the matter, there is a heavy positively charged mass (called nucleus) localized at the centre in a small spatial region. The light negatively charged particles (called electrons) are revolving around this nucleus in the elliptical paths. The laws of forces as a result of which the electron can stay in any of these orbits (called states) are rather well known: they are the electrostatic force of attraction (given by the inverse

2. This fact, often quoted in the Hindu philosophy is supported by *sa hi vaiṣṇavo yad vāmanaḥ; vāmano ha viṣṇurāsa* — *Śatpatha Brāhmaṇa*, 5.2.5.4 and 1.2.5.5, respectively. Another example to this fact can be cited from the biological evolution of the human Being. As a matter of fact a child in the womb of a mother during nine months period passes through the same stages as it has happened during the biological evolution of the human Being.

3. Though, to a good deal of accuracy the validity of this law is already known in the case of electromagnetic interactions between elementary particles, the validity is also noticed in recent times at the level of quark model for strong interactions; see for example, T. Appelquist and H.D. Politzer, *Phys. Rev. Lett.* 34 (1975) 43; R.S. Kaushal and D.S. Kulshreshtha, *Ann. Phys.* (N.Y.), 108 (1977) 198.

square law) and the centrifugal force experienced by the revolving electron. Depending on whether the energy is supplied to or extracted from the atom, the electron performs the transitions to higher or to lower energy states, respectively; otherwise it prefers to stay in the lowest energy state. As we go away from the centre, the spacing between successive energy levels decreases. This fact can be attributed to the nature of the law of forces on the electron.

On the other hand, every human Being (not restricted by the boundaries of caste, colour, creed or country) is considered to have the following essences of life, viz. worldly objects (WO), gross body (B), senses of knowledge and action (SE), mind (M), intellect (I), ego (E) and soul (SO). The existence of all these essences of life is necessary for a human being, no matter how their individual proportions may vary. However, some of them may be absent in the case of non-human Beings. Before describing the model exactly we first elaborate here on the meaning of various essences of life :

WO = Worldly objects like kith and kin, money, prosperity, lust, pleasure, fame, honour, etc.

B = Body: biological body of a human being.

SE = Sense organs responsible for knowledge and action — in all there are believed to be ten senses — five senses of knowledge and five senses of action. Senses of action are hands, feet, power of speech, copulatory organ and anus; and the senses of knowledge are ear, eye, skin, tongue and nose, whose corresponding sense objects are sound, form, touch, taste and smell. These five sense objects correspondingly have an intimate connection with the five *mahābhūta*s (*pañca mahābhūta*s), ether, fire, air, water and earth, through the five *tanmātra*s to which Harrison[4] identifies as the partons of modern physics.

4. David Harrison, *Am. J. Phys.* 46 (1978) 432.

M = Mind: particularly subconscious mind.

I = Intellect: the faculty of decision

E = Soul: the inner-most existence, the pure self characterized by consciousness and bliss and which is beyond the concept of space and time.

b = Human Being: the equivalent word is *jīva* or the seed of life.

With this elaboration of the essences of life and the ingredients of the model we describe the model as follows:

Consider the human Being b (now onward termed as only Being) as revolving around the nucleus of the worldly objects WO placed at the centre. The Being b can stay in any of the finite numbers of states specified by (see *fig*. 2.1) B, SE, M, I, E, SO. These states are multiply degenerate and do not have well-defined boundaries as well. In fact every state (except B) may be considered to have a gross and a micro component. The gross component along with a fraction of the micro component of each of the states SE, M, I, E, and SO constitutes the state B. In other words, the state B has very complicated and composite structure. At any instant the Being b is subjected to experience of two kinds of force — one is attraction which is towards the centre WO while the other is repulsion which is away from the centre. These two forces of attraction and repulsion on b, in Hindu philosophy, are known as *pravṛtti* (attachment to WO, which leads to the outward action) and *nivṛtti* (detachment from WO, which leads to the inward action), respectively. Of course, the attractive force always dominates as long as b is in the lower excited states. Note that the state B which is very close to the centre WO is the ground state of b.

The Being b can perform the transitions. The downward transitions (towards WO) from any of the states (except SO) are more likely and favourable than the upward transitions (towards SO). Generally, the upward transitions to the state SO are possible only from the states M and I, and that too after overcoming the subtle micro-component of E (cf. *fig.* 4.1 in the text). As we go from the state B to the state SO both the level-spacing and the level-width increase in such a way that in the region of SO onward there is all continuum (the shaded area in *fig.* 2.1). Furthermore, the pervading property also increases as we go from the state B to the state SO. The importance of the space-time concept is maximum at the level of B and decreases to zero at the level of SO. Even at the level of M it has a negligible importance. In other words, there are no space-time boundaries at the level of SO.

Having described this atom-type model of the human Being b next we bring out the domains of physics and philosophy in the light of this model.

Such a picture of human Being based on the Vedānta philosophy is termed as "patomic" model in its later applications[5, 6] and in the text. While the first letter "p" of the word philosophical is combined with the word "atomic" to make the word "patomic," the dictionary meaning of this latter word can be derived from the word "patois" meaning thereby "differing materially from the literary language," which in fact speaks of the correct spirit of the model proposed here.

A3. Domains of Physics and Philosophy

In Hindu philosophy Nature is described as consisting of two modes[7] one is lower (insentient) nature while the other is higher (sentient) nature. As far as the search for the laws of the natural sciences is concerned it does not go beyond the domain of these

---

5. Radhey Shyam Kaushal, "Patomic Model of Human Being in the context of Modern Science" Ph.D. Thesis (unpublished), University of Delhi, 1998. Also see, *The Philosophy of the Vedanta: A Modern Scientific Perspective*, Delhi: Sri Satguru Publications and Indian Book Centre, 1994.

6. Radhey Shyam Kaushal, *Structural Analogies in Understanding Nature* New Delhi: Anamaya Publishers, 2003.

7. *Śrīmad Bhagavad-Gītā*, chapter 7, verse 4 (cf. verse (2.1) in the text).

eight constituents of insentient mode of nature.[8] However, the classification and the understanding of all these constituents along with other essences of life, require the mind and the intellect to play a dual role.

In other words, in traditional philosophy there exists a much wider spectrum of the human Being; it starts with the WO and B level and after carrying through the SE, M, I and E, it continues up to the level of SO. For the purposes of studying the interaction of these essences of life with WO and also for the sake of classification of the details of these essences, the human Being again offers the mind and the intellect as the instruments. Thus, if one ignores that part of philosophy which can only be realized by Self but cannot be expressed by any means — what to say of words — then the role played by the mind and the intellect is rather twofold — as an object of study and also the subject. Moreover, science can only explain the genesis of life, while for a description of life one has to look into philosophy.

In this way philosophy leads us far ahead of the domain of science, however it does have — maybe in small proportion — an overlap region with science. This overlapping region of physics and philosophy (which is termed as "scientific epistemology" due to Eddington[9] is expected to have many ideas in common and mostly analogous. There are many examples of such analogies[10] including even the above atom-type model. In fact the analogy noticed by Harrison[11] between the confined

8. As far as the ordering of mind, intellect, ego and soul is concerned it is further supported by another verse (Ch. 3, verse 42) of *Śrīmad Bhagavad-Gītā* (*SMBG*). The Sāṁkhya philosophy, however, maintains another eightfold mode of nature, namely, *pradhāna, mahāttatva*, Ego and five *tanmātras*. Here, however, we shall adopt the eightfold (insentient) mode of nature as described in *SMBG*.

9. A.S. Eddington, *The Philosophy of Physical Sciences* (Cambridge: Cambridge Univ. Press, 1939), p. 7.

10. R.S. Kaushal, *Laws of Physical Sciences and the Human Behaviour*, (Delhi: Spiritual India and Kundalini, vol. II (1978), p. 17.

11. David Harrison, op. cit.

behaviour of partons and that of *tanmātras* also comes under this category.

According to Eddington[12] "the astronomer observes stars; the epistemologist observes astronomer." In other words, a physicist bothers himself only about the quantity and content of the knowledge of the world whereas the epistemologist has also to worry about the quality and the nature of the knowledge itself. Thus, though the foundations of the laws of physics, no doubt, have to be based on somewhat deeper philosophical interpretation, the degree of depth should be decided in view of the model discussed above in Section A2.

Although, generally we do talk about the limitations on the laws of science somehow, to some extent, one finds oneself incapable of thinking of or believing in the region which is beyond philosophy. In view of the limitations of mind and intellect of a Being, the philosophy may also have limitations. In philosophy, mind and intellect not only have to play a dual role but also make an attempt to go even beyond, delving up to the level of soul. The latter is a subject of realization only and hence expressible and understandable by taking recourse to examples and analogies.[13] This is meant by the *Kaṭhopaniṣad* when it says that reasoning is not capable of understanding the higher plans of spirit — *naisa tarken matir apaneya* (*Kaṭhopaniṣad* 1.2.9).

A4. Partons of Physics and Tanmātras of Hindu Philosophy

With a view to exploring further substructure of nuclear particles the concept of partons (quarks) was introduced[14] in modern physics about four decades ago. Gaisser and Gaisser[15] later pointed out that the idea of confined quarks or partons as constituents of elementary particles was already present in the

12. A.S. Eddington, op. cit.

13. Radhey Shyam Kaushal, 2003, op. cit.

14. M. Gell-Mann, *Phys. Lett.* 8 (1964) 214; J.J.J. Kokkedee, *The Quark Model* (New York: Benjamin, 1969) and the references therein.

15. Julia H. Gaisser and T.K. Gaisser, *Am. J. Phys.* 45 (1977) 439.

Greek atomic theory, particularly in the theory given by Epicurus (341-270 BCE). Harrison[16] while describing two other atomic systems of antiquity (including the Hindu philosophy), has identified these partons with five *tanmātras*. He argues that since *tanmātras* are confined in the sense of being observables, and so is the case with partons; therefore, the partons are *tanmātras* as described in Hindu philosophy. In spite of the consistent reasoning given by Harrison, this identification, in our opinion, is not completely convincing. However, within the framework of the present model it should be taken as a case of certain analogy.[17] In support of our statement the following reasons are in order:

(i) The laws of physics, which are supposed to be obeyed by partons, may not be applicable as such to *tanmātras*, because these laws have their own limitations (cf. Section 1.6). In fact in the domain to which these *tanmātras* belong (cf. the levels SE and M), precise laws, as in physics, are not known; (ii) The concept of *tanmātras* is rather subjective while that of the partons is objective. In other words, the concept of partons (or for that matter any sub-structure of partons talked about in recent[18] years) is supposed to explain the structure of matter whereas that of *tanmātras* is not only required to describe the structure of matter but also to describe the interaction of the Being b with the matter. As a matter of fact, all physical laws work well only for inanimate objects and in the absence of free-will; and (iii) had this identification been correct, then all the efforts made in search of quarks and their substructures should be stopped, which is not the case.

Though the arguments given by Harrison are appealing, they are so condensed that a student of science finds it generally hard to understand them. The purpose of the present paper is

16. David Harrison, op. cit.

17. Radhey Shyam Kaushal, 2003, op. cit.

18. H. Harari, *Phys. Lett.* B86 (1979) 83; M.A. Shupe, Phys. Lett. B86 (1979) 87.

not to advocate ontology of atomic systems adopted in antiquity by different races, but to provide a tool which may help in understanding the so-called difficult philosophical ideas.

A5. Applications of the Model

By using the philosophical atomic model the interaction of an individual with the world can be studied.[19] In fact the way in which an individual Being interacts with the worldly objects WO, very much depends on its frequency, whether the frequency corresponds to E level or to B level or lies in between. A man of perfection (whose frequency lies in the soul region, SO, and who, in different races, is variously known as supreme power, God, prophet, saint, *yogī* and so on) and a man who is totally involved in the worldly objects (whose frequency lies in B or at the most in SE region) are two extreme cases available in this world.

Though the downward transitions are always possible from any of the states, the upward transitions are not easily favourable if the Being is in the lower excited states, particularly from B or SE states. It should be noted that at any stage the Being b is not allowed to leave the force field created by WO. This is, however, possible if the Being b is in the continuum, i.e. in the language of Hindu philosophy only after attaining the state of salvation. Moreover, barring a few exceptions, most of the Beings in this world do not cross the state E. Anyway, upward transitions of b will provide peace whereas the downward ones, i.e. towards WO are the source of pleasure.

After making these general remarks we would like to mention that the behaviour of an individual Being, having the frequency corresponding to either of the states B, SE, M, I, or E has been described in different ways in different creeds. We restrict ourselves from going into these details here.

Apart from the fact that this model provides a clearer understanding of the abstract philosophical ideas and helps in

---

19. Radhey Shyam Kaushal, 1994, op. cit.

classifying[20] the human Beings, a large number of applications of this model in behavioural sciences, can be noticed. For example, the degree of compatibility of any two Beings in the same state can be realized. This degree would however reduce if these two Beings are in the nearby different states. Furthermore, even if they are in different states they may still co-exist. Similarly the behaviour of three or more Beings can be understood[21] through this model.

The model can also be used in understanding the behaviour of animal beings. The only difference would be that in animal Beings the state I is completely absent while a part of each of the states M and SE is also sometimes absent. However, a gross component of E already exists through B level in the animal beings.

Though the model described above seems to be designed on the basis of scientific reasoning and the observed empirical facts, the essences with which it deals with do not lie in the domain of science (except the nucleus WO and the states B and SE). They are much beyond the domain of science.

Like the atomic model of physical science the force laws are not known for this philosophical model. Moreover, the mass-like character of the Being b (as we have for the electron) cannot be assigned. Therefore, in the absence of such inputs the analogy with the atomic model remains incomplete and the more exact predictions about the Being cannot be expected on the basis of this model. Now the question is: can we think of a law of force for the type of Being under consideration? Or can we assign some mass-like character to the Being? Though these questions come under the category of open questions to a philosopher (which we want to avoid here), the answer is that we cannot.

Here we have refrained from going into the finer details of various states B, SE, M, I, E and SO. Indeed the detailed study

20. Radhey Shyam Kaushal, 2003, op. cit., chapter 1.

21. Radhey Shyam Kaushal, 1994, op. cit.

of each of these states leads to various modern disciplines of knowledge. Such a detailed study of these states with reference to their multiple degeneracy and to the laws of physics, along with other implications of the model, has become the subject matter of this book and of other works.[22, 23]

22. Radhey Shyam Kaushal, 2003, op. cit., chapter 1.
23. Radhey Shyam Kaushal, 1994, op. cit.

Appendix B

Modelling Game in Physical Sciences

B1. Modelling for Tools: Sub-structures of Matter

UNLIKE *pañca mahābhūtas* (*PMs*) in the Vedānta philosophy for the world we perceive, physics has been dealing with certain other model-constituents of Nature for centuries, even though with some limitation on their working(s). For a physicist, the matter and its dynamics in this universe is considered as an ultimate creation of the space-time structure of Nature (cf. Chapter 3). In the last century, while space and time are unified and a relation between matter and energy is found to exist in mathematical terms, with regard to the structure of matter models have been considered at different stages of granularity; for example, models exist for solids, liquids, gases, in general, and then for their constituents like molecules, atoms, nuclei, elementary particles and the like. Out of continuum and continuous spectra of space-time, only these few entities are identified so far by physicists to understand and describe Nature. The same is the case with regard to the rules of working of these entities in terms of space-time mediated interactions. We shall continue this in Section B2. In what follows, we briefly describe the models used for these entities in recent times in a rather reverse order, i.e. from the smallest to the biggest.

B1.1 MODELS FOR ELEMENTARY PARTICLES

In search of the ultimate building blocks of the universe, the concept of elementarity of a particle has been investigated in the past and the same has been changing with the improvement in the techniques used to detect them over the years. Once upon a time only electron, proton and neutron were considered as the fundamental building blocks of the universe, but after several stages of discoveries the present picture of elementarity of a particle has become somewhat different. In terms of lepton-hadron picture for the structure of matter at present, six quarks (u, d, s, c, b, t) six leptons $(e, \mu, \tau, \nu_e, \nu_\mu, \nu_\tau)$ in addition to their anti-particle counterparts and a few field quanta like gluon (g), photon (γ), weak bosons (W and Z) and graviton are found sufficient to describe the structure of matter. These are the entities still believed to be point objects and constitute a large number of other extended particles and resonances (higher excited states thereof) via various models for their interaction processes. Also various colour and Coulombic charges on them are considered in addition to their spin and parity quantum numbers. Among broad frameworks used to study the associated processes are those of potential and field theoretic approaches. In both cases one uses variety of models for the composite structures. In mathematical terms, group theory has also offered support to certain models and helped in classifying the particles and also in predicting several new particles and resonances.

Thus, models do exist to describe mesons and baryons and associated processes in terms of quarks and gluons. Many of these elementary particles while manifest themselves at high and ultra high energy beams of other lighter particles, their presence in abundance has been noticed in cosmic rays, inside the nucleus, during very early stages of evolution of universe and in relativistic heavy ion collisions. In particular, pion and nucleon (or neutron and proton) are found to constitute the nucleus of an atom.

B1.2 MODELS FOR THE ATOMIC NUCLEUS

In spite of the fact that a large number of ideas are now settled about the fundamental particles in terms of quark-picture, the atomic nucleus still remains a less understood object even after 100 years of its discovery by Rutherford. The fact that atomic nucleus matter shows up and behaves differently under different circumstances, e.g. in different nuclear processes does not allow one to use a particular model for it. About half a dozen models are available to explain successfully its various properties. Shell model picture of the nucleus successfully works for explaining magic numbers, spin, parity and magnetic moments of light nuclei. On the other hand, the properties of heavy-mass nuclei are explained by using collective model which in turn is an improved version of the liquid drop model. While for the purposes of understanding high energy processes the Fermi-gas model or statistical models of the nucleus are used, the success of optical model is known for the description of resonance scattering. Further, for the explanation of certain experimental data the field-theoretic concepts have also been applied through hole-particle model and by considering the filled shell(s) as core or the vacuum.

This is the situation in treating the nucleus as a many-body system; otherwise the problems do exist even today with regard to the understanding of two- or three-nucleon systems. The fact is that the nature of nuclear forces is not yet completely understood. The interesting point is that a variety of potentials are capable of explaining the same set of experimental data. In spite of all this the physics of the atomic nucleus has given a lot to mankind — both in positive as well as negative directions.

B1.3 MODELS FOR ATOMS

Historically, several models for the electrically neutral atom are discussed in the literature. Sir J.J. Thomson first proposed a model in which both negative and positive charges in the whole atomic volume are uniformly distributed. It was only the Rutherford experiment involving large angle scattering of alpha particles which supported the idea that the positive charge inside the atom is localized only to a very small volume in the centre — called nucleus, and the negatively charged electrons are revolving around this nucleus. Then came the Bohr's theory which supported the stability of this dynamical model and it successfully worked for the hydrogen atom or for the atoms having single electron in the outermost orbit such as sodium, etc. Bohr model of atom could explain a large number of properties necessary to differentiate atoms of different elements. In conjunction with Planck law, it could also throw light on the emission and absorption of radiation in terms of electronic transitions. Again some limitations of this semi-classical model were observed when applied to heavy atoms. Even the corrected version of Bohr model by Sommerfeld was found inadequate for this purpose. Some such problems were finally resolved by the induction of full-fledged quantum theory into the atomic physics. In particular, the quantization of electron orbits and an account of electron spin were the main ingredients for a successful explanation of several observed spectral properties of atoms.

Unlike the nuclear physics, the important ingredient which could provide a successful theory of atoms is the fair knowledge and applicability of the Coulomb's law of forces between the electrical charges. Such a law, till this date, however could not be established for the nuclear particles.

B1.4 MODELS FOR MOLECULES

Two or more atoms of the same or different elements constitute a molecule. As for the atom, the models for molecule are also equally successful as far as the explanation of observed properties is concerned. For a system of two atoms, called diatomic molecule, a dumble-shaped picture in which atoms are bound by a Morse potential is well known. In this model, the atoms first repel each other and then start attracting as the distance between the constituent atoms increases. As a whole the system remains bound. Similar models do exist for the systems containing three, four or higher number of atoms. The model for ammonia molecule (NH_3) consisting of four atoms is well known. With regard to the explanation of spectral properties of molecules, an account of other dynamic degrees of freedom, like the rotation, vibration, etc. of a molecule have played an important role.

Models do exist for long chain organic or for macro-molecules. In recent years, the studies of biomolecules have also become of considerable interest from the point of view of genetic engineering.

B1.5 MODELS FOR GASES

Gases basically consist of molecules (or of atoms, particularly the monatomic gas). For a gas in a container the model of kinetic theory is well known in the literature. To start with, molecules are considered as point particles moving randomly and freely (i.e. without interacting with other molecules or with the walls of the container and even not affected by gravity). However, they are constantly undergoing elastic collisions as a result of which the temperature of the gas is maintained. Such an ideal model designed for a gas explains quite a few of its properties, but for the explanation of some other, one needs to relax some of the assumptions of the model. For example, intermolecular forces and also the extended character of the molecule is accounted for in the Van der Waal model of a gas, thus making the model more realistic. In this way several properties such as conduction, diffusion, liquefaction of gases could be successfully explained. Not only this, this kinetic model developed for a gas has further suggested a basis for the branch of thermodynamics in terms of three basic laws, particularly after introducing other physical quantities like pressure, temperature, volume, entropy, etc.

Other alternative models for the gas used in the literature are in terms of the statistical descriptions of an aggregate of molecules. Models do exist for an aggregate of quantum systems heavily depending upon the concept of their indistinguishability which in turn is decided on the basis of their spin considerations.

B1.6 MODELS FOR LIQUIDS AND SOLIDS

Physical quantities like pressure, temperature, density, etc. play a crucial role in defining the state of matter. At a given temperature and pressure certain substances are gaseous, while others may exist in the form of liquid or solid. In general, as the temperature decreases a gas has tendency to condense and becomes liquid and in turn it becomes solid if the temperature decreases further. Sometimes two or all the three states of matter may coexist for a substance. In fact in between the gaseous and solid states of a substance, the latter goes through several transitions and processes with the variation of temperature and pressure. To describe each of these processes several theoretical models are used. Sometimes different models work in different temperature-pressure ranges.

Also models do exist for the description of metals and crystalline substances. The use of models in the study of magnetic materials (cf. Ising model) is well known. Free electron gas model of metal has formed the basis for the study of conductors. This is the case of outside-out (cf. Section 2.4.3) in the spirit of patomic model. In this case the valence electron(s) from each atom contributes to form the so-called "electron gas" and the analysis of this latter system provides explanation to various properties of metals/solids in general. Kroenig-Penig model in which an electron is considered to traverse through periodic potentials generated by the atom-sites is also used to describe conductivity of solids. While atoms arranged in an array constitute the solid state of matter, the use of models for the vibration of atoms connected by a spring-like force in this case is well known.

B1.7 MODELS IN ASTROPHYSICS AND COSMOLOGY

Starting with the planetary model for our solar system, several models are used for the heavenly objects in this universe. In spite of the fact that there are theories of several universes, models do exist for the origin of our own universe such as Big-bang or steady-state models. Further, with regard to the theories of early universe the explanations are prevailing in terms of physics of elementary particles. One important study in this direction is through the experiments on heavy-ion collisions at ultra relativistic energies. Once the universe has come into existence, then a variety of models are in use to describe its subsequent evolution and expansion (the so-called "inflation") in space and time in terms of potential function of a fundamental scalar field. Again there are questions relating to uniform or accelerating expansions of the universe which are yet to be resolved. In recent years the concept of accelerating universe has been found appealing to describe certain interesting features of the underlying theory. In particular while the existence of "dark" (cold and hot) matter in the universe is considered in certain contexts, the concept of "dark" energy is attributed to the accelerating feature of the universe.

With regard to structure formation in the universe, variety of models are in use particularly to describe the evolution of galactic structures and the underlying dynamics therein. In spite of all these developments there is only a limited experimental support to many of these theories. Several massive collaborative projects in the world are on their way to verify many of these ideas. Unfortunately, these are only the photons of different frequency range coming from these heavenly objects and are able to reveal the details about these objects.

B2. Models for the Rules of Game

Here we briefly outline the modelling used in physics for interactions and forces which are responsible for the existence of the entities discussed in B1. Also, we highlight the basis and limitations of the conservation laws used in establishing these naturally preferred interactions and forces.

B2.1 UNDERLYING FORCES AND INTERACTIONS

In the classical sense, force is an agent which causes motion or acceleration in a moving object. In mechanical systems while the concept of force by and large arises due to contact of objects, in several other cases however it is there even without contact, for example, the force due to gravity, due to electric charges or due to a magnet. This latter class of forces fall under the category of action-at-a-distance (AAD) type force and are characterized by its strength and range. Moreover, electricity and magnetism with regard to the force-laws were unified long ago by Maxwell and others. Force is translated into "potential" function in many non-relativistic situations and the same appears as "interaction" in the language of field theory. These are the only variety of forces with which physics or physical laws deal. In fact in physics one basically deals with four fundamental interactions leaving behind the case of contact force mainly for mechanical systems, namely gravitational, weak, electromagnetic and strong interactions with relative strengths of about 10^{-38}, 10^{-7}, 10^{-2}, 1, respectively, on the most microscopic scale, for example, for the two protons just touching at their surfaces. Further, gravitational and electromagnetic interactions are of infinite range and in the classical domain they are beautifully described by an inverse square law whereas the range of effectiveness for weak and strong interactions is very small but finite and varies from system to system. Again in terms of strength and range the last three (except gravitational) interactions are shown to be unified at very high energies and in view of the concept of asymptotic freedom. On the other hand, the beautiful theories (like string theory) do exist at present times in which the gravitational interaction is also accommodated in a unified manner by way of modifying the geometry in the language of general theory of relativity.

With regard to the existence of sequence of sub-structures of matter discussed above (cf. Section B1), all the four fundamental interactions are in active consideration in the domain of elementary particle physics. Recent studies going on in quantum cosmology or in quantum gravity theories do accommodate the gravitational interaction, which was once neglected for the data from accelerator-based experiments. For a lepton-photon system, the quantized version of the electromagnetic interaction still works successfully. However, for the case of lepton-hadron system the concept of weak force is introduced. Further, for the system consisting of hadrons (particularly the nuclear particles) the existence of strong force is established. Perhaps with a view to putting the available knowledge in a nut-shell, the efforts have been there to find a generalized framework in terms of colour and weak charges which will provide a unified description of these interactions and processes.

A successful force-law has yet to be found to describe the atomic nucleus which is a bound system of nucleons. While a variety of force-laws are found to work well for the two- and three-body nuclear systems, a successful model for the light nuclei is in terms of independent particle model based on the use of harmonic potential.

For the description of atoms Coulomb's law still works successfully. For molecules, however, in addition to some other laws like Morse potential, the Coulomb's law and its variants are found to work well. For the description of gases, liquids and solids, while several model-dependent force-laws are in use in the literature on the contextual basis, a unified description in terms of statistical mechanics has also been sought. The sanctity of inverse square law of gravitation is well established for the study of heavenly objects.

B2.2 CONSERVATION LAWS

After having described the sequence of sub-structures of matter and the associated force-laws for their existence, we now highlight another important ingredient used in these descriptions and that is the concept of "conservation" laws. In fact keeping in mind the universality of physical laws which basically are defined in the domain of space-time structure of Nature, physicists have postulated the concept of conservation laws.

There is an intimate connection between the symmetry of a system and the associated conservation law (Noether's theorem). As a matter of fact, to describe the dynamics or motion of a physical system certain physical quantities are assumed to remain fixed as the system evolves with time. This corresponding quantity is said to be conserved or it is said to be an "invariant" of motion. By and large the sanctity of conservation laws is maintained throughout the motion and the description of dynamics, as physics-laws work well for closed systems and any departure from this "closeness" is bound to bring problems for these beautiful descriptions.

In the classical domain, there are seven conservation laws which need to be obeyed, namely three components of each of linear momentum and angular momentum and the seventh one is energy. These seven laws respectively have the basis in the concepts of homogeneity and isotropy of space, and homogeneity of time for a physical system. In the quantum domain where systems are indistinguishable however one comes across several other conservation laws. For the present we restrict ourselves from going into these details here.

Appendix C

Modelling Game in Biological Sciences

EARLIER biology consisted mainly of a study of living organisms which includes the study of animals and plants. In recent times, however, many new subjects of interdisciplinary nature such as biochemistry, biophysics, molecular biology/genetics, etc. have emerged under the heading of bio-sciences. The science of biology has expanded beyond its classical concepts of anatomy, physiology, histology or taxonomy, etc. to include many new and developing branches of genetics and microbiology. Accumulation of all such knowledge necessitated development of some common models based on analogies. Such, modelling game does appear in other disciplines as well. For example, in order to study the effect of a drug on biological systems (bio-parts) the models of chemistry for understanding the underlying reactions are frequently used. Sometimes an account of time dependence in the decay and growth of reactants and products becomes important. Similarly, the models of physics are also in use to understand various aspects of bio-parts and their functioning. Note that the models of bio-parts are the realities in the space-time domain, i.e. they are visualizable at the levels of SE and M, contrary to those used in physical sciences (cf. Appendix B). Further, in comparison to physical sciences, here, there are only limited number of models for tools (bio-parts) but there are many to describe their functioning. A large number of models (concepts) borrowed mainly from physics and chemistry are in use. As a matter of fact, more analogies/models are needed to describe the invisible (as in physics) compared to the physically realizable objects (as in biology).

Poetic minds for centuries have been making full use of this perfect creation of God, the human body (particularly that of a female one), to express their emotions, sentiments and their concept of beauty with regard to both its description and functioning. Many similes, metaphors and alikes are used in a variety of literary works in different languages. The analogies of body parts and their operations are drawn with the objects and processes in Nature according to their (poets) liking. Here, we shall however restrict ourselves from going into such imaginative considerations and will adopt only a scientific outlook in this regard.

C1. Models for Tools (Body Parts)

Structure of a biological body of a living organism, particularly that of a human Being, is the example of the finest fabric which God has manufactured. While the understanding of its detailed structure, designing and functioning is still the subject of modern research, the description of some of its parts has been better understood through models. In fact both symmetry and geometry play important roles in understanding the design and structure of a body of an organism. However, standard symmetries of physics and standard geometries of mathematics are often found incapable of describing the body parts. For example, there may appear symmetries at the face value but it breaks down as soon as one enters deeper into the structure. Perhaps new symmetries start emerging. Similarly, standard Euclidean geometry or the rules derived therefrom for a description of body parts in terms of standard shapes of straight line, circle, rectangle, triangle, sphere, cylinder, ellipse, etc. do not work. Several million mile long capillaries distributed all over inside a finite size body or the fascinating structures inside the bones all over, constitute some of the fantasias of this great fabric of God. Still, in what follows, we present some representative models used for different bio-parts:

(a) Balls and Sockets are there at various joints in the body. Their functioning is beautifully controlled by muscles, tendons and there is an ideal co-ordination with the central nervous system.

(b) For the structure of heart and its functioning various models have been used. For example, a lot of work has been going on on the heart valve leaflet mechanics. To this effect, large-strain constitutive modelling of biological tissues has grown enormously over the years. Models do exist to estimate the chemicals like calcium in the heart-cells and to study the blood circulation in the body in general and in the heart in particular.

(c) Models do exist for the structure and functioning of the brain. While the details we postpone to the next section, three main functions of the brain, namely pattern recognition, analysis and motor control are better understood again in terms of certain models.

C2. Models for the Rules of Game

Complex systems in physics are studied by dividing them into simpler subsystems (cf. Appendix B) and by analysing the functioning of the latter as the isolated units. Thus, physicists attempt to construct complex from the simple and in the process the assumption of isolation is found very viable in framing the laws and subsequently the theories. This is possible mostly because systems or sub-systems in physics are the inanimate objects and as such they are free from the storage of effects of environment in their memories. In biology, however, this is not the case. The assumption of isolation for systems or subsystems is only partially valid; as such the application of physical laws fails to describe the complete working of the system. Also, the effect of environment (whether the system is inside or outside the body) plays a dominant role in describing its functioning. In fact biologist can only supply data about the working of the body parts with their plausible descriptions; otherwise for their analysis the use of physical laws with possible modifications is there in biosciences. We highlight some of these models below.

In fact in physics domain such biological systems are studied under the heading of "soft" matter.

C2.1. MODELS USED IN BIOMECHANICS

To understand the functioning of various bio-parts the concepts and models of mechanics are applied in different contexts. For example, the role of extensor muscles in head and of deltoid muscles in arms is studied by considering static equilibrium of forces in the respective parts of the body. As a matter of fact the muscles themselves work as machines which convert chemical energy obtained from food into the mechanical energy of motion by way of their contraction according to the sliding filament theory. The mechanism of muscle contraction in the presence of load is further understood in terms of series and parallel combinations of elastic components of a muscle in the same way as one studies about springs in physics.

Bones in the body, as mentioned before, constitute the lever arms of the bio-part, and their joints (called articulations) provide the example of mechanical coupling required for motion of one bone with respect to another. The load that a bone-system can bear depends on the strength of the corresponding bones. Further the structure and shape of a bone in different parts of the body is suitably adapted to the kind of stresses it is likely to be exposed to. The models of a cantilever or of a beam loaded at both ends are used to compute the strength of bones.

The questions like how one moves on earth, how birds fly in air, or how fishes swim in water are studied in the subject of bio-dynamics. To understand these processes the equilibrium of forces acting always on a particular organ is considered and in general these forces are the gravity force, elastic forces and frictional forces (like static or kinetic friction during locomotion on ground, or viscous forces during the motion in a fluid) in addition to some other forces. Laws of dynamics are frequently used for living organisms to understand their movement through the process of automation and locomation on land, air and water, etc. mainly on the basis of analogies; otherwise these laws show limitations when applied to living systems.

C2.2 MODELS FOR BIO-FLUID FLOW

Attempts are being made to use the physical theories of laminar and viscous flow, turbulence, thermal systems, plasmas, etc. to study the blood flow in organisms and the xylem flow in plant kingdom. In spite of the fact that the conditions for the application of these laws to bio-fluids do not prevail in an ideal sense, still many interesting results are derived by this kind of modelling at least in the lowest order. Not only this, these studies have given a feedback to improve upon the physical laws themselves in accordance with these new conditions. The subject of hemodynamics dealing with the blood flow in closed arterial to venous circulatory systems offers the example of flow of a viscous fluid through pipes for a physicist. On the other hand, the flow of water of varying density, pressure and temperature in the water conducting channels in plants constitute the subject of xylem and phloem transport.

While certain phenomena like the composition of blood in an organism in terms of blood cells and plasmas, the nature of blood flow and the construction of arteries and capillaries through which the blood flows have no exact parallels in the laboratory experiments, still the efforts have been there to create "nearly the same" conditions in the laboratory. Similar is the case with the studies of xylem and phloem transports in the laboratory. Even today, many questions pertaining to the dynamics of these bio-fluid flows in both organisms and plants remain unanswerable. For example, the study of hydrodynamical equilibrium of forces responsible for upward flow, the flux and velocity of flows and the resistance offered by xylem conduiting to the flow is not completely understood. Similarly, the study of hydrostatic equilibrium responsible for the upward flow in plants during nights (before the sun rise) poses several questions like what forces hold such a long continuous fluid columns in xylem channels which may be as high as a few hundred feet in certain trees, etc.

C2.3. MODELS FOR BIOGAS FLOW

Study of gas transport in living organisms (including plants) involves two kinds of physical processes, the convective transport and the diffusion of gas. For example, breathing or external respiration in animals transports oxygen (O_2) from and carbon dioxide (CO_2) into atmosphere through respiratory canals or airways, whereas the diffusion of O_2 and CO_2 takes place across membranes of lungs or other external respiratory systems. Also the exchange of O_2 and CO_2 between blood and body cells takes place by diffusion.

An analysis of the processes of gas diffusion in tissues was done by Krogh in 1919 by considering the tissue as a cylinder and a capillary (blood vessel) was considered to pass through this tissue-cylinder. Using such a model, Krogh studied the variation of pressure within the tissue as a function of radii of blood vessels. Models do exist for understanding the breathing mechanism in bio-systems. Interestingly, the deviations from the Boyle's and Charle's law of physics are more frequent here in bio-systems.

C2.4. MODELS RELATED TO VISUAL AND AUDIO SYSTEMS

An analogy of the structure of eye and its working with that of a camera is well known. A variety of laws of optics are applied to understand the working of human eye. A "reduced eye model" works well in vision technology. In this case all the different refractive surfaces inside the eye are replaced by a single thin lens of optical power + 60D (approximately). By taking an average value of the refractive index as 1.34 the equivalent focal length of this lens is computed which helps in designing the visual aid(s). Models do exist to understand the working of retina in terms of photo-sensitive cells and accordingly the conversion of light energy, first into chemical (via photo-pigment molecules) and then into electrical-like energy which later is transmitted to the brain by optical nerves, is considered. In fact the transmission of energy to brain takes place automatically after an appropriate amplification of the signal by means of natural biological amplifiers. The photo-receptors of eye containing photo-pigment molecules, are believed to behave as optical fibres.

Similarly, the study of the structure of ear and its working involves the use of different concepts and models of physics. Ear, in fact, is a device which converts sound waves in air into electrical signals of auditory nerves as in the case of eye. In the outer ear, the ear canal is considered as an organ pipe closed at one end and the same resonates at the fundamental frequency of 3300 Hz. In the middle ear, ossicles (three small bones) function as a lever with appropriate identifications of pivots and piston. To understand the vibrations of the eardrum, one employs the theory of membranes again. Recall that the theories of physics developed for ideal geometries are however applicable only approximately to these bio-systems. Also, an account of the non-linearity in the physical theories becomes desirable at different stages of application.

C2.5 MODELS USED IN NEURODYNAMICS

The mechanisms of excitations of neurons and conduction of nerve impulse are described in terms of the change of potential inside the plasma membrane of the nerve cell. While in the unexcited (resting) state of the cell this membrane is electrically polarized, its potential, however, gets altered locally in response to a suitable and sufficient stimulation. This change in potential then propagates along the nerve fibre to synapse and then to the next neuron. The mechanism therefore involves three distinct features namely, resting potential, generation of action potential and its conduction along the fibre, and synaptic transmission. The phenomenological theories advanced to understand these mechanisms have left options for use of various models for different underlying concepts in Neural Science.

For the diffusion potential, arising due to different ionic

concentrations of a particular ion across a permeable membrane, various functional forms such as Nernst potential, Hodgkin-Katz-Goldman (HKG) potential, Donnan potential, etc. are used in different situations.

Electric analogue of membrane: An element of plasma membrane at any localized region can be regarded electrically equivalent to a parallel combination of a capacitor and several resistors with a resultant resistance. The two surfaces of a membrane element are considered so as to form two plates of a parallel plate capacitor, separated by a distance equivalent to the membrane thickness, and raised to a potential across the plates.

Nerve excitations and the related mechanism: Both the nerve and muscle cells exhibit the interesting property, i.e. they are excitable. When an external stimulus triggers nerve cell at a synaptic junction it excites. A series of various quarries like (i) what happens to a nerve cell when stimulated? or (ii) What is the nature of initial excitation and how does it occur at the synapse?, etc. involves the applications of various analogue concepts (and laws) of physics which basically are developed and derived for inanimate objects. For example, the phenomena like depolarization of cell membrane and its revelation through voltage clamp technique, passive spread of depolarization along the membrane surface particularly from one membrane element to another, are the ones whose understanding is carried out in terms of analogous physical concepts. In the latter case, the behaviour of passive spread in axon is however described by considering the fibre as equivalent of an electrical cable consisting of combinations of a large number of capacitors and resistances.

The process of activation and de-activation of ion-channels during the action potential resulting in a refractory state of the fibre, are explained in terms of the so-called "gate mechanism" or "gate model." Gates, in fact, can be considered as analogues of molecular sensors which regulate ionic channels across the membrane.

C2.6 USE OF MODELS IN OTHER BIOLOGICAL CONTEXTS: CONCLUDING REMARKS

Models are also designed and used to understand the modern fields like cellular/molecular biology. These studies are carried out mainly as an extended version of the concepts and models in physics and chemistry but now in the context of (bio) cells and bio-molecules. In particular, molecular biophysics deals with the study of structures and functions of living systems in terms of physics of constituent bio-molecules, i.e. in terms of interactions between various bio-molecules and their subsequent dynamics.

The distinct nature of bio-molecular dynamics can be attributed to the specific structure of bio-molecules (unlike that of molecules in physics). In fact the large bio-molecules like proteins and nucleic acids exhibit first a basic primary structure and then a number of secondary structures. The primary structure is relatively more stable and secondary ones are rather weakly bound. This leads to the existence of two types of forces between bio-molecules, namely strong and weak forces. The strong part is short range, attractive and has physics-origin (in terms of ions and atoms), the weak part, on the other hand, is attributed to secondary structures and plays an important role in bio-molecular processes. These weak forces are of relatively long range, some of them simply have classical electrostatic nature and others originate from the quantum nature of the interacting systems.

Depending upon the nature of the bio-molecule in terms of its charge, size, dipole moment, etc. various force laws have been discussed in the literature, often as an extension of the laws applicable to a physical/chemical system. For example, with regard to the nature of long-range weak forces note that only dispersive and inductive forces act between a polar and a non-polar molecule, and all the three dispersive, inductive and electrostatic forces act between two polar molecules. The cumulative effect of any or all of the above three gives rise to the Van der Waal force.

Some other areas in biosciences where modelling game continues can be identified as follows:

(a) Water offers an easy environment for bio-molecules and as a result of their interaction one comes across the hydrophobic and hydrophilic forces and models them accordingly.

(b) A study of structural organization of proteins, nucleic acids and other macro molecules in terms of secondary structures, also requires certain degree of modelling. For example, each of the two sugar-phosphate chains comprising DNA molecules is a right-handed helix. Hence DNA molecule is a double right-handed helix which appears like a spiral stair-case, with A-T and G-C bonds forming the rungs of this helical ladder (Watson-Crick model of a DNA molecule).

(c) Models do exist for understanding the mechanism of genetic information transfer. Models based on group theory have also been very successful in understanding the mechanisms of transfer and transcription of genetic information.

(d) The studies of physics and chemistry of bio-membranes in cellular biology have basis in models again.

The basic unit of all living organisms is the living cell. Though the structure and shape of cells of different parts of the body are different, each cell is surrounded by a membrane. As a matter of fact, this membrane envelopes the cell and separates its internal contents from the external environment. The cell acts as an *open system*, being in non-equilibrium state continuously transports matter into and out of itself through its semi-permeable membrane (or plasma). Models do exist for the structure and functioning of these different types of membranes in terms of diffusion and osmosis processes.

(e) The entire activity of a living being, its growth and maintenance, needs energy. There has also been use of models in bioenergetics, i.e. in describing the energy transformation processes in the living systems.

It may be mentioned that the concepts and laws of physics are basically developed for (i) inanimate objects (termed as "hard" matter), (ii) isolated systems (not interacting with surroundings) and for (iii) countably small number of particles (as far as their accuracy in terms of the predictive power is concerned) or for the objects assumed as "rigid" bodies and like that. These laws when used in chemistry already undergo one order of approximation since the systems in the latter case are bigger in size and large in numbers. Sometimes they are not isolated. Not only this, they may also deal (as in bio-chemistry) with animate (so called "soft" matter) objects. The application of these laws for the systems in cellular and/or molecular biology naturally involves one order higher approximation than that in chemistry as far as their predictive power in concerned. As a result, in the biological context the existing laws of physics/chemistry require a new dimension of modification not only in terms of complexity and non-linearity of the underlying dynamics but also for the "life-substance" prevailing in these systems. It remains a big question mark as to what extent the present studies in terms of linear physics models are successful. In fact linearity (in terms of algebraic or differential equations) and/or simplicity (in terms of harmonic forces) in physical theories appear rather uniquely; on the other hand, there is enough scope of plurality of ways for accounting for the nonlinearity and complexity in the theories developed for bio-systems.

Appendix D

Pañca Mahābhūtas and the Treatment of Diseases

D1. Introduction

MODERN scientific researches have shown that there is no life on every planet and also for the existence of life certain optimum conditions in terms of percentage of air, water, etc. need to be fulfilled. On the other hand, Vedānta philosophy has been repeatedly emphasizing[1] the role of *pañca* (five) *mahābhūtas* (*PMs*) namely earth, water, air, fire and ether, not only in the creation and actions of a Being[2] but also in its survival[3] in this world in the form of eightfold insentient mode of Nature (cf. verse (2.1), chapter 2).

In fact in Vedic literature an equilibrium between the life (i.e. the existence of Being b) and its interactions with *PMs* has been discussed at length (see, for example, citation 4 and the references[4] therein) in terms of the *pañcīkaraṇa*-rule and the five *tanmātras*.[5] These

1. See, for example, verse (2.1) in chapter 2 (from *SMBG*).
2. Verses (2.4) and (2.5) of chapter 2 (from *SMBG*).
3. See, for example, the concept of *kṣara* and *akṣara* in chapter 13 of *SMBG*.
4. Radhey Shyam Kaushal, *The Philosophy of the Vedanta: A Modern Scientific Perspective*, Garib Das Oriental Series no. 179, Delhi: Indian Book Centre, 1994; also see, "Patomic Model of Human Being in the Context of Modern Science", PhD. Thesis (Unpublished), University of Delhi, 1998.
5. Radhey Shyam Kaushal, 1994, op. cit., chapter 4.

tanmātras basically are the five quanta of interactions of the Being with each *mahābhūta*. When any disturbance in this equilibrium takes place (often by an "ill-action" of the Being, particularly by a human Being since he has more degrees of freedom to think and perform the newer actions in this life), then the role of *PMs* in the deeds of Being need to be redefined in the form of treatment for his further survival. Thus arises the need for treatment of diseases of a Being using *PMs* through, so-called "naturopathy." Within the framework of *aṣṭāṅga prakṛti* (cf. verse (2.1)) this disease could be at both mental and physical levels. While other "pathies" deal with the use of *PMs* in their other variant forms, Āyurveda in general and naturopathy in particular deal with a direct use of *PMs* for the treatment of diseases.

Another unaccepted science that is popular with common mass and followed only hesitantly all over world in different styles is astrology. In astrology one studies and investigates the effect of other planets (if at all it is there) on the life and actions of a Being on this planet earth. For non-humans while this effect may go unnoticed, for human Beings, however, this effect at times is considered very crucial in terms of auspicious times for the sake of performing an action by the individual. In some sense this seems to be quite logical but represents only a partial truth. In fact the ether, mostly responsible for this effect, is only one of the five *mahābhūtas* and for the totality of truth the effect of the remaining four *PMs* needs to be accounted for. Therefore, the accuracy of predictions in this exotic science of astrology, as will be argued in Section D5, remains questionable.

In the next section we elaborate on these five cosmic elements (*PMs*) in the context of modern science. In Section D3, we discuss the origin of a disease as an outcome of disturbance of equilibrium maintained by the Being with *PMs*. Methods of attaining this equilibrium by way of using *PMs* again are discussed in Section D4. In Section D5, a basis for the science of astrology is highlighted. Finally concluding remarks are made in Section D6.

D2. An Explanation of PMs in the Context of Modern Science

According to *Śrīmad-Bhagavad-Gītā* (*SMBG*) (cf. verse (2.1), Chapter 2) the *PM*s in addition to mind, intellect and ego constitute the insentient mode of Nature. Clearly, these *PM*s have dual role to play in the life of an individual, i.e. in their physical forms as external agents responsible for the survival of the Being in this Universe and in their micro form as important factors affecting the behavior and actions of a Being in the day-to-day life. In conjunction with the micro-body (i.e. mind, intellect and ego) of a Being the effect of latter type of role of *PM*s becomes more realizable for humans than for non-humans. Studies of the former type of role of *PM*s, in fact, is the subject of objective science in which the individual is an observer, whereas for the latter role it is the subject of humanities since the individual now becomes the part of the system and the role of micro-body also comes into existence.

In view of the fact that *PM*s form the basis of survival of the Beings in this Universe, in Hindu mythology they are personified sometimes with divine powers and as a result they are worshipped by a common man in all rituals. To understand their role better, these five cosmic elements are further redefined in Vedic sciences through a so-called *pañcīkaraṇa* rule.[6] According to this rule the actual earth which we *perceive* is not the *physical* earth alone; rather it is the composite of 50 per cent of the physical earth and 12.5 per cent each of the remaining four physical *mahābhūtas*. Similarly, the actual water which we perceive is not the physical water alone but it is a composite of 50 per cent of physical water and 12.5 per cent each of the remaining four physical *mahābhūtas*, and so on. Thus, if we denote $\tilde{E}_a, \tilde{W}, \tilde{F}, \tilde{A}, \tilde{E}_t$ as the redefined[7] *PM*s corresponding to each

6. See, for example, *Sadānandayati Pranītaḥ Vedāntasāra* ed. Pt. Ram Govind Shukla, Delhi: Bharatiya Vidya Prakashan, 3rd edn., 1992, pp. 45-47.

7. It should be noted that in citation 6, the words *pañcīkṛta* and *apañcīkṛta* are used respectively for the "perceived" and "physical" *mahābhūtas*.

physical *mahābhūta*, namely earth (E_a), water (W), air (A), fire (F) and ether (E_t), then according to *pañcīkaraṇa* rule we have[8]

$$\begin{aligned}
\widetilde{E}_a &= \tfrac{1}{2}E_a + \tfrac{1}{8}W + \tfrac{1}{8}A + \tfrac{1}{8}F + \tfrac{1}{8}E_t \\
\widetilde{W} &= \tfrac{1}{2}W + \tfrac{1}{8}A + \tfrac{1}{8}F + \tfrac{1}{8}E_t + \tfrac{1}{8}E_a \\
\widetilde{A} &= \tfrac{1}{2}A + \tfrac{1}{8}F + \tfrac{1}{8}E_t + \tfrac{1}{8}E_a + \tfrac{1}{8}W \\
\widetilde{F} &= \tfrac{1}{2}F + \tfrac{1}{8}E_t + \tfrac{1}{8}E_a + \tfrac{1}{8}W + \tfrac{1}{8}A \\
\widetilde{E}_t &= \tfrac{1}{2}E_t + \tfrac{1}{8}E_a + \tfrac{1}{8}W + \tfrac{1}{8}A + \tfrac{1}{8}F
\end{aligned} \tag{D.1}$$

and hence note that

$$\widetilde{E}_a + \widetilde{W} + \widetilde{A} + \widetilde{F} + \widetilde{E}_t = E_a + W + A + F + E_t, \tag{D.2}$$

which implies that the net effect of the five perceived *mahābhūta*s on Being b is the same as that of all five physical *mahābhūta*s provided the perception process is duly accounted for. This is understandable because of the fact that *PM*s also constitute the measuring instrument, i.e. the biological body (B) of the Being in addition to other essences of life like SE, M, I, E, of course in the background of SO (cf. Appendix A). In Vedic science the concept of five *tanmātras* $\tau_{ea}, \tau_w, \tau_a, \tau_f, \tau_{et}$ (which can be considered as analogous to the quanta of interactions in modern physics) corresponding to each *mahābhūta* is introduced and they can be considered as to provide a connection between the perceived mahābhūtas and the physical ones through the process

$$\widetilde{E}_a \rightleftharpoons E_a + \tau_{ea},\ \widetilde{W} \rightleftharpoons W + \tau_w,\ \widetilde{A} \rightleftharpoons A + \tau_a,\ \widetilde{F} \rightleftharpoons F + \tau_f,\ \widetilde{E}_t \rightleftharpoons E_t + \tau_{et}.$$

In other words, the perception of physical *PM*s by a Being b is translated into the role of five *tanmātras* in the interaction process.

8. With regard to the ordering of *mahābhūta*s according to their fineness *air* (A) comes after *fire* (F) in Vedānta philosophy (see, for example, verse (2.1) in chapter 2 (from *SMBG*) citation 6 above). However, we treat F after A, mainly because later on we shall identify F with the plasmonic state of matter in the universe which basically is a stage higher than air as one considers it as a collection of ions. Moreover, according to modern astrophysics, it is the (electromagnetic) radiation (a characteristic of F) which is all-pervading through photons of different frequency ranges and not the air.

To this effect a particular *tanmātra* is considered to carry the net effect of interaction of the micro-body $\mathcal{M}$, SE and B with the corresponding *mahābhūta* and some effect of other *mahābhūta*s as well. In some sense these *tanmātra*s are the micro-versions (or the seeds) of physical *mahābhūta*s which in turn participate not only in the biochemical reactions and physiological changes in the body but also in all actions of day-to-day life of b and at both mental and physical levels. Since perception process starts at the B and SE levels of b (cf. Appendix A) and continues up to M, I and E levels (i.e. up to the level of micro-body $\mathcal{M}$ = {M, I, E}), the physical *mahābhūta*s do have an effect on the essences of life of an individual. Not only this, a little extrapolation of the role of *tanmātra*s in the perception process (i.e. via the role of consciousness) of a physical phenomenon can lead to offer their link with the "quantum measurement problem" of modern physics[9] or with the "field quanta" of quantum field theories. In fact there also exists a mention of *mahābhūta*s and the associated *tanmātra*s in other modern context.[10, 11] We refrain ourselves from going into these details here.

Earlier we have argued[12] that SO of b is the second quantized version of the field of cosmic consciousness prevailing all over the universe. Now the question arises as to what the *PM*s of Vedānta philosophy represent? In fact the *mahābhūta* ether (or *ākāśa* or firmament) already represents the all-pervading space in the universe and this space is filled with both physical and non-physical matter.[13] In view of the concept of *tanmātra*s presented

9. See, for example, Amit Goswami, "Consciousness in quantum physics and the Mind-Body Problem", *Journal of Mind & Behaviour* **11** (1990), 75-96.

10. David Harrison, *Am. Journal of Physics* **46** (1978), 432.

11. C.W. Misner and J.A. Wheeler, "Classical Physics as Geometry", *Annals of Physics* (NY) 2 (1957) 525 (Footnote no. 9a); E. Schrodinger, *My View of the world*, translated by C. Hastines (Cambridge: Cambridge Univ. Press, 1964), p. 18.

12. Radhey Shyam Kaushal, 1994, op. cit., chapter 6.

13. Radhey Shyam Kaushal, 1994, op. cit.

above, the physical *PMs* account only for the physical matter and energy in the universe whereas the perceived ones are related to both physical and non-physical matter in the universe since the role of M, I and E enters in the perception process. In other words, in the presence of the field of cosmic consciousness all the five *mahābhūtas* are dressed up and become the objects in the process of perception. In this way, while the physical ether (E_t) is already finest among all the five *mahābhūtas*, the perceived ether ($\tilde{E}_t$) and the corresponding *tanmātra* become still finer as far as the all-pervading property is concerned. This will explain as to how both physical and non-physical matter of the universe can affect the actions of an individual and subsequently become the cause of both first mental and then physical diseases or the other way round. For further details see Chapter 6.

According to another interpretation of *PMs* of Vedic science, they are considered[14] as representing the five states of matter and energy of modern physics. For example, earth accounts for all solids or solid states in the universe; water for all liquids or liquid states; air for all gases or gaseous states; fire for all plasmonic states; and ether for the whole space in the universe in which all physical fields are considered as present. This may be true with physical *mahābhūtas*; otherwise the perceived *mahābhūtas* through *tanmātras* go one step ahead as they become the part of $\mathcal{M}$ of b via *tanmātras*. The medical system of Vedic science, called "Āyurveda," is based on this philosophy and the treatment of both physical diseases pertaining mainly to B and SE and mental diseases (pertaining to M, I and E) using *PMs* can easily be understood within this framework. At the face value of physical *mahābhūtas* it can be noticed that both their subtle character and the pervading property increase as one proceeds from earth to ether.

14. These days there exists a huge literature on naturopathy as the West has also accepted this system of treatment of diseases. Here, however, we have cited only a few cases from the Āyurveda system of treatment. For further details, see, for example, *Prākṛtika Ayurvijñāna* ed. originally by Dr. Ganga Prasad Gaur "Nahar" and revised by Dr. Rakesh Jindal, Modi Nagar: Arogya Seva Prakashan, 1994.

D3. Disease, Pain and Worry

D3.1 DISEASE: AN OUTCOME OF DISTURBANCE IN THE EQUILIBRIUM

A wonderful super equilibrium in a working body (consisting of active micro and gross bodies) of a Being b is maintained by Nature among various essences of life in conjunction with *PMs*. While the *yogī* category of persons is capable of overcoming (maybe for a short while) any disturbance in this or other partial equilibria, other categories (cf. Chapter 1) of persons including non-humans and plant kingdom find it difficult to tolerate any, even an infinitesimal, disturbance in this super equilibrium; their body starts decaying unless efforts are made to restore first the partial and finally the super equilibrium by the method of curing. In fact the super equilibrium is the outcome of several partial equilibria which are maintained locally not only by inner and outer essences of life among themselves but also by their interactions with the external world including *PMs* in the domain of WO. This decaying of body in the absence of treatment again consists of two aspects — one is normal decay, i.e. ageing[15] and the other is due to the deficiency of a cosmic element in B. It is the latter aspect which is repairable by the method of curing and the same sometimes can also affect the former aspect of decay. Thus, the curing is a process to bring in the missing cosmic element from outside in B so that the same can assist in restoring the partial and subsequently the super equilibrium in the body. While the super equilibrium can be attributed to an overall interaction of b with the Nature, the partial equilibria, on the other hand, are the outcome of interaction of individual essences of life with Nature. In the same tone one can define peace corresponding to the former case and the partial pleasures corresponding to the latter. Again it is the stability of these

---

15. In fact the biochemical processes in the body undergo two types of time-dependences. The first one is fast and of short duration related to the decay and attributed to the deficiency of a *mahābhūta* and the second one is slow and continues till the death of a Being .

equilibria which is desirable for peace; otherwise their unstability leads only to momentary peace or partial pleasures.

D3.2 PAIN, WORRY AND DEPRESSION AS SYMPTOMS OF DISEASES

The additional essence of life in the human being, i.e. the intellect, makes him different from other species on this earth. As a result, human Being tries to have the best of all in Nature — starting from the materialistic gains to spiritual achievements. For this, he makes efforts at various levels and as an outcome he draws peace (linked with the stability of super equilibrium) and pleasure (linked with the stability of partial equilibria) from the interactions with Nature. In fact peace and pleasure appear to be the two sides of the same coin[16] and also are the end-products of two different classes of actions. While the peace is realizable at the innermost existence, with the pleasure one feels satisfied at different levels of the patomic modẹl (cf. Appendix A) out of the partial equilibria maintained with Nature at these levels.

Note that the nucleus WO in the patomic model also includes the *PM*s of Vedānta philosophy. To understand this, we recall the extended version of the *pañcīkaraṇa* rule[17] in terms of associating the sense objects with each perceived *mahābhūta*. For example, *dhvani* (or sound) with the perceived ether E_t, sound and touch with the perceived air A, sound, touch and shape

16. Radhey Shyam Kaushal, "Structural Analogies, Abstraction and Mathematical Concepts in Vedic Sciences", *Indian Philosophical Quarterly* (Poona) 33 (2006), 125-46.

17. Note that *PM*s do appear in WO in various forms and proportions. In fact any sense object or the objects of mind in this world whatsoever are not free from the realm of *PM*s since they are interwoven in one form or the other in all the objects perhaps by way of an extended *pañcīkaraṇa* rule, i.e. the *asthikaraṇa* rule, as M, I, E also play the role in the choices of objects of WO and also of their interconnections (cf. Chapter 5). Their existence in WO is also due to a certain equilibrium which the objects separately maintain with *PM*s. For example, a mango is fit for eating if it is properly ripe and in the process of ripening all the *mahābhūta*s do play a role.

with the perceived fire F, sound, touch, shape and taste with the perceived water W, and sound, touch, shape, taste and smell with the perceived earth E_a. Again it is worth recalling the link and correspondence of these five sense objects with the five senses of knowledge, viz.

> Ether–sound–ear; air–touch–skin; fire–shape–eyes;
> water–taste–tongue; and earth–smell–nose. (D.2′)

In Vedānta philosophy the origin of *mahābhūta*s is attributed to God, particularly that of ether, and from ether originate the other *mahābhūta*s. In fact as one proceeds from ether to earth the characteristics associated with a *mahābhūta* increase. For example,

> Ether – one quality – sound of a generalized nature, i.e. *nāda*
> Air – two qualities – sound+touch
> Fire – three quantities – sound+touch+shape (D.3)
> Water – four qualities – sound+touch+shape+taste
> Earth – five qualities – sound+touch+shape+taste+smell.

In the light of above correspondence between the sense objects and the *PM*s, the concept of partial equilibria and also the origin of pain and worry experienced by b, can be understood better.

Once the equilibrium of a localized nature between B and WO through SE is arrived at, then for b this amounts to a physical pleasure felt by M and stored in E. Any disturbance in such equilibrium causes a disease that manifests through pain which again is felt by M and stored rather deeply in E. At the next stage and maybe in a different situation, when b does not feel satisfied by this pleasure, then several pros and cons in terms of desires, which of course are guided by I, arise in M of b and again there are efforts of b to attain an equilibrium with WO, but now through SE and B. At this stage the pain is taken seriously by b. At another higher stage, when several guidances are provided by I, each of them appears to have priority and appeal over the other and leading to several pros and cons of desires in M with a possibility of their fulfilment, then another equilibrium among I, M, SE and B with WO is required to draw the pleasure of a higher order;

otherwise it causes worry to the individual. Thus, pain and worry experienced by b are the indications of diseases of mental domain. Their combined effect on b sometimes leads to depression — a mental setback. While pain has some physical content, worry, on the other hand, is the symptom purely of a mental disease and if the latter persists for a long time then this mental disease leads to a fast decay of B as a result of several instabilities in M. Note that both deficiency and excess of a *mahābhūta* in the system causes a disease in B in general and its cure again lies in readjusting this deficiency or excess from outside. In fact modern researches have shown as to how the pain and worry originate as a result of the brain-functioning or the functioning of the nervous system as a whole in B via biochemical reactions which in turn lead to a faster decay of B.

D4. Treatment of Diseases Using PMs: An Attempt to Restore Equilibrium

As mentioned, the *PM*s are not only the part of B, SE and WO in certain proportion[18] but also play an important role in the functioning of a Being. While the absence of any one of the *mahābhūta*s in the composition of B, SE or WO can cause the physical death of a Being, the deficiency or excess of any of them in this composition at any time or place can cause a disease in the body. This disease can be treated by compensating for the missing *mahābhūta* from the outside. In fact this treatment helps in restoring first a partial equilibrium between b and *PM*s which was initially disturbed and later the super equilibrium between the b and the cosmos.

While the cosmic consciousness field (the *mahātattva* of Vedānta[19, 20]) provides the background for everything in this universe, the deficiency or excess of a *mahābhūta* in the body can occur at all levels of essences of life, i.e. at physical, mental and/

18. See, Note 17.
19. See, the reference in citation 6.
20. See, Note 14.

or soul levels. It is the *mahātattva* of Vedānta philosophy which is responsible for bringing the spirituality in the life of a Being and that cures the last category of disease by way of transforming the lifestyle into a spiritual one;[21] otherwise for the cure of mental and physical diseases *PMs* come for help. In fact the "prayer" lies in the domain of *mahātattva* and the same also cures a disease or diseases. When a doctor fails and declares himself as incapable of curing a disease and the patient is striving for survival, then it is the prayer (or the realization of God in a true sense) which comes to rescue. Many patients have gone through such experiences and finally got cured of their disease. In what follows we briefly discuss some methods of curing of diseases in which *PMs* directly play their role, as it happens in naturopathy.

D4.1 ETHER/ĀKĀŚA MAHĀBHŪTA-BASED TREATMENT OF DISEASES

The existence of ether in the theories of physics was ruled out by Michelson-Morley experiment long ago. This perhaps was due to the limitations of the instrument used for the purpose or else the intuition that led to such a postulate in the theory was not well-founded. However, recent researches[22] have again started arguing for the existence of ether when experiments are performed using the laser beams. Otherwise the Vedānta ether or *ākāśa* (a synonym of space), as old as the Vedic literature, is all-pervading, a subtlest possible entity (of course still not as subtle as the field of cosmic consciousness or the *mahātattva*) in

21. Generally a ten-point programme is highlighted by saints to achieve the spirituality in life and these points are: (i) faith in God, (ii) chanting God's name and glory, (iii) thinking of God, (iv) surrender to God, (v) feeling one with God, (vi) meditation, (vii) straightforwardness, (viii) free from all conflicts, (ix) silence, and (x) feeling unattached to everything.

22. See, for example, M. Consoli and E. Costanzo, "From classical to modern ether-drift experiments: The narrow window for a preferred frame", *Phys. Lett.* A333 (2004) 355-63, and the references therein; Also see, *Phys. Lett.* A361 (2007) 513-14, for the reply to the comments by other authors.

this universe. Even in certain frameworks of modern physical theories, the concept of a fundamental or basic physical field is again cropping up[23] in recent years. If at all such an entity is established, this will be just an *apañcīkṛta* ether[24] of the Vedānta philosophy.

The use of *ākāśa mahābhūta* manifests directly or in conjunction with other *mahābhūtas* in the treatment of many diseases. Here however we highlight only a few treatments/prescriptions in which *ākāśa mahābhūta* plays a dominant role compared to others. In fact it appears that all the eight components of *rāja-yoga* of Patañjali hint towards the use of ether not only in treating a particular disease but, in general, in keeping oneself overall fit for attaining the ultimate truth/reality in Nature. To this effect, we discuss the control of mind, fasting and a few more (unusual) treatments which at their end-points result in the cure of a variety of diseases of both physical and mental levels. It may be mentioned that it is the instability of mind and the irregularity in the intake (sun, air, water, heat, food) of physical body which disturbs the corresponding partial equilibria of b with *PMs*.

(a) Control of Mind: For physical fitness, the mental fitness is necessary. On the other hand, for mental fitness a feedback comes from physical fitness of the body. In view of the *kārmika* theory discussed in Chapter 4, mental fitness in terms of control of mind plays an important role in the process of constructive (positive) pursuits. Thus the control of mind tantamounts to a channellizing of the mental energy so that the latter, when projected on to the physical space-time domain, gives rise to maximum output via the "principle of minimum efforts" (cf. Section 4.4). Otherwise, the mental energy is distributed all over in the medium like ether. This also includes the energy of mind/subconscious mind used on its other functions like dream, imagination, feeling, emotions, etc. which in some sense are

23. See, for example, C.M. Bender, D.C. Brody and H.F. Jones, *Phys. Rev. Lett.* 89 (2002) 270-401; *Am. Jour. Phys.* 71 (2003) 1095.

24. See the references in Notes 7 and 14.

beyond the space-time domain. Thus, the ether helps in curing of mental diseases of b by way of restoring a partial equilibrium of b with *PMs*. Similarly, if one regulates the functions of senses of knowledge and action by way of controlling them with mind as a seer, then this will further add to a directed flow of the mental energy. For this purpose, the instruments of SEs like ear, nose, throat, eyes, etc. (the parts of body) have to be in perfect order. Any defect in them needs to be cured using other *mahābhūtas* directly or indirectly. Once they are set in order and in tune with their corresponding sense objects, then their efforts for constructive pursuits treat the mental disease of b, via ether.

(b) Fasting: Dozens of diseases get cured by observing fast for a day or two. Fasting is of various degrees depending upon a check on the quality, quantity and frequency of intake during the day. While over-eating can cause a disease, under-eating is also a source of disease for a common man. For *yogīs*, however it is possible to survive with an intake of only one or a few of the *mahābhūtas* and to restore the equilibrium of their body with Nature. Fasting, in fact, resets the spacing not only among various inner organs of the body but also among blood cells and blood vessels which in turn further reflects on the skin and face of the person observing the fast. Fasting in general restores several partial equilibria of b with *PMs* and it is attributed to the *mahābhūta* ether. Fasting also improves the work efficiency at the level of both mind and physique by way of enhancing concentration. Not only this, the working of the nervous system also improves by observing a fast.

(c) Some other treatments and symptoms: There are several other phenomena whose occurrence in the body also sets the inner system in order and sometimes they are the indications of a disease in the body. For example, yawning (*jamhāhi*: opening the mouth wide as effect of drowsiness — it is due to the stimulation of certain centres in medulla oblongata); burping or belching (*dakāra*: emitting wind noisely from throat); sneezing (*chīṅkanā*: irritation inside the nasal mucosa or making an explosive sound in involuntarily expelling anything that irritates interior of nostrils — in this case olfactory fibres are stimulated producing this reflex via cranial nerves 9th and 10th); hiccup (*hicakī*, involuntary spasm of respiratory organs with sudden closure of glottis and thus making characteristic sound periodically); and farting or release of gastric gases (*pāda*: discharge of gas generated in the alimentary canal or of wind in the stomach — it is a release of gas produced by anaerobic bacteria in alimentary canal via anal opening), etc. In addition to them, "liberal laughing" and "submissive crying," leading sometimes to tears in eyes, recreation and sound sleep are also counted as best ways of self-purification of the body. These so-called natural phenomena (whose occurrence to some extent can again be attributed to the quality, quantity and the frequency of the intake in the body), do occur for all Beings in certain proportion and in one form or the other. Since the occurrence of some or of all these phenomena in the body has something to do with the resetting or readjustment of space among inner organs at the micro-level, their origin, in fact, is the direct attribute of the *mahābhūta* ether, with a little credit to other *mahābhūta*s as well. Perhaps, for this reason only the occurrence of some of them with an individual is considered as the indication of good or bad omens in some societies, particularly that of sneezing and hiccups.

D4.2 FIRE MAHĀBHŪTA-BASED TREATMENT OF DISEASES

In this wonderful machine of human body, the temperature — a measure of hotness is maintained at 37° Celcius or 98.4° Fahrenheit for a considerable period of time or as long as the human Being survives in this world. In some sense the role of fire *mahābhūta* in our life is attributed to the hotness of the sun and of the associated planets of our solar system including earth. Since the sun is a permanent and main source of heat and radiation and so are the planets, the fire *mahābhūta*-based treatment of diseases are nothing but the applications of direct sun, sunrays, heat and light in one form or the other. Not only this, in order to cure certain diseases hot air, hot water, hot earth (in the form of hot mud, brick or stone) and/or hot oil are used. Some examples to this effect are the following:

Steam bath cures a number of diseases. It could be a full steam bath (i.e. of the whole body) or a partial one (i.e. of a part of the body). Similarly, the use of hot water cures a number of diseases when used in different ways. For example, the drinking of hot water cures the cold or throat infection when used with black pepper and a pinch of sugar; continuous application of mildly hot water mixed with a bit of salt cures the muscular pain and helps in restoring the displaced nerves and in curing the pain at joints of body and so on.

Often the baking using the hot brick piece or hot mud is carried out to activate different muscles and nerves in various parts of the body and thereby providing some relief in the pain in that part. In fact there exists an altogether separate branch for the treatment of diseases using the sun, called *sūrya cikitsā*.

With regard to curing of diseases using the radiation or light, the system of chromotherapy had been used not only in India but also in Rome, Greece, Egypt and China since ancient times. Later in the nineteenth century other European countries also picked up the system and used it for curing some diseases. Chromotherapy, also called colour therapy, is an alternative medical approach in which therapists use colour and light to treat different health problems. In modern colour therapy, the different light spots depending on the type of disease are focused on body's acupuncture points and meridians. The light releases hormones in the body and influences reactions in the brain.

Indian Āyurvedic medicine system associates colours with the seven main *cakras* — spiritual centres in the body assumed to be located along the spinal cord. However, these seven points in modern times, in some sense are identified with seven nerve plexus as the centres of energy. According to *rāja-yoga*, during *samādhi* the life energy stored generally in the *mūlādhāra cakra* gets activated and raised up step by step to the levels of *ājñā* and *sahasrāra cakra*s by a *yogī*.

The colour convention found useful in treating various diseases in this case is that of the visible part of the long electromagnetic spectrum in the order of VIBGYOR. The top most *seventh sahasrāra cakra* in the brain is considered to be sensitive to *violet* colour and this colour treats lymphatic system, spleen, soothes organs, relaxes muscles, calms nervous system, etc. The *sixth ājñā cakra* in the forehead is sensitive to *indigo* colour and this colour provides treatment for eyes, ears, nose, mental problems, sedative, calming effects etc. The *fifth, viśuddhi cakra* assumed to be located in throat, is sensitive to *blue* colour and this colour provides relief in headaches, migraines, pains of stomach, muscle cramps, liver disorder and also leaves positive effects on all kinds of pain conditions. The *fourth, anāhata cakra* located near heart, is sensitive to *green* colour. The use of this colour provides relief in bronchitis, inflation of joints, swelling, cysts, eye diseases, diabetes, etc. It also promotes relaxation of organs and stimulates general detoxification. The *third, maṇipūraka cakra* located at *nābhi* (navel) is sensitive to *yellow* colour. This colour combats glandular diseases, diseases of lymphatic system, strengthens nervous system and assists metabolism and glandular activity. The *second, svādhiṣṭhāna cakra* located between *nābhi* (navel) and anus is sensitive to *orange* colour. This colour treats mental illness, depression, discontent and pessimism, loss of appetite, anaemia, anorexia and digestive system discomforts. The *first* one at the bottom, *mūlādhāra cakra* located in anus is sensitive to *red* colour. The use of this colour can increase pulse rate, blood pressure, rate of breathing, etc. However, it claims to combat anaemia, asthma, disease of larynx, certain skin diseases and chronic coughs, etc.

With regard to application of colours in clinical methods it may be noted that these colours of sunrays are used in various ways, for example, coloured glasses, colour-operated water, colour-operated oil, colour-operated clay, etc. are used in various diseases. In addition to this, the visibility of colours in Nature, colours of various chemicals and of other objects, which we see in day-to-day life, also have roots in the colour of sunrays. In fact liking and disliking of a colour by an individual can also be attributed to the deficiency or excess of a *mahābhūta* in the body. For further details on this science of chromotherapy.[25]

D4.3 AIR MAHĀBHŪTA-BASED TREATMENT OF DISEASES

Air in the atmosphere of earth-planet is an important ingredient in the existence of life on this earth. For any creature, particularly for the human Being it is rather impossible to survive even for a few minutes without inhaling the air. On the other hand, a regulated circulation of air inside the body among various organs including blood is also essential for survival. Any excess or deficiency of air in this process disturbs the equilibrium of b with the air-*mahābhūta* and thereby cause diseases. The *prāṇāyāma* component of *rāja-yoga* in Vedic sciences offers variety of methods to restore the stability of this equilibrium and thus offers cure of a large number diseases. According to Caraka there are three basic causes (i.e. *vāta, pitta* and *kapha*) of all diseases in the body, and air (*vāyu or vāta*), counts only for one cause and the same also offers treatment in a variety of cases. Some examples of such treatments are the following:

- Air bath or daily morning walks cure a number of diseases.
- A regulated breathing during *prāṇāyāma* or *apānāyam* also offers prescription for a number of diseases.
- Massage (dry or otherwise) helps in various disorders and diseases.
- Exercises until sweating or dry friction baths cure variety of disorders and diseases.

25. See the reference in Note 14.

- Various *yogāsanas* are recommended to cure variety of diseases.

D4.4 WATER MAHĀBHŪTA-BASED TREATMENT OF DISEASES

Like air and fire, water is also an important ingredient for survival of Beings on this earth. Though there is plenty of water on earth its presence in the body is always in a definite proportion and that maintains stable equilibrium of b with water *mahābhūta*. Like other *mahābhūtas*, excess or deficiency of water in the body causes a number of diseases. There is about 80 per cent water in human body. Not only this, teeth, the so-called hardest part of the body, contain 4 per cent water, bones contain 11-14 per cent, muscles 75 per cent, blood 80-87 per cent of water. Water is also a very important component of full food. It is water which helps in blood-flow through micro-components and organs of the body. Extra water in the body comes out in the form of sweating, vapour, urine etc.

Water at different temperatures is used for curing different diseases and such a use finally helps in maintaining the body temperature at 37° C. Not only this, the use of the same cold, hot or normal water, at times leaves short- and long-term effects in the body as a result of different biochemical reactions. Some treatments in which water is directly used in curing of diseases are the following:

- Normal daily bath provides a lot of relief from various diseases.
- In fact there are variety of ways in which bath can be taken with cold, hot and normal water and this recommends the prescription for various diseases and disorders in the body. For example, swimming in river, bath in rain, bath in ocean, bath in a mineral stream, and shower bath are recommended in different diseases.
- Partial bath or washing of a part of body using water is also recommended. For example, hip bath, spinal bath,

hot foot bath, steam bath, etc. are recommended according to various types of diseases.

- Towel bath, periodic friction bath or the use of cold and hot wet bandages or sheet in different parts of the body such as at forehead, chest, joints, back, etc. are also recommended in different cases.
- Daily washing of eyes, nostrils, mouth, head, etc. using water gives a lot of relief to these parts of the body.
- Use of cold or mild hot water through enema is normally a prescription in various abdominal diseases and disorder.

D4.5 EARTH MAHĀBHŪTA-BASED TREATMENT OF DISEASES

While earth is one of the five *mahābhūta*s of Vedic science, it is also one of the nine planets of our solar system. Earth in the form of clay or mud is easily available for any kind of treatment. The clay while considered as a neglected item, in fact, is full of positive qualities as far as its use in curing of a disease is concerned. For example, it can destroy bad smell, it can easily bear hotness and coldness at par, it can clean water, it can absorb poison, clay can check the flow of water, hotness of fire and the flow of air as well. The clay when combined with water, can take different shapes. Clay can be used to cure diseases in a variety of ways and some of them are the following:

- Walking bare foot on earth gives relief in various diseases.
- Taking bath using both dry and wet mud at times is useful in some diseases.
- Like the use of hot and cold water bandages, hot and cold bandages of mud are the assets in some diseases.
- Some naturopathists do not hesitate in recommending the swallow of clean sand, as it contains variety of minerals in general.

As a matter of fact whatever we eat everyday, most of these items are produced from earth. As a result a new branch of treatment based only on diet control has evolved. Not only this, the use of spices, fruits, vegetables in the meal also takes care of any harm from diseases.

In summary, the direct use of *PM*s does help in recovering from various diseases, no doubt at times at a slow pace, but the effects are definitely positive. In fact for any disease there are two types of causes, namely objective (external) and subjective (internal). While working against the doctrines of health and body maintenance is the root for the external cause, harmful worries and imaginative fear constitute the internal cause of a disease. Vedic science, combined with the balanced use of *PM*s and spirituality, is the best remedy to become free from these diseases.

D5. A Case for Astrology as a Science

In terms of belief, people in a society are divided over the acceptance of astrology as a science because of its 'not so sound' predictions. This is understandable in view of the definition of a perfect science given in Chapter 1. In fact there are certain prerequisites to be fulfilled by a model in science to provide ideal predictions and it is not so even with the so-called exact science like physics when combined with wonderful mathematical tools. Normally, the predictions of a theory are expected to be good if the initial conditions are "precise and stable" and the space-time evolution of the so-called "closed" system proceeds in a "linear" fashion. In the absence of any of them, the predictions of a theory cannot be reliable in terms of accuracy. Similar are the shortcomings with the science of astrology, which of course has a theory to predict the nature of actions and behaviour of a living system, particularly that of humans. Some of the difficulties with this science of astrology are as follows:

Firstly, treating the living system as a closed one is questionable even if the initial space-time conditions (e.g. the place and the time of birth of a Being) are known with a fair degree of accuracy. Secondly, for living systems the space-time is only one aspect in the super set of initial conditions (whether they pertain to physical birth of a Being or to the time and place of conception); otherwise several other parameters related to micro and causal bodies of a Being also come into existence. Thirdly, the space-time evolution of a Being does not take place in a linear fashion (it is rather highly non-linear) because of the presence of several other uncontrollable parameters and variables associated with the essences of life (cf. patomic model, Appendix A) of an individual. Fourthly, the space-time evolution of a Being (in spite of being non-linear) takes place on several fronts of the system, i.e. at the levels of biological body (B and SE) and micro-body (M, I and E). Of course, the causal body remains unaffected by these evolutions during the lifespan of a Being except for its role as an ultimate observer.

As mentioned in Section D2, each of the perceived *mahābhūtas* has some component of physical ether which in fact carries the effect of the entire universe, since all stars and planets are situated in it. In this way, the individual Being while on the earth, not only during its lifespan but also before the birth and after the death, is continuously exposed to the effect of these stars and planets, at least of those which are in the close proximity of the earth. As *per se* (cf. verse (2.1)), the micro-body of a Being through an extended *pañcīkaraṇa* (or rather some sort of *asthikaraṇa*, see Chapter 8) rule plays the role in the interactions of a Being with the cosmos, or conversely the stars and planets do affect not only the space-time evolution but also the mental evolution of the Being. Recent researches in astrophysics have shown that each planet or star has its own characteristic radiation; as a result its existence in the universe is detected by sophisticated instruments. These radiations received on the earth differ mainly in terms of frequency range in the electromagnetic spectrum. Furthermore, the intensity or energy of these radiations varies with the time scale variation on earth and also depends on the distance of a particular star or planet at a given time, its mode of rotation (intrinsic as well as orbital) and perhaps on the position of an observatory on the earth. Thus, it is not illogical to say that the radiation from these distant stars or planets can affect not only the growth of physical body but also the functioning of the micro-body of a Being. Perhaps future researches will reveal more on this front. Once the essences of life M, I and E get affected by the interactions of various *tanmātra*s, physical actions and behaviour of a Being also get affected.

It may be mentioned that a great deal of actions of a Being takes place in a domain which is beyond the space and time, i.e. at the level of micro-body and if other essences of life have to do something with this domain then the question is: at which stage of evolution the space and time enter? Indeed a certain fraction of it enters at the time of conception and most of it at the time of the birth of a Being when the physical body of the newly born baby is exposed to this physical universe. It is quite possible that the effect of planets and stars having dominant intensity in the radiation received on the earth at that point of space and time can affect the growth of both physical and micro-body of the baby in question. But note that ether/*ākāśa* is only one of the five *mahābhūta*s which the astrology mostly accounts for; otherwise other *mahābhūta*s do have a role to play in these evolutions of a Being. Therefore, the predictive power of the science of astrology remains rather poor. It provides only the pathways, directions and the trends of actions of a Being in the context of past, present and future, sometimes with large errors and uncertainties. These errors are natural since we have not accounted for the effect of other *mahābhūta*s or uncontrollable parameters of micro-body in the theory except for the ether/*ākāśa*.

D6. Concluding Discussion

With a view to exploring a justification to and a link between the two obscure sciences, namely naturopathy and astrology a framework in Vedānta philosophy has been revisited in the context of modern science. It is suggested that there exists a kind of super equilibrium between the workings of a Being and *PMs* of Vedānta philosophy. For peace, while humans and the like species have to make good use of their God-given extra essence of life that is intellect to maintain this super equilibrium with Nature, for pleasure, however, they have to maintain several partial equilibria with *PMs* at different levels of the patomic model (cf. Appendix A). Non-humans however feel satisfied with partial pleasures drawn out of these partial equilibria in the light of the "survival of the fittest" principle. In fact the super equilibrium is an outcome of all interactions of b with *PMs* via *tanmātras* whereas a partial equilibrium is attributed to the individual interaction of an essence of life of b with any or all five *mahābhūtas*.

Since the body of a Being is composed of *PMs*, it is argued that any deficiency or excess of a *mahābhūta* in the body of a Being causes a disease. Subsequently the adjustment of the corresponding *mahābhūta* from outside to the extent of restoring the equilibrium again is the cure of that disease in the science of naturopathy. To this effect several examples are cited in Section D4.

In view of the fact that planets and stars have their own characteristic frequency range in the electromagnetic radiation received from them on the earth, a basis for the science of astrology is sought in terms of the effect of these radiations on the Being. In reality while other *mahābhūtas* can also play a role in producing such an effect on b, astrology seems to account mostly for ether/*ākāśa mahābhūta* in terms of certain interactions via *tanmātras*. In fact in view of the *pañcīkaraṇa* rule the *tanmātra* associated with a given *mahābhūta* also carries some effect of other *mahābhūtas* beside the one of ether. Thus, whether the treatment of a disease in naturopathy or the predictions of astrology on the basis of effect of planets and stars, all this is an amalgamated effect of *PMs* in general. However, a particular *mahābhūta* dominates the scene in a particular situation. It is argued that once the Being is born and exposed to this physical universe, its evolution takes place on several fronts (cf. Section D5) and that too in a non-linear fashion. The predictions can be accurate only with respect to some of these evolutions, for example, for the physical evolution it is possible if and only if the initial conditions with respect to space and time (i.e. the place and time of birth or of conception) are known accurately. Since these space-time-based initial conditions are only one aspect of a bigger set of initial conditions, the predictions made from astrology regarding the behaviour of a Being remain rather poor.

Appendix E

A Generalized Hamilton Principle and the Derivation of Space-Time-Consciousness Evolution Equations for EP Matter

In this Appendix, in continuation of Section 8.7.1, we derive the space-time-consciousness (STC) evolution equations for the EP-matter using the methods of calculus of variation and in the spirit of Hamilton principle of least action in classical mechanics. A generalized version of the latter principle will be used here in the sense that now we account for the consciousness attached with the P (physical) matter and note that P matter plus consciousness is defined as the EP (epiphysical) matter. The role of consciousness in the action integral is considered by introducing a meditation parameter μ in the Lagrange function L, and by treating μ on par with the time variable t. Again, we shall carry out the derivation of STC evolution equations for two different cases, namely (i) when the Lagrangian L(q, $\dot{q}$, $\overline{q}$, t, μ) remains real, and (ii) when L(q, $\dot{q}$, $\overline{q}$, t, μ) becomes complex, viz. L = L_1 + I L_2, as a result of complex extensions of the coordinate q and the velocity p (=$\dot{q}$) in the form $q(t,\mu)=q_1(t)+iq_2(\mu)$, $p(t,\mu)=p_1(t)+ip_2(\mu)$ with $p_1=\dot{q}_1$ and

$$p_2=\frac{\partial q}{\partial \mu}=\overline{q}_2.$$

For further details see Section 8.7.

E1. Conscious Action: The Case of a Real Lagrangian

For the conscious action K, in this case, we write

$$K = \int_{t_1}^{t_2}\int_{\mu_1}^{\mu_2} L(q, \dot{q}, \overline{q}, t, \mu) d\mu dt. \tag{E.1}$$

Following the standard procedure based on the calculus of variation,[1] we proceed to find the stationary value of the functional integral (E.1). For this purpose, we introduce arbitrary parameters α with reference to t- variable and β with reference to μ- variable and write the integral (E.1) as

$$K(\alpha, \beta) = \int_{t_1}^{t_2}\int_{\mu_1}^{\mu_2} L(q(t, \mu, \alpha, \beta), \dot{q}(t, \mu, \alpha, \beta), \overline{q}(t, \mu, \alpha, \beta), t, \mu) d\mu\, dt. \tag{E.2}$$

Note that these infinitesimal parameters α and β defining the neighbouring paths vanish at the end-points of physical trajectory. Since K is the function of two variables now, the condition for stationary action demands that

$$\left(\frac{\partial K}{\partial \alpha}\right)_{\substack{\alpha=0\\ \beta=0}} = 0, \qquad \left(\frac{\partial K}{\partial \beta}\right)_{\substack{\alpha=0\\ \beta=0}} = 0, \tag{E.3a, b}$$

which in turn lead to the equations

$$\int_{t_1}^{t_2}\int_{\mu_1}^{\mu_2}\left[\frac{\partial L}{\partial q}\cdot\frac{\partial q}{\partial \alpha} + \frac{\partial L}{\partial \dot{q}}\cdot\frac{\partial \dot{q}}{\partial \alpha} + \frac{\partial L}{\partial \overline{q}}\frac{\partial \overline{q}}{\partial \alpha}\right] d\mu . dt = 0 \tag{E.4a}$$

$$\int_{t_1}^{t_2}\int_{\mu_1}^{\mu_2}\left[\frac{\partial L}{\partial q}\cdot\frac{\partial q}{\partial \beta} + \frac{\partial L}{\partial \dot{q}}\cdot\frac{\partial \dot{q}}{\partial \beta} + \frac{\partial L}{\partial \overline{q}}\frac{\partial \overline{q}}{\partial \beta}\right] d\mu . dt = 0 \tag{E.4b}$$

After simplifying the second and third terms in these equations in conjunction with the requirement that

$$\left(\frac{\partial q}{\partial \alpha}\right)_{t_1} = \left(\frac{\partial q}{\partial \alpha}\right)_{t_2} = \left(\frac{\partial q}{\partial \beta}\right)_{\mu_1} = \left(\frac{\partial q}{\partial \beta}\right)_{\mu_2} = 0,$$

one obtains

---

1. See, for example, H. Goldstein, *Classical Mechanics* (Addison-Wesley Publishing Co., 1981), chapter 2.

$$\int_{t_1}^{t_2}\int_{\mu_1}^{\mu_2}\left[\frac{\partial L}{\partial q}-\frac{\partial}{\partial t}\left(\frac{\partial L}{\partial \dot{q}}\right)-\frac{\partial}{\partial \mu}\left(\frac{\partial L}{\partial \overline{q}}\right)\right]\frac{\partial q}{\partial \alpha}\,d\mu.dt=0 \qquad \text{(E.5a)}$$

and

$$\int_{t_1}^{t_2}\int_{\mu_1}^{\mu_2}\left[\frac{\partial L}{\partial q}-\frac{\partial}{\partial t}\left(\frac{\partial L}{\partial \dot{q}}\right)-\frac{\partial}{\partial \mu}\left(\frac{\partial L}{\partial \overline{q}}\right)\right]\frac{\partial q}{\partial \beta}\,d\mu.dt=0 \qquad \text{(E.5b)}$$

Since $(\partial q/\partial \alpha)$ at any arbitrary value of t or μ is not zero, eq. (E.5a) yields the evolution equation as

$$\frac{\partial L}{\partial q}-\frac{\partial}{\partial t}\left(\frac{\partial L}{\partial \dot{q}}\right)-\frac{\partial}{\partial \mu}\left(\frac{\partial L}{\partial \overline{q}}\right)=0 \qquad \text{(E.6)}$$

Interestingly, the same STC evolution equation is obtained from (E.5b) by noting that $(\partial q/\partial \beta)\neq 0$ for arbitrary values of t and μ.

E2. Conscious Action: The Case of a Complex Lagrangian

With a view to investigating the nature of eigenvalues for a non-Hermitian Hamiltonian in quantum mechanics and certain aspects of classical mechanics, earlier an extended complex phase space approach is adopted by us to solve the Schrodinger equation[2, 3] in the former case, and to develop a method for constructing the dynamical invariants in the latter case.[4, 5] Super-symmetric quantum mechanics is also worked out[6] within the same framework. The role of imaginary parts in the coordinate and momentum variables has led to several interesting results and interpretations in these works. In the same spirit we continue here with a complex coordinate q and a complex velocity p in the forms

2. R.S. Kaushal, *J. Phys. A: Math & Gen* 34 (2001) L709.
3. R.S. Kaushal and Parthasarathi, *J. Phys. A: Math & Gen* 35 (2002) 8743.
4. R.S. Kaushal and Shweta Singh, *Ann. Phys.* (NY) 286 (2001) 253.
5. R.S. Kaushal and H.J. Korsch, *Phys. Lett.* A276 (2000) 47.
6. Parthasarathi, D. Parashar and R.S. Kaushal, *J. Phys. A: Math & Gen* 37 (2004) 781.

$$q(t,\mu)=q_1(t)+iq_2(\mu), \quad \text{(E.7a)}$$

$$p(t,\mu)=p_1(t)+ip_2(\mu), \quad \text{(E.7b)}$$

where $p_1=\dot{q}_1$ and $p_2=\dfrac{\partial q}{\partial \mu}=\bar{q}_2$; and with a complex Lagrangian as

$$L(q,p,t,\mu)=L_1(q_1,p_1,q_2,p_2,t,\mu)+IL_2(q_1,p_1,q_2,p_2,t,\mu) \quad \text{(E.8)}$$

In eq. (E.7), while real parts q_1 and p_1 correspond to the case of physical reality associated with the object, the imaginary parts q_2 and p_2, on the other hand, are the measures of non-physical reality and in turn account for the role of consciousness in the realization of the given object (cf. Section 8.7). In (E.8) we have split the complex Lagrangian L into real and imaginary parts where "I" instead of "i" is used with the imaginary part L_2. This is mainly because there is no reason why the dreaming of an object be the same as the dreaming of an action on it. They might belong to different imaginary planes. In the mathematical terms, we are considering different imaginaries with a complex number system and with the mappings on it. As we shall see, this is done at the cost of analyticity of the complex Lagrangian function L.

Note from (E.7) that

$$\frac{\partial}{\partial q}=\frac{\partial}{\partial q_1}-i\frac{\partial}{\partial q_2}, \qquad \frac{\partial}{\partial p}=\frac{\partial}{\partial p_1}-i\frac{\partial}{\partial p_2}, \quad \text{(E.9)}$$

and for the complex Lagrangian $L(q_1+iq_2,\ p_1+ip_2,t,\mu)$ we write the conscious action as

$$K=\int_{t_1}^{t_2}\int_{\mu_1}^{\mu_2} L(q_1(t)+iq_2(\mu),\ p_1(t)+ip_2(\mu),t,\mu)d\mu.dt \quad \text{(E.10)}$$

Now, as in the previous section, we introduce the parameters α and β corresponding to t and μ variables and write the action integral (E.10) as

$$K(\alpha,\beta)=\int_{t_1}^{t_2}\int_{\mu_1}^{\mu_2} L(q_1(t,\alpha)+iq_2(\mu,\beta),\ p_1(t,\alpha)+ip_2(\mu,\beta),t,\mu)d\mu.dt \quad \text{(E.11)}$$

and demand $\left(\frac{\partial K}{\partial \alpha}\right)_{\substack{\alpha=0\\ \beta=0}} = 0$, $\left(\frac{\partial K}{\partial \beta}\right)_{\substack{\alpha=0\\ \beta=0}} = 0$,

for the stationary action K. These conditions lead to

$$\int_{t_1}^{t_2}\int_{\mu_1}^{\mu_2}\left[\frac{\partial L}{\partial q}\frac{\partial q}{\partial \alpha}+\frac{\partial L}{\partial p}\frac{\partial p}{\partial \alpha}\right]d\mu . dt = 0, \tag{E.12a}$$

$$\int_{t_1}^{t_2}\int_{\mu_1}^{\mu_2}\left[\frac{\partial L}{\partial q}\frac{\partial q}{\partial \beta}+\frac{\partial L}{\partial p}\frac{\partial p}{\partial \beta}\right]d\mu . dt = 0. \tag{E.12b}$$

As before, we solve and simplify the second integral in these equations by noting that

$$\frac{\partial p}{\partial \alpha} = \frac{\partial p_1}{\partial \alpha} = \frac{\partial \dot{q}}{\partial \alpha} = \frac{\partial}{\partial t}\left(\frac{\partial q_1}{\partial \alpha}\right);\ \frac{\partial q}{\partial \alpha} = \frac{\partial q_1}{\partial \alpha}$$

$$\frac{\partial p}{\partial \beta} = i\frac{\partial p_2}{\partial \beta} = i\frac{\partial \overline{q}}{\partial \beta} = i\frac{\partial}{\partial \mu}\left(\frac{\partial q_2}{\partial \beta}\right);\ \frac{\partial q}{\partial \beta} = i\frac{\partial q_2}{\partial \beta}$$

and require that $(\partial q_1/\partial \alpha) \neq 0$ for (E.12a) and $(\partial q_2/\partial \beta) \neq 0$ for (E.12b) for arbitrary values of t and μ, then eqs. (E.12a) and (E.12b) respectively yield the following evolution equations with respect to the complex variables q and p:

$$\frac{\partial L}{\partial q} - \frac{\partial}{\partial t}\left(\frac{\partial L}{\partial p}\right) = 0, \tag{E.13}$$

$$\frac{\partial L}{\partial q} - \frac{\partial}{\partial \mu}\left(\frac{\partial L}{\partial p}\right) = 0. \tag{E.14}$$

In its component form eq. (E.13) is equivalent to the following set of equations

$$\frac{\partial L_1}{\partial q_1} - \frac{\partial}{\partial t}\left(\frac{\partial L_1}{\partial p_1}\right) = 0 \quad , \quad \frac{\partial L_1}{\partial q_2} - \frac{\partial}{\partial t}\left(\frac{\partial L_1}{\partial p_2}\right) = 0, \tag{E.15a, b}$$

$$\frac{\partial L_2}{\partial q_1} - \frac{\partial}{\partial t}\left(\frac{\partial L_2}{\partial p_1}\right) = 0 \quad , \quad \frac{\partial L_2}{\partial q_2} - \frac{\partial}{\partial t}\left(\frac{\partial L_2}{\partial p_2}\right) = 0, \tag{E.15c, d}$$

when "i" ≠ "I". Now if "i" = "I", then eq. (E.13) yields the following pair of equations

$$\frac{\partial L_1}{\partial q_1}+\frac{\partial L_2}{\partial q_2}-\frac{\partial}{\partial t}\left(\frac{\partial L_1}{\partial p_1}\right)-\frac{\partial}{\partial t}\left(\frac{\partial L_2}{\partial p_2}\right)=0, \tag{E.16a}$$

$$\frac{\partial L_2}{\partial q_1}-\frac{\partial L_1}{\partial q_2}-\frac{\partial}{\partial t}\left(\frac{\partial L_2}{\partial p_1}\right)-\frac{\partial}{\partial t}\left(\frac{\partial L_1}{\partial p_2}\right)=0, \tag{E.16b}$$

Similarly, eq. (E.14) is equivalent to

$$\frac{\partial L_1}{\partial q_1}-\frac{\partial}{\partial \mu}\left(\frac{\partial L_1}{\partial p_1}\right)=0 \quad ; \quad \frac{\partial L_1}{\partial q_2}-\frac{\partial}{\partial \mu}\left(\frac{\partial L_1}{\partial p_2}\right)=0, \tag{E.17a, b}$$

$$\frac{\partial L_2}{\partial q_1}-\frac{\partial}{\partial \mu}\left(\frac{\partial L_2}{\partial p_1}\right)=0 \quad ; \quad \frac{\partial L_2}{\partial q_2}-\frac{\partial}{\partial \mu}\left(\frac{\partial L_2}{\partial p_2}\right)=0, \tag{E.17c, d}$$

when "i" ≠ "I". Now if "i" = "I", one obtains the following pair of equations

$$\frac{\partial L_1}{\partial q_1}+\frac{\partial L_2}{\partial q_2}-\frac{\partial}{\partial \mu}\left(\frac{\partial L_1}{\partial p_1}\right)-\frac{\partial}{\partial \mu}\left(\frac{\partial L_2}{\partial p_2}\right)=0, \tag{E.18a}$$

$$\frac{\partial L_2}{\partial q_1}-\frac{\partial L_1}{\partial q_2}-\frac{\partial}{\partial \mu}\left(\frac{\partial L_2}{\partial p_1}\right)+\frac{\partial}{\partial \mu}\left(\frac{\partial L_1}{\partial p_2}\right)=0, \tag{E.18b}$$

For the case when "I" = "i", we make use of the Cauchy-Riemann conditions for a complex function of two variables, namely

$$\frac{\partial L_1}{\partial q_1}=\frac{\partial L_2}{\partial q_2}, \frac{\partial L_1}{\partial q_2}=-\frac{\partial L_2}{\partial q_1} \quad ; \quad \frac{\partial L_1}{\partial p_1}=\frac{\partial L_2}{\partial p_2}, \frac{\partial L_1}{\partial p_2}=-\frac{\partial L_2}{\partial p_1}, \tag{E.19}$$

And their by-product as[7]

7. See, for example, V.S. Vladimirov, *Methods of Theory of Functions of Many Complex Variables*, (MIT Press, Cambridge, MA, 1966).

$$\frac{\partial^2 L_j}{\partial q_1^{\,2}}+\frac{\partial^2 L_j}{\partial q_2^{\,2}}=0 \quad , \quad \frac{\partial^2 L_j}{\partial q_1 \partial p_1}+\frac{\partial^2 L_j}{\partial q_2^{\,2}}=0 \qquad \text{(E.20a, b)}$$

$$\frac{\partial^2 L_j}{\partial p_2^{\,2}}+\frac{\partial^2 L_j}{\partial p_1^{\,2}}=0 \quad , \quad \frac{\partial^2 L_j}{\partial q_1 \partial p_2}-\frac{\partial^2 L_j}{\partial p_1 \partial q_2}=0 \qquad \text{(E.20c, d)}$$

For j = 1, 2, i.e., L_1 and L_2 are bi-harmonic functions and solve the Laplace equation $\Delta_j L_i = 0$. As a consequence, they cannot have a minimum in configuration space. The use of (E.19) in (E.16) and (E.18) respectively yields

$$\frac{\partial L_1}{\partial q_1}-\frac{\partial}{\partial t}\left(\frac{\partial L_1}{\partial p_1}\right)=0 \quad ; \quad \frac{\partial L_2}{\partial q_1}-\frac{\partial}{\partial t}\left(\frac{\partial L_2}{\partial p_1}\right)=0\,, \qquad \text{(E.21a, b)}$$

and

$$\frac{\partial L_1}{\partial q_1}-\frac{\partial}{\partial \mu}\left(\frac{\partial L_1}{\partial p_1}\right)=0 \quad ; \quad \frac{\partial L_2}{\partial q_1}-\frac{\partial}{\partial \mu}\left(\frac{\partial L_2}{\partial p_1}\right)=0. \qquad \text{(E.22a, b)}$$

It can be seen that eqs. (E.21a) and (E.21b) (or eqs. (E.22a) and (E.22b)) are the just two equations of the set (E.15) (or the set (E.17)). Two equations in each set are still left which are the outcome of non-analyticity property of L. In fact these two remaining equations further reduce to one in each case using the additional conditions (E.20) for analyticity.

It can be seen that the case of complex Lagrangian turns out to be much richer than the real one as far as the description of non-physical reality in Nature is concerned. In particular, when we relax the analyticity property of the complex function,[8] several interesting features emerge in mathematical terms. Some of these features are as follows:

---

8. The non-analytic nature of the conscious Lagrangian seems understandable in view of the fact that like time, consciousness can-not be fragmented in general and the nature of implicit dependence of q and p on μ variable remains in the background of such a requirement.

(i) The appearance of imaginary part of L, i.e. L_2, in eqs. (E.15) to (E.22) represents the effect(s) of non-physical action (i.e. the dreaming or imagination) in the space-time consciousness evolution of the system. On the other hand, in these equations the terms involving the imaginary parts of q and p, i.e. q_2 and p_2, accordingly represent the non-physical aspects associated with the realization of an element in WO. In general, the terms like

$$\frac{\partial L_2}{\partial q_2} \text{ or } \frac{\partial}{\partial \mu}\left(\frac{\partial L_2}{\partial p_2}\right)$$

have their origin purely in the domain of consciousness whereas the terms like

$$\frac{\partial L_2}{\partial q_1}, \frac{\partial L_1}{\partial q_2}, \frac{\partial}{\partial t}\left(\frac{\partial L_2}{\partial p_1}\right), \frac{\partial}{\partial t}\left(\frac{\partial L_2}{\partial p_2}\right), \frac{\partial}{\partial t}\left(\frac{\partial L_1}{\partial p_2}\right), \frac{\partial}{\partial \mu}\left(\frac{\partial L_1}{\partial p_1}\right), \frac{\partial}{\partial \mu}\left(\frac{\partial L_2}{\partial p_1}\right) \text{ or } \frac{\partial}{\partial \mu}\left(\frac{\partial L_1}{\partial p_2}\right)$$

in eqs. (E.15) and (E.17) originate from the domains in which the space, time and consciousness co-exist either pair-wise or otherwise, namely the domains of M, I and E.

(ii) It is not difficult to realize that eqs. (E.16) and (E.18) (corresponding to the case when "I" = "i") respectively are certain combinations of equations in sets (E.15) and (E.17). In fact the addition of (E.15a) and (E.15d) or the subtraction of (E.15b) from (E.15c) lead to eqs. (E.16a) and (E.16b) respectively. Similarly, the addition of (E.17a) and (E.17d) or the subtraction of (E.17b) from (E.17c) gives rise to eqs. (E.18a) and (E.18b). Further use of Cauchy-Riemann conditions (E.19) reduces eqs. (E.16) and (E.18) into some simpler versions. It can be seen that the pairs of these simpler versions in (E.16) and (E.18) are just the two equations of sets (E.15) and (E.17). In fact the additional two equations in each of these sets are the outcome of non-analyticity property of L. As a matter of fact the relaxing of the analyticity property of the complex function L results in a fine-tuning of the effect of consciousness. Further, since the consciousness cannot be fragmented like time, this non-analyticity of L in some sense becomes desirable.

(iii) An interesting feature to be noted from the sets of eqs. (E.15) and (E.17) is that eq. (15a) describes exclusively the evolution of physical aspect and that eq. (E.17d) describes exclusively the non-physical aspect — the two extreme situations with regard to the evolution of the system. The remaining equations (namely eqs. (E.15b)-(E.15d) and (E.17a)-(E.17c)) however, account for the evolution in mixed situations in which all three space, time and consciousness play their roles in certain proportions.

(iv) Finally, we remark on the choice "I" ≠ "i". Note that for the case when $q_1=0$, $q_2=1$, $L_1=\mathbb{Z}$ (zero transformation) and $L_2=\mathbb{1}$ (identity transformation), "I" will map "i" alone to give the image I(i), i.e. I as some function of i. Now, if I(i) is an even function of i, then this will result in the function I to be a real one and so is the transformation $L=L_1+IL_2$. Therefore, for a complex transformation, I(i) has to be an odd function of i and for this case I(i) in its most general form, can be written as I(i) = ai + b, with a and b as real constants. However, the property I(-i)=-I(i) implies b=0, leaving behind I(i)=ai. Thus, without any loss of generality the constant a can be chosen as unity and perhaps for this reason I=i is used all throughout the theory of functions of complex variable. In the present case, however, neither q_1 can be zero nor can the real part L_1 be a zero transformation since we are basically building up a theory on the ground of physical reality (cf. Chapter 8). Therefore, in general, "I" ≠ "i" is considered here.

Appendix F

Some Exotic Phenomena in the Realm of Human Behaviour

THIS Appendix provides some details of the ideas presented in Section 6.3 and pertains to some exotic phenomena which also lie in the domain of human behaviour and actions. Two such phenomena, namely out-of body experiences (OBE) and near-death experiences (NDE) which an individual might have at the time of death and the explanations of the same may have its roots in biological science, are already discussed there. A basis of several other spurious phenomena like dowsing, levitation, remote viewing, or the ones pertaining to hypnosis or the ones that fall in the domain of parapsychology will be discussed here. In spite of a great deal of research to understand this latter class of phenomena being in progress, above experiences by an individual, if at all they are there (in the sense that many of us have not undergone any of such experiences while their occurrences cannot be ruled out), still qualify to be called as *mystiques*. Here, keeping the framework of patomic model in mind, we shall look for a possible basis for the occurrences of these peculiarities in the human and non-human behaviour and actions. These peculiarities basically are the outcome of interactions beyond the space-time Cartesian grid (STCG); however their effects are noticed in the domain of STCG.

These phenomena basically originate when an individual is put under some abnormal conditions willingly or unwillingly; of course, in both the situations the behaviour of the individual turns out to be different from the normal. It may be mentioned that as for the existence of human race on this planet certain optimum physical and biological conditions (like pressure, temperature, environment, etc.) are necessary, in the same way for a person to have normal behaviour and living a particular setting of his mindset $\mathcal{M}$(m, i, e; σ) is necessary. Any drastic change (not adjustable under given circumstances, σ) in the parameters m, i and e (manifestations of inner EOLs M, I and E) can lead to an abnormal behaviour of the person. To understand such abnormalities in the behaviour, another analogy from atomic physics will be useful here at the outset.

F1. An Illustrative Analogy

Recall that an atom in itself has an intrinsic electricity and magnetism and the corresponding fields inside, but when placed in an external electric or magnetic field it shows abnormal behaviour in the form of Stark, Zeeman, or Faraday effect. In the same way, a conscious individual who himself has "soul" or "spiritual" energy fields (translasted into the mindset $\mathcal{M}$ above), when placed in an external but "soul" or "spiritual" energy field is bound to undergo a change in its mindset or the behaviour. The later phenomenon is abbreviated as *"K-effect."*[1] Note that in the case of an atom the electric or magnetic field inside and outside the atom, are in no way different as far as their fundamental features in space-time are concerned. The only thing is that these two categories of fields are separated by space-time boundary to term them as "inside" and "outside" fields and what appears in the observed data is the resultant effect of the interactions between the two. On the other hand, when an individual undergoes an intense or specially designed psychic

1. To cut short the phrase, let us abbreviate it as "K-effect." This effect no doubt can be noticed in the above context but basically is a change in the mindset of one person by the presence of the other and observed by the third with reference to the first. In the language of Chapter 9, this is the case of three interacting persons (like mother-father-child etc.) in which the effect of the interaction is noticed by the third person on one of the participating persons. The exchanges are not balanced and are unidirectional in certain sub-domains.

zone, then a variety of phenomena with regard to the behaviour of the individual are bound to appear as a result of interactions. In the latter case, however, each — the external psychic zone and the psychic zone associated with the individual — has a number of constituents (like M, I and E) to interact with. Therefore, there is a possibility of appearance of a variety of phenomena as a result of interactions in the K-effect.

Unlike the atomic case, here the individual acts as an open system as far as the space-time boundary or the associated (physical) processes are concerned. These are basically the psychic processes or the fundamental processes that occur and are discussed in this book. Therefore, there is no range of interaction in physical terms or the sharp boundary in space-time to define "inside" and "outside." Moreover, in the atomic case while forces are AAD-type, in the K-effect, however, the forces could be any one type or all the three AAD-, AAT- and AADT- types in addition to the contact force. This latter feature of the fundamental processes suggests the possibility of occurrence of phenomena like remote viewing, remote sensing, tele-therapy, and unexplained acoustics, etc. which in fact are beyond the reach of common-man experiences.

In atomic case it is the detecting apparatus which converts the "interaction-effects" of the two category of fields into an "observable-effect," i.e. in the form of splitting of spectral lines etc. in the Stark or Zeeman effect. In the K-effect however the affected individual (who is also a living Being) himself acts as an instrument and his behaviour as noticed by a third normal person, becomes observable in terms of abnormality. Note that this abnormality in his behaviour appears from the point of view of a normal person.

Finally note that in the atomic case the electric or magnetic field is not considered (and in fact it is not) the part of cosmic electric or magnetic field (if at all it is there, it is not yet investigated in the present-day physics), as a result only a part of interaction manifests in the experiments. On the other hand, in the K-effect since both intrinsic and extrinsic soul energies are part of cosmic consciousness field, the problem is more complicated and the occurrence of a variety of phenomena is possible. It is not that these phenomena are the recent discoveries in Nature; rather people have been noticing their occurrence since time immemorial and in different societies and cultures. It is only in recent times, that efforts have been made for some systematic studies and to look at them in a scientific framework if possible. Now the question is as to what extent the individual undergoing the external psychic zone will get affected; of course, this will depend upon the development of his FOUs and on several other factors. In what follows, we first highlight and list a few phenomena and the related case-studies pursued systematically is recent times and then try to categorize these exotic phenomena[2] with some plausible explanation(s) within the framework of patomic model.

F2. A brief Survey of Exotic phenomena

Although these phenomena (seen rarely in the human behaviour and actually fall within the realm of parapsychology) have been known ever since, only in recent years some systematic studies (see, for example[3, 4, 5, 6, 7, 8]) have been carried out, even though

2. At times these phenomena are cited as "mystiques" as their explanation remains beyond the reach of space-time-mediated physical laws or beyond the reach of level of development of FOUs of a common man.

3. See, for example, June G. Bletzer at the website http://www.world-mysteries.com/sci_4.htm.

4. Scott Prieskop, at the website http://www.tomzap.com/sounds.html.

5. Paul H. Smith, at the website http://www.world-mysteries.com/sci_remotev.htm.

6. See the website http://www.dowsing.com/dowsing/dqonda.htm

7. David Pratt, "Gravity and Antigravity", Feb. 2005 http://ourworld.compuserve.com/homepages/dp5/gravity2.htm.

8. David Pratt, "Consciousness, causality, and quantum physics", http://ourworld.compuserve.com/homepages/dp5/jse.htm (2007)

without any general theoretical framework for the analysis of the data so collected. Also, there does not exist a unifying mechanism to understand various phenomena observed in diverse and often disconnected situations. With a hope that patomic model of human Being can provide an explanation for some (if not for all) phenomena, we review briefly here some of these works.

June G. Bletzer[9] groups these phenomena into the following sixteen classes on the basis of some of the similarities noticed perhaps in their noticeable effects:

(i) Telepathy, tele-empathy;
(ii) Clairvoyance, Precognition, Premonition;
(iii) Remote viewing, Psychometry, Psi-detectives;
(iv) Dowsing, Earth radiation;
(v) Deja Vu, psychic archaeology;
(vi) Out-of-body Experiencs (OBE), Near-death Experiences (NDE), Dreams, Psychic dreams, Hallucinations;
(vii) Hypnosis;
(viii) Telekinesis-Psychokinesis, Levitation, Teleportation;
(ix) Psychic healing, Influencing plants, Influencing weather;
(x) Prophesies, Divination-auguri, Oracles;
(xi) The pendulum, Reading cards;
(xii) Automatic writing, Quiza board;
(xiii) TV Psychics, Communication with animals;
(xiv) Trance mediums, Spirit doctors;
(xv) Psychic photography, Psychic audio contacts, Haunting, Poltergeists; and
(xvi) Reincarnation.

Note that all these sixteen classes are not completely independent as far as roots of their origin and the domain of their occurrence are concerned.[10] In view of analogy of Section

9. June G. Bletzer, see citation 3.

10. Raj Kumari Bahl, "Mystiques and Science", Orientation Course Project (OR-46), CPDHE, University of Delhi, 6 December 2005 – 4 January 2006.

F1 above, most of these phenomena concern an individual and originate from an affected psychic zone of that individual as a result of (i) his *saṁskāras* of previous birth, (ii) the development of his extra-sensory perception in terms of dressing of his EOLs with consciousness, (iii) the presence of another abnormal psychic zone around, or (iv) the presence of extreme external physical conditions, i.e. environment and/or circumstances, causing a change in the neurodynamics of brain. Further note that these phenomena appear to be strange for a third person with a normal psychic zone and some of them if not all may not be exotic for him if he himself also has a matching psychic zone in terms of development of his FOUs and/or abnormality desired for.

Next we define the terminology for some and highlight a selective categorization of these phenomena, used in recent studies.

(A) ***Psi***: A neutral term used for parapsychological phenomena. Psi, psychic, psychical are the synonyms.

(B) ***ESP (Extra-sensory perception):*** a general term used for obtaining information about events beyond the reach of normal senses (i.e. beyond the domain of space-time Cartesian grid). Some phenomena listed under this category are:

(1) *Telepathy:* Direct mind-to-mind communication (the word "mind" needs a clarification in the present context of patomic model). Another related phenomenon is the *tele-empathy* in which one feels the physical pain or the mental and emotional situation of somebody else that destroys the peace of mind.

(2) *Precognition:* Obtaining information about future events where the information could not be inferred through normal means. Precognition can happen to anyone. It does not require a special talent. Another related phenomenon is *premonition* in which one feels about

something to happen in a specific way without any details given.

(3) *Clairvoyance:* Obtaining information about events at remote location beyond the reach of the normal senses. This French word means "clear seeing." Clairvoyance is the ability of a person to "clearly see," present or future or situations at will. Another phenomenon related to this is the *Remote viewing*.

(C) ***Psychokinesis (PK) and Bio-psychokinesis (BPK):*** PK deals with direct mental interaction with physical objects (animate or inanimate), whereas BPK deals with direct mental interaction with living systems (Beings).

(D) ***NDE, OBE and Reincarnation:*** These are the cases discussed already in Section 6.3.

(E) ***Haunting:*** Recurrent phenomena reported to occur in particular locations that includes apparitions, sounds, movement of objects and other effects.

(F) ***Poltergeist*:** Large scale PK phenomena often attributed to spirits but which are now thought to be due to a living person, frequently an adolescent.

(G) ***Non-humans also show exotic phenomena:*** As mentioned in Chapter 10, there are several non-humans who show the symptoms of ESP, particularly rats, dogs, cats, etc. Even among them there are exceptions which have stronger sense perception. According to a Reporting,[11] a nursing home cat is found capable of sensing death coming to patients. When the cat (named Oscar) visits residents of Steere House Nursing and Rehabilitation Centre in Providence, Rhode Island, the staff jumps into action — Oscar can sense within hours when someone is

---

11. "Nursing home cat can sense death coming", Reporting in *Times of India*, 27 July 2007, p. 21, based on a Reporting by Dr David Dosa of Brown University in Providence in *New England Journal of Medicine*.

about to die. It is not that the cat is consistently there first, but the cat always does manage to make an appearance and it always seems to be in the last two hours. Oscar has visited at least 25 persons on the death bed according to Dr. Joan Teno (Professor of Community Health); the cat does not appear to be psychic, but there is probably a biochemical explanation of the phenomenon.

(H) ***Some other related phenomena of particular interest:***

(1) *Dowsing*: With the help of one's superconscious mind, using a suitable device, one may gain unseen information at a distance, (even through material barriers), about a person, creature, object, substance, place or "thing" beyond the limitations of one's five senses and his so-called logical, thinking mind.

(2) *Levitation:* Transportation, lifting or floating of a heavy load (as heavy as beyond the human or instrument capacity in the air without any sign of physical connection, is termed "levitation." While some researchers attribute this phenomenon to spiritual energy of an individual, other mainstream scientists try to find reasons in the concept of antigravity.[12] Particularly, the acoustic and magnetic levitation techniques, currently under development, are expected to provide a force stronger than the force of gravity. It will take a long way to find answers to the question as to how the use of heavy loads in Haṛappan or Mayan civilization was made.

(3) *Telekinesis and Teleportation:* Use of one's spiritual energy to levitate some material object is called "telekinesis." On the other hand, *teleportation* is the transport of something through the quantum vacuum to a different location. As this happens in the realm where there is no space and no time, this process is instant. Further, someone,

12. David Pratt, 2005, op. cit.

with sufficient spiritual prowess can teleport himself to a different location or can move an object this way.

Note that for some of these phenomena (like NDE, OBE, reincarnation, hallucination, etc.) an explanation has already been sought in terms of fundamental processes taking place inside a human being, and for some (i) an induction of action-at-a-time (AAT) type forces in physical theories, (ii) the case of highly dressed inners EOLs, and (iii) the illustrative analogy of Section F1 can offer explanation in the present work, at least qualitatively.

Further, different categories of researchers have different interests in the study of these phenomena. For example, *physicists* tend to be interested in parapsychology because of the implication that we have a gross misunderstanding about space and time and transfer of energy and information. *Biologists* are interested because "psi" implies the existence of additional unexplained methods of sensing the world. *Psychologists* are interested for what "psi" implies about the nature of perception and memory. *Philosophers* are interested because psi phenomena specifically address several age-old philosophical problems, including the role of the mind in the physical world, and the nature of the objective *vs.* the subjective. This is partly the reason for listing these phenomena at this place. *Theologians and general public* are also interested in these phenomena because personal psi experiences are often accompanied by feelings of profound, ineffable meaning. As a result, "psi" is thought by some to have "spiritual" implications.

F3. Possible Available Explanations

Clearly, the exotic phenomena do occur. They are exotic because none of the categories of experts mentioned above have a convincing and logical explanation for them. Not only this, there exists a category of scientists that outrightly rejects even the occurrence if not of all but of some of these phenomena unless the concerned scientist himself undergoes (or has undergone) these strange experiences. For the explanation of their occurrence, however, a scientist does not want to go beyond the domain of STCG, whereas going beyond this domain is a must as many of these phenomena lie within psychic zone. On the other hand, as these phenomena over centuries have become a part of life in different cultures, their comprehensive study and a unified explanation in scientific terms is necessary. The patomic model in conjunction with several other ideas advanced in this book, perhaps can be helpful in providing plausible explanation if not for all but for most of these phenomena.

Note that the studies based on Western philosophy (including the scientific thoughts of STCG domain) are highly sketchy and at times inconsistent in themselves mainly because this philosophy, as discussed in Chapter 3, lags behind in presenting a comprehensive picture of the phenomenon of consciousness that prevails in a living Being and his actions. Yet for the sake of completeness a couple of such explanations available[13, 14, 15, 16] are given below before emphasizing the viability of patomic model in this regard.

F3.1 EXPLANATIONS BASED ON WESTERN THINKING

From the materialistic point of view, one of the foundations of the current scientific explanation of these phenomena is the following: Human consciousness is considered as a resultant product of the functioning of brain, body and nervous system (BBNS) (cf. Section 11.2). That is, no matter how different mind may seem from solid stuff like bodies, it is generated solely by the electrochemical functioning of the BBNS, and so it is absolutely dependent on it. When the BBNS dies, so does the consciousness. From this perspective, claims of survival of bodily death, or ghosts, or apparitions, must be due to wishful thinking. Furthermore, the limits of material functioning automatically

13. June G. Bletzer, op. cit. in citation 3.
14. Scott Prieskop, op. cit.
15. Paul H. Smith, op. cit.
16. See, website cited in 6.

determine the ultimate limits of mental functioning. Thus, the phenomena like ESP and PK appear to be impossible, particularly when our current understanding about how the world works is given.

Note that Psi phenomena occurred in all cultures and continue to occur, and the occurrence of some more phenomena reported have been persuasively verified using scientific methods. Since Psi seems to transcend the assumed limits of material thinking (and therefore of BBNS), some persons interpret Psi as supporting the idea that there is something more to mind than just the BBNS and it is some sort of "soul" or the like. Such a non-physical aspect in fact does not seem to be as tightly bounded by STCG as the present scientific models require and the same might survive the bodily death in para-psychological studies.

1. First note the difference between two types of para-psychological studies, namely one type are the findings that have implications for spiritual concepts and in other case parapsychologists are driven by some hidden spiritual agenda, like religious motives in which they try to prove the existence of soul. Since spiritual concepts also end up at the level of soul or in its cosmic links then these aspects of study are complementary, particularly within the framework of Vedic science.
2. ***Goddess Psyche and the source of psychic phenomena:*** The word psychic describes anything related to psyche. This word dates back to ancient times when a goddess by the name of Psyche was in charge of all the invisible but essential part of human existence. Over the period of time the word and its meanings evolved and at present the synonyms used for this word are: Mind, soul, self, subconscious, spirit, subliminal self, inner self, ego and individuality. While these words have wide range of meanings, the source of psychic phenomena by analyst is sought in the following framework; in particular the

work of Professor Fredric Schiffer of Harvard University[17] is well known in this context.

(i) One starts with two types of energies, namely the "energy of matter," and the "energy behind matter." In a religion, the latter is a synonym of spiritual energy and in physical science it is called the energy of the quantum vacuum. Thus there are matter phases and the phases of the associated energy of matter. The energy of matter oscillates between the stages of energy and of matter. The energy behind matter is very different from the energy of matter. The former always remains energy and, therefore, does not constitute space and/or time. In this realm of pure energy everything is inter-related.

(ii) The succession of matter phases marks the change, which was achieved in the energy phase and expresses it in a material dimension in the form of geometry (space), whereas the progression of matter phases creates time, the fourth dimension of matter.

(iii) Any kind of change for matter happens in its energy phase. When the oscillation of matter stops in matter phase, everything would stop dead at this instance. For example, when a body moves, the displacement takes place in the energy phases and matter follows energy's lead in consecutive matter phases, thus expressing the movement which has taken place in the preceding energy phases. For movement to take place a command has to be issued. The processes,

17. Fredric Schiffer, "Brain may have two minds of its own" (Researchers study novel ways to ease depression), *Harvard University Gazette,* 4 April 2002; also see, "Of Two Minds: Revolutionary Science of Dual-Brain Psychology" (New York: The Free Press, 1998).

that determine as to what matter has to do, take place in the realm of spiritual energies. An appropriate command to matter energies comes from this domain and the same decides the kind of action the energies of matter took.

Refrigerator example: Consider a person who wants to go to the refrigerator. First comes the thought in his spiritual energies. This thought issues a command to the energy of matter, which then progresses towards the refrigerator. The movement of the energies of matter is expressed in consecutive matter phases as this person walks to the refrigerator.

Thus, every movement of a person's life involves spiritual activity. Without the directions given to a person by the energies behind matter — the spiritual energies — nothing can happen in the realm of matter.

3. ***Schiffer's computer-working-analogue of psychic processes:***[18] In the spirit of discussions in Section 6.5, Schiffer here also looks for explanation of psychic phenomena in the analogy of a computer-working. According to him the left and the right side of the brain of a human Being, respectively corresponding to conscious and unconscious aspects of mind, act like a biological computer. The conscious correspond to the processor and the working memory of the machine whereas unconscious acts like a hard-disc, i.e. memory storage. Consequently, every person has two minds and together they constitute his personality.

Further, conscious mind puts data into the unconscious mind with thoughts, words and actions. This data is stored and retrieved when a situation arises for it can be used. If such data is used to make the conscious mind to do something specific on

---

18. Fredric Schiffer, op. cit.

a specific occasion, then this works like a computer programme that makes the machine to perform a certain task.

At the time of birth the conscious mind of a baby is blank since it has no memory. All of its skills have to be learned and developed as the baby grows up. On the other hand, the unconscious mind is the spirit (!) of a person and it contains all the data put in during all previous births (lifetimes). With its access to memories of previous lifetimes the unconscious mind also has access to a vast reservoir of previous experiences from which the conscious mind can draw if it pays attention to feelings and hunches etc. mainly because the unconscious mind cannot talk (or communicate), it just transmits images or feelings. Every time the conscious mind thinks or plans, the unconscious mind checks on the information stored in its energies and issues responses in the form of feelings and images. Since this check is done by spiritual energies, the information is provided instantly mainly because in the spiritual realm the concept of time is not there.

Note that the occurrence of a large number of psychic phenomena listed in Section F2 has been understood within these frameworks. However, the patomic model of Vedic science offers explanation of these phenomena in a more elaborative and fine-tuned manner.

F3.2 EXPLANATIONS BASED ON PATOMIC MODEL OF VEDIC SCIENCE

With regard to the explanation of various exotic phenomena the limitations of physical and biological theories are already discussed in Chapter 6. Further, it can be seen that the explanations advanced above too suffer from certain links as far as the understanding of these phenomena in totality is concerned. For example, (i) the postulated spiritual energy (i.e. the energy behind matter) is a "black-box," nothing is clear as to how different phases of energy arise in it or as to what the varieties of energy of matter linked with different phases of matter are; (ii) as to how the spiritual energy transmigrated from one life span of a person to his another life span and what is carried over in the process, and (iii) many loop-holes can be found in the refrigerator-example or in seeking the explanation in terms of analogy with computer-working. In a nut-shell, the phenomenon of consciousness of a Being is not understood in these theories.

On the other hand, within the framework of Vedic science (i) patomic model clearly takes care of various EOLs and their functioning in the field of WO and SO; (ii) inner EOLs contribute to spiritual energy and also to its different phases (cf. Section 13.2); (iii) the description of a Being as consisting of causal- micro- and gross-bodies clearly defines different domains of working of a Being in terms of newly introduced *tanmātra*s (cf. Chapter 9); (iv) energy of matter is nothing but five *tanmātra*s discussed in Vedic science and corresponding to interaction with five different phases of matter i.e. *pañca-mahābhūta*s, and so on. Further, the introduction of AAT- and AADT-type forces in the domain of spiritual energy will be an asset in these explanations. Finally, it is the transmigration of micro-body in conjunction with SO, that carries the experiences of one life to another life of a Being. For further details we refer to appropriate chapters.

F4. K-Effect, Patomic Model and the Exotic Phenomena

Returning back to the illustrative analogy of Section F1, when the mindset $\mathcal{M}_1$(m, i, e; σ) of an individual is placed in the vicinity of another different but "intense" mindset $\mathcal{M}_2$ (m, i, e; σ) then the former undergoes various types of changes (depending upon the dominating variable(s) in $\mathcal{M}_2$) as a result of interaction with the latter. If these changes supersede the limits of a normal person, then they become abnormal and the person exhibits exotic behaviour (phenomenon). Note that all this takes place in the domain of inner EOLs and hence not of much relevance to as far as the domain of outer EOLs is concerned. However, the abnormalities are seen on different fronts in the domain of outer EOLs (since inner EOLs do control the working of outer

EOLs) with reference to a third normal person. If e of $\mathcal{M}_2$ dominates, then $\mathcal{M}_1$ can carry extra memories or he becomes capable of recalling remote past or far future; if i of $\mathcal{M}_2$ dominates, then $\mathcal{M}_1$ can develop extra analysing power, and if m of $\mathcal{M}_2$ dominates then $\mathcal{M}_1$ can be tuned with for extra emotions as compared to a normal person. These abnormalities form the basis of different psychic phenomena listed in Section F2. In addition to these cases, several other phenomena of mixed nature also appear when any two or all the three m, i and e of $\mathcal{M}_2$ dominate and affect some or all the three m, i and e of $\mathcal{M}_1$ at the same space-time point and under the same circumstances σ.

Further note the difference between a person undergoing the above psychic changes and an MC person discussed in Chapter 10. The former, in fact, is an induced effect due to the presence of another $\mathcal{M}$ whereas the latter is the case of a missing inner EOL.

One can as well proceed for a mathematical modelling of the K-effect on the lines of Zeeman or Stark effect, but only under highly simplifying assumptions. However, we refrain ourselves from going into such details here.

ॐ पूर्णमदः पूर्णमिदं पूर्णात्पूर्णमुदच्यते।
पूर्णस्य पूर्णमादाय पूर्णमेवावशिष्यते।।

— ईशवास्य उपनिषद्

āum pūrṇamadaḥ pūrṇamidaṁ pūrṇād pūrṇamūdacyate ।
pūrṇasyaḥ pūrṇamādāya pūrṇamevā vaśiṣyate ॥

– *Īśavāsya Upaniṣad*

That is whole, this is also whole, the whole or fullness originates again from the whole, if one takes away the whole out of the whole only the whole remains.

Bibliography

Bagchi, B., "Position Dependent Mass Models and Their Nonlinear Characterization", *Journ. Phys.* **A**: Math & Gen **40** (2007) F1041.

Bahl, Raj Kumari, "Mystiques and Science", Orientation Course Project (OR-46), CPDHE, University of Delhi, 6 December 2005 - 4 January 2006.

Balasubramaniam, R. and M.T. Turvey, "Co-ordination Modes in the Multisegmental Dynamics of Hula Hoping", Bio, Cybern. 90 (2004), 176-90.

Balsekar, Ramesh S., "Consciousness Pervades the Real and Unreal", The Speaking Tree Column, *Times of India*, 20 Ferbruary 2008.

Basu, Amitava, "The Speaking Tree", *Times of India*, 4 January 2007.

Bṛhadāraṇyaka Upaniṣad, Gorakhpur: Gita Press.

Blakeslee, Sandra, "Experts Recreate Out-of-body Experience", in *Times of India*, 25 August 2007, "Times Trends", p. 21.

Blakeslee, Sandra, "Out-of-body experience? Blame the Brain", *Times of India*, 4 October 2006, p. 33.

Bohm, D., B.J. Hiley, and P.N. Kaloyerou, *Phys. Reports* 144 (1987), 323.

Bohm, David, *Quantum Theory*, Englewood Cliffs, New Jersey: Prentice Hall, 1951.

Chakraborty, Shatarupa, "Out-of-body Experiences Remain an Enigma", *Times of India*, 15 July 2007.

Chalmers, D.J., *The Conscious Mind: In Search of a Fundamental Theory*, New York: Oxford University Press, 1996.

Chaplin, J.P. and T.S. Krawiec, *Systems and Theories of Psychology*, New York: Holt, Reinhart and Winston, Inc., 1968.

Chattopadhyay, Rabindranath, "On the mas-energy relation within human body", *Bulletin Ind. Association of Phys. Teachers*, January 1997.

Chevreul, E., Lettre' A.M. Ampere', "Surne Classe Particuliere de Mouvemens Muscularies", *Revue des Deus Mondes* **2** (1833), 249-57.

Chopra, Deepak, "Time is an Illusion", a reporting in the Times Wellness Column, *Times of India*, 31 December 2007.

Clayton P. and P.C.W. Davies (eds.), *The Re-Emergence of Emergence*, New York: Oxford University Press (in press).

Dalmia, Himani, "Spiritual Link Between Human and Animals", The Speaking Tree Column, *Times of India*, 29 March 2008.

Eccles, Sir John, "How the Self Controls its Brain" (Springer, 1993).

Eddington, A.S., *The Philosophy of Physical Sciences*, Cambridge: Cambridge Univ. Press, 1939.

Ellis, G.F.R., "Physics and the Real World", *Physics Today*, July 2005, pp. 49-54, the World Year of Physics 2005 issue.

Feynman, R.P., *Theory of Fundamental Processes*, New York: Berjamin, 1962.

Fisher, Ian, and Correlia Dean, "Darwin Vs. 'Design': Evolution Still Rules", The Speaking Tree, *Times of India*, 20 January 2006.

Flintoff, John-Paul, "Feel Factor: Emotions not Just for Humans", Times Trends column, *Times of India*, 25 August 2008.

Fragopanagos, N. and J.G. Taylor, "Emotion Recognition in Human-computer Interaction", *Neural Networks* **18** (2005), 389-405.

Gaur, Ganga Prasad "Nahar" (ed.), *Prārtika Ayurvijñāna*, revised by Rakesh Jindal, Modi Nagar: Arogya Seva Prakashan, 1994.

Glicksohn, J. and S. Lipperman-Kreda, "Time, Thought and Consciousness", *The Journal of Mind and Behaviour* **28** (2007), 289-306.

Goldstein, H., *Classical Mechanics*, Addison-Wesley Publishing Co., 1981.

Goswami, Amit, "Consciousness in Quantum Physics and the Mind-Body Problem", *Journ. Mind and Behaviour* **11** (1990), 75.

Haken, H., A. Karlquist and U. Svedin (eds.), *The Machine as Metaphor and Tool*, Springer series on Frontiers in Science and Philosophy, 1993.

Haken, Hermann, *Synergetics*, 2nd edn., Springer-Verlag, 1978, vol. 1.

Hamalainen, M., R. Hari, R.J. Lmoniemi, J. Kanuutila, and O.V. Lounasmaa, *Rev. Mod. Phys.* **65** (1993), 413-97.

Hawking, Stephen, as quoted in "Nature Rewrites Laws of Universe" and reported by Jonathan Leake in *Times of India*, 10 September 2001.

Isadi Nau Upaniṣad, tr. in Hindi by Harikrishna Das Goyanka, Gorakhpur: Gita Press, 1994.

Jalm, Robert G. and B. Dunne, *Margins of Reality: The Role of Consciousness in Physical World*, Harcourt Brace Jovanovich Publishers, 1987.

Jammer, Max, *The Philosophy of Quantum Mechanics*, New York: John Wiley & Sons, 1974.

Jhunjhunwala, Bharat, "Intelligent Design and Darwin go together", The Speaking Tree, *Times of India*, 21 December, 2005.

Kana, Santosh Kumar, "You are a Continuous Process, not Product", The Speaking Tree Column, *Times of India*, 25 August 2007.

Kant, Emmanuel, *Metaphysical Foundation of Natural Sciences*, London: Bell Publishers, 1883.

Kaushal, R.S. and D. Parashar, *Advanced Methods of Mathematical Physics*, 2nd edn. (New Delhi: Narosa Pub. House and London: Alpha Science, 2008), chapter 8.

Kaushal, R.S., *Classical and Quantum Mechanics of Non-central Potentials: A Survey of Two-Dimensional Systems*, New Delhi: Narosa, Heidelberg: Springer-Verlag, 1998.

Kaushal, R.S., *Laws of Physical Sciences and the Human Behaviour*, Delhi: Spiritual India and Kundalini, vol. II (1978).

Kaushal, R.S., "A Model for Quark-gluon Plasma with Pentaquark Baryons and Tetraquark Mesons", *Ind. Journ. Phys.* 82 (2008), 891-906.

Kaushal, R.S., "The Conscious Pendulum: A Physicist's Approach", *Indian Philosophical Quarterly* **29** (2002), 65-78.

Kaushal, Radhey Shayam, "Patomic Model of Human Being in the Context of Modern Science", Ph.D. Thesis (unpublished), University of Delhi, 1998.

Kaushal, Radhey Shyam, "Discretization of Characteristics : A Concept prevailing in Mathematical and Behavioural Sciences", presented in National Conference of History of Mathemetics and Recent Developments, held at Rohtak, Dec. 20-23, 2006, (to be published).

Kaushal, Radhey Shyam, "A Complex Domain Analysis of Actions of a Consciousness Human being", the paper presented in Int. Conf. on Advances in Mathematics: Historical Developments and Engineering Applications, held at Pant Nagar (India), 19-22 December 2007, Abstract no. 35; *Ganit Bharati* **30** (2008), pp. 99-113; *Pramana — J. of Phys.* **73** (2009), 287-97.

Kaushal, Radhey Shyam, "Human Being : From the Point of View of a Philosophical-type Model", *Journal of Scientific and Ind. Res.* (New Delhi) 49 (1990) 578-82.

Kaushal, Radhey Shyam, "Modelling in science and religion : From the point of view of Ancient Hindu Philosophy", *Science-Philosophy Interface* (Calcutta) **1** (1996) 40-53, No. 1.

Kaushal, Radhey Shyam, "Plurality of Consciousness in Vedantic Philosophy and its Role in Scientific Observations" in *Scientific and Philosophical Studies in Consciousness*, ed. Sangeetha Menon et al. Bangalore: National Institute of Advanced Studies, 1999, pp. 346-61.

Kaushal, Radhey Shyam, "Structural Analogies, Abstraction and Mathematical Concepts in Vedic Sciences", *Indian Philosophical Quarterly* (Poona) 33 (2006), 125.

Kaushal, Radhey Shyam, *Structural Analogies in Understanding Nature*, New Delhi: Anamaya Publishers, 2003.

Kaushal, Radhey Shyam, *The Philosophy of the Vedanta: A Modern Scientific Perspective*, Garib Das Oriental Series 179, Delhi: Indian Book Centre, 1994.

Kokkedee, J.J.J., *The Quark Model*, New York: Benjamin, 1969.

Krishnamurti, Jiddu, "Creative Thinking is Infinite Movement of thought", The Speaking Tree, *Times of India*, 27 May 2009.

Kriyananda, Swami, (J. Donald Walters), *The Art and Science of Rāja Yoga: Fourteen Steps to Higher Awareness* (based on the Teachings of Paramhamsa Yogananda), Delhi: Motilal Banarsidass.

Kundu, M.N., "Death Does not Mean the End of Consciousness", The Speaking Tree, *Times of India*, 4 April 2006.

Laughlin, R.B., *A Different Universe: Re-inventing Physics from the Bottom Down*, New York: Basic Books, 2005.

Lea, S.N., "Limits to Time Variation of Fundamental Constants from Comparison of Atomic Frequency Standards", *Reports on Progress in Phys.* **70** (2007), 1473-1523.

Lindsay, A.D., *The Philosophy of Immanuel Kant*, T.C. & E.C. Jack, 67 Long Acre, W.C. and Edinburgh and New York: Dodge Publishing Co. Rare collection.

Madradihassan, S., "The five elements of Chinese Cosmology in the Dialecticism", *Ind. Journ. Hist. Sc.* (New Delhi) 27 (1992) 1-3; Also see, *Ind. Journ. Hist. Sc.* (New Delhi) 24 (1989), 181-85.

Mandler, G., *Consciousness Recovered: Psychological Functions and Origins of Conscious Thoughts*, Amsterdam: John Benjamin, 2002.

Mandler, G., "Consciousness: Respectable, Useful and Probably Necessary", in *Information Processing and Cognition*, Proc. Loyola Symposium, ed. R.L. Solso, Hillside, New Jersey: Lawrence Erlbaum Associate, Inc., 1975.

Marathe, M.P., *Study of Jainism* ed. M.A. Kelkar and P.P. Gokhale (Pune: I.P.Q. Publication, 1984).

Mehta, Neelam, "Age of Consciousness Just Round the Corner", The Speaking Tree Column, *Times of India*, 13 March 2007.

Misner, C.W. and J.A. Wheeler, "Classical Physics as Geometry", *Annals of Physics* (NY) 2 (1957), 525.

Naficy, Kambiz, "Are You Tuned into the Right Frequency?", The Speaking Tree Column, *Times of India*, 31 December 2007.

Naficy, Kambiz, "Metaphysics of the Physical World", The Speaking Tree Column, *Times of India*, 23 January 2007.

Narlikar, J.V., *General Relativity and Cosmology* (The Macmillan Company of India, Ltd. 1978), Lecture 1.

Narlikar, J.V., "Cranks' Constant : Popular Science and Vulgar Factions", *Times of India.*

Narlikar, J.V., "Past Perfection: Science in the Service of Arts", *The Times of India*, 10 February 2004.

Natsoulas, T., "The Concept of Consciousness: The General State Meaning", *Journ. for the Theo. of Soc. Behaviour* **29** (1999), 59-87.

Neumann, J. von, *Mathematical Foundations of Quantum Mechanics*, Princeton, New Jersey: Princeton University Press, 1955.

Nicolis, G. and I. Prigogine, *Self Organization in Non-equilibrium Systems*, Wiley, 1977.

Nolting, B., *Methods in Modern Biophysics*, Berlin-Heidelberg: Springer-verlag, 2004.

Osho, "Transfer Heat to Light with Inner Alchemy", The Speaking Tree Column, *Times of India*, 3 March 2007.

Pai, Hung-I., Chih-Yuan Tseng and H.C. Lee, "Identifying Biomagnetic Sources in the Brain by Maximum Entropy Approach", arXiv:q-bio.NC/0508040 v1, 29 August 2005.

Panda, N.C., *Maya in Physics*, Delhi: Motilal Banarsidass, 2005.

Panikkar, R., "Towards a Typology of Time and Temporality in the Ancient Indian Tradition", *Philosophy East and West*, **24** (1994) no. 2, pp. 161-64.

Penner, A. Raymond, "The Physics of Golf", *Reports on Progress in Physics* **66** (2003), 131.

Penrose, Roger, "Physics of Tao", *Times of India* (New Delhi), 28 January, 2003.

Penrose, Roger, *Shadows of the Mind: A Search for the Missing Science of Consciousness*, Oxford University Press, 1994.

Penrose, Roger, *The large, the Small and the Human Being*, Cambridge: Cambridge University Press, 1997.

Pink, T., *Free Will : A Very short Introduction*, New York: Oxford University Press, 2004.

Rampal, V.V., "Universal Consciousness and Cosmic Energy", The Speaking Tree column, *Times of India*, 12 February 2007.

Ranade, Deepak M., "Sever Connections Overcome Illusion", The Speaking Tree Column, *Times of India*, 30 Novermber 2007.

Ranade, Deepak, "Is Realization Nothing More Than a Chemical Reaction", The Speaking Tree Column, *Times of India*, 5 March 2009.

Ranade, Deepak, "Of Memory Templates and Free Will", The Speaking Tree Column, *Times of India*, 12 Sptember 2007.

Ranade, Deepak, "Search for the Centre of Consciousness", The Speaking Tree Column, *Times of India*, 10 April 2007.

Ranade, Deepak, "Stages of Knowledge for Becoming Aware", *Times of India*, Speaking Tree Column, 17 December 2007.

Ranade, Deepak, "The Democratic Nature of All Creation", The Speaking Tree Column, *Times of India*, 26 March 2008.

Resenblum, Bruce, and Fred Kuttner, *Quantum Enigma: Physics Encounters Consciousness*, New York: Oxford Univ. Press, 2006.

Richards, Jay, "Intelligent Design Theory: Why it Matters?", an Article by Jay Richards, Sr. Fellow, Discovery Institute's Centre for the Renewal of Science and Culture in Seattle, USA, on Thursday, 25 February 1999.

Robert, Galambos, *Nerves and Muscles*, Bombay: Vakil, Fefferand Simons Pvt. Ltd., 1972.

Saha, M.N. and B.N. Srivastava, *A Treatise on Heat*, Allahabad: The Indian Press Pvt. Ltd., rpt. edn. (1972). and 1st edn. (1931).

Savari Raj, L. Anthony, "Towards Trans-historical existence: Cross-cultural Relations on Human Time-consciousness", *Indian Philosophical Quarterly*, 34 (2007) no. 1, pp. 61-74.

Schiff, L.I., *Quantum Mechanics*, 3rd edn., New York: McGraw-hill, 1968.

Schrodinger, E., *My View of the world*, tr. by C. Hastines, Cambridge: Cambridge Univ. Press, 1964.

Searle, J., "Minds, Brains and Programs", *Behaviour and Brain Sc.* 3 (1980) 412; P. Churchland, *Neurophilosophy* (Bradford Books, 1986).

Sharma, Mukul, "Ape and Awareness", *Times of India*, 1 Novermber 2006.

Sharma, Mukul, "Organic Machines," *Times of India*, 12 July 2001.

Shri Yogavashishtha Bhasa (Hindi) Pt. I and II, Trilok Nath Road, Lucknow: Tej Kumar Depot (Pvt) Ltd, 2003.

Shukla, Pt. Ram Govind (ed.), *Sadānandayati Pranītaḥ Vedāntasāra*, Delhi: Bharatiya Vidya Prakashan, 3rd edn., 1992.

Sikdar, J.C., "Fabric of life: Paryatpi Pranapan in Jain Agam", *Ind. Journ. Hist. Sc.* (New Delhi) 27 (1992), 221-29.

Sisodiya, Avnish Kumar, R.S. Kaushal, D. Parashar and V.S. Bhasin, *Journ. Phys.* **G:** Nucl & Part **34** (2007), 929.

Spitz, H.H. and Y. Marcuard, "Chevreul's report on the mysterious oscillations of the hand-held pendulum: A French Chemists' 1833 open letter to Ampere" (translated from French), *Skeptical Inquirer* **25** (2001), no. 4, pp. 35-39.

Srimadamritcandsurikrit, *Tattvārthasāra* ed. Pt. Pannalal Sahityacarya (Sri Ganesh Prasad Varni Granthmālā, Varanasi, 1970).

Śrīmad Bhagavad-Gita (SMBG), Gorakhpur: Gita Press.

Srivastava, B.N., *Proc. Roy. Soc. Lond.* 175 (1940) 26.

Stapp, H.P., *Mind, Matter and Quantum Mechanics* (Springer, 1993).

Sur, Mriganker, "Brains, Computers and Intelligence", Lecture delivered at INSA, New Delhi, 16 December 2008.

Tao of Jaina Sciences, Delhi: Arihant Publications, Dariba, 1992.

Theophil, Marguerite, "Bonding and Understanding Through Storytelling", "The Speaking Tree" column, *Times of India*, 5 July 2007; ibid., 6 August 2007.

Tripathi, G.S., "Life Without Dream is Colourless", The Speaking Tree Column, *Times of India*, 15 May 2007.

Vedānta-Darśana (Brahmasūtra), Śrīmanmaharṣi Vedvyāsa Praṇīta, tr. in Hindi by Harikrishna Das Goyanka, Gorakhpur: Gita Press, 1999.

Venkatramani, S.H., "Self-awareness Makes us a Unique Species", The Speaking Tree Column, *Times of India*, 10 January 2008.

Victor F. Weisskopf, "Frontiers and Limits of Science", *American Scientist* **65** (1977) 405.

Vivekacūḍāmaṇi, Ādiśaṅkarācārya racita tr. in Hindi by Muni Lal, Gorakhpur: Gita Press, 1966.

Vivekananda, Swami, *The Yoga-Sūtras of Patañjali*, Delhi: Motilal Banarsidass.

Vladimirov, V.S., *Methods of Theory of Functions of Many Complex Variables*, Cambridge, MA: MIT Press, 1966.

Wade, Nicholas, "Baboon use Their Brains to Socialize", in *Times of India*, 10 October 2007.

Werner, H., "The Concept of Development from a Comparative and Organismic Point of View", in *Developmental Processes: Heinz Werner's Selected Writings*, New York: International Univ. Press, 1978, vol. 1.

Weyl, Hermann, Frank Wilczek (Introduction), *Philosophy of Mathematics and Natural Science*, Princeton University Press, 2009.

Yoganand, Paramhansa, *Autobiography of a Yogi*, Bombay: Jaico Publishing House, 1994.

Yoganand, Paramhansa, *Vākya Sudhā*, Agra: Vedanta Kesari Karyalaya.

Index